WITHDRAWAL

White Man's Club

Indigenous Education

SERIES EDITORS

Margaret Connell Szasz
University of New Mexico

Brenda J. Child
University of Minnesota

Karen Gayton Swisher
Haskell Indian Nations University

John W. Tippeconnic III
The Pennsylvania State University

JACQUELINE FEAR-SEGAL

White Man's Club

Schools, Race, and the Struggle of Indian Acculturation

University of Nebraska Press   Lincoln & London

Library of Congress Cataloging-in-Publication
Data

Fear-Segal, Jacqueline.
White man's club : schools, race, and the
struggle of Indian acculturation / Jacqueline
Fear-Segal.
p. cm. — (Indigenous education)
Includes bibliographical references and index.
ISBN 978-0-8032-2024-9 (hardcover : alk.
paper)
1. Indians of North America—Education.
2. Indians of North America—Government
relations. 3. Indians of North America—Social
conditions. 4. Education and state—United
States—History. 5. Discrimination in
education—United States—History. 6. United
States—Race relations. 7. United States—
Social policy. I. Title.
E97.F43 2007
323.1197—dc22
2007015448

For Lucas and Oscar, with love

Contents

Illustrations

Acknowledgments

This project became a reality during a year spent on an academic exchange at Dickinson College, Carlisle, Pennsylvania, but my work on Indian education, and the scholarly and personal debts I have incurred, go back much further.

While researching I have benefited from generous support and advice from many individuals and institutions across the United States. I would like to express my thanks and gratitude to archivists and librarians at the following: National Archives; Smithsonian Institution; Beinecke Rare Book and Manuscript Library, Yale University; Houghton Library, Harvard University; Hampton University; Dickinson College Archives and special collections; Nebraska State Historical Society; Minnesota State Historical Society; Historical Society of Pennsylvania; Newberry Library; U.S. Army Military History Institute; St. Augustine Historical Society; Cumberland County Historical Society.

Numerous scholars and friends have given their time, help, and encouragement. Among these are Mick Gidley, David Murray, John Zvesper, Eric Homberger, Michael Coleman, Richard Ruland, K. Ian Grandison, David Stirrup, Sam Maddra, Claudia Haake, Deborah Madsen, Richard Tritt, Jim Gerencser, Tess Eichenberger, Carole-Ann Johnston, John Bloom, Amy Farrell, Neil Weissman, Susan Rose, Clyde Ellis, Margaret Jacobs, Cliff Trafzer, David Adams, and Margaret Connell-Szasz. Deserving special mention are: Sharon O'Brien and Ellman Crasnow, who both offered ongoing intellectual and emotional support; Lonna Malmsheimer, who not only welcomed me to Dickinson's American Studies Department but open-handedly gave me access to her own Indian School archival resources; and Barbara Landis, of the Cumberland County Historical Society, who contributed to the fabric of this book by generously sharing documents, ideas, stories, jokes, and road trips.

Colleagues at the University of East Anglia have waited long years for this book. In particular, I would like to thank Richard Crockatt, Tim Marshall, Cath Sharrock, Allan Lloyd-Smith, Clive Scott, and Rebecca Tillett for their unfailing support.

I owe a special debt to many Indian people and especially those who directly told me about their experiences or answered my endless questions: Daniel Castro Romero Jr., Donna Herne, Diane Herne, William Herne, Jim Anquoe Sr., Jim West, Juanita Neconie, Anne Wheelock Gonzales, Gigi Pilcher, George Yuda, the late Maggie Lazore Tarbell, the late Andrew Cuellar, the late Ruth Fire, the late Rev. Clive Estes, and the late James Hamilton.

Finally, I owe my deepest debt of gratitude to my family. To Allan, who cooked the meals, endured the absences, and kept the faith, and to Lucas and Oscar, who held me in the stream of life, where real understanding of the issues examined here is to be found.

Introduction

> There was a feeling among our people that some of our young men
> should be educated so that they could read and write and understand
> what was written in the treaties and old documents in our possession.
> ... Or, as one chief put it, "it would enable us to use the club of white
> man's wisdom against him in defense of our customs and our Mee-
> saw-mi as given us by the Great Spirit.
>
> —Thomas Wildcat Alford, *Civilization*

THIS OLD SHAWNEE CHIEF, optimistic about the advantages to be
gained from white schooling, uses "club" unambiguously. For him it is
a weapon, a means to power he would like his people to acquire. Today, the reader of "white man's club" inevitably perceives it as a racial
enclave, with implications of self-definition and self-assertion gained
through restricted access and privilege. Nor is it inappropriate to read
these implications back into the nineteenth century, where they serve
as synecdochic representations of larger, national concerns; the 'club'
extends to a society and a culture and access appears as acculturation
with its own agendas and prohibitions while exclusion carries singu-
lar penalties.

In the final quarter of the nineteenth century, the federal government
enrolled thousands of Native American children in white-run schools
in a campaign to eradicate native cultures and communities and incorporate all Indians, as individuals, into the United States. This book explores how these schools, supposedly established to educate native children for citizenship, became arenas where whites debated the terms of
that citizenship and where native peoples, struggling in this convoluted
context against the total erasure of their cultures, claimed, adapted, or

deflected the "white man's club" and in the process, realigned and re-defined tribal and Indian identities.

American nation building necessitated and justified Indian territorial and also cultural dispossession. The United States was by now techno-logically and demographically dominant and well positioned forcibly to incorporate Indian lands. Asymmetries of power underpinned all as-pects of Indian-white relations—military, economic, legal, social, cul-tural, and linguistic. Reluctant to embark on an open policy of geno-cide, white Americans instead organized to incorporate the surviving remnants of Indian tribes into the nation through cultural reeduca-tion. For contemporaries, the ethnocidal task of the schools was sani-tized by being narrated within the ideological frame of national expan-sion or "manifest destiny." The process was not always cold-blooded or undertaken at a deliberate, conscious level, but neither does it have to have been. As Foucault makes clear, any analysis of power relations "should not concern itself with power at the level of conscious inten-tion or decision"; rather, "what is needed is a study of power at its ex-ternal visage, at the point where it is in direct and immediate relation-ship with that which we can provisionally call its object, its target, its field of application . . . that is to say—where it installs itself and produc-es its real effects."[1] The construction of American nationality involved the destruction—geographical, legal, political, and cultural—of Indian nationalities. But the prospect of an Indian U.S. citizenry raised thorny problems. For whites, it meant contending with the issue of Indian dif-ference and the place Indians could and could not occupy in the Amer-ican nation. The school was the institution recruited to accomplish this task. For Indians, it meant positioning themselves, both as individuals and communities, where they could best ensure that inclusion did not entail obliteration. Schools inevitably had a powerful impact on native lives and also purloined a place in native agendas.

White-run schools for Indians were institutions where American his-tory and Indian histories converged. Monuments to the white educa-tional campaign they spearheaded, they embroiled Indians and whites in two separate yet interlocking dialogues driven by very different mo-tivations and supported by unequal power. The strands of this asym-metric interaction provide a frame for this book, enabling me both to interrogate the overt and covert agendas of white educators and to uncover some of the actions and reactions of the Indians who were made the targets of these programs.

Today, the blinkered ethnocentrism of white educators and the corrosive long-term legacy of the schools are generally acknowledged.[2] But the complexity of their professed goal—to rapidly assimilate Indians and absorb them into the mainstream—and its engagement with issues centering on race has not been fully unpacked. The issue of race lies at the core of this study, which considers the different discourses of race that have not yet been fully integrated into scholarly analyses of Indian schooling to argue that from the start, an upbeat rhetoric of Indian inclusion and assimilation cloaked a fierce dispute about racial ability. The rhetoric of Indian schooling pointed to an ideology of universalism, which in this context derives from an Enlightenment ideal. It is the Enlightenment claim for universal human capacities that feeds into the familiar egalitarianism of the Constitution.[3] Although this was an eighteenth-century concept, it was still potent in nineteenth-century debate, even if by then it was accompanied by a distinctively different set of ideas: those surrounding the concept of evolutionary development and the application of this biological theory to social development.[4]

The Indian school system was built during an era of intense racial debate. The United States was struggling to find a way to replace the brutal rules and laws of slavery, which had controlled political and social relations between two socially constructed and defined races since colonial times and become embedded in the institutions and psyche of the new nation. Thousands of immigrants, streaming into the United States from countries as diverse as China and Italy, were joining the work force and yet, to varying degrees, were being classified as nonwhite. Definitions of race in the late nineteenth century were fluid, changing, and associated with amorphous ideas that blended notions of blood, culture, and peoplehood in what George M. Fredrickson has termed "romantic racialism." The range of nineteenth-century racial ideologies was, as Peggy Pascoe reminds us, "much broader than scientific racism," but increasingly, race would become tied to strict scientific categories that measured, categorized, and separated one group from another.[5]

At issue was a contest between two different sets of ideas and attitudes, both central to western thought and both powerfully influential on American society and culture. Many white Americans were never able to concede full equality to Indians and progressively situated them within the developing discourse of scientific racism. So from the outset, opposing racial discourses about Indians interwove and became incarnated in the structures and practices of education. When interrogated, these reveal the conflicted racial agenda of the schooling campaign and challenge the hinged interpretation of Indian education, first marked out by Frederick Hoxie, whereby the late nineteenth century is regarded as optimistically assimilationist and the early twentieth century is identified as the time when a more pessimistic judgment of Indian capacity became established.[6] Recent studies of individual schools have focused almost exclusively on the last few years of the nineteenth century and the beginning decades of the twentieth. They provide substantiating evidence of Indian educational programs founded on an assumption of Indian intellectual inferiority.[7] By the turn of the century, the school system was fully fledged, the doctrine of social evolution well entrenched, and a restricted vision of what Indian schools could and should aim to achieve had been institutionalized in the government's prescribed *Course of Study for the Indian Schools* (1901). Indisputably, the white assumption that Indian children's racial inheritance was limited shaped twentieth-century schooling programs, but *White Man's Club* explores and reveals how this restricted view of Indian capacity was already evident in the formative years of the schooling system and inseparable from the drive to educate Indian children.

Scholarship on Indian schools focusing on the work of Christian reformers has sometimes contributed to the distortion of the broader picture. Nineteenth-century Indian educators shared a united front and their forceful profile and committed, upbeat rhetoric served to mask darker, more pessimistic views about Indians.[8] As the acceptable face of U.S. nation building, schools formed part of a master narrative of optimism, individual possibility, and progress. *White Man's Club* investigates the shadow narrative, in which, from the beginning, Indian schools are integral not only to a story of land theft, ethnocide, and cultural erasure but also to a pattern of progressive racialization as yet unexplored in scholarship on Indian schools.[9]

Recent research on race has outlined for us the social construction of racial ideologies and also demonstrated the extent to which the hierarchies of scientific racism ended up being imposed on all aspects of social life.[10] Historians focusing on "people of color" and studying America's racial history have developed a paradigm that argues racial categories are neither biologically determined nor static but historically constructed; although often seen as immutable, they are always in a state of flux. These scholars' work opens the possibility of looking beyond the Indian school as a component in a political program to view it as a site where whites, influenced by their historical experience of dealing with other racialized groups—Chinese, Italian, and Jewish immigrants and, most notably and enduringly, African Americans—debated and enacted not only Indian education but also racial formation.[11]

Including Indians in the United States necessitated counteracting America's own intellectual, historical, and political past.[12] The proposition that all native peoples should become citizens was a radical departure: it contravened the very fabric of the Constitution, which had specifically located Indians outside its purview and categorized them as separate and "other." Once co-opted into the nation, time-honored strategies for designating Indian difference and separateness became redundant. Americans instead progressively included and enmeshed Indians in discourses and practices derived from the nation's racial past and lexicon. No longer separate and outside American society, they were steadily constructed as separate inside the nation, and the extent and nature of their differences were fiercely debated. From its foundation, I argue, the Indian school system was both the location of this debate and the institutionalization of its outcome.

I am indebted to scholarship published over the last thirty years, but this study does not pretend to be a comprehensive analysis of the Indian school system.[13] Looking at the history of an educational debate by concentrating on a single narrative line or an abstract theoretical analysis would be restrictive, so while consistently privileging racial concerns, my aim is twofold: to interrogate the overt and covert agendas of white education programs and to probe the actions and reactions of Indians who struggled to resist as well as claim the power of white schooling. There are four areas I consider in addressing these concerns. First, the

problematic and thorny questions associated with conflicting white notions of savagery and race, inflected by the wider racial debate. Second,
the white-managed restricted environments where the projected transformation of Indians was to take place: principally schools, both on and
off the reservation, but secondarily, by extension, the reservation itself,
with its defined borders, administrative links to Washington, and nearby military back-up. Third, the input and response of Indian people to
the workings of a system dedicated to their transformation and geared
to altering their worldview and their loyalties, in a context where survival and resistance often necessitated borrowing the weapons of the
enemy. And fourth, the shift from a series of atomized missionary ventures with Christian conversion at their core, to a centralized, federal,
educational endeavor driven by a national Americanizing agenda that
forefronted the English language.[14]

Macrobiographies of key representational figures, white and Indian,
are used in this study to explore the diversity and detail of the educational project. Microbiographies of Indians provide snatches of individual lives to illustrate particular points, often when fragmentary evidence
is all that has survived. This is a study of a school system that touched
thousands of young Indian lives, so stories of individual Indians shape
the narrative and, in the final section, carry it into the twenty-first century.[15] In the years leading up to 1900, the first generation was taken from
homes mostly untouched by American culture and channeled through
the schools with no one ahead to lead the way. The majority left behind
no record of their experiences. Some of their stories were never told.[16]
Others were recounted privately and then passed down from generation
to generation, carried in the living memory of Native American communities. Many have been lost or buried. But traces of some have been preserved within the written record and can be unearthed from the archives
and pieced together to create etiolated, firsthand accounts of individual children's responses to their schooling.[17] The stories assembled here
stand in for the many others that have been effaced, lost, or forgotten.
The schools were organized specifically to transform identities and dis-
locate loyalties and so these fragmentary life studies are often contex-
tualized to privilege issues of identity and allegiance, endorsing Simon
Jenkins's observation that "social identity is never unilateral."[18] Exca-

vated from a larger record, which consistently privileges the booming tones of white authority, they enable us momentarily to hear the whisper of some Indian voices and to perceive that sometimes, although threatening cultural annihilation, the "club" of white education could be grasped as a weapon with which to confront the new asymmetries of power and actively shape the meaning and structure of what it meant to be Indian in the United States.

The paucity of sources inevitably frustrates and preoccupies any historian of Indian education. It is not only that Indian cultures were oral or that whites produced most of the written record; it is also that without doubt, Indian people concealed their activities and clouded or obscured their opinions in ways common to many subordinate and threatened groups.[19] So the challenge to detect and interpret Indian voices and views in the official archival record, and sometimes even to infer them when absent, is qualified always by the awareness that the evidence thus provided is always partial and curtailed. Despite this constraint, the letters received by the Bureau of Indian Affairs and those sent back from the reservations to Carlisle and Hampton offer a source for gaining understanding of some of the attitudes and experience of members of the first generation of white-educated children. Moreover, school newspapers, and particularly Carlisle's *Indian Helper*, provide rich information about school life. Articles in them often represent the "hidden transcripts" to which James C. Scott has alerted us and can be interrogated to reveal evidence of the children's responses to their schooling experience.

The official written record—reports of commissioners, superintendents, inspectors, agents, teachers—inevitably exerts a strong centripetal pull on interpretation and encourages us to take at face value the stated intentions of white educators and overlook the muted voices of Indians. In an effort to correct this imbalance and unveil the "hidden transcript of white rule that could not be openly avowed" as well as the Indian "critique of power spoken behind the back of the dominant," I analyze the white-managed built environment of schools (Santee Training School and most notably the Carlisle Indian School) using techniques and concepts borrowed from landscape historians and human geographers, as well as those more familiar to historians.[20] Archival photographs, maps and charts, school buildings, structures and circulation elements (roads, paths, fences, entrances, and exits) are treated here as primary sources for spatial analysis.[21]

My analysis of all aspects of Indian lives that are hidden and of the posturing and self-dramatization on the part of dominant whites is indebted to the work of James C. Scott.[22] His studies of dissident subcultures and the politics of disguise, although never explicitly engaging Native American educational history, offer a theoretical frame for scrutinizing forms of domination that share family resemblances and for understanding the related responses of subordinate groups. Like any other historian concerned with issues of power, my thinking has been massively shaped by the work of Michel Foucault, and for close-up study of boarding schools, *Discipline and Punish* has been indispensable. Michel-Rolph Trouillot's work on history and power has also played an important role in alerting me to how power operates in the processes of making and recording of history and how overlapping historical narratives often mean that those produced by the least powerful can easily be obscured by evidentiary silence.[23] Over the years, my ideas have developed through my engagement with Benedict Anderson's brilliant classic study of nationalism; his book is an important foundation stone of this work. Anderson's comment that "communities are to be distinguished, not by their falsity/genuineness, but by the style in which they are imagined," and his observations on patriotism and racism, have afforded me ways of understanding how racist strands in American nationalism impeded many whites' capacity to imagine Indians as members of their own limited, sovereign community and prevented them from including native peoples in the "deep, horizontal comradeship" that underpins a nation.[24] Anderson's clarification of how language and the printed text are intrinsic to the forging of modern "imagined communities" extends beyond the realm of nations to elucidate our understanding of bonds established within the white-created community of educated Indians. It also throws into much larger perspective the determined efforts of individual Indians, like Harry Hand, a Dakota from Crow Creek Agency, to establish and maintain their own small, local newspapers.

Structurally, *White Man's Club* reflects the book's focus on the foundation years of the Indian school system, 1875–1900, starting with the organization of the first nonmission school, with prisoner-pupils in Fort Marion, Florida, and ending with the publication of a standard, common curriculum for an extensive national system of Indian schools and the simultaneous cessation of government funding for mission education. As a study of institutions and events that carry a powerful and enduring legacy that cannot be consigned to the resolved past, the biographical studies in the last section and the epilogue carry the story into the twenty-first century.

While many white-educated children survived their experience and found ways to use their schooling, many more were culturally maimed and psychologically scarred. As an English woman, I come from a nation that in the nineteenth century built a system of boarding schools to educate a ruling class who would go out to administer and control a worldwide empire. These schools taught values and beliefs shared by ambitious, high-class parents and gave a privileged education to a juvenile social elite. Yet today, it is recognized that they also caused crippling emotional harm to boys and young men separated from the love and support of family. These findings alert us to the proportionally greater crushing impact of Indian schools on children of a racial minority already politically, socially, and culturally undermined. The extent of the damage inflicted by these schools is beginning to be openly acknowledged and in Canada, the legal testimony of survivors and the resulting reparations have brought into the public domain the enduring and painful legacy of the schools.[25] Nineteenth-century American Indian children who attended militarisitic, boarding institutions far from home where they forewent contact with their families over several years, were an extremely vulnerable group and totally dependent on the compassion, kindness, and morality of their white carers; we know that frequently these virtues were not forthcoming. It is not my purpose in this study to explore or expose this abuse, yet it inevitably haunts the analysis and cannot be forgotten.

The prologue starts with a defining historical event: the capture, deportation east, imprisonment, and schooling of the group of Plains Indians who were made the first federal school pupils. Organized to prefigure some of the questions and issues to be examined in the book, the prologue outlines the historical context of the schools' organization, for both Native nations and the United States.

The first part of *White Man's Club* considers white theories about Indian education alongside Native views and responses. One tradition of white thought deemed Indians capable of achieving equality with whites; a second condemned them to a permanently inferior status. Chapter 1 briefly describes this debate, analyzes the universalist/evolutionary frame that surrounded it by the late nineteenth century, and locates the major white educators within this, arguing that a shared ideological commitment to American nation building enabled them all to work together for the cause of Indian education, despite their different judgments of Indian capacity and projected place she or he should find in American society. Chapter 2 focuses on the native peoples who were made the subjects of this program of Americanization. Far from composing a single entity, native communities enjoyed separate histories, cultures, and languages, which they passed down to younger generations through stories, ceremonials, and day-to-day events. Inseparable from daily life, these educational practices were distinct and unique and few tribes willingly gave them up. White-run schools were therefore involved in an extensive program of reeducation. This chapter sketches but does not survey the complex patterns of traditional education that white schools sought to displace. Framed within the new asymmetries of power, it demonstrates how Indian ambivalence and hostility toward white values was often balanced by acknowledgment of a pressing need to learn white skills and become knowledgeable about the white man's world. Indian peoples across the United States were all subjected to identical offensives of land theft and cultural obliteration. This often fostered shared critiques and cultural survival strategies that they used to defend their own identities and resources

Chapter 3 examines the missionary foundations on which the federal school system was built, revealing how, in the short term, the Christian doctrine of the unity of mankind was able to intersect with the new secular ideology of national universalism. Using the Dakota Mission and the Santee Normal Training school as examples, it charts the gradual shift from mission-centered schooling to a centralized federal educational endeavor with its secular curriculum forefronting individualism, practical skills, and the English language. It also explores how the seemingly parochial contest over the use of the Dakota language as a medium of instruction was embedded in a much more fundamental and far-reaching dispute about the true nature of the Indian, the best means to bring him or her to civilization, and his or her future status in the American nation.

The second part of the book directs attention to the first two off-reservation schools established in the East: Hampton and Carlisle. Hampton Institute in Virginia, founded by Samuel Chapman Armstrong to educate freed slaves, hosted the first formal Indian schooling program. Chapter 4 examines Hampton's Christian, national, social evolutionary philosophy and the curriculum Armstrong developed to educate what he called America's "despised races." It investigates the long-term impact of the theory and practices of this race school on the developing Indian school system. In chapter 5, the biographical study of a Hampton-educated Shawnee Indian shows how white schooling changed his life and forced realignments in his Indian identity.

The next four chapters focus on the Carlisle Indian Industrial School in Pennsylvania, which lies at the hub of this study. A living experiment watched closely by officials in Washington, Carlisle marked the transfer from mission to federal control of Indian schooling. The first government boarding school, set up in the buildings of a disused barracks far from Indian Country, this militaristic institution supplied the blueprint for the dozens of government schools that, by the turn of the century, dotted the western territories. Although never the main focus of any academic publication, scholars in the field all acknowledge Carlisle's key role in the Indian school movement.[26] Analyzing this prototypical institution will help us understand the broader federal education program. Chapter 6 examines the philosophy and pedagogy of the school's founder, Richard Henry Pratt, in conjunction with the national universalist mission to which he dedicated his school and his bold prediction that a Carlisle education and total separation from tribal communities would Americanize native children in a single generation. In order to look behind Pratt's assimilationist rhetoric, in chapter 7 the built environment of the Carlisle campus is enlisted as a primary source. I look at maps and photographs, alongside more traditional sources, to disclose patterns of racial separation and segregation that contradict Carlisle's acclaimed universalist mission. Chapter 8 interweaves close study of the spatial layout of the built environment with scrutiny of the school newspaper, the *Indian Helper*. Analysis of the editorial practices of the man-on-the-bandstand, the paper's invented editor, not only exposes the intense surveillance to which the children were subjected but also reveals some of the ploys and tactics the children used to undermine and resist the school's purpose. To go one step further in exploring an aspect of Carlisle's history that was shielded from public view, chapter 9 focuses on the school cemetery. Never photographed and only fleetingly mentioned in archival sources, the cemetery's creation, expansion, removal, and reconstruction are read here as an allegory of the school's purpose and history. It is the surviving physical manifestation of a white discourse about race and dispossession that also supplies evidence of Carlisle's compromised mission.

Part 4 engages with the legacy of Carlisle and, by extension, the federal school system. Two quite different life studies are presented as examples of how native histories and cultures have survived into the twenty-first century despite the campaign to expunge them. In chapter 10, I piece together the story of a Carlisle student who left behind no written record using archival sources, photographs, newspapers, interviews, and internet searches. Kesetta's life embodied the educational campaign at its most absolute and brutal, but it also stands as evidence of the endurance of a native community and the power of its oral traditions to sustain memory when surrounded by silence. Chapter 11 looks at the life of Susie Rayos Marmon, who returned to her pueblo home and used her white education in ways never anticipated by Carlisle. She merged her dedication to book learning with her determination to help her people preserve elements of their culture and independence in more traditional ways. Teaching Pueblo children their own heritage by telling stories passed down through the generations was, for Marmon, as vital as instructing them to read and write in order to navigate their way in the white world. Recovered from archival material, newspapers, and stories of family members, Aunt Susie's story is not uncontested and reengages with the complex issue of English language usage (examined in chapter 3). It is reconstructed here as the life of an individual equally committed to Pueblo and white educational methods yet unswervingly loyal to her Laguna community.

Finally, the epilogue returns to Carlisle and Powwow 2000: remembering the Carlisle Indian School. At this event, descendants of children sent away to Carlisle returned for the first time to reclaim the grounds of the old school. Dancing, singing, drumming, speeches, ceremonies, and give aways reflected the vibrancy of powwow—the fastest growing intertribal phenomenon in Indian Country today—and confirmed the survival of tribal cultures Carlisle had worked to destroy. Funded by the local white community and attended by Indian people from across the United States, this memorial event is presented as reflecting a mounting awareness among both groups of the need to acknowledge and understand the legacy of Indian schools.

White Man's Club

Prologue:

Prisoners Made Pupils

IN THE LATE spring of 1875, the ancient seaport town of St Augustine, Florida, witnessed the beginnings of an educational campaign that would have an impact on every Indian nation in the United Sates. Here, in a forbidding, shell-proof fortress, built by the Spanish to defend the east coast of Florida, the first lessons for Indians were held in ammunition storage casemates. At Fort Marion, adult Indian prisoners, not children, walked to class past mounted cannon and piles of old cannon balls. Their jailer, Captain Richard Henry Pratt, had made himself their self-appointed teacher. By turning prisoners into pupils, Pratt was determined to demonstrate to white Americans that savage fighters could readily be tamed and civilized.

Education had been intrinsic to Indian-white relations since the days of first contact and also inseparable from native subjugation and dispossession. So the prison venture at Fort Marion fell into a long-established tradition. Yet it also displayed a range of important new elements that would shape the Indian school Pratt went on to establish in Pennsylvania and influence, too, the future trajectory of Indian schooling in the United States.

Pratt was a serving army officer and the education program he organized at the fort was militaristic in style. In the past, missionaries and churchmen had run all schools for Indians, introducing Christianity as the foundation stone of civilization. At Fort Marion, the schooling venture was organized under the auspices of the War Department and the federal government. Pratt played a vigorous personal role and he introduced subtle changes to past educational emphases. While he deemed Christianity of fundamental importance, Christian teaching did not constitute the central core of his program. Pratt worked to teach the ex-warriors English as well as "proper" habits of discipline, work, and clean-liness. Convinced that a military regime and instructions in how to "read and talk [English]" were the best means to ensure that, on their re-turn home, the young men "would be a strong civilizing element around their people," he positioned Christianity as a vital but subsidiary con-cern. Bishop Henry Whipple of Minnesota, who arrived to spend the winter in St Augustine, became a regular visitor to the fort and Pratt welcomed his presence and support. Nevertheless, he considered Whip-ple's contribution to be aiding, not driving, his "system of instruction." Convinced his own style of management was very different from that practiced by the Bishop, he self-assuredly explained to General Sheri-dan, "Bishop Whipple . . . has given much good help and is converted to Army management of the Indians."[1]

"Army management of the Indians" had secured the prisoners' cap-ture. Thirty-four Cheyenne, twenty-seven Kiowa, nine Comanche, two Arapahoe, and one Caddo had been transported from Fort Sill in Indian Territory in chains, with Pratt as their escort. Among them were Heap of Birds, Eagle's Head, Gray Beard, White Horse, and Lone Wolf, some of the proudest fighting chiefs of the southern plains, all now "prison-ers of war" of the U.S. government. Their captive status supplied ev-idence not only of fast-changing power relations in the West but also the coercion that underpinned this fortress educational venture. In the small, contained, controlled environment of Fort Marion, this young army officer built the bones of an educational program that later he would flesh out at the Carlisle Indian School, making him the nation's best-known Indian educator.

Defeat, imprisonment, and exile meant that Pratt's Fort Marion edu-cational project could operate in complete isolation from the prisoners' home communities. This convinced Pratt that total cultural severance created ideal conditions for obliterating Indian cultures. Despite the spe-cial and multifarious conditions attending the Indians' schooling in St. Augustine, for Pratt, their separation from what he called "camp soci-ety" was crucial and would provide the key rationalization for choos-ing the eastern location of Carlisle for his school. All subsequent off-reservation boarding schools would follow his model.

Local white populations represented an audience that Pratt quickly realized he could engage to aid his experiment. He made the fort into a living exhibit where visitors were welcome and persistently courted local and national publicity for this showcase of Indian transformation. He had been alerted to the public's intense interest in Indians by the huge crowds that awaited the shackled prisoners' arrival at all the large stations—Indianapolis, St. Louis, Louisville, Nashville, Atlanta, Jacksonville—during their long journey across the United States, to St. Augustine. Pratt openly scorned this white fascination with Indian exoticism. Yet he was not immune to it himself and, as we shall see, during his early career, he often made a spectacle of Indian cultures to bring notoriety to his work. Although sometimes treading a dangerous line in his relationship to Indian cultures, he always eschewed racial categorization. Insisting on Indians' capacity for equality with whites, Pratt seized every opportunity to "correct the unwarranted prejudice promoted among our people against Indians through race hatred and false history."[2] Yet from the start, Pratt's project was entangled within a preexisting racial discourse and debate. Even those most impressed by what they saw at Fort Marion often still described and categorized the prisoners in racial terms. Harriet Beecher Stowe, with her reform and abolitionist past, visited Fort Marion and became a staunch advocate of Indian education. She wrote enthusiastically about Pratt's work in *The Christian Union*, yet she sited her praise and optimism within a racial frame. Categorizing Indians as a race, she then compared them favorably with African Americans and pronounced them "a strong, thoughtful, sensible race, not emotional, like the negro, or liable to shifting phases."[3] Intended as a tribute, Stowe's language and judgment nonetheless presage how America's racial history would inform and infect white efforts to school Indians.

Racial bias and ethnocentrism prevented whites from crediting the prisoners with their own independent purposes and agendas. In the penal environment of Fort Marion, change and accommodation were invariably interpreted as a direct response to white example and pressure. Thus the younger men's willingness to attend school was construed as endorsement of the superiority of white society. Yet, in their attitude to white education, White Horse's great-grandson, Jim Anquoe Sr., suggests that the Kiowa were more nuanced and sophisticated. Many took home with them a determination not to emulate whites but instead to send their children to school so they could "fight back peaceably."[4] Substantiating Anquoe's observation, in 1880, after the prisoners' return, the Kiowa agent reported a new and positive attitude in the tribe with many parents keen "to have their children educated in the schools."[5] Agent P. B. Hunt read this unambiguously as evidence of the Kiowa's readiness to abandon Indian ways. He did not entertain the possibility that they might be seeking to harness white education for their own purposes.

Historical Context: Whites

The fortress school in St. Augustine achieved wide and favorable coverage in the national press. Pratt's experiment was timely. The special Peace Commission, created by Congress in July 1867 to consider how to bring peace to the plains, had recommended "endeavoring to conquer by kindness." The spirit of this new endeavor was reflected in the educational clauses incorporated in the Treaties of Medicine Lodge and Fort Laramie, signed in 1868 with the Indians of the northern and southern plains respectively. These treaties incorporated many of the commission's recommendations and included an active plan for Indian civilization.[6] They drew new, tighter boundaries for reservations, and gave assurances to tribes that the government would furnish seed, agricultural implements, instructors, and other essentials to enable the Indians to farm. Clothing and food would be supplied to them while they learned. Judged by scholars to be a cynical means to acquire Indian lands, these treaties all strongly emphasized schools and education.[7] Earlier treaties had sometimes included vague educational clauses. The one signed with the Lower Brule in 1865 was typical: "When the Secretary of the Interior may so direct, schools for the instruction of the said band may be opened on said reservation."[8] In 1868, however, the "necessity of education" was stressed. White officials situated schools at the heart of all treaties and educational clauses were prescriptive and detailed. Indians were now required to compel their children to attend school, agents were ordered to enforce this, and the government committed itself to providing a schoolhouse and a teacher "for every thirty children."[9] The Treaties of Medicine Lodge and Fort Laramie thus represented an important and open shift in the way the government defined its relationship with Indians. Education had been made an integral part of an aggressive policy of pacification.

Driven by the pressing demands of national expansion, officials in Washington had never set down coherent plans for the future of Indian communities. Concentration on reservations had gradually replaced removal as a means of segregating Indians from the white population and avoiding conflict. Yet confusion reigned over whether the promised schools should merely appease Indians and render them safe neighbors or instead provide an educational bridge into white society. Francis Walker, the famous New England educator, economist and statistician, and President Grant's commissioner of Indian Affairs, addressed the problem directly, in 1874: "The Indian question naturally divides itself into two: what shall be done with the Indian as an obstacle to national progress? What shall be done with him when . . . as he ceases to obstruct the extension of the railways and settlements?"[10] Walker supplied his own harsh answer to the second part of his question. Envisaging the reservation as a type of reform school, where Indians would be forced to learn habits of industry and sobriety, he argued that the United States should be liberal and generous. The government should provide both schools and equipment, but he was adamant that "the Indians should not be allowed to abandon their tribal relations, and leave their reservation to mingle with the whites, except upon express authority of law." Walker opposed any scheme for assimilation that might "hasten the time when these tribes shall be resolved into the body of our citizenship." In his view, they would be pitifully unable to compete with superior Anglo-Saxon stock. Conceding that it was likely that their numbers would decline, he postulated that it was also possible that "the Indian [might] bear restriction as well as the Negro has borne emancipation."[11] Harsh in his judgment of Indian capacity, Walker's chilling scheme for a series of permanent, policed, Indian compounds reiterated both a well-entrenched belief in the obduracy of Indian inferiority and a time-honored commitment to Indian separation and seclusion.

In the past, this policy of separation had been backed by a series of laws. Legally identified as ineligible for citizenship by the Constitution and again specifically barred by the Naturalization Act of 1790 with its "free, white person" clause, Indian exclusion from U.S. society had been reaffirmed by Congress during debates surrounding the Fourteenth Amendment.[12] Indian citizenship had been consistently refused and the tribes' status as separate nations insisted on. Chief Justice Marshall had circumscribed but not ended their separate national status in his 1832 Supreme Court decision, which declared them "domestic dependent nations." Then, in 1871, the tribes' long-standing status as individual nations was brusquely and unilaterally ended. A single sentence, tagged onto the Indian Appropriation Act, terminated the tribes' national status and brought to an end the long era of treaty making, which dated back to British colonial days:

"Hereafter no Indian nation or tribe within the territory of the United States shall be acknowledged or recognized as an independent nation, tribe, or power with whom the United States may contract by treaty."[13] This unilaterally imposed new status meant that Indian tribes were no longer defined or treated as legally discrete and sovereign nations. They were now "wards" of the federal government—a unique, hazy, and untested category.

The complexity of the Indians' new legal status was highlighted after the capture and imprisonment of raiding Kiowa, Comanche, and Cheyenne Indians ended the Red River War (1874–75) in the Southwest. The Indians were charged with crimes ranging from murder to petty depredations. General Sheridan had planned for all the accused to be tried by a military commission.[14] Military trials, however, could only be held in times of war and the attorney general quickly ruled that, "a state of war cannot exist between a nation and its wards." With a military trial now out of the question, President Grant had been forced to come up with a solution that was as unprecedented as it was arbitrary: indefinite incarceration in an eastern fort. This harsh decision reflected the asymmetries of power that now governed Indian-white relations. It also threw into sharp focus the complex issues raised by the inclusion of 250,000 Indians in the American nation as "wards." The prisoners never stood trial. Instead, as already noted, they were sent to Florida to be made subjects of a very different kind of trial—a trial to test and prove the educability of their race.

Defeat of the Kiowa, Comanche, and Cheyenne brought the beginnings of peace to the southern plains. Although Geronimo and his band would not be captured until 1886 and minor clashes not cease until the early years of the twentieth century, modern military historians confirm contemporary observations "that the defeat of the Plains tribes in the mid-1870s was decisive."[15] What was less decisive was how Indians would survive on reservations and the place whites would grant their new "wards" within the nation.

Historical Context: Indians

Reservation life was hard. For the Plains tribes the calamitous disappearance of the buffalo made them economically dependent on the government and forced home the distressing bleakness of their situation. Carved in two by the transcontinental railroad, in just over a decade almost the whole five million buffalo herd had disappeared, the southern portion being the first to go. In 1876, Kiowa chief, Big Bow, begged "Washington" to help: "We wish you to understand that we consider ourselves passing away as our buffalo are passing away. We shall soon be gone. This is what weighs down the hearts of the Kiowa people with a heavy grief."[16] In the summer of 1879, when food supplies at the agency were exhausted, the agent sent the Indians out to hunt, but not a single buffalo was to be found and the Kiowa were forced to eat their ponies. A pictograph, showing a horse's head instead of a buffalo head on the Sun Dance Lodge, recorded the gravity of the situation that summer in the Set-t'an Kiowa calendar, where important tribal events were logged.[17] A frightening and unwelcome change had been forced on the Kiowa's most important ceremony. For Indians across the plains, the sudden and ruinous destruction of the buffalo herds heralded economic misery along with cultural disruption and devastation. The destruction of the economic base of their cultures forced many tribes to end their movements across traditional hunting grounds and settle on reservations, where they were pressured to enroll their children in white-run schools.

That commandeering Indian lands and schooling Indian children were inseparable processes was made glaringly obvious to the Sioux. The same tall, commanding military officer, who had visited their reservations in 1879 to collect children for his new Indian school in Carlisle, would return less than a decade later heading a federal commission hoping to persuade the different bands to sign away more of their land. The government was determined to open the Dakotas for settlement by breaking up the Great Sioux Reservation, guaranteed to the Indians by treaty in 1868. Richard Henry Pratt and his fellow commissioners were unsuccessful in their endeavor, but a second commission, led by General George Crook, secured its goal. In February 1890, before the boundaries of six, small, new reservations had been determined, President Harrison had thrown open the ceded lands for white settlement.[18] Across the West, native peoples were confined on ever-diminishing tracts of land. As "time went by," the Keeper of the Cheyenne Sacred Arrows reflected, "we became a small island . . . in a rising ocean of White Men."[19]

The speed of this confinement and loss forced changes hard to envisage or endure. The Kiowa chief, Kicking Bird, who led a peaceful group, was worried that the Kiowa could never adapt to life on the reservation. But at about the same time that he wrote a desperate letter to the commissioner, outlining his fears for the survival of his people, Kicking Bird also invited the Quaker missionary Thomas Battey into his camp to set up a school and teach the Kiowa children.[20] The government was forcing the Kiowa down "a new road" and Kicking Bird concluded that the children needed to learn white skills if the Kiowa were going to survive.

A respected leader, Kicking Bird led the peaceful two-thirds of the Kiowa who had not joined the Red River War. Later, he would be persuaded by Pratt to reveal details of raids carried out by individual Kiowa and so become instrumental in determining who would be imprisoned and sent to Fort Marion.[21]

Turning Point for Tribes of Southern Plains

The banishment and incarceration of their chiefs and warriors in Fort Marion marked a definitive and bleak moment for the tribes of the southern plains.[22] It dramatized the loss and defeat experienced by all Plains Indians, even if for some this was less abrupt.[23] Kiowa historian Anko kept a calendar in a small notebook to record major events in the history of his tribe.[24] To mark the summer of 1875, when the prisoners were transported east, he drew a dark, black pencil picture of Fort Sill, where the prisoners had been incarcerated for six months and from where they departed into exile. This pictograph of the fort formed part of the continuous spiral of figures Anko had drawn to record the significant events of Kiowa history. The work of a single individual, it nevertheless carried meaning for all the Kiowa people.[25]

Two thousand miles east in Florida, some of the younger prisoners also recorded their departure from Fort Sill. Kiowa artists, Wo-Haw, Zotom, and Etahdleuh, and Cheyenne artist, Nock-ko-ist (Bear's Heart, the only one to sign his drawings with his English name), all drew pictures of the start of their fateful journey. But unlike in Anko's calendar, they did not integrate this event into a preexisting spiral of history embracing a continuing story of the Kiowa people. Instead, it stood as the first of what was often a series of drawings depicting the different stages of their journey from Indian Territory to Florida. Fort Sill marked the beginning of their exile—the start of a new era of separation from their communities and histories as well as their forced and sudden encounter with white ways.

Significantly, when Zotom made sketches for his sequence of pictures depicting the different stages of the journey not only did he start with Fort Sill, but he also laid out his sketches in a linear pattern that read from left to right, rather than in the traditional spiral or circle. This new organization of space was just one indication of how at Fort Marion the prisoners were beginning to be influenced by white traditions. Adapting and reshaping a tradition of Plains narrative art already well developed by 1875, they borrowed from white systems of presentation and representation to chronicle the tumultuous changes they were experiencing.[26] Traditionally, Plains Indian men focused public attention on their military prowess by recording the precise details of their brave deeds on buffalo hide robes, tipi covers, and linings. These pictures' prime purpose was not decorative but helped establish status. As early as the 1860s, Plains Indians began to use pages of white-manufactured ledger books for drawings and this new surface carried their art in fresh directions.[27]

At Fort Marion, when the prisoners began drawing, their pictures still exhibited many traditional characteristics of the warrior painting tradition, but they also began to develop innovative techniques and styles that allowed the portrayal of unfamiliar subjects and alien experiences.

1. Indian prisoners leaving Fort Sill, 1875. Drawing by Bear's Heart. Courtesy of the Beinecke Rare Books and Manuscript Library, Yale University.

If we focus on just one of the many drawings made at Fort Marion—Bear's Heart's rendering of "Prisoners Leaving Fort Sill"—we can observe some of these developments (fig. 1). Horses, so rarely absent from any Plains painting, are here drawn lovingly and accurately and their movement is from right to left, as was traditional. The meticulous attention to detail that was such a distinctive feature of traditional paintings is also evident in the harness of the horses, the soldiers' weapons, and the roofs, chimneys, and windows of the fort. Here the similarities end. While Plains' narrative paintings are generally alive with movement and often depict a courageous and heroic accomplishment, Bear's Heart's drawing is static and instead of a triumphant act of war, it depicts his people's conquest. The detailed precision with which the white soldiers and fort are presented contrasts sharply with the empty forms of the Indians. Their unadorned heads are void and even the spoked wheels of the wagons have been given more embellishment. It is not the victorious individual that is important here but the vanquished group. Bear's Heart's drawing is the antithesis of the triumph of counting coup; it is a picture of subjugation and defeat. In the middle of the drawing, sketched with detail and hugely out of scale, flies the American flag: the ruling motif of the whole picture. Bear's Heart and the other prisoners fully comprehended the reality of this new politics of supremacy. They

2. Miss Nannie Burt's class, Fort Marion. Drawing by Bear's Heart.
Courtesy, National Museum of the American Indian, Smithsonian
Institution (206231.000). Photograph by NMAI Photo Services Staff.

also grasped the scope of the new powers that attended it. When classes
for the younger prisoners exposed them to reading and writing, they
actively turned to traditional art forms to portray, assess, and explore
their awareness of this new power. Many of their drawings feature the
vaulted casemate, where the Indians attended school.[28]

As a point of comparison with his Fort Sill picture, it is interesting
to explore how Bear's Heart depicts his understanding of the power relations of the classroom. Presented as being associated with the mystery and preeminence of literacy, his drawing of "Miss Nannie Burt's
Class" explores the source of her power (fig. 2). A group of Indian
men, uniformed and seated in rows on benches, await the arrival of
their teacher. Representation of the Indians is highly stylized with the
only detail being trappings from the white world: collars, shoes, and
short haircuts. There is no visual evidence to indicate that they are Indians. Regimented, docile, and attentive, their heads are turned toward
their arriving teacher who provides the only movement, or action, in
the picture. Her appearance is sharply contrasted with the passivity and

uniformity of the Indians. The detail of her spotted suit, the ribbons hanging from her hat, and the frills on her collar and bustle stand out; these are the trimmings of civilization. She is a figure of power and intimidation advancing toward a lone, wheelback chair, unknown to native society. Standing in the very center of the picture, it appears to represent the quintessence of the white world. From here, a woman will deliver the secrets of civilized life to a group of grown men. It is Miss Burt who is in control here. There are no instruments of brutal coercion visible, but the central chair has a partner in the top left corner of the picture. Here we can see the accessories of her trade—books, inkwells, wooden desk with turned legs, and chair—the source of her power, both threatening and desirable. All are drawn with care and detail, showing that Bear's Heart clearly understood the dynamic of power in which the skills he was learning were enmeshed.

It is not surprising therefore that Bear's Heart was ready to continue his schooling when released from Fort Marion. Several years later, he would describe his Fort Marion English lessons in the auditorium of the Hampton Institute in Virginia to a white audience that included President Rutherford B. Hayes and Secretary of the Interior Carl Schurz: "By and by teacher she comes with pictures of dog, cat, cow and tell us every day nine o'clock morning we go to school stop at twelve o'clock."[29] Yet Bear's Heart's picture of his lesson with Miss Nannie Burt conveys more about his Fort Marion classroom experience than this short passage spoken in broken English.

The work of a range of scholars has explored and investigated the unique flowering of Plains art that took place when, "for three years, Fort Marion was a hive of artistic creativity."[30] The intention here is not to further this investigation but rather to enlist these scholars' work as evidence of how Pratt's planned program to transform the prisoners was accompanied by unplanned transformations as well as enduring stabilities. The prisoners' drawings illustrate how changes in their ways of seeing and representing did not interrupt their powerful relationship with their own artistic and cultural traditions. They remind us, too, that the educational experiment at Fort Marion was accompanied by many creative and unforeseen responses from those on who it was carried out.

In what has to be judged an extraordinary intercultural transaction, Bear's Heart made a present of his pictures to Pratt, including the one of prisoners departing from Fort Sill. Pratt had been the commanding officer escorting them and Bear's Heart must necessarily have included himself among the featureless figures in the wagons. This gift from an Indian prisoner to his white jailer carries several possible different meanings, both obvious and implied. Among these is the gift's symptomatic marking of the unusual relationship and pattern of custody Pratt was cultivating with the prisoners at Fort Marion. He began as their military guard, but he progressively presented himself as their father figure, comrade, confidant, teacher, and friend. Hard on the heels of their military defeat and exile from their own people in chains, at Fort Marion Pratt took it upon himself to make their imprisonment both gentle and instructive. He quickly set up a system of benign policing and organized an education program for their improvement.

In his study of colonization, *The Intimate Enemy: Loss and Recovery of Self under Colonialism*, Ashis Nandy identifies two separate stages in the process, which are enforced by two different generations of people. Nandy contends that men of violence, intent on conquest, were succeeded by "people who . . . sought to be helpful." This second generation was motivated by a peaceful mission and sought to colonize minds in addition to bodies. The impact of this peaceful mission was more potent than its military counterpart, because, he argues, it "released forces within the colonized societies to alter their cultural priorities once for all."[31] The focus of Nandy's study is the British, engaged in overseas colonialism, but many scholars have argued that America's relationship to its native peoples was one of internal colonialism. And certainly, Nandy's two separate stages are still evident in the United States, although here they can be seen to have overlapped.

At Fort Marion, this merger was exemplified physically in the fortress classrooms where the prisoners attended school and personally in the figure of Captain Pratt. After eight years as an Indian fighter, Pratt began his new career as an Indian educator without even shedding his army uniform. The title of his autobiography aptly encapsulates this abrupt switch: *Battlefield and Classroom: Four Decades with the American Indian 1867–1904*. Pratt's life spanned a period when history crossed that invisible line that separates one historical time zone from another: conquest by fighting was over; the new battle was for hearts, minds, and loyalty.[32] Yet because the two stages had collapsed into each other, the battlefield would taint the classroom and leave its mark on how the nascent school at Fort Marion and the subsequent Indian educational program was both developed and experienced. The pupils in the casemate classrooms were all prisoners of war, and the man who organized the classes was an officer in the U.S. Army who, four year later, would found the Carlisle Indian School. While several scholars acknowledge that Pratt's time at Fort Marion constitutes an early episode in the wider story of Indian education, the enduring impact of this formative period has not been fully explored.[33]

Fort Marion, St. Augustine, Florida

One vital aspect of the Fort Marion period, as yet unanalyzed, is the complicated interplay between Pratt's schooling program and the use he made of the layout of the fort and it environment. An examination of this relationship can provide insight into the later workings of the Carlisle Indian School (discussed in chapters 7, 8, and 9) and also supply clues for understanding the enduring impact of the embryonic Fort Marion program in shaping the complex dialectical power relations at work in the white-Indian education process.

Fort Marion's monumental structure was designed by Spanish engineer Ignacio Daza as a state-of-the-art defense for Spain's vast New World empire. The Castillo de San Marcos, as it was then called, was built between 1672 and 1695 in the local porous, pink, coquina stone. A bird's eye view shows a square courtyard surrounded by battlements (fig. 3). Each corner of the fort was protected by a diamond-shaped bastion, allowing every wall to be seen from some vantage point inside the fort. Situated at the waterside, close to the town wall on the northern edge of St. Augustine, its shape would remain unchanged for the following two centuries. The fort was used by the Spanish, British, Confederacy, and United States: it was subject to changing names and ownership but never defeat. When ceded to the Americans in 1821, the old castillo was renamed Fort Marion and almost immediately it was written into the story of white conquest of the continent when it was

3. Aerial view of Fort Marion, St. Augustine, Florida.
Photograph by John Cipriani.

used to imprison a group of local Seminoles. Squeezing through a nine-inch-wide window located fifteen feet above the floor of their casemate prison, the Seminoles made a dramatic escape from the fort. A month later their leader, Coacoochee, would lead the fight against Colonel Zachary Taylor at Okeechobee and go on to engage in armed struggle for a further three years.

Less than forty years later, the frontier had moved on but the story had not changed. Fort Marion was deliberately chosen as a prison for the Kiowa, Comanche, Cheyenne, and Arapaho hostages in the hope that its eastern setting would make their escape or rescue impossible. Yet memories of that earlier successful escape plot dominated building and repair works at the fort as officers made it ready to receive the Plains prisoners. The colonel in charge of these arrangements was determined to block off any possible escape route and suggested that "a strong barricade [be] erected with thick planks, across the ramp leading to the terreplein" and that measures be taken to close the "casemate loop holes."[34] When Pratt arrived, he would quickly adopt a quite different strategy. Nevertheless, the architecture of the fort would form a vital component in the prisoners' experience.

Confinement and enclosure were written into the fort's structure. Its massive walls were twelve feet at the base and over thirty feet high.

Once having passed under the spiked portcullis, the only views of the outside world were from the high outer wall, or terreplein. The day the Indian prisoners arrived in St. Augustine, the Georgian poet, Sidney Lanier, happened to be visiting the town assembling material for his book about Florida. Joining the crowd that gathered at the station to watch the prisoners' arrival, he was stunned by their dignity and grace and in a letter to his wife, Lanier pronounced Fort Marion as "unfit for them as they for it."[35] The Georgian author made this judgment having seen only the forbidding, jagged exterior of the fort.

Inside the scene was even more dismal. Once across the ravelin and through the twelve-foot wall, the Indians were housed in the damp, coquina stone vaults, which faced onto the small, central courtyard and had been built originally for storing ammunition rather than human habitation. Before the hot and humid Florida summer was over, three Kiowa were dead (Ih-pa-yah, Co-a-bote-ta and Maman-ti).[36] It quickly became obvious to Pratt that if the prisoners were kept confined in the dark, leaking casemates, their sentence meant not exile but death.

Pratt demanded from his military superiors "more liberty of judgment in methods of care," and once this was granted, he took a series of bold decisions. Bringing the prisoners out of the casemates, he had their shackles removed and organized them to construct a large, makeshift structure on the upper level of the whole northern terreplein of the fort. Total confinement—enforced on the prisoners by the design of the fort and imprisonment within its casemates—had been suddenly partially lifted. This new use of space within the fort brought increased comfort to the prisoners and also softened its silhouette, changing the skyline of the old fort for the first time in over three centuries. Where previously only cannon had jutted and soldiers stood guard, an improvised ramshackle shed now sprawled, so that locals, taking evening strolls on the outskirts of the town, often glimpsed the unregimented figures of the Indians moving about the terreplein, high over the moat.

The fort's monumental architecture, which had been recruited to enforce as well as legitimize the authority of the United States, had now been subtly modified. Yet if Pratt's set of practical, pragmatic decisions had moderated the fort's harsh outline, they did not weaken or undermine his authority. That complex dialectic, often identified by architectural historians, whereby overt expressions of power in space tend toward an inverse relation to the security of that power, was strongly at work in St. Augustine.[37] No one was in any doubt about who was in control, so Pratt was able to redefine the conditions of the Indians' detention as well as the terms of his own stewardship, with no loss of authority.

The new living quarters played a powerful symbolic as well as practical role in the relationship Pratt was developing with the prisoners. Just as built forms can produce illusions of permanence and stability, so too innovation and change can create a sense of progress. So, while the material conditions of the prisoners had undoubtedly improved, their situation as prisoners and exiles was unchanged. Pratt was, however, now confidently presenting himself as the prisoners' helper and friend and only incidentally their jailor. Over the three years the prisoners remained in St. Augustine, the schooling program became an increasingly important part of the daily lives of the younger men. But their lessons in spoken English were always accompanied by an unspoken penal message; the fortress setting of their schoolroom provided a constant reminder that they were prisoners and could not go home. They were encouraged to talk with the many tourists who came to the fort and even to visit the town, but they could never walk through the forbidding gateway without a pass.

The entrance to the old fort was both visually and spatially one of its essential features (fig. 4). Designed for defensive purposes, it was turned 160 degrees away from the town. Entry into the main body of the fort was achieved only by turning through a 90 degree angle to cross the moat. This meant the courtyard was not visible until you were in it. But an entrance is also an exit, and a concomitant of this design, crucial to both Pratt and his prisoners, was that from inside the fort this exit was invisible. Here was a totally enclosed space over which surveillance was assured and from which escape could be prevented. Pratt could be compassionate and lenient in his treatment of the prisoners because he was readily able to enforce his power. So, for example, when he heard that the Kiowa were planning a secret escape, he speedily ordered "the massive entrance doors closed." By simply and instantly sealing off the whole fort, he was able to lock up the ringleaders.[38]

4. Entrance to Fort Marion, St. Augustine, Florida.
Photograph by John Cipriani.

It seems probable that the design of Fort Marion was at the back of Pratt's mind when he later reorganized the Carlisle Barracks into the Indian school campus. At Carlisle, he remodeled the school's gateway to match the single-access, oblique angle of the fort's entrance and then gradually constructed new buildings until the interior space of the school replicated the enclosed environment of the fort (more on this in chapter 7). Pratt's three years at Fort Marion gave him the opportunity to test and shape his ideas about educating Indians, but before focusing on the nascent education program he organized at the fort, we will follow the path that led him to St. Augustine.

Richard Henry Pratt

The planned deportation of the Indian prisoners from Fort Sill to Fort Marion in 1875 had signaled a career opportunity for this ambitious thirty-five-year-old army officer. As soon as the prisoners' fate had been decided, Pratt wrote to General Sheridan to suggest that "while undergoing this banishment, [the prisoners] should be educated in English, trained in our industries, and brought in contact with our civilization as much as possible."[39] A month later he sent a second letter, putting himself forward as the man for the job. "If, in the care of these Indians east, the government requires an officer of my rank, I want to go."[40] It was a bold initiative that secured him command over the prisoners, the chance to initiate his "educational experiment," and a permanent shift in the direction of his army career.

Like so many of his generation, Richard Henry Pratt had joined the U.S. Army after the bombardment of Fort Sumter in 1861 and spent four years fighting on the Civil War battlefields. After the war, following a brief, undistinguished spell as a civilian, he applied for a commission in the regular army. Having signed up with the newly organized Tenth United States Cavalry, where black enlisted men were under the command of white officers, he spent eight years pursuing, fighting, and negotiating with the tribes of the Southwest and became confident he understood and knew how to work with Indians. He would rely on this double interracial experience to substantiate his simple, egalitarian racial philosophy (examined in chapter 6).

Photographs of Pratt at Fort Marion show a gaunt, unprepossessing young man; there is no visible evidence here of the stature or confidence he would display in later years. Enlistment in the army had given Pratt an opportunity his limited elementary education had denied him, but it was his stint as Indian jailer in Florida that laid the foundations for his lifelong career as Indian educator. These three years, capped by a year at the Hampton Institute, would provide him with the experience and training necessary to establish and run the Carlisle School. Although he remained in the army, Pratt never returned to regular duty. A minor and unknown officer, he would eventually rise to the rank of brigadier general through his work schooling Indian children. For Pratt, when the army wagons rolled out of Fort Sill to transport the prisoners from Indian Territory to Florida, they set him on a new and successful career path.

At Fort Marion, Pratt was instructed to take charge of the prisoners' welfare and he gave these orders his own free and very personal interpretation. Having unchained and rehoused the Indians, transforming their material circumstances, he quickly moved to implement more fundamental alterations to their minds and bodies. He began with their clothes. Issuing them with surplus army uniforms, he ordered their white soldier guards to teach them how to crease their trousers, clean their shoes, and polish their buttons and caps. Within six months not only did the younger men look like soldiers, but Pratt also had fifty of them drilling and marching in the grounds of the fort as a military unit with sergeants and corporals. He even armed them with old guns. Convinced he could win their loyalty and transform them from captives to cadets, Pratt requested military authority to allow the prisoners to guard themselves. Having received conditional agreement from his superior in the local barracks, he put his own army commission on the line and dismissed the U.S. Army guard. By this time he had significantly changed the conditions of the prisoners' imprisonment. They now lived in a rooftop shed instead of barred casemates; they attended school, strolled the streets of St. Augustine, and interacted with the tourists who visited the fort. Yet their orders and rewards still came from Pratt.

Pratt was engaged in an elaborate exercise of intimidation and seduction. The intimidating and deadly effects of the chilling fort were softened by the new, airy living quarters. The unnerving presence of the American army guard had been replaced by a carefully selected Indian guard. But the startling dissonance of Indians dressed as U.S. soldiers, their so-recent enemy, offered the prisoners a constant visible display of Pratt's unabashed purpose. Seduction, as Stephen Lukes suggests, is always a highly sophisticated form of power hinged to constructions of self-identity.[41] In an intimidation/seduction dialectic, the subject is made aware of implied force yet is often seduced into connivance or even admiration—simultaneously belittled and impressed, he or she internalizes oppression.

At Fort Marion, Pratt's confidence in his capacity to use minimal force to maintain the good behavior and compliance of the Indian prisoners began to develop and blossom.[42] Dismissing the U.S. Army guard and beginning to use the prisoners to guard themselves was the first step in a system of self-surveillance that Pratt would outline in St. Augustine and elaborate at Carlisle. It necessitated a realignment of the men's loyalty and identity, and Pratt knew that this was essential. Otherwise, his plans to educate the prisoners were destined to fail. A single incident, when the Kiowas planned their secret escape and flight to the Southwest, nearly ended the experiment and Pratt's army career at the same time. When he had dismissed the U.S. Army guard and wagered his commission on his faith in the prisoners' good behavior, what was really at stake was not Pratt's lackluster army career but his new mission to civilize Indians.

Convinced that Indians had the capacity to succeed in the white world and only lacked opportunity and training, Pratt saw his responsibility for some of the fiercest Plains warriors as an opportunity for them as well as himself. Work and the English language would be the key to their advance. From the moment he unshackled them, Pratt kept the prisoners busy—polishing "sea beans" for the tourists, picking and packing oranges, clearing land, portering at the station—no work was too lowly or temporary if it introduced the prisoners to the rigors of the Protestant work ethic. After six months, with the help of five ladies, he organized formal English classes for fifty of the younger men. Behind all his actions lay a set of simple yet deep convictions: the Indian prisoners were capable of joining white society; they badly needed white help and instruction; they themselves knew this and were now keen to leave their old ways behind; and white Americans must be made to realize the capabilities of the race.

St. Augustine, Florida

When the prisoners arrived in Florida, St. Augustine had recently become the winter home of hundreds of well-to-do northern tourists. They filled guesthouses and two giant luxury hotels, bringing their servants with them and not returning north until springtime.[43] Visits to the old fort, to watch the activities of the Indians, added excitement to their usual entertainment of concerts, carriage parades, and dances. These visitors supplied Pratt with a teaching force—dedicated leisured women from New England keen to help "civilize" young "savages"—and also brought notoriety to his educational experiment. Harriet Beecher Stowe, Bishop Henry Benjamin Whipple, Spencer Fullerton Baird (secretary of the Smithsonian Institution), and many other notables wintered in St. Augustine.

Keen to ingratiate himself with both locals and visitors, Pratt organized the Indians to provide entertainment for them. One of his earliest

efforts, a bull fight to amuse St. Augustine's Spanish settlers and show
off the Indians' buffalo hunting skills, did not go quite as planned. Pratt
brought a large bull from the Everglades and locals shut off one of the
principal streets in the town before crowding the stands and balconies.
The crowd's first shock was the Indians' garb. Instead of the finery of a
Spanish toreador, the two Indians entered the arena on horseback wearing only their G-strings. Then, when the bull had been despatched with
no ceremony or extravagant gesture and "before Lt. Pratt could inter-
fere," an onlooker reported that, "Tsen-T'Aint, also known as 'White
Horse,' slashed the bull's side, scooped out one of the animals kidneys
and began to eat it."[44] Pratt gives no mention of this unfortunate event
in his autobiography but understanding the allure of Indian performance, he exploited the Indians' traditional cultures in different ways
to draw his crowd. Archery in St. Augustine's market square, advertised
as an afternoon competition—"over thirty of the Braves will compete
and pierce a target at the extraordinary distance of 200 yards"—was
followed by an evening program of Indian dancing and singing in the
courtyard of the fort. From special reserved seats, costing fifty cents, or
a standing place on the ramparts for twenty-five cents, white spectators
were invited to view a Kiowa ring dance and an Osage war dance "in
costume" and with horses.[45] Half a dozen years before William Cody
invented the Wild West show, which Pratt would so fiercely condemn
for being the antithesis of his own educational program, he himself was
creating roles for "authentic" Indians on stage and producing his own
commercial, Indian entertainment.[46]

Pratt justified this activity because it advanced his mission to school
Indians. A sentence at the bottom of one publicity poster explained,
"The Fund raised by Admission to the Fort is to be devoted to the education of one of the Indians." The profits of an Indian performance for
a white audience would be used to purchase a white schooling. These
shows were indeed miniature dramatic renderings of the terms of exchange that were exacted by white schooling: Indian cultures were the
forfeit for white education.

Yet at these dances other exchanges took place, neither noticed nor
comprehended by Pratt. Indians, dancing and singing for their own purposes and pleasure, borrowed and learned from each other in a series of

intertribal exchanges. For White Horse, the Kiowa chief who had led the failed escape plot, the greatest legacy of his Fort Marion days was the famous Omaha dance he learned from the Cheyenne and brought home to teach the Kiowa. Several years after his return, in response to Pratt's enquiry about White Horse's progress, the Kiowa agent reported with perplexity that he "runs well in the white man's road for a long time and then comes a dance or Indian orgy and he flops." Neither he nor Pratt understood the vital cultural importance of dance to Indians, nor did they realize that this chief had used his supposedly civilizing years in the East to invigorate dance traditions among his people.[47] Dances organized at the fort to satisfy a white desire for thrill and exoticism had been made to serve a quite different Indian agenda. Despite prohibition and bans imposed by the government, down the years the Kiowa secretly continued to dance the Omaha dance that White Horse had learned at Fort Marion.

Indians Racialized

Beguiled by the exoticism of Indians, many Americans were also fixated on the question of their racial difference. Pratt, with his leveling universalism, insisted always that their intellectual capacity was equal to that of whites. Yet, even as he worked to promote their civilization and acceptance, he also willing participated in a procedure that aimed to measure and display the Indians' supposed physiological differences, which carried with it a covert message about their mental abilities. At the request of Spencer Fullerton Baird of the Smithsonian Institution in Washington, Pratt allowed a sculptor to visit the fort to make plaster casts of the prisoners. Describing this venture in the "Proceedings of the National Museum for 1878," Baird expressed his delight with this opportunity to use life models, because it had "always been difficult to obtain face casts of the North American Indians. They manifest a deeply rooted aversion to the process required." At Fort Marion, Baird had sitting targets who, at Pratt's persuasion, submitted to the procedure of being encased in plaster. Although the sculptor pronounced Zotom a perfect "specimen of physical manhood" and insisted on making a cast of his entire body, the main focus of the project was on the Indians' heads: the seat of intelligence.[48] Samuel Morton had used Indian skulls as a means to demonstrate that different races of humans had different skull shapes and sizes. In his well-known *Crania Americana* (1839), Morton went on to argue that these physical traits also had moral and intellectual concomitants. So when Pratt persuaded the Indians to participate in the Smithsonian's "scientific" project, he was drawing them into a long-standing study of Indian crania that was already informed by racial hierarchy and tainted by faulty methodology.[49] This move subtly compromised Pratt's long-term goal to gain full acceptance for the Indians in white society. It can be seen to reflect not only his desire for renown for himself and the prisoners but also his own complicity in the racial discourse and categories being constructed in America at this time. Sixty-four casts were made of the Indians at Fort Marion and taken to Washington to be placed on conspicuous display in showcases at the Smithsonian as representative specimens of their race.[50]

The full impact of this long-established pattern of racial classification was brought home to Pratt when he was unable to find schools or colleges willing to include Indians in their student body. After three years, when the government released all the prisoners, Pratt managed to persuade twenty-two not to return home but instead to continue their schooling in the East. White fears about the inherent savagery of the race plagued his frantic efforts to find state agricultural colleges willing to enroll his protégés; college after college rejected his request. Significantly, it was General Samuel Chapman Armstrong, principal of Hampton Agricultural School for Negroes in Virginia, who came to Pratt's rescue. Armstrong was already engaged in an experimental program of race schooling for the recently freed slaves and agreed to take first one Indian and finally, when no other institutions opened their doors, a group of seventeen.

These Fort Marion students enabled Armstrong to extend his racial project by providing the base for a Hampton Indian Program. Armstrong quickly sought and won government support to enroll fifty more Indian students and Pratt went west to do the recruiting. Although he met fierce opposition, Pratt and his wife nevertheless managed to return to Virginia with a party of forty boys and nine girls.[51] So the first government-sponsored Indian schooling program was set up in the nation's premier industrial school for African Americans and was run by a man who believed that "both races need similar methods."[52]

Pratt was ordered to help run the Hampton Institute's new Indian program, but he did not regard this work as long-term. Impatient over being cast as Armstrong's number two, he also had qualms about Armstrong's racial philosophy. He openly let the General know about his "dissatisfaction with systems to educate the Negro and Indian in exclusively race schools and especially with educating the two races together." Loath to see Indians forced into an association with a group condemned to live at the bottom of society, he insisted that "participation in the best things of our civilization through being environed by them was the essential factor for transforming the Indian."[53]

Carlisle Indian School

Pratt was keen to found an institution dedicated exclusively to educating Indians. Despite having benefited from only a few years of elementary schooling himself, his three years in charge at Fort Marion had left him confident and bold. He presented his idea for an Indian school to the secretary of war and also Carl Schurz, secretary of the interior. Within a day, he had won authority to convert the disused army barracks in Carlisle into a school for Indians and permission to recruit 125 students. Driven by Pratt's boundless enthusiasm and keen support in Washington, events moved with extraordinary rapidity and on November 1, 1879, the Carlisle Indian School opened.

The first names recorded on Carlisle's student record files belonged to fifteen of the young men Pratt had escorted from Fort Sill in chains, guarded at Fort Marion, and then accompanied to Hampton. By now in their twenties, all had been regulars at the fortress school.[54] Pratt called the group his "Florida Boys" and relied on them as a vital source of support during the school's first year. He sent his trusted quartermaster sergeant from Fort Marion, the Kiowa, Etahdleuh, as well as the Cheyenne, Okahaton (Making Medicine), back to their reservations to recruit pupils. The others assisted with setting up the school before returning home. Zonekeuh (Teeth), however, did not make it back. The twenty-two-year-old Kiowa died on the way home and was brought back to Carlisle to be buried in the school cemetery, his marker representing a permanent connection between Carlisle and the Fort Marion prisoners. Only Etahdleuh, Pratt's star pupil stayed more than a year, but all

Pratt's "Florida Boys" had provided far more than practical help. They supplied the living testimony Pratt needed to prove that neither background nor race prevented an individual Indian from behaving and living like a white man. But Pratt's Carlisle project was very different from its Fort Marion prototype because it targeted children, the most vulnerable and malleable members in any community.

Pratt and the government's goals were extensive as well as ambitious. This was an educational experiment intended to demonstrate that separating members of the younger generation from their home environment and intensively schooling them in white ways offered a means of obliterating tribal cultures and acculturating a whole race. Having eschewed the race education he had witnessed for African Americans at Hampton, it is important to note that Pratt was now targeting and simultaneously constructing a different race: Indians. Although he began with a contingent of Dakota and Lakota children, historical and cultural differences were irrelevant to Pratt. He deliberately aimed to embrace as many tribes as possible in his experiment. Within three months, he was enthusiastically planning to sign up a group of Navaho and by the end of his time at Carlisle, he had enrolled children from almost every Indian agency in the United States.[55]

Pratt's educational project was unprecedented. It intentionally overrode native history and geography in its diasporic recruitment of students. For the first time too, conversion and the saving of souls was not the prime goal but instead the training of citizens. Just as at Fort Marion Pratt had treated Bishop Whipple's presence as important but secondary, so too at Carlisle the children's religious instruction was seen as vital yet subordinate to their practical instruction and the teaching of "a common language, a unity and loyalty of thought and effort."[56]

Shortly after Christmas, Carl Schurz visited the experiment he had authorized. He brought with him members of both the Board of Indian Commissioners and the House Committee on Indian Affairs. They visited the classrooms and trade shops to see the children at work and watched Pratt put them through their paces on the parade ground. Just three years after the combined forces of the Northern Cheyenne and Lakota had wiped out Custer's Seventh Cavalry, at a time when fear and revulsion as well as fascination with the Indian was at its height, here was a school demonstrating it could pacify and civilize. Pratt's school was given unhesitating official approval. His optimistic insistence on the possibility of Indian assimilation in a single generation suggested to government officials that the long-entrenched Indian Problem could be solved, without resort to continuous military force.

I

The Development of an Indian Educational System

1. White Theories: Can the Indian be Educated?

THE GOVERNMENT'S NEW COMMITMENT to educating all Indians and assimilating them into the Republic preempted the answer to a question that had been long debated and still haunted the minds of many white Americans. Could white schooling prepare native children for equal citizenship? After the Civil War, advocates of federal Indian education were engaged in a new and controversial venture. Outspoken in their views, they appeared to constitute a united group as they worked to find ways to persuade the tribes to abandon their traditional habits, dress, beliefs, and customs and adopt those familiar to Americans. Yet the common goal of reformers masked a fundamental division in their perceptions and constructions of the Indian. In deliberating over how to transform the Indian, they were forced to broach the thorny problem of racial difference; to ask not only in what ways Indians were dissimilar to whites but to confront the essence and source of that difference. Some Indian educators believed the task could be simply and rapidly accomplished while others envisaged a far more difficult, long-term project. United in their determination to work toward the same broad but vague goal of Indian civilization, they were divided in their perception of the precise and necessary means to achieve this as well as the place Indians would be granted in United States society.

Dual Tradition of Racial Thought

In America, a dual tradition of thought about Indians had developed almost as soon as Europeans set foot on the continent and the thrill of exploration gave way to exploitation and settlement. Rooted in European philosophical and religious doctrines, this tradition depicted the Indian as either a noble, generous, wise, and virtuous savage or alternatively, as a base, depraved, and worse than bestial one. Although articulated in different terms at different times, the pattern remained unchanged: Indians were found to be either essentially redeemable or incontrovertibly damned.[1] The important difference between colonial ideas about savagery and those of the late nineteenth century was the authority that defined them: the former was religious, the latter scientific. Yet both strands of this long-standing tradition remained potent after the Civil War and independently informed the thinking and actions of Americans who formulated Indian education policy as well as those who worked to implement it.

One set of ideas and attitudes was informed by universalism, an eighteenth-century concept deriving from the Enlightenment. It was still highly potent in nineteenth-century debate but was increasingly accompanied by a distinctly different set of ideas: those surrounding the concept of evolutionary development and the application of biological theory to social development.[2] "Science" now challenged theology and moral philosophy and was enlisted to explain social, cultural, and physical variances among peoples. Recruited to classify different societies into a hierarchical scheme, "science" played an important role in suggesting that nonwhite "savages" were socially inferior to members of civilized society and that their social inferiority had a biological or racial counterpart. This more pessimistic discourse denied the possibility of change and attributed to individuals and groups inherent and permanent characteristics.

The broad American discourse on race ascribed to Indians a subsidiary but vital supporting role.[3] The major focus of this discourse was always African Americans, but in scientific inquiry as much as popular thought, America's nonwhite peoples could not be considered separately and judgments about African Americans influenced opinions of Native Americans. Scientific journals and illustrated monthlies enthusiastically explored race theory and discussed racial attributes. By the end of the nineteenth century, the forces of scientific racism had triumphed. Yet white thinking about race did not, as Bruce Dain reminds us, move tidily from "a shallow Enlightenment environmentalism to a deep biology; nor were the two positions mutually exclusive. Nature and nurture intertwined."[4] In the final quarter of the nineteenth century, whites striving to reconcile Christian values with scientific theories spanned a wide range in their opinions. For social gospel prophets addressing the future of African Americans, this spectrum ranged from "Josiah Strong's radical assimilationism to Josiah Royce's conservative assimilationism and from Edgar Gardner Murphy's conservative separatism to Thomas Dixon Jr.'s radical separatism."[5] Whites committed to Indian education spanned a parallel breadth of opinion. Convinced that the only solution to the "Indian problem" was for the remnants of Indian tribes to be absorbed into the Unites States, they nevertheless held sharply contrasting views about Indian capacity, the place the educated Indian should be assigned in the nation, and the best means of preparing him for his new situation.

Racial Fault Line in Reform Thought

The fault line that ran through the ranks of those who worked to educate the tribes was most notable when it separated the two army officers who publicly pioneered the cause of Indian education and made their respective institutions into living showcases for this experiment to "transform a race." Both Samuel Chapman Armstrong and Richard Henry Pratt believed fervently in the need for Indians to be Americanized and agreed that the best answer to the age-old "Indian Problem" lay in education.[6] Yet although Hampton and Carlisle were generally perceived by Americans concerned with Indian affairs as twin, flagship institutions and were often referred to in the same breath, the two military men who ran them held very different views about both the aptitude of Indians and their future within the United States. Armstrong subscribed to a philosophy that relegated Indians to a lowly place within the nation, close to "Negroes," and did not foresee that either race could readily attain equality, because, as he explained, "these people, who are with us and with whom we share a common fate, are a thousand years behind us in moral and mental development. Substantially the two races are in the same condition."[7] Although Armstrong's evolutionist position had rapidly gained ascendancy in the post-Civil War era, Pratt totally rejected it. Throughout his life, Pratt argued forcefully and persistently that with the help of white education, Indians were capable of achieving total equality with whites.

Despite these differences of opinion, Indian educators like Armstrong and Pratt closed ranks when fighting for their cause. The campaign for Indian education was new and untested, and in the broader society it was often greeted with skepticism and hostility. The battle lines were drawn between those who supported the new commitment of the government to Indian education and those who were against it. Differences of opinion amongst the educators seemed unimportant when the whole experiment was being contested. "The problem to me," Pratt explained, "seems not how it is done, but to get it done at all."[8] Until the experiment was secure and schooling for Indians generally accepted, disagreements were downplayed or aired in environments where a consensus on the topic already existed.

The main forum for discussion of Indian education was the annual Lake Mohonk conference. Starting in 1883, Albert Smiley, the affluent Quaker philanthropist who had served as a member of the Board of Indian Commissioners since 1879, brought Indian reformers together at the beautiful holiday resort he had developed on the shores of Lake Mohonk, New York. Smiley's aim was to "unite the best minds interested in Indian affairs, so that all should act together and be in harmony, and so that the prominent persons connected with Indian affairs should act as one body and create a public sentiment in favor of the Indians."[9] Within a decade the conferences were being attended by over 150 people calling themselves "friends of the Indian." Well-educated, middle-class Protestants, the men and women who gathered to listen to one another in the meeting rooms of Smiley's resort hotel or who strolled on the pathways admiring the colors of fall, represented a powerful segment of American society.[10]

Although the Lake Mohonk conferences had no official standing, the attendees published their proceedings, made their opinions known in the press, and worked to have their views implemented in Washington. During the early years, their crusade was uncoordinated, but within a short time the delegates had focused their attention on developing and executing a political program in which individual ownership of land, citizenship, and education played a key role. Unified by this agenda, they unanimously supported Senator Henry Dawes in 1886 when he sketched out the bill he was about to present to Congress. Merrill E. Gates, president of Rutgers College, was fulsome in his praise, but he also hinted at some of the rifts that had been healed by the reformers' shared determination to support what would become the Dawes Act: "To me one of the most encouraging features of this conference . . . is the fact of the coming together of minds that several years ago differed widely on these matters. It seems to me this Dawes Bill furnishes a solution of this."[11]

At Lake Mohonk conferences, men and women subscribing to diametrically opposed views of Indian difference and adhering to two different traditions of racial thinking could work side by side for the common cause of Indian education without always acknowledging the extent of their differences. Their political and social cohesiveness meant they all decried the Indian's "savagery," testified to the importance of "education," insisted on the necessity of "schools" to redeem the "race," and incessantly spoke of the Indian's need for "civilization." These abstract words, which peppered the reports of the Lake Mohonk conferences and were echoed in Congressional speeches and commissioners' reports, served to shroud contradictions and inconsistencies in policy and obscure differences of opinion among the educators. Sometimes they were used to smooth over latent disputes—everyone could assent to "schooling" without having to sign up to a declared set of educational and social goals. But this facile agreement masked an important shift taking place in the meaning and use of some key words.

"Civilization" was, indisputably, the word that tripped most frequently from the lips and pens of reformers when they expounded on the failings and needs of the Indian and the glories of their own society. Even this apparently untroublesome word was used in different ways, as becomes clear when we examine how it was employed by two separate speakers at Lake Mohonk in 1886. Herbert Welsh, cofounder, secretary, and leading light of the Indian Rights Association, described the main task of "friends of the Indian" gathered at Lake Mohonk as being to guide the Indian "from the night of savagery into the fair dawn of Christian civilization."[12] Welsh here equates the age-old polarities of savagery and civilization not only with darkness and light, but also (by implication) with paganism and Christianity. Yet he implies that the Indian can be helped to progress from one state to the other—from savagery to civilization—quite easily and naturally, in the same way that the "fair dawn" breaks after the night. Welsh's natural and optimistic imagery is nourished by a positive Enlightenment vision.

Yet, just a few hours before Welsh addressed the Lake Mohonk conference, Philip Garrett, a member of the Board of Indian Commissioners, had spoken to the same assemblage. He employed the word "civilization" in a very different context, with a quite different inflected meaning from the one it had in Enlightenment discourse. Garrett called on the Indian to "Lay aside his picturesque blanket and moccasin, and, clad in the panoply of American citizenship, seek his chances of fortune or loss in the stern battle of life with the Aryan races. . . . If civilization is a blessing, then in the name of Christianity let us offer it as a boon, even to the untutored savage."[13]

What is interesting about this speech is that an invitation to claim citizenship is followed by a forceful statement about the racial makeup of the population the Indian will be joining, "the Aryan races." Not only have all nonwhites conveniently been eradicated from the population of the United States, but the Indian's entry into American society is presented here in racial terms. More specifically, that entry is couched in the competitive language of evolutionism; the reference to "fortune or loss in the stern battle of life" is a restatement of the social Darwinian notion of the "survival of the fittest." The implicit suggestion here is that the "untutored savage" should be allowed the opportunity to join American society, but that he might not be a survivor because of the disadvantage of "race."

Garrett's reference to "the Aryan races" at Lake Mohonk signaled the new way "race" was increasingly being constructed and discussed in the broader society. Bolstered by scientific research, long-accepted differences between "races" were now being measured and charted onto an organized hierarchy. "From the mid-nineteenth century on," Audrey Smedley argues, "science provided the bases for the ideological elements of a comprehensive worldview summed up in the term 'race.'"[14] Cultural differences between "racial" groups in America had always been remarked and constructed into a narrative of differentiation, because without such a narrative, "the entire rationale of domination and exploitation would crumble."[15] For many years the word "race" was multidimensional and used in various contexts that combined elements of nation and culture as well as biological inheritance. By the 1880s, however, the use of the word had become more restrictive and specific. Over the course of the nineteenth century, the physiological aspects of "race" had been progressively privileged and scientific attention became focused on all aspects of bodily difference. Audrey Smedly suggests that "the greater the number of variables that could be noted and measured, the stronger the argument for vast gulfs between the races."[16] Fixed physical differences between the "races" were increasingly identified as the correlatives of social and intellectual states.

While everyone who met at Lake Mohonk could agree that the main obstacle standing in the way of civilizing Indians was savagery, what was not completely clear was the true nature of this savagery. Did it represent a stage through which Indians could happily pass, or was it a state in which they were compelled to live? Often the answer to this question was not clear-cut, and even the opinions of a single individual could waiver or be confused. But the speeches of Welsh and Garrett make plain that among those concerned with Indian affairs, two quite different discourses about "race" were running concurrently. For all of them, however, a strong commitment to Christianity allowed them to work toward a common cause.

Christian values mollified differences in opinion among the reformers. An atmosphere of deep religiosity pervaded the Lake Mohonk conferences; over a quarter of those present were ministers and wives of ministers, and everyone else also claimed strong religious motivations for their work for Indians. Christianity could be invoked to smooth over differences or disputes. "It may be taken for granted," the Congregational minister Lyman Abbott declared in 1885, to the growing number of delegates who assembled at Lake Mohonk, "that we are Christian men and women; that we believe in justice, good-will, and charity, and the brotherhood of the human race."[17] But reminders of Christian commitment to the "brotherhood of the human race" such as this could spring from the same lips as racial opinions that separated men into mutually discrete groupings.

Abbott, who had been executive secretary and spokesman for the American Freedman's Union Commission since 1866, was well known for his efforts to obtain social justice for the freedmen. Yet while he insisted that the races should all enjoy "the same rights, immunities and opportunities," he suggested that wise friends of the freedmen should not claim that "the

African race is equal to the Anglo-Saxon." So on the question of schooling, he argued that "equal—not necessarily identical—educational advantages [needed to] be offered to both races." He steered a similar course for Indians. Adamantly against assimilation, he openly criticized missions if they aimed "to make Malays and Hindus and Negroes and Indians into second-hand Puritans," maintaining, "the less we have of such missions the better." The damaging implications of Abbott's racial philosophy provoked W. E. B. Du Bois to describe him as "the most subtle and dangerous enemy of the Negro in America." It was Abbott's amalgamation of Christianity, morality, and racial inequality that Du Bois found so offensive. Not only did he use "every art of his remarkable gift of casuistry to put the religion of Jesus Christ into the service of caste," Du Bois protested, but he did it with "so straight a face and such an assumption of high motives and impeccable respectability that thousands of well-meaning Americans followed his lead." [18] At the Lake Mohonk conferences where "friends of the Indian" assembled, there was no need for the scores of "well-meaning Americans" gathered there to follow Abbott's lead because they already shared his opinions. Like Jonathan Baxter Harrison, member of the Indian Rights Association and agency inspector, who worked consistently to better the situation of Indians in the United States, they too believed Indians to be "as a race, far inferior to white men in intellectual vitality and capacity." [19]

Whenever problems developed in the education of Indians, the white delegates in the racially exclusive environment of Lake Mohonk habitually attributed them to the Indians' lesser intellectual capability. No Indians were ever present to refute this claim; those invited were invariably cast as ventriloquists of a white script. One reason the Mohonk Conference on the Negro Question only lasted two years, when it was planned to duplicate the annual pattern of the Indian model, was that here, too, the future of black people was presumptuously pondered without consulting them. At the Negro conference, only Albion Tourgee, the maverick Ohio-born carpetbagger, protested against this, and in the absence of any black delegates, he took it on himself to rail against the evil influence of slavery, insist on the need for racial justice, and accuse Abbott of reducing the conference to an absurdity by denying the existence of a serious racial problem. Contemptuous of Mohonk's "watering-place gushiness, which seeks to bait the Devil a little way towards heaven by agreeing not to say anything about the 'airs of hell' which cling to his clothes," Tourgee concluded, "for the Indian and Negro, you might as well try to cure cancer by giving me treacle as expect any good from such gathering."[20] Failure to include black spokesmen prompted some, like George Cable and Joseph Cook, to shun the conference, but no similar boycott of the Indian conference was ever staged. Instead, doubts about Indian educability constantly surfaced in muted guises and time and again the Indian's inherent difference from whites was cited as an explanation. Even the tragic collapse of children's health was attributed by Frederick Treon, doctor on the Crow Creek reservation for six years, to the inferiority of the Indian children's mental powers: "Up to the age of twelve or fourteen they learn rapidly. . . . After that age, however, education proves a task and they soon tire or fall behind. Whenever an Indian is placed in a situation where he must think for himself and assume mental responsibility, he soon sickens and breaks down under the strain."[21]

All apparent setbacks in Indian advance were accounted for in similar ways. In 1890, on reservations across the West, tribe after tribe was hit by an atavistic movement that looked to the resurgence of Indian people and a return of the buffalo. When hopeless and starving adult Indians listened to the prophesies of an Indian messiah and danced for days at a time in a vain attempt to assist this renaissance, white Americans looked on aghast. Meeting some months after the Ghost Dance movement had led to the tragic massacre at Wounded Knee, delegates at the Lake Mohonk conference were chilled by what they interpreted as a sign of the yawning and impassable gulf between Indians and Americans. Merrill Gates, president of both Lake Mohonk and Amherst College, offered a judgment which no one present disputed:

> I believe that the Dakota disaster shows that we shall not need to have taught us again the lesson of the difference between savagery and civilization. As we watched the progress of the disasters that began these disorders, as the reports of eye-witnesses came to us, . . . we saw that for one brought up in the atmosphere of Christian civilization to enter the consciousness of the savage at such a time is almost as impossible as it is for us to get behind the great, blue limpid eyes of the ox as he chews his cud in the pasture, and know how the world looks to him.[22]

All trace of belief in a universal family of man is absent here. When confronted with an incomprehensible and unacceptable aspect of native culture, the "friends of the Indian" could only explain it by emphasizing the unbridgeable gap between themselves and Indians and by relegating the latter not just to a lowly situation but to a position closer to beast than man. Savagery here is not just a state but an unalterable condition as fundamental as the divide between man and beast that was laid down in the book of Genesis. The crucial significance of this biblical divide was that, according to Christian doctrine, man was given dominion over beast and, by extrapolation, whites at Lake Mohonk and across the nation assumed it was their natural right to hold dominion over Indians.

In one of his extraordinary acts of intellectual racial chicanery so hated by W. E. B. Du Bois, Lyman Abbott successfully merged the two divergent discourses subscribed to by "friends of the Indian." In an article laying out what he described as "the Basis of Anglo-Saxon Understanding," Abbott claimed indisputable rights to world power for whites while continuing to pay lip service to the "brotherhood of man" and its ties to "the kingdom of God": "I am proud that I belong to that race which dominates the world, whose branches stand together shoulder to shoulder, hand to hand, promoting intelligence, liberty, culture and civilization. . . . The Anglo-Saxon race is to act as leader, and in the United States is to take no inferior place in leadership toward that brotherhood of man founded on justice and liberty which is the kingdom of God."[23] Just as Abbott could collapse together two separate outlooks and gloss over the inconsistency of enlisting "the brotherhood of man" in the service of "that race which dominates the world," so too many white reformers were able to overlook their contradictory racial perspectives and unite behind what for them was a more fundamental issue: U.S. expansion and white power. Herbert Welsh spoke for the majority of reformers when he explained, "we cannot stop the legitimate advance of emigration and civilization . . . and, we add most emphatically, we would not if we could."[24]

Whether reformers regarded Indian societies as the main obstacle or saw the problem as rooted more deeply in the Indian himself, they were all united in their hostility to everything they saw represented by "Indianness" and so dedicated themselves to its rapid eradication in every form. Their ethnocentrism allowed them to ride roughshod over Indian cultures and values and approve the seizure of Indian lands that was "legalized" by the Dawes Act as well as parallel plans to enroll native children in white schools. When Commissioner of Indian Affairs Thomas Jefferson Morgan outlined to delegates at the seventh Lake Mohonk Conference of Friends of the Indian his scheme for an integrated system of government Indian schools, they cheered. Morgan's projection, that Indian children would advance from reservation day school to reservation boarding school and then on to the militaristic off-reservation institutions that stood at the apex of the system, presented reformers with the orderly and coherent educational scheme they longed for to render Indians harmless.

Three years later, when Morgan outlined further details of his plan and alluded to the physical force that might be necessary to ensure it was put into practice, there was no dissent. Reformers stood firmly behind him and included in their conference platform a provision that "In cases where parents, without good reason, refuse to educate their children, we believe that the government is justified, as a last resort, in using power to compel attendance. We do not think it is desirable to rear another generation of savages."[25] Compulsory attendance at school would thus ensure, in a single generation, the obliteration of savagery, despite the fact that reformers had never reached accord about the true essence of savagery and its relationship to race. At Lake Mohonk and in the larger society, both strands of the well-entrenched dual discourse used to characterize and discuss Indians remained potent and unresolved.

Dr. Thomas A. Bland: Lone Voice of White Dissent

The bedrock of unity that lay at the core of the reformers' campaign and allowed them to work together manifested itself in their dealings with Indians. It was, however, most starkly and tellingly revealed in their fierce opposition to a compatriot and fellow reformer, who refused to toe their line: Dr. Thomas A. Bland. Bland's Quaker background and dedication to Indian reform should have enabled him to mix effortlessly with the reformers who assembled at Lake Mohonk, but his views progressively diverged from theirs.

In 1881, after the death of Colonel Alfred B. Meacham, he had taken over editorship of the *Council Fire* and reaffirmed the journal's commitment to "justice to the Indians and arbitration as a remedy for war."[26] The

goals of the *Council Fire* did not obviously conflict with that of other reformers and an early issue gave a very favorable assessment of one of the
major reform groups, the Women's National Indian Association, and even
reprinted one of its petitions.[27] However, Bland began to use the pages of
the *Council Fire* to critique government policy and soon started a lengthy
and increasingly acrimonious campaign against the mainstream reformers. He became critical of them because they failed to present "the Indians' side of the story" and pointed out that in their determination to dis-
mantle both tribes and reservations, they rode roughshod over Indians'
rights.[28] Confident in Indian capacity, Bland went beyond the universalist reformers in his support for Indians; he recognized both the strength
of native institutions and the legitimacy of Indian wishes. Convinced that
only through gradual change, implemented in close consultation with Indians themselves, could the tribes' property rights be protected, he used
the pages of the *Council Fire* to speak out vociferously in defense of tribal
governments and community ownership of land.

Believing that Indian institutions should be enlisted to facilitate the tribes'
transformation instead of being destroyed, Bland demanded that whites
listen to Indian views before enforcing policies to enable Indians to share
in American progress rather than be undermined by it. Bland promised
to throw his weight behind severalty legislation but only with Indian con-
sent.[29] When he realized that mainline reformers were determined to use
"individual title to land" as the "entering wedge by which tribal organization" was to be "rent asunder," he changed his mind and began a vocif-
erous campaign against the Indian Rights Association.[30]

Founded in late 1882 by Herbert Welsh and Henry S. Pancoast, the Indian Rights Association had quickly claimed the position of most important reform organization. Powerful in Washington as well as at Lake Mohonk, the association was vehemently committed to a policy of allotting
Indian lands and destroying tribal organization. To thwart its influence, in
1885 Bland set up a rival organization, the National Indian Defense Association. "The fact that powerful organizations are already advocates of the
policy to be opposed," the National Indian Defense Association platform
declared, "renders it necessary that the effort to counteract their influences
should be an organized effort also."[31] The National Indian Defense Association was small and the *Council Fire* made far less of a show than the

stream of publications pouring out of the Indian Rights Association. Despite this, Bland's clash with reformers is important for our purposes here because it revealed the latter's uncompromising belief in white power, which buttressed their national-racial vision. This vision allowed them to work cooperatively. Despite their contradictory views about the future place of the Indian in U.S. society, they were prepared to forfeit Indian rights and were happy to see tribal cultures and institutions destroyed.

In stark contrast, the new association made clear its favorable attitude to tribal organization: "The immediate dissolution of the tribal relation would prove to be an impediment to the civilization of the Indians by depriving them of a conservative influence tending to preserve order, respect for person and property, and reduce vagrancy and vagabondage."[32] Rather than abolishing tribal governments, members of the National Indian Defense Association looked to these as important controlling and stabilizing forces that would, "with such modifications as may be necessary[,] . . . eventually merge into some political institution in harmony with the general system of Government."[33] Indian control over their own affairs was deemed crucial.

Bland was, however, a strong advocate of white schooling, seeing it as the best way to prepare Indians for life in American society. When Secretary Henry Teller made a speech at Carlisle, emphasizing the importance of education over "land in severalty," Bland published it word-for-word in the *Council Fire*.[34] But the reformers' growing commitment to rapid, single-generation transformation of all Indian children, which was accompanied by their enthusiasm for boarding schools, led Bland to counsel prudence. He published an article suggesting that day schools were better, because they were linked to Indian communities. Once again, Bland was out of step with his fellow reformers, but most Indians shared his views.

Chief Standing Bear had allowed his son, Ota Kte (Luther Standing Bear), to make the long journey from Dakota to Pennsylvania. He believed in the importance of white schooling, but in an 1883 letter to the *Council Fire*, written when his son had been at Carlisle three-and-a-half years, Standing Bear voiced his support for schools closer to home:

> We have no Church or School and hav [*sic*] to send our children away
> to school. Your plan of schooling children at home is what al [*sic*] the

Indians want, then they can se [*sic*] their children when ever their parents want to. If they are sent away and are sick and in som [*sic*] cases die and their parents and relations can't go to se [*sic*] them, it makes us feel bad, where if the school was on our agency we could se [*sic*] them when we wanted to.[35]

When Chief Standing Bear wrote this letter, whites concerned with civilizing Indians were determinedly placing their faith in the power of boarding schools to reconstruct and transform Indian children and, increasingly, in the efficacy of institutions far from Indian Country. That same year, Congress approved the founding of four new, off-reservation schools in Chilocco, Oklahoma; Genoa, Nebraska; Albuquerque, New Mexico; and Lawrence, Kansas. Bland was working against the grain of mainstream Indian reform. His was a lone voice that would be drowned out by the noisy unanimity of mainstream reformers who drove Indian policy.

Bland was a maverick among reformers as well as in the wider U.S. society, where few questioned white prerogative to quash Indian cultures and decide Indian futures.[36] "The white man has legislated for him," Commissioner of Indian Affairs Daniel M. Browning pronounced unashamedly. "His circumstances are not an outgrowth from himself, but something to which he must grow up—an unnatural process, but inevitable when civilization and barbarism collide."[37] However, certainty about the power and authority of whites could not conceal confusion about the ability and status of Indians, nor could it effectively fuse the dual discourse.

Dual Racial Discourse in Chicago

This dual racial discourse was publicly displayed at the 1893 World's Columbian Exposition in Chicago. On the banks of Lake Michigan, the high achievements and progress of American civilization—technological wonders, industrial might, scientific triumph, and artistic accomplishments—were exhibited in cream-colored edifices in what became known as the White City. At the same time, the architecture and layout of the exposition also carried within it a covert message about racial and cultural superiority/inferiority, and the Indian exhibits perpetuated the now-familiar twin discourses.

On the opposite side of the river, segregated from the White City, was a second section of the fair known as the Midway. Here popular entertainment—the freak show, the honky-tonk bar and Ferris wheel—intermingled with living ethnological exhibits of "savage villages." The villages were arranged in an obvious evolutionary and chromatic hierarchy, with the darker peoples situated at the bottom of the Midway and the lighter peoples at the top, closest to the White City. Furthest from the White City stood the African Dahomey village. Sixty-nine imported living "exhibits," described by reviewers as being "degraded as the animals which prowl the jungles of their dark land," titillated visitors with the thrill of a glimpse of "darkest Africa." After Africa, villages of progressively paler and more "advanced" "savages" marked the mile-long journey to the riverbank with its views of the gleaming White City. On opposite sides of the river, the accomplishments of the civilized world were "counterposed to [the] ignorance, dirt, smells and brown bodies" of the Midway.[38] Crossing from one side to the other, visitors moved between the white civilized world to the non-white world of the savage. These, Robert Rydell suggests, were not antithetical constructs but instead represented "two sides of the same coin—a coin minted in the tradition of American racism."[39]

At the exposition, there was no equivocation about the low status of Africans, and their direct links to African Americans were made explicit. But the organizers vacillated in their presentation of Indians. Eventually, two separate displays were planned reflecting the two separate and irreconcilable discourses and judgments of Indians with which we have become familiar. The Bureau of Indians Affairs mounted a display of modern Indians in federal schools to demonstrate the Indian's capacity for citizenship. This, however, was featured alongside a second Indian exhibit on the Midway showing traditional camp life. Frederick Ward Putnam was professor of anthropology at Harvard's Peabody Institute and also director of the Midway project that was responsible for organizing "strictly scientific" representations of the primitive conditions of indigenous life. His exhibit gave no suggestion of the possibility of indigenous change or advance. The progress demonstrated by Indians in the second exhibit was presented as being entirely the product of their government schooling.

Emma Sickles, chair of the Indian Committee of Universal Peace Union, who had been given a post in the Midway Project, was outraged at the implied narrative of Putnam's projected Midway exhibit. She denounced the "low and degrading phases of Indian life" Putnam was presenting and suggested that the Indians' own role and participation in the process of civilization should be shown. Putnam was unrepentant and immediately dismissed her. Sickles retaliated by publishing an article in the *New York Times*:

> Every effort has been put forth to make the Indian exhibit mislead the American People. It has been used to work up sentiment against the Indian by showing that he is either savage or can be educated only by government agencies. This would strengthen the power of everything that has been "working" against the Indian for years. Every means was used to keep the self-civilized Indians out of the Fair. The Indian agents and their backers knew well that if the civilized Indians got a representation in the Fair the public would wake up to the capabilities of the Indians for self-government and realize that all they needed was to be left alone.[40]

Sickles's article indicated that she, too, read the Chicago displays as mirroring the dual discourse that did not permit the Indian any influence over his own destiny or development. Like the entire exposition, setup on two sides of the river in Chicago, the two Indian exhibits represented opposite sides of the same white-minted coin of American racism. It was a coin that at all times allowed "friends of the Indian" to deal in a common currency, despite their differing racial views.

For those reformers who felt uneasy about the inclusion in American society of a group they judged to be racially inferior, Merrill E. Gates supplied an historical model and reminded them of "the stupendous precedent of eight millions of freed men made citizens in a day."[41] The secretary of the interior, a little more exact with his figures, supported Gates. He was confident that "after swallowing four million black slaves and digesting that pretty well, we need not strain at this."[42] But by 1885, the political and social strains of "digesting" four million exslaves were already becoming starkly evident in American society and would (as chapter 4 shows) have a deepening impact on the project to include Indians, another nonwhite group, in America's citizenry.

The attitudes of excluded groups were discounted by whites but critical to their educational project. The freedmen had always been part of U. S. society and generally were eager to embrace education and the full rights of citizenship previously denied them. Indians, however, living in their own separate communities apart from whites, had developed quite different opinions about white schools and frequently associated them with danger and the threat of annihilation. American history and belief structures caused many whites to feel uneasy or hostile towards the prospect of including Indians in their nation. Indian views on the same subject were varied and complex and displayed even greater concern.

2. Native Views: "A New Road for All the Indians"

As he watched the Great Plains of the Southwest being staked out, Kicking Bird, the Kiowa chief, was afraid for his people. He wanted peace and "had given his hand to the white people, and had taken a firm hold of theirs," but he was fearful the Kiowa could never adapt to the new life demanded of them.[1] In a letter to Washington he explained: "The Commissioner has required a hard thing insisting the Indians stay on the reservation, which was not in the road our fathers traveled. It is a new road for us. . . . It is a new road for all the Indians in this country." And he confessed to his overwhelming sense of doom. "The white man is strong, but he cannot destroy us all in one year, it will take him two or three, maybe four years and then the world will turn to water or burn up. It cannot live when the Indians are all dead."[2]

The dramatic shift in the balance of power on the Plains after the Civil War placed all Indians who lived there in a desperate situation. With armed resistance progressively less possible, they were forced onto reservations where strong measures were taken to ensure that their children enrolled in white-run schools. Hundreds of Indian communities were subjected to the same process. They did not represent a single monolithic culture and the responses of different individuals and societies to the new situation varied enormously. Yet, for the first time, a unified government program of educational instruction was being enforced on all their children and the reactions it elicited from Indian people fell into identifiable patterns. Open defiance was a fading possibility, yet passive compliance with white demands and acceptance of cultural suicide was equally out of the question. In the vast terrain between the polar opposites of these responses, Indian leaders and their people worked to protect and reshape worlds they recognized as their own. In their struggle to do this, they often resisted white schooling or grudgingly accommodated its demands, but sometimes they were able to claim and adapt for their own purposes the new skills and perceptions taught in the schools.

In the early days, although forced to sign treaties with strict educational clauses, many tribes held out resolutely against any proposal that their children should be sent to white schools. Speaking through an interpreter at the Council of Medicine Lodge, the Kiowa chief Satanta (White Bear) doggedly informed white negotiators, "I don't want any of the medicine lodges within this country. I want the children raised as I was."[3] The medicine lodges he referred to were the schools and churches written into the terms of the Treaty of Medicine Lodge. For Satanta and many others at the council, including Satank (Sitting Bear), E-si-sim-ers (Lone Wolf), Woman's Heart, and Isa-tah (White Horse), these white institutions, specifically devised for education and worship, were extraneous and offensive to a people well able to care for and instruct their own children. Edward Red Hand, the Cheyenne Keeper of the Sacred Arrows, shared their opinion and some years later recalled: "We did not want our children to learn the White Man's ways. We had our own ways and we liked them better. It was still our country and we did not want anyone to tell us what to do."[4] While Indians retained their economic and political independence, the majority felt no incentive to relinquish their own cultural practices, particularly the education of their children.

Native Patterns of Education

As with all peoples, the training of Indian children reflected individual cultures and histories. Each tribe had developed clearly defined ways to ensure the survival of its own beliefs into the next generation. It is not within the scope of this study to begin to offer a full account of these many patterns of traditional native education. Instead it supplies a backdrop against which the reeducation program attempted in white schools can be more accurately assessed.

Despite many cultural differences, some fundamental assumptions shared by tribes were reflected in their child-rearing practices. For example, in no native community was education a discrete endeavor conducted in a separate institution. It was always woven into everyday patterns of living and took place informally in daily interactions between children and their elders. As in all traditional societies, children learned from example and informal lessons as well as by participation in more formal ceremonies and rites. This training was essential to their own survival as well as the continuation of the identity and worldview of their tribe. Charles Eastman's extensive white schooling, which came hard on the heels of a traditional Dakota childhood, induced him to write about and elucidate the special nature of Indian society and educational practices for a white audience. Countering a contemporary supposition that "there is no systematic education of their children among the aborigines of this country," he explained that "nothing could be further from the truth. All the customs of this primitive people were held to be divinely instituted, and those in connection with the training of children were scrupulously adhered to and transmitted from one generation to another."[5] In his autobiographical book, *Indian Boyhood*, Eastman describes the strict training given Dakota boys and his own careful instruction by his uncle and other elders. He felt a pressing need openly to counter white misconceptions and stereotypes. "It seems to be a popular idea that all the characteristic skill of the Indian is instinctive and hereditary. This is a mistake. All the stoicism and patience of the Indian are acquired traits, and continual practice alone makes him master of the art of wood-craft."[6] Outlining how he developed the athleticism, patience, restraint, courage, and generosity required of a Dakota man, Eastman detailed how he also gained intimate knowledge of the natural world from the numerous suggestions and snippets of information spoken by his uncle. "It is better to view animals unobserved. I have been witness to their courtships and their quarrels and have learned many of their secrets in this way."[7]

Acquaintance with the animal kingdom was common to all Indians, wherever they lived. In *Apache Mothers and Daughters*, Narcissus Duffy Gayton tells how, in the Southwest, a Chiricahua Apache mother would warn her child about dangerous animals, like bears and snakes, and carefully explain the correct way to treat them. "Don't ever say snake's name. It must be addressed in terms of respect, in the third person. It is a relative. Call it 'father's father.' Always be careful of snake. It is dangerous. It crawls."[8] Accounts like these give a glimpse of how Indian children were taught to live safely and properly in the natural environment. For hunting tribes, understanding the animals was essential to survival, but beyond this, all Indians believed they were members, not masters, of the natural world. The Christian cosmology, in which man stands above the animals, created in the image of god, was utterly alien to them. For all Indians, the animal kingdom was an intrinsic part of both their physical and spiritual world.

Spirituality pervaded all aspects of Indian life and was never absent from a child's instruction, supplying "the basis of all Indian training."[9] By watching and listening to his or her elders, the child understood his or her place within both the social and spiritual world. Everyday actions were performed with habitual reverence. Among the Pawnee, as in many tribes, "when the pipe is lighted, the first whiff is blown to the Deity. When food is eaten, a small portion is placed on the ground, or in the fire, as a sacrifice to them."[10] In the same way, stories passed down from generation to generation, carrying the traditions, history, and values of a people, were told always with respect and reverence. John Stands-in-Timber remembers the preparations an elder would make before he told a story:

> An old [Cheyenne] storyteller would smooth the ground in front of him with his hand and make two marks in it with his right thumb, two with his left, and a double mark with both thumbs together. Then he would rub his hands, and pass his right hand up his right leg to his waist, and touch his left hand and pass it on up his right arm to his breast. He did the same thing with his left and right hands going up the other side. Then he touched the marks on the ground with both hands and rubbed them together and passed them over his head and all over his body. That meant the Creator had made human beings, and that the Creator was witness to what was to be told. They did not tell any of the old or holy stories without that.[11]

The experience of telling or listening to a story was as important as the story itself, instructing and including the children while binding the generations together. Charles Eastman recalled how: "Very early, the Indian boy assumed the task of preserving and transmitting the legends of his ancestors and his race. Almost every evening a myth, or true story of some deed done in the past, was narrated by one of the parents or grand-parents while the boy listened with parted lips and glistening eyes. On the following evening he was usually required to repeat it."[12]

A hidden educational task figured in many apparently neutral activities.[13] In many tribes, names carried important social information and were used to mark different stages of life. Thus an individual could be awarded several different names in the course of a lifetime. Eastman, the last of five children, whose mother died shortly after his birth, was called Hakadah, "the Pitiful Last," before he became known to his people as Ohiyesa. Sitting Bull was called Jumping Badger before his deliberate ways earned him the nickname Hunkesni or "Slow." Then, at the age of fourteen, after counting his first coup in a fight against the Crow, his father honored him with the ultimate accolade, his own name, Tatanka-Iyotanka, Sitting Bull.[14] Employed more often to refer to than to address an individual, Indian names were therefore not just sounds, like John or Mary, but also often carried a record of a person's life. Among the Apache, a new name might be given to a child as protection from the ghost of a deceased parent and the accompanying ceremony on such occasions was serious and sedate.[15]

Ceremonies of all kinds were essential to the educational process. All Indian children learned about their own tribe's traditions and were embraced within them by participating in ceremonies of both a public and personal nature. Ella Deloria makes clear how "what we might call the formal education of Dakota youth was centered in tribal ceremonies."[16] On the plains, the Sun Dance was the greatest religious ceremony, bringing together whole tribes at the height of summer for a massive social and religious gathering.[17] Sun Dance rituals were religiously adhered to, although they varied from tribe to tribe. For the Cheyenne, John Stands-in-Timber recounts, there were "many, many steps in the ceremony, far too many to explain here, and certain songs to be used and prayers and offerings to be made."[18] This community act of worship, with its many separate elements, would be widely misunderstood and condemned by whites. In 1882, the government banned the Sun Dance, and for many years it could only be practiced in secret.

Individual ceremonies marked and celebrated the stages of life differently in different tribes, but all initiated the child into his/her people's guiding principles. Among the Dakota, the Hunka ceremony placed a young child at center stage and the accompanying giveaway to honor him/her was intended to commit that child to generosity, "even if at times it might involve great personal sacrifice."[19] Among the Apache, there was a ceremony to celebrate a child's first steps and for a girl, the most important ceremony was the puberty rite, a four-day feast with dancing, held to mark her passage from childhood to maturity and initiate her into the knowledge and mysteries of womanhood.[20]

Underpinning all ceremonials was a complex system of human relations—kinship systems—into which Indian children were progressively initiated. The pattern of relationships and duties associated with them varied from tribe to tribe, but attachments always extended far outside the nuclear family of parents and children and carried a matching network of responsibilities. "The ultimate aim of Dakota life, stripped of accessories was quite simple," Ella Deloria explained. "One must obey kinship rules; one must be a good relative. . . . In the last analysis every other consideration was secondary—property, personal ambition, glory, good times, life itself."[21] Through the kinship system a child was constantly reminded how one individual should both treat and address another. "It was improper to plunge into conversation without first using the polite term of kinship"; this was the means by which a child was taught good manners.[22] "Among my earliest recollections," recalls Omaha Francis La Flesche, "are the instructions wherein we were taught respect and courtesy toward our elders; to say 'thank you' when receiving a gift, or when returning a borrowed article; to use the proper and conventional term of relationship when speaking to another; and never to address anyone by his personal name."[23] The kinship system, with its parallel demands and responsibilities, exerted such power that even at school, when forced to speak English, depriving them of access to the extensive case system of their own language that carried a host of special nuances, children still often refrained from using personal names. One white teacher at the Kiowa school indicated she had gained an inkling of the responsibilities of kinship when, in a letter to her mother, she explained, "They call each other 'brother' and 'friend' and that word is the talisman by which one does everything for the other."[24] Her observation stands as a reminder that Indian children carried with them a deep awareness of traditional kinship obligations. Sometimes, even when children lived within the rules and strictures of white-run schools, these could work to reinforce and deepen tribal loyalty.[25]

The Need to Adopt White Ways

Even though children carried within them many traditional values, as more and more of them were packed off to boarding schools, the communities where these values were rooted were undergoing drastic change. On the Plains, it was tribes that had already experienced the devastation of removal who were most alert to the ongoing threat of white expansion. They recognized its fatal implications for their own nation and all Indian people. In 1870, Lewis Downing, a full-blood elected Cherokee chief and Baptist minister, who spoke only Cherokee but had fought for the Union as a colonel, voiced his sense of doom about what was now happening on the Plains. He called upon the people of the Cherokee Nation to pray to Almighty God as the only means left to them by which they might preserve their national integrity:

> Today, the Cherokees, and the whole Indian race are in distress and danger. Powerless we lie in the hands of the United States [that] can bring the weight of forty millions of people, and untold wealth, power and skill to crush us in our weakness. . . . Especially are we alarmed, when we read in the short history of the United States name after name of mighty nations of red men who once occupied this vast continent, but who are now swept from the face of the earth before the white man. . . . Viewed in every light, and from every standpoint, our situation is alarming. The vortex of ruin, which has swallowed hundreds of Indian Nations, now yawns for us.[26]

Downing acknowledged both the commonality as well as the gravity of the situation for the Cherokee and other tribes. In his speech, he openly linked the fate of all the "nations of red men" on the continent, drawing them together under the unified title of "Indian Race." The following year, in 1871, the Cherokee and the other so-called Five Civilized Tribes called a council to meet with and advise their Indian neighbors in Indian Territory. The Kiowa, Comanche, and Cheyenne had experienced far fewer years of contact with whites and their Indian neighbors now strongly advised them that military struggle was futile and that they should instead fight to protect their rights by adopting and adapting the ways of whites.

At this time, with the buffalo dwindling but still in evidence, these Plains tribes were not ready for such a dramatic change. A decade later, after the Kiowa, Comanche, and Cheyenne had suffered military defeat and confinement on reservations, they were more receptive, because they were now alarmed by the mounting threat posed by the surrounding white population. The encroachment of cattle and settlers, the construction of railroads on their land, and the imminent threat of allotment motivated these tribes to send representatives to another intertribal council called by the Cherokee specifically to address these issues.[27] Again the Cherokee would repeat the recommendations they had made a decade earlier, which were rooted in their own history and experience.

Even before removal, groups within the Cherokee Nation had recognized that there was strategic advantage to be gained from learning white skills and had invited missionaries into their communities to set up schools. Yet while they wanted their children to gain the benefits of a white education, they held no intention of adopting Christianity.[28] After removal to Indian Territory, the Cherokee purposefully established their own school system. For many in the nation, Cherokee-run, white-style educational institutions seemed to offer the best way to protect their nation and identity.[29]

Separate Peoples

The Cherokee strategy was founded on a conviction that assertion of their rights and interests as Indians required adaptation and appropriation of white skills and expertise. Forceful and dynamic, the same approach would be adopted in a range of guises by many tribes over the years. Yet within many Indian communities, this compliant adaptive approach was flanked by a more steely and intractable stance. Ever since the Revolutionary era, relationships between whites and Indians had grown "increasingly antagonistic as they found themselves in competition for the same land."[30] For many Indians, just as for many Euro-Americans, Daniel Richter argues, "purging the other from the land—and, just as important, cleansing one's own community of those who still believed in accommodation with the hated other—was integral to the creation of a national independence and racial identity."[31] This viewpoint was founded on the belief that Indians and whites were, in all ways, mutually discrete and separate peoples. Stories, including creation narratives, were told within many tribes supporting this proposition.[32] Anthropologist Clark Wissler recorded the detail of one such story. Recounted by a judge in the agency court, it made clear not only that Indians were totally distinct from whites but also that they were superior:

> The Great Spirit made the world. He made two great bodies of land, separating them by water. . . . There being two separate lands, he decided to make two kinds of people—Indian and White. . . . The Great Spirit first made the Indian. He said to him, "you are the one I love the most, you are my favorite son." He spent several days instructing the Indian how he was to live, all of which he was expected to remember and pass on from generation to generation without change.[33]

Such accounts were often organized to deny the possibility of any "middle ground" where negotiation and adjustment might legitimately take place. Accommodation, within this frame of reference, was presented as being tantamount to capitulation.[34]

Sitting Bull, the Indian best known to whites in the late nineteenth century, appeared to represent as well as articulate this view.[35] His well-reported role in the Battle of the Little Big Horn and subsequent self-exile in Canada had ended in capture and a period of imprisonment in Fort Randall. When finally forced to settle with his people on the Standing Rock reservation, Sitting Bull developed a combative yet cordial relationship with Mary Collins, the local Congregational missionary. She reported how she once nursed a dangerously sick child of Sitting Bull's and insisted that "we were always good friends personally." At the same time she recalled how Sitting Bull "hated Christianity and found great satisfaction in taking my converts back into heathendom, while of course I felt equal satisfaction in converting his heathen friends."[36] It was to Mary Collins that Sitting Bull confided, "I would rather die an Indian than live a white man."[37] Yet despite the obduracy of this statement and the uncompromising position it affirms, Sitting Bull's life on the reservation provides evidence of careful and selective adaptation and use of white patterns of behavior to aid the survival of both himself and his people.

"Not the Road Our Fathers Traveled"

Sitting Bull had been born into a distinguished Hunkpapa family and as a young man had quickly proved himself a faultless horseman and courageous warrior. Later, he would become a great war leader as well as Wichasha Wakan, a holy man, capable of perspicacious dreams and visions. Admired and respected among his own people, Sitting Bull was also the subject of continuing publicity among whites. After the Battle of the Little Big Horn, splashy publicity announced that he had joined William Cody's Wild West spectacular. Later, the mature Sitting Bull struck fear in the hearts of many Americans when it was reported that he was taking part in the Ghost Dance.

Sitting Bull never relinquished the ways of his ancestors or the battle to protect his people, but on the reservation he was forced to find new weapons. Scrutiny of Sitting Bull's life in these later years reveals a far more complex picture than the one that comes down to us in contemporary reports of his unyielding statements. The Standing Rock agent, James McLaughlin, and Sitting Bull were at loggerheads, and McLaughlin seized every opportunity to foster the old chief's reputation as arrogant and rigidly conservative. Yet Robert Utley, Sitting Bull's most recent biographer, paints a much more intricate picture, which includes details of Sitting Bull's adaptation to a variety of white ways as well as evidence of how he put these to Indian use. During his years on the reservation the Hunkpapa chief lived in a cabin, cultivated land, owned chickens and cattle as well as horses, and, most significantly for the interests of this study, sent all his five children to the Congregational day school on the reservation.[38] While still imprisoned at Fort Randall, he had also agreed to his stepson being sent away to the Yankton boarding school. So though Sitting Bull's public statements were forceful and unrelenting and the official white record, carried in McLaughlin's reports, always portrayed him as deeply intransigent, the chief's actions hint at a more ambiguous and shrewd position.[39] They reveal an unpublicized determination to exploit white ways for Indian purposes.

In July 1889, when General George Crook returned to the Sioux at the head of yet another commission bent on extracting two-thirds of the adults' signatures necessary to secure the sale of Indian land, Sitting Bull worked strenuously to keep his people from capitulating to Crook's demands and signing away their lands. Playing a powerful and persuasive role behind the scenes, Sitting Bull recruited white-educated Sioux boys to take notes, so that everything said at the councils could be written down, reported to the Indians, and maintained as a record independent from that made by the white commissioners.[40] On countless previous occasions, Indians across the United States had been duped into signing agreements that did not reflect their wishes, because they had not understood white words or practices. "What do we know of the manners, the laws, and customs of the white people?" Black Hawk demanded. "They might buy our bodies for dissection and we would touch the goose quill to confirm it and not know what we were doing. This was the case with me and my people."[41] Sitting Bull was determined the Hunkpapa Sioux should not fall victim to the same deception and that white education would be harnessed to serve Indian needs.

Three years later, the Pawnee employed a similar tactic and turned to their white-educated kinsmen in their tribe's struggle to resist land "sales." After being browbeaten by the Jerome Commission, which was determined to allot Pawnee land and buy what remained, the Pawnee chiefs insisted they would not agree to sell any land at less than $1.50 an acre. After a deadlock of twelve days, the chiefs grew concerned that their opinions were not being correctly translated. They informed the commissioners that they would authorize seven young, educated English-speaking Pawnee to take over negotiations in the next council. Pawnee elders then met with educated youngsters and discussed the tribe's needs and demands. Using skills they had learned in white schools, the young men wrote a report in English, stating what the tribe wanted. Dressed in "civilian" clothes, to confront the commissioners on their own terms, the young Indians called a meeting with Jerome, at which Carlisle-educated Samuel Townsend handed over the report. In discussions that followed, the group of young men quickly indicated that they were well informed about events outside Indian Territory and that their boarding school experiences had provided them with personal contacts in other tribes.

Samuel Townsend had been a star pupil at Carlisle Indian School and a leading light in the school debating society. Appointed head printer by the white woman who ran the school print shop, Marianna Burgess (about whom we will hear more in chapter 8), he had also successfully shouldered the responsibility of producing the school paper in her absence. Now, utilizing skills he had honed in the school debating club, Townsend argued with the commissioners over the price to be paid for Pawnee land. The Sioux and the Cherokee had received $1.50 an acre, he reminded them. This price had been unfair, he insisted, because the Sisseton (Sioux) land had almost immediately sold for $2.50 an acre.[42] The Jerome Commission was relentless and the Pawnee eventually were paid only $1.25 an acre, but the young white-educated Pawnee had played an important and unprecedented role alongside the traditional elders. Schooling, intended by whites to suppress Pawnee culture, had instead been enlisted by these chiefs to defend Pawnee interests.

Although Indians often viewed schools as alien and dangerous places, many knew schools also proffered skills for survival in a white-dominated world. "One would be like a hobbled pony without learning to live like those amongst whom we must live," Charles Eastman's father explained, before sending his son away to school.[43] For Eastman, school was a new battlefield, where honor could be won in defense of the people. "Remember, my boy, it is the same as if I sent you on your first warpath. I shall expect you to conquer."[44] Eastman's father no longer harbored Satanta's hope that Indian children could continue to be raised in the ways of their ancestors, but when explaining to his son the need for white education, it was the Dakota standards of bravery, honor, and service through warfare that he evoked. These were values his son had been thoroughly and carefully taught throughout his Dakota education. They now needed to be enhanced with white skills—in particular, reading and writing.

Literacy and Power

For many Indians, literacy and the written word were indissoluble from white strength. Yet because written treaties always robbed them of their land, literacy was also linked to white perfidy. The Indian judge, who told Clark Wissler some of the "sayings of our fathers as they came down to us," specifically identified the written word as an indicator of white limitations:

> Whenever white people come together there is much writing. . . The white people must think that paper has some mysterious power to help them on in the world. The Indian needs no writings, words that are true sink into his heart where they remain; he never forgets them. On the other hand, if the white man loses his papers he is helpless. I once heard one of their preachers say that no white man was admitted to heaven unless there were writings about him in a great book.

But the same man, it should be remembered, also admitted the power of the written word, most notably the Bible. "Naturally, the white man possessing a book in which was written the way of life and signed by the Great Spirit, has a great advantage over the Indian, eventually surpassing him and overrunning the whole earth."[45]

Across the United States, Indians desperate to stand up to whites overcame their instinctive apprehensions and sent their children to school to learn to read, write, and become familiar with the English language. Some even allowed them to leave the reservation in the hope that they would secure a more thorough grounding in these necessary skills. The risks were high. After careful deliberation, Shawnee chiefs sent Thomas Wildcat Alford from Indian Territory to the Hampton Institute in Virginia, to train for tribal leadership (see chapter 5). At Rosebud Agency in Dakota, Spotted Tail, the principal Brulé chief, was persuaded by Richard Henry Pratt to allow his children to enroll at Carlisle after being reminded how ignorance of the English language had so often spelled doom for his tribe in their negotiations with whites.[46] But Spotted Tail's enthusiasm for his children to learn English was quickly dissipated when he visited Carlisle. He was horrified to see Indian children marching in white soldier uniforms and to learn that one of his sons, as punishment for a minor misdemeanor, had been shut away in the barracks' guardhouse. Spotted Tail decided on the spot that he would take all the Sioux children home with him, although he was prevented from doing this and allowed to remove only his own. For Spotted Tail, the price of white schooling proved too high to pay.[47]

But by the 1880s, the overt defiance that Satanta had displayed at the

Council of Medicine Lodge was no longer a viable strategy for most Indian people. The challenge now was to claim vital skills, like literacy and fluency in English, without undermining key values or threatening individual or tribal integrity. The real struggle for all Indian people was to ensure that their children grew up as Kiowa, Apache, Dakota, Winnebago, Omaha, Crow, or Osage, even as the terms of these tribal identities were in the throes of seismic change. The "new road" and lessons taught in white schools offered useful skills but they also generated confusion, anxiety and doubt. They unleashed forces into Indian communities that changed them forever.[48]

The founding of a school on any reservation Omaha anthropologist Francis La Flesche explained, "marked an epoch in the tribe."[49] It introduced new forces that interrupted and contested traditional educational patterns and, backed by powerful external sources, these invariably brought division and fragmentation. La Flesche himself was sent to school by a father who was part of a group described by whites as "progressive." These Indians lived in houses, wore citizen's clothes and believed that by sending their children to school "some good will come of it . . . in the future."[50] More traditional Omaha disparagingly described them as "make-believe white-men," yet for this group, the school was not just a passively received institution of instruction; it was also a site of resistance where they fought to maintain a hold over the education of their children.

These Omaha persistently insisted that they be permitted to participate in the running of the school, until finally the government sent an inspector to investigate their request. Acting on advice in his report, the agent changed his approach and "appointed two of the councilmen as inspectors, to visit the school at least once a week for a month, to be succeeded by two others for the following month."[51] This was a rare achievement for any Indian tribe, particularly one not yet fully competent in English and requiring a full-time interpreter to conduct their affairs.[52] To the Omaha who sent their children to school, the agent admitted the Indian inspectors had made a big difference. "To these men the parents state their grievances, real or imaginary, and they lay the matter before the superintendent and an explanation follows, and in nearly every case everything is adjustable harmoniously."[53] Two Crow was quick to capitalize on this experience when he wrote to the commissioner the following year demanding greater powers for the Omaha in running their affairs:

> When the Inspector came he said you wished us to fill both schools. In less than two weeks we filled both schools to overflowing with scholars. The Inspector allowed us at least to share in the management of the schools, and they were immediately filled with children. This he did by appointing school directors among the Indians. If we were allowed only a little share in the management of our affairs, I think we would get along much better. We hope we will hear good news from you soon.[54]

On nearly all reservations, the management of schools was a common cause of complaint. Bad sanitation leading to poor health, overwork of the children, physical abuse, and inadequate instruction triggered protests and when these went unheeded led to a sense of outrage and impotence among the Indians. With few means of leverage, one of the most frequent recourses was to withhold the children from school. When the Omaha were sent a new agent whom they judged corrupt, they organized a campaign to get rid of him. Led by Young Prophet, they refused to send any children to school.[55] At Crow Creek the story was similar. When the Lower Yanktonai chief, White Ghost, complained bitterly about corruption in the school, he announced to the commissioner that unless something was done quickly, it would mean an end to all white education on that reservation.[56] Yet however organized and forceful Indians might be, they were never granted more than a peripheral role in the control of their schools. When the explicit purpose of white education was to wipe out Indian cultures, the white educational process was inevitably accompanied by terrible risk.

High-Risk Strategy
Almost a century after the first Sioux child had been sent east from the Crow Creek reservation, elderly Indians there remembered that the reason parents opposed their children's schooling was fear of losing them. "Too many children died," Ruth Fire explained succinctly.[57] Disease and death were rife at all boarding schools and the greatest fear of all

parents was that their children would never return home. Even when schooled closer to home, the health of children attending the reservation boarding schools was also a constant source of anxiety to their parents. On one occasion, when a epidemic of measles struck the Crow Creek school killing two children, the agent was agreeably surprised to report that "the parents of those who died were careful to let us know, even in their grief, that they did not blame anyone and were grateful for what had been done."[58] Fear of physical death was unremitting but uncomplicated. Fear of cultural obliteration was more tortuous.

Speaking to the Indian agent about the effect of government schools on his people, Che Sah Hunka, the Osage chief, voiced measured yet deep-seated fears about the wisdom of the enterprise:

> At this school they make our young men do things like white man; but he is Indian. . . . This is not good I believe. I am troubled in my mind about these things. I do not know if it is good for Indian to learn from white man. Indian knows many things, but white man says that these things are not good. I believe that white man does not know many things that Indian knows. . . . But my mind is troubled about my people. I think they are like dog who has lost trail; they run in circles saying, "here is trail, here is trail," but trail is lost and they sit down like dog that has lost trail, and wait with no thoughts in their head.[59]

Many Indians shared this judgment of schools as a dangerous force undermining Indian cultures, as well as confidence and initiative.

The English language brought many advantages but also carried corrosive risks. Although literacy and English were the skills Indians most often welcomed when deciding to send their children to school, long years spent in boarding schools meant that many of the younger generation returned home incompetent in their mother tongue and so unable to communicate with their own people. Even those who returned still fluent in their own language often carried a time bomb planted by the schools. They had been so humiliated for speaking "Indian" that they chose not to teach their native tongue to their own children. Maggie Tarbell Lazore, a Mohawk from St. Regis, gleefully remembered at the age of ninety-nine how she had proudly led "Section A" as it marched on the parade ground at Carlisle. She had been a good

student and proud of her education and later returned to foster education among her own people. Yet while a schoolgirl at Carlisle, she admitted that after hours secretly in their bedroom on the third floor of
the girls' dormitory, she and her cousin had always loved talking "Indian" together. When she returned to raise a family on the reservation,
however, she did not teach any of her seven children the Mohawk language.[60] In this, as in so many other ways, the dark shadow cast by the
schools stretched across the generations. It also fell on the older generation of Indians, who had parted with their children, and reached deep
into their home communities.

On the reservation, the separation of adults and children imposed by
boarding schools created a series of social vacuums. Traditional education was always a community project in which all reputable adults participated and the beliefs and loyalties of the adults were reinforced through
teaching the children.[61] Without children, adult Indians suffered not just
loneliness but cultural disruption, as everyday activities were robbed of
their pedagogical role. With the children no longer there to be gently instructed, to hear and later repeat myths and legends or participate in the
ceremonies, these activities lost some of their cultural purpose.

At the same time, older Indians' role as educators also suffered. Luther Standing Bear described how Lakota adults were perpetually vigilant, so that "Children were taught the rules of *woyuonihan* and that
true politeness was to be defined in actions rather than in words. They
were never allowed to pass between the fire and an older person or a visitor, to speak while others were speaking, or to make fun of a crippled
or disfigured one. If a child thoughtlessly tried to do so, a parent, in a
quiet voice, immediately set him right."[62] Once at school, elders were
no longer able to shape their children's behavior or influence who they
mixed with. Francis La Flesche remembers how at home children were
always warned against playing with the children of persons of poor
character, but "at school we were all thrown together and left to form
our own associates."[63] At home, adult Indians no longer able to guide
their children also felt far less need to monitor their own behavior. "In
their sphere," Luther Standing Bear explained, "children were a power
in the home." This was because "the hardest duty in the performance of
parent-hood was not so much to watch the conduct of their children as

to be ever watchful of their own—a duty placed upon parents through the method used in instructing their young—example."[64] In a wide array of activities, from mundane social interactions and the telling of stories to the practice of sacred ceremonies, the absence of this "power in the home" impoverished the lives of elders, already severely challenged by the strictures of reservation existence. Deep-seated hostility to white society often attended fears of loss of tribal identity.

It was frequently the mysteries surrounding death that revealed anxieties about the adoption of white ways and a continuing intense belief in Indian separateness. When an Osage girl requested that she be clothed in a dress and buried in the white cemetery after she died instead of being placed on the traditional raised platform, her mother was filled with confusion and panic: "it was bad that Indian should be placed in ground where it is dark; where sun can not be seen at dawn, but my daughter wanted this thing."[65] After the funeral service, but before her daughter was buried, the mother painted her face: "I have looked at my child in white man's coffin, and I said it is good. He [*sic*] wanted to be buried in burying ground of white man. I said it is good to be buried in white clothes of white woman. I do not know about these things. I looked at the face of my girl and I said he is Indian, my girl. They will not know who he is. It will be good if we paint the face of my girl."[66] Conceding the white clothes, coffin, and burial, this Osage mother nevertheless found a way to maintain a clear distinction between whites and Indians. She assuaged her disquiet about the confusion of her child's acculturated identity by unequivocally marking her dead child's Osage identity on her face. This mother was not alone in her anxieties about the ambiguous identity of the acculturated Indian after death.

George Sword, Oglala Sioux political leader, tribal court judge, and spiritual head, played a creative intermediary role for his tribe, walking "the tightrope strung between competing loyalties with agility, integrity and unfailing dignity."[67] Literate and well versed in white ways, Sword was baptized a Episcopalian. Yet on his chest he bore the scars that proved he had participated in the Sun Dance, and he admitted that he still feared the Indian gods, "because the spirit of an Oglala may go to the spirit land of the Lakota."[68] Despite his conversion to Christianity and other outward signs of acculturation, Sword had not wholly relinquished his belief that whites and Indians were two distinct and separate peoples. As the Norwegian anthropologist Fredrik Barth suggests in his study of group identity markers, "The important thing to recognize is that the drastic reduction of cultural differences between two ethnic groups does not correlate in any simple way with a reduction in the organisational relevance of ethnic identities, or bring a break-down in the boundary making process."[69] In other words, even when traditional practices were being undermined and educated Indians wielded power playing new roles and practicing an alien religion, they did not cease to be Indian or to define themselves as such.

For many, like Sword, traditional spiritual beliefs lay at the core of their identity. The Shawnee chiefs who sent Thomas Wildcat Alford east to Hampton wanted him "to learn the white man's wisdom." They were apprehensive, however, that his beliefs, values, and loyalties would change and so they were adamant that he "should not accept the white man's religion; [he] must remain true to the Shawnee faith."[70] These chiefs, like many others, had come to realize that Christianity was an exclusive religion and that whites would never accept it could legitimately be practiced alongside traditional Indian ceremonies. Christianity, all Indians were forced to realize, was deeply implicated in white educational processes and represented the edge of a powerful cultural wedge.

3. Mission Schools in the West: Precursors of a System

CHRISTIAN MISSIONARIES LAID THE deep and diverse foundations on which the federal system of Indian schools was built. The campaign to convert and educate the native peoples of America had been fought on multiple fronts over many centuries, with missionaries always at the forefront of the endeavor. From the start, they had worked to claim souls for Christ, and the school had always been vital to their project. But, as James Axtell and others have shown, they also sought to nurture loyalty to their own nation-states.[1]

After the founding of the United States, Washington, Jefferson, and Monroe, planning nation building on American territory, envisaged the incorporation of Indian tribes into the body politic. Unhesitatingly, they turned to mission groups to accomplish this end.[2] In 1819, Congress created a Civilization Fund to encourage and support schools for Indian children, and the monies were channeled through missionary groups. In the early years of the republic, the goals of government and missions seemed to overlap so neatly that it appeared there was no conflict of interest.[3]

From one point of view this is surprising, because Enlightenment thinking, from which republican values derived, carried within it a fundamental critique of the Christian worldview, stressing the primacy of reason for acquiring knowledge and understanding the world and advocating a strict division between the power of church and state.[4] Yet the ardent anti-ecclesiasticism that accompanied intellectual debate in the salons of Paris did not cross the Atlantic. In the New World, there was no oppressive established church to oppose. More importantly, Enlightenment ideas, on which the United States was founded, incorporated unequivocal beliefs about the universal qualities possessed by all men. The republic's founding documents enshrined Enlightenment's central precept, the essential uniformity of human nature, and this was a principle that echoed Christianity's doctrine of the "family of man." The confluence of these two positive and universalist doctrines meant that, despite the Enlightenment commitment to scientific enquiry and the preeminence of empirical materialist knowledge, for the purpose of civilizing Indians, republicanism and Christianity did not appear contradictory.

America's new secular ideology of national universalism could, in the short term, run smoothly in parallel with the Christian doctrine of the unity of mankind. When invited to educate and prepare Indians for life within the republic, protestant missionaries' response was enthusiastic. The American Board of Commissioners for Foreign Missions represented all protestant missions when it unselfconsciously identified the republic as the purveyor of hope and Christian values. In 1824, with the aid of financial support from the government, the board opened its first mission in Brainerd, Tennessee, and openly correlated its work educating and schooling Indians with the larger mission to "elevate our national character and render it exemplary in the view of the world."[5]

Yet, in the New World, Christian commitment to the unity of mankind had been compromised from the start by its inherent links to colonialism and tacit acceptance of doctrines in support of a white nation. Papal bulls issued in Rome, following the "discovery" of the new continent, gave Christian validation from the highest authority to European expansion, native dispossession, and the sovereignty of invaders over indigenous populations.[6] This was the shadowy side of Christian theology, conscripted to condone physical bloodshed and cultural violence. It was matched by an equally dark thread that ran through the fabric of Enlightenment thought. In the United States, this thread was spun thick and wide and would be progressively woven into an uncompromising racial tapestry of inequality.

Enlightenment Thought and the Pseudoscience of Racial Difference
Bruce Dains, in his study of American race theory, acknowledges that racial prejudice was endemic in colonial America but suggests that systematic race theory began to be formulated shortly after the Revolution, when Enlightenment natural history attempted to answer new questions about racial difference raised by the issue of slavery and morality.

Enlightenment methods of enquiry were scientific and empirical, creating a dilemma for "men of reason": how to reconcile god's intentions with the findings of science. Scientists, attempting to reveal the foundations of racial difference through biological investigation, oscillated in their conclusions about whether or not nonwhite peoples possessed the same faculties of reason and sensibility as Euro-Americans. Generally, attention focused on the head, the seat of human intelligence. The most comprehensive as well as authoritative study of cranial capacity, and, by doubtful extrapolation, of the comparative intelligence of the different races, was Samuel George Morton's, *Crania Americana*, published in 1839. In this, his first and largest work, Morton sought to prove that a ranking of races could be established objectively by comparing physical characteristics of the brain, particularly its size.

Morton painstakingly assembled and measured 144 American Indian skulls. On average he found them to be five cubic inches smaller than the Caucasian norm, and from this he concluded that "the structure of [the Indian] mind appears to be different from that of the white man." Morton's opinion was already widely accepted in the nonscientific population; he was reiterating in scientific language the conventions of the Great Chain of Being, which located whites on the top, Indians halfway down, and blacks at the bottom. Using a wealth of apparently neutral data, Morton had made the fateful link between physiology and mental capacity and extended this to embrace social competence: the two races could not, he claimed, "harmonize in social relations except on the most limited scale." Morton went further and suggested that ameliorating this condition was unlikely, because Indians "are not only averse to the restraints of education, but for the most part are incapable of a continued process of reasoning on abstract subjects."[7] As the century proceeded, discussions about racial attributes were conducted increasingly in the language of pseudoscience, and American scientists were at the forefront of this. Their work did not silence the traditional political discourse of Enlightenment universalism nor the Christian belief in human brotherhood. Instead, an uncomfortable, flanking, dialectical relationship developed between science, on the one hand, and Enlightenment and Christian ideals, on the other, in which the findings of "science" progressively undercut these more optimistic perspectives.

President Grant and the Missions

But after the Civil War, it was not to America's scientists that President Grant would turn when, in his inaugural address, he asserted that "the proper treatment of the original occupants of this land—the Indians— is one deserving of careful study. I will favor any course toward them which tends to their civilization and ultimate citizenship." Instead, in a determined move to pacify Indians by incorporating them into the nation, Grant, like those before him, engaged Christian missionaries. In an unprecedented move, inaugurating what became known as his peace policy, Grant invited America's Quakers to run affairs at the northern and central Indian superintendencies, explaining to Congress that "The Society of Friends is well known for having lived in peace with the Indians. . . . They are also known for their opposition to strife, violence and war, and are generally noted for their strict integrity and fair dealings."[8]

Grant had initiated a period of federal-mission relations that, for a short time, would be more intense than ever before or since. Quakers were the group most unequivocal in their universalist beliefs. Their commitment to equality was not just political; it was the fundamental principal that infused all aspects of their day-to-day as well as spiritual lives. Quakers had been at the forefront of abolitionism and were now keen to shape government dealings with the Indians. This enthusiasm matched federal objectives. By drafting Quakers into active involvement in the implementation of Indian policy, Grant could publicly present the most acceptable face of national expansion. James C. Scott's understanding of the "public transcript" elucidates this relationship:

> The public transcript is, to put it crudely, the self-portrait of dominant elites as they would have themselves seen. . . . While it is unlikely to be merely a skein of lies and misrepresentations, it is, on the other hand, a highly partisan and partial narrative. It is designed to be impressive, to affirm and naturalize the poser of dominant elites, and to conceal or euphemize the dirty linen of their rule.[9]

Their engagement with the peace policy drew many individual Quakers who had no previous active experience among Indians into Indian affairs. Lawrie Tatum, a Quaker living in Springdale, Iowa, was one such individual. Appointed Indian agent to the Kiowa and Comanche, in

Indian Territory, Tatum had never before worked in the field, although he vigorously supported the new peace policy and had been active in the antislavery campaign. The Iowa yearly meeting nominated Tatum for the post of agent, as part of Grant's peace policy, because he was a respected and upstanding member of his local Quaker community who was judged to possess the moral stature and strength of character necessary for the work. As the snows began to melt on the prairies of northeast Iowa in the springtime of 1869, this bald, dutiful, forty-six-year-old farmer left the community he had helped found in Cedar County, where he had lived for a quarter century, and made the long journey south, to take up residence at the Kiowa and Comanche Agency. He had been appointed to administer, pacify, and civilize more than six thousand Indians from nearly ten separate tribes, who had recently been confined on a reservation by the terms of the Treaty of Medicine Lodge. Tatum brought firm Quaker convictions, spiritual dedication, and a wealth of practical pioneering and farming experience to the task.

The orthodox Friends' assumption of responsibility for the Indians of the central superintendency brought with it a dramatic collision of values. If most of the Quaker agents were honest and capable men, in the judgment of historian Richard N. Ellis, "some, like Lawrie Tatum, were exceptional."[10] Yet when Tatum became agent of the Kiowa and Comanche, his deeply held Quaker pacifist beliefs would be challenged and tested. "There was no more incongruous spectacle," historian William Hagan notes, "than that of a Quaker agent preaching the virtues of peace and agriculture to a plains warrior," certain that an Indian "could be brought to see the error of his ways by compassion and sweet reason."[11] Four years later, Tatum had not persuaded the Indians of his agency to cease raiding. Frustrated and perplexed, he resigned his post: "We were all sadly disappointed," Tatum acknowledged in his autobiographical account, "that those 'spoiled Indians' would not be brought into subjection by peaceable means."[12]

Religious conviction led many individual Quakers to work with Indians, but Quaker churches gradually withdrew from the Quaker-government experiment. By this time, however, Grant had enlisted "the cooperation of the entire religious element of the country, to help, by their labors and counsels, to bring about . . . the civilization and Christian-ization of the Indian race."[13] He placed the religious, educational, and administrative responsibility for all Indians living on reservations in the hands of the Christian churches.[14] Eli Parker, Grant's commissioner of Indian affairs, a Seneca and the first Indian to hold this post, made the government's goal and program clear in his 1871 report: "The policy is to prepare them as rapidly as possible to assume the relation of citi-zenship. By granting them increased facilities for the education of their young; by habituating them to industrial pursuits, and by the incentive to labor incited by a sense of ownership in property which the allotment of their lands would afford, and by the benign and elevating influences of Christian teachings."[15]

These "increased facilities for education" were to be paid for by the federal government. Starting in 1870, Congress began to allocate funds specifically for Indian education. Every year the amounts rose: $992,800 in 1885; $1,348,015 in 1889; $3,080,367 in 1901.[16] The fig-ures reflected not only increased funding but also the growing propor-tion of government spending on Indians that was being channeled to schools.[17] In the early 1870s, only 0.8 percent of Indian Office expen-ditures went to schools. By 1885 this figure had risen to nearly 20 per-cent and a decade later to over 30 percent.[18] Although churches con-trolled Indian agencies only for about ten years, missions developed and expanded their schools for Indians for more than twenty years with di-rect support from the federal government. The number of both gov-ernment and mission schools grew quickly, but up until the end of the 1880s, enrollment in mission schools increased at a faster rate than in the institutions run by the Bureau of Indian Affairs.[19]

Indian schools varied enormously in their size and organization. Small day schools on the outskirts of Indian villages gave way increasingly to large boarding schools located in agency towns. Off-reservation gov-ernment schools, modeled on Carlisle, were gradually established across the West in the midst of white populations. The administration and fi-nancial support of all these different types of school was equally di-verse. Missions continued to fund a substantial number entirely from their own monies. With government encouragement, they also built new schools, and the government paid the mission an annual fee for every student enrolled. Simultaneously, an increasing number of new schools were built and run by the Bureau of Indian Affairs, under direct supervision of the agent.[20]

Progressively, the federal government took control of this fragmented educational activity to forge a system that was administered and financed by Washington. This shift in authority and control took place gradually but perceptibly. When John D. C. Atkins became commissioner of Indian affairs (1885–88), he was determined to establish at least one government school on every reservation, even if a mission school already existed. Simultaneously, he cut funds to mission schools in an effort to sharply reduce both the work and influence of all religious groups.[21] His successor, John H. Oberly, continued this gradual transfer of power from missions to government. He had worked as Atkins's superintendent of Indian schools and although he served as commissioner for less than a year (1888–89), he eagerly seized the opportunity to extend the power and duties of his former post. Aggressively implementing a new provision in the Indian Appropriation Act, Oberly authorized the superintendent of Indian schools to appoint and dismiss reservation teachers and other school personnel directly from Washington.[22] He also standardized school rules and regulations and introduced a schedule of regular inspections for every school receiving federal funding.[23]

Thomas Jefferson Morgan and a System of Indian Schools

By the time Thomas Jefferson Morgan was appointed commissioner of Indian affairs, in 1889, the role of the missions was already being seriously challenged and curtailed by the Bureau of Indian Affairs. Morgan's systematization of all Indian schools would further concentrate authority in Washington. Cannily, Morgan enlisted the reformers' support when he presented his plans to the Lake Mohonk conference: "I come here," he told delegates, "where the Christian Philanthropic sentiment of the country focuses itself, to ask you what will satisfy you." Speaking for nearly an hour, Morgan laid out his thirteen-point scheme for a totally integrated school system. Curriculum, methods of instruction, and textbooks as well as goals would be identical in every Indian school across the United States. His system was organized to enable the smooth progress of Indian children from elementary reservation day schools, through to agency boarding schools, and on to higher levels of study in off-reservation institutions. Indian schools, Morgan projected, would mirror and eventually merge with white schools. Buoyant and optimistic, Morgan communicated his confidence "that under a wise system of education, carefully administered, the condition of this whole people can be radically improved in a single generation." The shrunken role envisaged for missions was mentioned only in his thirteenth and final point. Their function would be the same as in the wider society, so that "just as the work of the public schools is supplemented in the States by Christian agencies, so too will the work of Indian education by the government be supplemented by the same agencies."[24] Morgan was keen to demonstrate that his projected system would resemble America's common schools and to signal that Indian schools would enjoy the same separation of church and state.[25] Yet what is of most interest to the present argument is his near silence on Christianity and his ascription of a much-diminished role for the missions.

In the past, school and church work had been inseparable, with the former always acting as handmaiden to the latter. Now, instead of conversion and Christian teaching being presented as the best means to civilize Indians, Morgan assigned the prime role to the school. Significantly, he used the language of religion to describe what would be accomplished in the schools. "Education," Morgan insisted, "is the Indian's only salvation." Yet, in the future, he projected, the educational burden would no longer be shared with the missions: "This grave responsibility, which has now been practically assumed by the Government, must be borne by it alone."[26] Morgan had wrested Indian education from the church groups and delivered it into the hands of the federal government.

Thomas Jefferson Morgan's ability to secure support for this dramatic move can be attributed in part to the developing trajectory of reform thought but also to Morgan's many-sided professional and personal background. He had accepted the post of commissioner with no previous experience in Indian affairs, but his background made him appear eminently qualified for the job.[27] An ordained Baptist minister, Morgan was also a veteran colonel of the Union army who had organized and led the Fourteenth United States Colored Infantry. His main career, however, was as an educator and he had been president of three state normal schools in Nebraska, New York, and Rhode Island. In his person he represented the three groups most actively engaged in Indian affairs—army, churchmen, and educators. Literally as well as figuratively, Morgan could speak to the delegates of Lake Mohonk as easily as to those at the National Education Association and was just as comfortable meeting his old Civil War commander President Benjamin Harrison, to whom he owed his Washington appointment. A pivotal figure in Indian schooling, Morgan's discourse resonated with the precepts and concerns of men-of-god yet pointed toward the broad, nationalizing, desires of white educators and officials in Washington. "When we speak of the education of the Indians," he told fellow reformers at Lake Mohonk, "we mean that comprehensive system of training and instruction which will convert them into American citizens and enable them to compete successfully with the white man on his own ground and with his own methods."[28]

Morgan's scheme was founded on a publicly articulated belief in the Christian family of man and a passionate conviction that Indian children were "made in the image of God, bearing the likeness of their Creator, and having the same possibilities of growth and development that are possessed by any other class of children."[29] He smoothly transposed this Christian faith into a republican universalism, enabled by education and framed by a white citizenry:

> Education is to be the medium through which the rising generation of Indians are to be brought into fraternal and harmonious relationship with their white fellow-citizens, and with them enjoy the sweets of refined homes, the delight of social intercourse, the emoluments of commerce and trade, the advantages of travel, together with the pleasures that come from literature, science, and philosophy, and the solace and stimulus afforded by true religion.[30]

Morgan had relegated "the solace and stimulus afforded by true religion" to the very end of a long list of benefits conferred by education.

Not only had missionary organizations and personnel been sidelined by government schools, but in the emerging federal system of Indian schools, the secular had trumped the spiritual.

Despite Morgan's ringing success at Lake Mohonk and the subsequent progressive implementation of national legislation to build the system of schools he had drawn up, the uncoupling of schooling and mission work was unprecedented and did not go uncontested. At the Dakota Mission, missionaries had welcomed federal support for their ongoing enterprise, but they were horrified when new government policies began to prescribe methods and practices diametrically at odds with their own carefully thought-out teaching and mission work—in particular, their Dakota language-based educational program. At the Dakota Mission, three generations of one family, father Stephen Riggs, son Alfred Riggs, and grandson Frederick Riggs, contributed over a century to a thriving missionary and educational venture that, with the help of government support, saw its heyday in the 1890s. The Dakota Mission's grand scale, longevity, and tri-generational projects distinguished it from many less ambitious protestant ventures. So too did the symbiotic program of conversion and education, rooted in the Dakota language, which the missionaries developed and elaborated into a spiritual and pedagogical philosophy. Emblazoned in capital letters across the front cover of every issue of the mission's bilingual newspaper, *Iapi Oaye/The Word Carrier*, was the statement: "For Indians we want American education! We want American homes! We want American rights! The result of which is American citizenship." From this it appeared that the goals of the Dakota Mission perfectly matched those of the government. However, their respective emphases were very different.

The missionaries regarded conversion and schooling as linked and intimate processes, involving infiltration and disruption of fundamental belief structures. From the early days, they became convinced that the best means of gaining access to Dakota hearts, minds, and souls was by using the Dakota language. They first introduced the Indians to Christianity by speaking to them in Dakota and then taught them to read and write in their own language.

When the government began to formulate an educational policy hostile to the use of native languages, the missionaries of the Dakota board saw the foundations of their work under threat and fought hard to protect and preserve the pedagogical methods they had developed over four decades. Indispensable to their program, the Dakota language was the fault line that would gradually shift to expose a rift between the principles driving the government program of assimilation and the ideals of the Dakota Mission.

In the collision between the Dakota Mission and the Bureau of Indian Affairs, the dispute turned on the issue of Dakota as an appropriate language for instruction. Yet far more than pedagogy was at stake. Pronouncements about language are rarely neutral, particularly in a situation where language is involved in the establishment or maintenance of relations of dominance. The missionaries' struggle to uphold their linguistic strategy was, in essence, a multidimensional contest to maintain their power. Firstly, and most obviously, missionaries were implicated in the wider campaign to obliterate native cultures through a program of cultural imperialism. This was a fight, dating back to colonial days, now being conducted asymmetrically between whites and Indians on reservations across the United States. Secondly, missionaries were striving to defend the centrality of Christianity to the civilizing process and to resist secularized definitions of Indian advancement. This was a battle waged directly against the federal government over linguistic policy but also indirectly against the rising tide of secularism within American society. Thirdly, missionaries fought to valorize the Dakota language, both as a medium of instruction and as a language in its own right. This conflict was waged on the didactic front against any who suggested that Dakota was not a fit medium for conversion and tuition and on the political front against those who insisted that Indian transformation could be achieved speedily, with scant attention paid to inner spiritual change.

More than a component in a political program, the Indian school was a key site where whites debated and enacted Indian education, transformation, and racial formation. The seemingly parochial contest between government and mission over use of the Dakota language was embedded in a much more fundamental and far-reaching dispute about the true nature of the Indian, the best means to educate him/her, and his/her future status in the American nation.

The Dakota Mission

The American Board of Commissioners for Foreign Missions, which ran the Dakota Mission, represented the protestant group boasting the longest association with Indians and, before the Civil War, had sent out more missionaries than any other church society. In 1837, Stephen Riggs and his wife, Mary, journeyed to Minnesota to join John P. Williamson at the board's nascent mission at Lac-qui-parle. They quickly became fluent in Dakota.[31] Working with the help of a French-Dakota interpreter, John Akipa Renville (Ah-kee-pah), they began to adapt the Roman alphabet to accommodate Dakota sounds and give the language a written form. Uniting in a collective effort to puzzle out the grammar and gather vocabulary, they built on the work already accomplished by two Congregational missionaries, Samuel W. Pond and Gideon H. Pond, and between them devised the first systematic orthography for writing Dakota.[32] Williamson immediately began translating and transcribing the Bible. Although it would take him until 1878 to finish the whole text, he published the separate books as he completed them so they could be used by the Dakota Mission and other denominations working with the different bands of Sioux (Dakota, Nakota, and Lakota).[33]

This translation work was of fundamental importance to the American Board of Commissioners for Foreign Missions because it aimed to train a team of native teachers and pastors to aid efforts to reach "all the Indians in that part of the country."[34] The board regarded its early work among the Mdewakanton and Wahpekute bands of Dakota, who were more settled than their Yankton and Teton western neighbors, as the first step toward achieving this wider goal. The missionaries looked to a day when, served by native ministers and teachers, groups of hard-working, moral, Christian, Indian families, mostly making a living from the land, would live together quietly and peaceably alongside whites. In these "imagined communities," Indians would retain their ties and loyalties to their own people. And although they might continue to use their own language, their traditional customs and tribal relations would be replaced by a new pattern of relationships, with the Christian church at their hub.[35] The privileging of a native language, the emphasis on Christianity, and the deliberate nurturing of native communities clearly differentiated the Dakota Mission's project from the educational program that was being developed by the government.

In his study of education and imperialism, Martin Carnoy has argued strongly that colonial educators always deliberately frame educational aspirations in individual rather than collective terms and work to elevate subjugated peoples separately rather than collectively.[36] If the building of the federal Indian school system is viewed as an exercise in internal colonialism, this point is fully substantiated in the national Indian educational program outlined by Thomas Jefferson Morgan.[37] At the Dakota Mission, missionaries took a different approach and disparaged the single-generation transformation advocated for individual Indians in Morgan's schooling plan. They remained convinced that true conversion and civilization could only be achieved gradually, over generations, and needed to embrace and include the whole community.

To achieve this, the Dakota board had developed an interdependent program of Christian conversion and schooling—but with the emphasis always on conversion. In his account of the mission's early years, Stephen Riggs explained that the school was "a most important and indispensable auxiliary," but he was adamant that for the missionaries, "the school was always subordinate to the preaching of the gospel."[38] Secular schooling, on its own, was spiritually and morally dangerous: "We recognize their need for a moral power in their lives, without which," the board insisted, "education will only give them sail for their more speedy destruction."[39]

In the early years of the Dakota Mission, success, as judged by the missionaries, had been painfully slow and elusive, with few conversions and only a handful of Indians willing to attend services. Subscribing to a patriarchal model of society, the missionaries experienced a sense of failure when most of the Indians they could persuade to attend church were women, or men who were part white and therefore living only on the fringes of Indian society. When a young man called Simon Anawangmane (Walks Galloping On) joined the church, he was welcomed with enthusiasm as their first full-blood Dakota convert, but very few followed him. Large-scale conversions, with the associated impact on the wider Dakota society, eluded the missionaries, until after the Dakota Uprising.

Stunned by the strength of the uprising, the missionaries were equally shocked by the ferocity of its crushing, which occurred after six weeks of attacks and fighting and the deaths of hundreds of settlers as well as Indians. On December 26, 1862, in Mankato, Minnesota, thirty-eight Dakota were publicly hanged, in the largest mass execution ever in the United States.[40] Nevertheless, they interpreted the apparent mass conversion that took place at this time as the triumphant product of almost thirty years mission work among the Dakota.

The Indians were traumatized and in disarray, with hundreds in prison awaiting execution and the surrounding white population in a hostile and vengeful mood. Many Dakota spiritual practices had been disrupted or suppressed and, when offered support by the missionaries, large numbers began to attend church and send their children to school. We know from the writings of Charles Eastman that for his father, who spent three years in prison, the Dakota Uprising represented a turning point; the historical moment when he understood the inescapable strength of the whites and the need for his son to gain the skills necessary to survive in a white-dominated world. The Dakotas' relationship to Christianity intensified at this time, but, as Virginia Driving Hawk Sneve has shown, it also became more complex. Many never fully abandoned their Dakota traditions. Their conversion was superficial and they used Christianity as an enabling survival mechanism.[41]

For the missionaries, however, Dakota church attendance and the Indians' new willingness to adopt white ways represented an unequivocal success. They felt particularly gratified when key Dakota men, such as Artemas Ehnamane (walks-among-the-people), not only converted but also began to play an active role in the church. Son of a war prophet and himself a skilled hunter, Ehnamane's lifestyle and outlook appeared to have been transformed by defeat and exile. He abandoned his previous life to become pastor of one of the burgeoning local communities, at Pilgrim Church, after the Dakota had been moved to Nebraska. According to Alfred Riggs, before his death, Ehnamane's father had told him that "The white man is coming into this country, and your children may learn to read. But promise me that you will never leave the religion of your ancestors." Riggs was convinced that after the uprising, men like Ehnamane came to believe that the Indian gods had been beaten by the white man's god. For all the missionaries of the Dakota Mission, such developments represented an unambiguous and welcome indication that the Dakota, having witnessed the incapacity of their own gods to protect them from the revenge and justice of the whites, now recognized the power of the "one true God."[42]

Missionary Construction of the Dakota Religion

Close association with the Dakota over the years afforded these missionaries many privileged glimpses of Dakota spiritual rituals and practices; habitually, they saw and interpreted these through the grid of Christian dogma. Stephen Riggs, struggling to understand the belief system he was working to displace, attended ceremonies and studied the spiritual manifestations of Dakota society. Although he gained some knowledge of important Dakota gods, he judged them, "so far as forms and names are concerned . . . the creation of their own deluded and foul imaginings." In a book describing and publicizing the work of the mission, he attempted to describe Dakota religion for a white audience. For him it was a highly elaborate system of superstition. Noting four varieties of Ha-yo-ka, or antinatural god, Riggs resorted to ridicule and derision in his descriptions: "They are all armed with the bow and arrow and the deer-hoof rattle, which are charged with electricity. One of the varieties carries a drum and for a drumstick holds a little wake'yan god by the tail, striking the drum with its beak. This would seem an unfortunate position for a god to be in, but it must be remembered that it is *wakan*, and the more absurd a thing is, the more *wakan*."[43]

Riggs's humor was rooted in contempt, but it was also a strategy for confronting his own fear because he regarded the Indian gods as dangerous. Confessing his belief that "the worship of the Dakota does not fall on vacancy," he fell back on the dualism of Christian theology, insisting that "it is consciously paid to spiritual beings, which can be none other than the spirits of darkness."[44] When his wife's brother was drowned in the river, in his grief Riggs let slip a moment of doubt and made an oblique nod toward the power of Indian gods: "The Indians said their water god, Oonktehe, was displeased with us for coming to build here. He had seized the young man. It did seem at times as though God was against us."[45]

Recognizing that Dakota spiritual beliefs infused and determined not just religious behavior but all Dakota social customs and activities, Riggs's binary belief structures and the malign potency he accorded to Indian gods prompted him to insist that the Indian "must be a *savage* as long as he is a *pagan*."[46] His black-and-white style of thinking was quickly picked up on by the Dakota, who became conscious of the absolutism that was being demanded of them. "From the time the chief men came to understand that the religion of Christ was an exclusive religion and that it would require the giving up of their ancestral faith," Riggs observed, "they set themselves in opposition to it."[47] It was to counter this opposition that three generations of the Riggs family dedicated their lives to converting and educating the Dakota.

The degree to which Alfred Riggs's views echoed those of his father was revealed in a little pamphlet where he addressed the question, "What Does the Indian Worship?" Insisting that "the Indian is eminently religious, he has noble aspirations and a spiritual interpretation of the Universe," he nevertheless concluded, "he has entirely departed from the worship of the One Great God and father, and has taken up with the worship of gods that are no gods, to whom he vainly prays and sacrifices." Riggs then enumerated the countless ways in which this false worship had a devastating impact not only on individuals but also on the daily life of Indian communities: it affected them economically, because it induced families to impoverish themselves for a whole year when they held a Sun Dance or ceremonial feast; it affected their health, because it made them turn to medicine men for what Riggs deemed counterfeit cures for disease; it affected them spiritually, because it forced them to live in constant fear of what he described as "ghosts and evil spirits in need of placation."[48] For Alfred Riggs and the other missionaries, therefore, it was imperative not just to convert individual Indians but to reach into and change whole communities, so these false beliefs could be thoroughly rooted out. Indisputably, missionaries worked to save individual souls, the Christian religion allowing only for the salvation of individuals, not groups. Yet to keep heathenism at bay and sustain the reconstellation of the spiritual and symbolic universe of individual Indians, support from the wider community was essential. If this was not forthcoming, Riggs admitted the missionaries would be impotent to combat the continuing power of traditional beliefs because, as he put it, "the gods of the forest and prairie, of the water and air still whisper to them in the leaves and grass and winds."[49]

The Santee Normal Training School

The missionaries worked to drown these whispers and neutralize their power by educating the whole Dakota community. With the Indians defeated and cowed in the wake of the Dakota Uprising, the missionaries accompanied them on their move to the Santee reservation. Here, in 1871, they opened the Santee Normal Training School, headed by twenty-five-year-old Alfred Riggs. Santee was an institution with an openly acknowledged ambitious educational agenda. It started with an enrollment of 100 students from the local reservation and by 1884 had grown to 144 students, representing ten different Sioux agencies from Dakota Territory.[50] Numbers would continue to climb. During half a century, more than 2,500 students passed through the doors of the Santee Normal Training School. A few, like Henry Roe, Gertrude Simmons, and Charles Eastman, would play a role on the national stage and become known to the broader white public, but the vast majority of Santee's alumni returned to live and work among their own people, and this was Riggs's intention. Unlike Pratt at Carlisle, Riggs and the Dakota Mission did not want Santee to sever the students' links and ties to their homes and communities. "While we plan to fit them as individuals for citizenship with us," he explained, "we are also careful to maintain their common interests and sympathy with their own race." Riggs felt confident that Santee, "more than any other school in the country," stood at "the high water mark of Indian advance."[51] His opinion was endorsed by Charles Eastman, an alumnus of Santee, who described the Santee Normal Training School as "the Mecca of Sioux country."[52]

The curriculum and general activities of the children at Santee have a familiar ring to anyone who has read the scholarship or trawled through the archives of Indian schools. Boys and girls were housed separately and followed a curriculum that matched American society's gender expectations. Girls received a practical training in housekeeping, while boys were taught how to farm and given the basics of white trades in the shoe, carpenter and blacksmith shops. Indeed the Santee school shared

much in common with the government boarding schools that were being set up on reservations across Indian Country. But at Santee, a single, vital attribute differentiated it from any government school: it was
conceived, built, and animated by a religious agenda.

Christian homes lay at the core of the new-style Indian communities Riggs was working to create, so Indian children were not housed in
large dormitories. Instead they were organized into quasi families, with
children of different ages living together under the care of a surrogate
parent.[53] Quick to point out that the Dakota had no word for "home"
and to compensate for this perceived deficiency, Riggs commissioned
the building of small cottages, each under the charge of a white, Christian lady, to set the example and teach the skills and values deemed essential to Christian living.[54]

Evidence of the school's religious agenda can be seen visually proclaimed in its campus design (fig. 5). The chapel was accorded the supreme central position. Standing in splendid isolation, close to the street
that bisected the campus, the chapel was the tallest building with the
largest footprint.[55] Cross-shaped, it commanded the central point of
the site and the open space that surrounded it ensured that it was always highly visible to all residents of the school and to visitors traveling
to and from Niobrara and the agency. The school's other main buildings—principal's residence, Dakota Home, dining hall, Bird's Nest— all
toed the same building line at the back of the campus, behind the chapel. The flagstaff, located equidistant between the principal's residence
and the Dakota Home (the original children's dormitory), was also set
back. The stars and stripes was assigned a position less prominent than
the chapel, the school's design thus mirroring its philosophy.

As Santee's enrollment lists grew, so too did the number of "homes"
as well as the rest of the school's plant and facilities. By 1885, Riggs had
overseen construction of eighteen separate buildings on the school's 480-
acre site, which was located southwest of the Santee Agency town. Yet
he had allowed none of these to compromise the preeminent position
conferred on the chapel. Instead of filling in the street-side plots situated beside the chapel on the main site, Riggs ordered the new "homes"
and trade shops to be constructed on the north side of the street. Physically as well as spiritually, the chapel retained its place at the hub of
the school's enterprise.

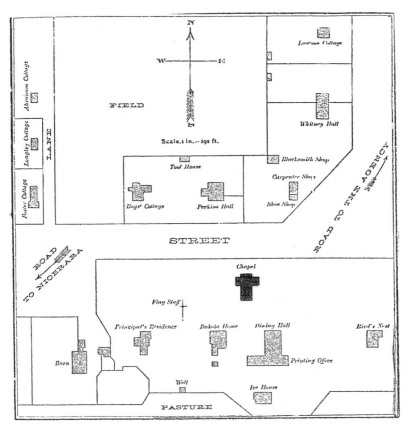

5. Plat of Santee Normal Training School, from Alfred L. Riggs, "Santee Normal Training School," n.p., ca. 1885, adapted by the author.

Writing about the early aspirations of the American Board of Commissioners for Foreign Missions, Stephen Riggs explained that "in carrying to the Indians the religion of the Bible," the missionaries also "desired to carry to them the education of the Bible, education in the most extended sense."[56] At the Santee Normal Training School, Alfred Riggs had realized his father's dream and had also rooted the school's curriculum firmly in Stephen Riggs's extensive linguistic work.

Dakota Language

Over the years, Stephen Riggs and his son wrote and translated a whole library of Dakota books. In addition to Stephen Riggs's Dakota Bible, there were dozens of religious texts, volumes of hymn and prayer books, as well as dictionaries, grammars, and an ever-growing range of schoolbooks.[57] The demanding task of transposing Christian theology into Dakota and elaborating the niceties of mathematics had forced the missionaries to grapple with the workings of Dakota culture and come face-to-face with some of its startling differences. Baffled by the apparent absence of conceptual words for "color," "time," or "space," they had nevertheless been impressed by the complexity of the Dakota verb. Stephen Riggs observed that it is "peculiarly complex and by means of inflections expresses certain shades of meaning not expressed by any of the languages of civilization without the introduction of adverbial phrases."[58] Discovering that the Dakota language of counting was limited, Stephen Riggs devised terms for fractions and other arithmetical concepts. Having begun this linguistic work in his youth, he devoted much of the rest of his life to deepening his knowledge and understanding of the Dakota language. He and the other missionaries had all come to regard it as the key instrument for instructing the Dakota who "cannot be easily educated except through a familiar language."[59] After thirty years' mission work, Stephen Riggs claimed the major lesson he had learned was that "as a means of evangelization, education should be in the vernacular. Men's hearts are reached through their understanding."[60]

So predictably, the main language of instruction at the Santee Normal Training School was Dakota. At the beginning of each day, services in the chapel were conducted in Dakota. The children then went to their classrooms to learn geography, history, and arithmetic from books written in their own language.[61] Some of these texts were bilingual. The first English-Dakota reader was published in 1875, at the encouragement of the commissioner of Indian affairs, and paid for mainly by government funds.[62] The school's monthly newspaper, *Iapi Oaye/ The Word Carrier*, was also bilingual. Here, Alfred Riggs described the activities of the school and outlined the ideas animating them. On one occasion he reiterated his father's philosophy and explicitly extended it to the schoolroom:

> It is the province of the teacher to make himself understood by his scholars, and not of the scholars to expend all their strength in vain efforts to understand what the teacher means. It is sheer laziness in the teacher to berate his Indian scholars for not understanding English,

when he does not understand enough Indian to tell them the meaning of a single one of the sentences he is trying to make them empha-
size properly.[63]

This linguistic strategy lay at the core of both school and church work
at the mission, and although it might appear to suggest a tolerance and
acceptance of Dakota culture, it can more accurately be interpreted as
a strategy of control.

This approach has been analyzed by Gwyneth Tyson Roberts in her
study of the imposition of English in Wales. Roberts draws attention to
two contrasting linguistic strategies used by colonial powers to exert
their authority. She describes the harsh approach of the Portuguese in
India, who approved the destruction of local Goan temples, drew up a
plan to kill every member of the local community who refused to convert, required all religious instruction to be in Portuguese, and banned
all use of the local language in schools and seminaries. By comparison,
she notes, the British approach was more conciliatory. In the long term,
however, Roberts argues that it was more insidiously effective, because
the British worked to educate a class of "natives" who would "consci-
entiously devote their working lives to serving the purposes of the power
which had colonized them."[64]

There were, of course, huge differences in the situation and histories
of American and Asian Indians as well as in the policies of America and
Britain on the two continents. Yet a parallel evaluation of the two is instructive here. While reminding us of the essential colonizing nature of
the missionary venture, it also underscores the potency of the gentle yet
resolute tactic employed by the missionaries as they worked to convert
and school a team of Dakota teachers and preachers who would promote the Christian cause out of the strength of their own convictions. In
a small pamphlet published at the school, where Alfred Riggs outlined
his approach to school discipline, he provides insight into this process:
"To many minds discipline means simply punishment or correction. But
with the word discipline take the word disciple and think a moment. . . .
A master implies mastery and subjection. But in discipline the subjection is voluntary; it is self-subjection."[65] Self-subjection and complicity
lay at the heart of the missionary educational endeavor.

The potency of the Dakota Mission's linguistic program was demonstrated in a brief incident that was written up in the school paper of the Carlisle Indian School. At Carlisle, an English-only language policy was strictly enforced and students caught speaking "Indian" were punished. (Carlisle's different strategy to achieve self-subjection will be explored in chapter 8). When Stephen Riggs visited Carlisle during a trip to the East, the very first delegation of Sioux children had been attending the school for just over a year and a half. Riggs made a tour of the classrooms, quietly talking to the Dakota students in their own language. The strong reaction this visit provoked in the students was described in caricatured terms in the school newspaper, where it was presented as proof of Indian capacity for emotion.

> Anyone seeing the astonishment and pleasure of the Sioux pupils in the different rooms, as they were addressed by Dr. Riggs in their own tongue, would forever relinquish the idea that the Indian does not exhibit emotion. Many of the boys and girls, Indian like, put their hands over their mouth, opened their eyes wide and rolled them around and then laughed heartily and some of them, with pleasure and surprise in their faces, clapped their hands, as Indians often do when surprised and pleased.[66]

For the white editor, it was the display of emotion by Indian children that warranted reporting, although the complicated source of these emotions was neither acknowledged nor examined. For the modern reader however, the account carries within it a series of quite different messages. The students' amazement at the incongruity of hearing an unknown white man speaking their language startles us into remembering the total ban Carlisle placed on Indian languages; students were not allowed to speak Dakota, yet here was a white man breaking the rules. This account serves, too, as a forceful reminder not just of the delight engendered in these children on hearing their "clandestine" mother tongue but also of the attendant potential power of this vernacular language when employed as a tool of transformation. The Dakota Mission had harnessed this power to reach into the hearts and minds of Indians as well as to maintain the authority of their Christian mission.

In a straightforward relationship between white colonizers and the colonized, such as the one depicted by Daniel Defoe between Crusoe and Friday in *Robinson Crusoe*, the white man traditionally demanded that the native learn his skills and, most importantly, his master's language. "I . . . made it my business, " Crusoe explains, "to teach him everything that was proper to make him useful, handy, and helpful; but especially to make him speak and understand me when I spoke."[67] Crusoe had the advantage of dealing with a lone individual of "humble thankful disposition," eager to be instructed and given language. At the Dakota Mission, while the missionaries' end goal was essentially the same, their approach was more convoluted. Confronting a whole society neither "humble" nor "thankful" in its attitude to whites, the missionaries wanted not only to teach the Dakota to "speak and understand" them (and be useful, handy, and helpful!); they also wanted to secure and maintain power within the communities. For this, knowledge of the vernacular, combined with its new literary status, was vital.

In Europe, Benedict Anderson argues convincingly that the birth of separate national consciousnesses was fostered in part by the "dethronement of Latin" and the accompanying rise of local or vernacular languages. Access to the printing press elevated these previously oral languages "to the status of languages-of-power." In Europe, it was the people who spoke these vernaculars who, by joining with the forces of capitalism, were able to harness the power of the printed text to forge separate, national identities. Although Anderson's model cannot be neatly applied to America, his observations about the dynamics of power do shed light on the processes at work at the Dakota Mission and their use of the printed word.

The missionaries had not only given Dakota a written form, but it was they who selected all texts that were printed and distributed in Dakota as well as all information disseminated in the newspaper, *Iapi Oaye/The Word Carrier*. In 1897, the agent estimated that 790 of the 988 Indians living on the Santee reservation could read, but he also reported that only 500 had "enough English for ordinary conversation." It is clear from this that more than a third of those who could read were literate only in Dakota and not in English. The missionaries therefore held full control over what these Dakota Indians read.

The move from orality to literacy is seismic for any society or community.[68] For one Indian tribe, the Cherokee, this step had been taken when Sequoia codified their language, enabling widespread Cherokee literacy. The creation of a newspaper, the *Cherokee Phoenix*, facilitated the growth of a shared group awareness and contributed to the birth of a national consciousness of the type described by Benedict Anderson. What is significant here is that the *Cherokee Phoenix* was managed and edited by Cherokee, not whites. When reading the newspaper and other Cherokee texts, members of the Cherokee tribe "gradually became aware of the hundreds . . . in their particular language-field, and at the same time that *only those* hundreds . . . so belonged. These fellow-readers, to whom they were connected through print, formed, in their secular, particular, visible invisibility, the embryo of the nationally-imagined community."[69]

Although schisms and factions within Cherokee society meant that the development of this nationalism was not uncontested, it is nonetheless very obvious that the Dakotas' transition from orality to literacy was very different from that of the Cherokees. For the Dakota, literacy was initiated and orchestrated by white missionaries, who strove to manage and control all aspects of the transformation that literacy brought to the Dakota people. The missionaries' hegemony was not enduring and men like George Sword quickly understood and claimed the power of the written word.[70] But in the early days, none of the information or values disseminated in print in the Dakota language was Dakota in its source or content. Quite the contrary—the missionaries consciously used their knowledge of the Dakota language to penetrate and inscribe new parameters on the Dakota people in an unremitting campaign to establish their own version of an "imagined community" of Christian Dakota. Their resolute determination to sustain this community and maintain their control over it through use of the Dakota language was reflected in their resistance to the dictates of federal policy. When it became necessary, they were even prepared to sacrifice vital federal funding for the Santee Normal Training School in order to protect their linguistic policy and, by extension, their hegemony in the community.

English Only

No other mission school had invested in an Indian language to the same degree as the Santee Normal Training School. The government's introduction of an English-only policy for Indian schools receiving federal monies directly challenged the very raison d'être of missionary work and threatened the funding of Santee. The policy developed gradually. In 1880 the Indian Bureau issued its first regulation linking funding to the teaching of English. The rule was not assiduously enforced and Alfred Riggs deftly succeeded in evading it by applying for funds exclusively for the English Department of Santee.[71] Progressively, however, more stringent orders and declarations were issued in Washington. In 1881, Commissioner Hiram Price insisted that "The Indian must be made to understand that if he expects to live and prosper in this country he must learn the English language." Six years later, in 1887, Commissioner John D. C. Atkins took a far more extreme position when he openly forbade the use of Indian languages in any Indian school, stating explicitly that "the rule applies to all schools on Indian reservations, whether they be Government or mission schools." The rationale behind Atkins's order directly undermined the linguistic strategy of the Dakota Mission. "The instruction of the Indians in the vernacular is not only of no use to them, but it is detrimental to the cause of their education and civilization, and no school will be permitted on the reservation in which the English language is not exclusively taught."[72]

Alfred Riggs was outraged. In a hyperbolic headline in *Iapi Oaye/ The Word Carrier*, he pronounced that the severity of the new policy sounded the death knell of all mission and educational work for Indians: "No more Indian Schools! No more Indian Bibles! No more Missions!" For Riggs, the threat appeared so great that he feared this would be "the logical result of the present policy of the Indian Bureau, as shown in the astonishing rules against the use of Indian languages."[73] Riggs was joined in his criticism by missionaries from other denominations who also used Dakota texts in their work. Although the commissioner took a step back and conceded that there might be a place for Indian languages in church services, he remained totally obdurate about the schools: "No text-books in the vernacular will be allowed in any school where children are placed under contract, or where the Government contributes to the support of the school; no oral instruction in the vernacular will be allowed at such schools. The entire curriculum must be in the English language."[74]

The educational methods of the Santee Normal Training School were now under direct assault. Riggs refused to compromise the school's pedagogy and so was forced to battle hard to protect its funding.[75] The new commissioner, John H. Oberly, showed himself to be a little more conciliatory when he upheld the Indians' right to worship in their own language, explaining: "It is not the intention of the Indian Bureau to prohibit the reading of the Bible by any Indian in any language." Nevertheless, pedagogical practices at Santee were now completely out of step with federal policy. Bureau officials who visited the school felt suspicious when Riggs spoke to the children in Dakota. Even when such conversations were allegedly about religious topics, they were unable to understand and so reported his activities to Washington. By 1888, official pressure had become so intense that Riggs felt it necessary to terminate his Dakota language theology class.[76]

The federal funding of the Santee School was at stake. Rations for all the schoolchildren were paid for by the government, and in 1880 Riggs had made a successful request for tuition payment too. To start with, fees for just thirty students were federally funded, but the number of students supported and the sums of money granted rose rapidly. By 1883, and for the following decade, the federal government annually paid a sum of at least $12,000 to the Santee Normal Training School.[77] By ducking and diving around the regulations, the school managed to retain this level of support for a few more years, even as progressively more stringent orders were issued by successive commissioners.[78]

Santee was just one among twenty-two mission boarding and sixteen mission day schools receiving federal monies at this time. Their relationship with the government was symbiotic. The federal system of schools was not yet fully developed, so there were not enough places for the children in government schools. The established religious "contract schools" were thus in a position to increase their enrollments and benefit from government funding.[79] At Santee, the size of the operation, the scale of its ambition, and the missionaries' refusal to compromise their well-honed pedagogy meant that this institution was more exposed and had the most to lose. When the school's language policy became the target of fierce and unrelenting criticism, Riggs felt compelled to write to the Bureau of Indian Affairs repeatedly to explain his methods and justify his position.

Riggs was now struggling against a strong and rising tide. The English language was no longer something Americans vaguely thought of as important to the civilization of Indians. Rather, by the mid-1880s, English had become identified as a vital building block in a clearly defined program of Americanization. In 1867, Indian peace commissioners, sent out to discover the source of friction between Indians and whites in the West, had declared that "in the difference of language today lies two-thirds of our trouble." Their advice to the government was to make Indian children attend schools where "their barbarous dialects should be blotted out and the English language substituted."[80] This aggressive and linguicist attitude to languages other than English was, over the years, progressively translated into Indian policy.

By the time Thomas Jefferson Morgan laid out his scheme for a national system of Indian schools, learning English was no longer viewed as just a matter-of-fact necessity because the language had been elevated to a blessing in its own right. The impact of this new clarity in official thinking is tangibly represented by the short history of the Dakota Mission's *English-Dakota Reader*. First published by the Santee Normal Training School in 1875, in response to encouragement from the commissioner of Indian affairs, the reader had been substantially funded by the government and rapidly became a central text in the Santee curriculum.[81] A dozen years later, after English had been elevated to a new status and positioned as a vital element in the civilizing program, this same text had become a banned book.

The fate of the *English-Dakota Reader* was just one tiny manifestation of forces at work in the American nation that oscillated in its attempt to determine the place of the Indian in its society. Thomas Crowley, in his examination of the significance of language in the unfolding of historical events, reminds us that "in order to understand language in history, we have to read the debates, claims and representations carefully and in relation to the history in which they are set." Crowley's work has particular significance for the study of the English language within the Indian school system. He alerts us to the "contextual interrelation of language and race" and cogently argues that "these interrelations are constantly shifting, contested, won and lost; that is that they are dialogic, forever at stake and always up for grabs."[82]

While the government was building the Indian school system, the political, economic, and social as well as racial status of the Indian was in flux in the United States and debates over the use of the English language provided an arena for contests in which a great deal more was "up for grabs." For the Indians, who were the subject of these debates, patterns of exclusion and forms of silencing implemented at this time as a product of the debates were to have a legacy that would endure into the twenty-first century. For the Dakota missionaries, active and anxious participants in these debates, defeat of their linguistic strategy signaled the official unyoking of schooling from conversion and the collapse of their dream of creating self-sustaining, Indian Christian communities. More generally, it marked a break with long-established definitions of civilization as bonded to Christianity. The undermining of the Santee program presaged the growth and expansion of a predominantly national system of schools and the triumph of a correspondingly secular curriculum.

In 1893, when the government finally terminated the contract that had subsidized the Santee Normal Training School for over a decade, Alfred Riggs and the Dakota Mission finally lost their long-fought battle.[83] The demise of federal support for the most renowned mission-run Indian school in the West was an unambiguous sign of the waning of church influence in Indian affairs, and it was an unstoppable trend. Of equal and parallel importance, was the triumph of the government's English-only policy. It marked Washington's imposition of authority over Indian education and clearly defined a national perspective on Indian languages. Previously tolerated and even harnessed as a vehicle for introducing English, from the 1880s on, native languages were deemed unacceptable and progressively positioned as inferior.

It is possible to interpret the linguistic experiment at the Dakota Mission as a minor irregularity in a much broader, relentless campaign to suppress Indian languages. This is the line taken by Ruth Spack. In her excellent study of what she cogently terms "America's second tongue," Spack tracks both the development and implementation of the United States' language policy for indigenous people and "the shifting ownership of English, as the language transferred from one population to another and as its uses were transformed."[84] Yet it is also evident, as we have seen demonstrated and as Spack also acknowledges, that the missionaries were fighting their own linguistic battle against the government. If we therefore position the missionaries as unsuccessful contenders in a contest over language, we are able more meticulously to nuance the nature and significance of both their defeat and the government's victory.

For Commissioner John D. C. Atkins, English was unquestioningly "the language of the greatest, most powerful, and enterprising nationalities beneath the sun."[85] His veneration for English extended beyond national chauvinism when he attached it to a theory of social development. English was not just a symptom of social advance, but other, lesser languages represented an active impediment. Directly referring to Indians and collapsing them into a single entity, he insisted that "the barbarous language of the people is the greatest object in the way of civilization." For Atkins, Indian languages were both symptoms and perpetrators of the savage state: "These languages may be, and no doubt are, interesting to the philologist, but as a medium for conveying education and civilization to savages they are worse than useless; they are a means of keeping them in their savage condition by perpetuating the traditions of carnage and superstition."[86]

The explicit correlation of Indian languages with "carnage and superstition" repeats a well-entrenched pattern whereby stigmatization of dominated languages is accompanied by glorification of the dominant language. Atkins's assertion that Indians would benefit from using the "superior" English language has many historical parallels. The Greeks stigmatized non-Greek speakers as "barbarians"; the English described the Welsh as "foreigners who spoke a strange language"; and the French belittled local languages for their "incapacity to serve beyond their limited frameworks."[87] Such claims represent an obvious attempt to legitimate social, political, and linguistic hierarchies and are frequently made over the course of colonial relationships. What should also be noted, however, was that the strident voice of linguistic imperialism, adopted by Atkins and progressively all other officials, was for some time accompanied by a cacophony of other voices that were not its exact echo.

Indian Languages

The official English-only policy that accompanied the drive to include Indians in the United States, which remained in force from the 1880s until the 1930s, was challenged from a variety of different perspectives.

Divergent viewpoints on Indians and their capacities were recapitulated in judgments of their languages, which ranged from romantic to repugnant. "The whole poetry of our American woods, rivers and lakes seems embodied in [Indian] speech," a writer in the *American Catholic Quarterly Review* pronounced in 1878. Praising their sonorous and melodious tones, he judged Indian languages to be superior even to Latin and Greek and designated them the linguistic correlative of the American continent as well as an eloquent gauge of the "mental capacity of American Indians."[88] At the other end of the spectrum, Captain Edward Butler pontificated on *Our Indian Question* and arrived at the conclusion, that Indian languages were nothing more than a string of grunts, seriously lacking in conceptual vocabulary. Identifying them as a negative marker of intelligence, he asserted that it is "generally the most debased in morals and the lowest in intellectual capacity who readily obtain some knowledge of the Indian tongue orally."[89] Such extreme and definitive pronouncements about Indian languages were nothing new.

From the time whites first set foot on the continent Indian languages had been keenly noted and studied. It seemed that they might hold the key to the Indian's origin, the future of whites in America, and even the secret of man's creation. Washington, Franklin, and Jefferson had all been compulsive amateur collectors of Indian vocabularies. By the 1880s, however, Indian languages had become the subject of calibrated scientific scrutiny at the Bureau of American Ethnology, from where they were used to legitimate and underwrite federal policy.

Under the directorship of John Wesley Powell, the Bureau launched a program to collect and organize all available material on Indian languages. During his epic journey of discovery down the Colorado River, Powell learned to speak the languages of several local tribes. Ten years later, from his Washington base, Powell hoped to gain some comprehension of the relationship of all languages, which might point to an explanation of both the origin of language and its future trajectory. Language was being treated here as a subject for study, rather than as a medium of communication, but Powell's investigation was shaped by intellectual parameters that incorporated a powerful covert political agenda.

Unapologetically evolutionary in an age when it was hardly possible to be scientific without using evolutionary categories, Powell believed that language, like society, evolved through recognizable stages that paralleled the so-called three grand stages of culture: savagery, barbarism, and civilization. His supposition was that "the evolution of language, in all times and among all peoples, has been toward the better expression of thought."[90] For Powell, Indian languages represented a stage in the development of a single, perfect language.[91] Disagreeing with many earlier philologists, he thought that inflection, found in Indian languages and Latin and Greek alike, indicated a lower stage of evolution. For him, economy of speech was the force that drove linguistic development. Judged on these terms, he found Indian tongues to be "of a very low grade" and placed English, French and German at the top of the scale. Using this same criterion, Powell concluded that the simplicity of English grammar meant that "English stands alone in the highest rank."[92] Powell's evolutionary linguistic paradigm made him confident that when savage or barbaric peoples associated with civilized peoples, the former would readily learn the language of civilization and abandon their own and that despite the savage's imperfect grasp of the new language, his power of expression would be "greatly improved thereby."[93] Powell's elaborately detailed theories gave scientific support to the realities of power, justifying American authority over the Indian as well as the enforcement of the English language in Indian schools. They replicated in scientific terms the thinking of many of his contemporaries but ran directly counter to the views of the Dakota missionaries.

Dakota Mission and Dakota Language

At the Dakota Mission, the Riggs's evaluation of language was founded on theology rather than science. The doctrinal belief that man was created in the image of God allowed Stephen Riggs to argue that all language was therefore of "divine origin"—the product of the human mind that, Riggs insisted, even "in its untutored state is God's creation."[94] At the Dakota Mission they fiercely rejected any nationalist or evolutionary paradigm that relegated the Dakota language to an inferior status. Eight years before Commissioner Atkins issued his ban on Indian languages, when the English-only campaign was in its infancy, the Dakota Mission vehemently protested against this line of thought in their bilingual newspaper: "No Jew was more bigoted against those he termed

Gentiles nor any Greek more full of contempt for the learning of those he termed barbarians, which included the rest of the world, than we are in our supreme egotism over the English language."[95]

For Stephen Riggs, Dakota was a language on a par with English and its grammar was comparably pure. Sounding like a supporter of Noam Chomsky's linguistic theories, he explained that in the everyday use of Dakota, "No ungrammatical expression can come in that will not be rejected." More than this, Dakota was a language fully able to express the subtleties and complexities of civilized life. Stephen Riggs confessed that he often thought and dreamed in the language. His original sense that it was "barren and meaningless" had long since passed and it had become for him "a heart language," equally as capable of expressing his profoundest thoughts as English.[96] Riggs was fully aware of contemporary pseudoscientific research, which found the Indian skull to be smaller than the white man's and concluded that Indian intelligence was similarly diminished. For him, however, this alleged disparity in skull sizes had a religious rather than an evolutionary cause and had had no negative impact on the Dakota language. Conceding that the "Indian cranium had been belittled by centuries of paganism," he wrote, "Do not imagine that the Indian languages are the product of the present degenerate race. . . . Those best acquainted with our aboriginal tongues are most astonished at their wonderful preservation in the hands of these unlettered savages."[97]

The Dakota Indians might be unlettered, but the missionaries could bring them literacy and the word of God in their own language: unequivocally the best vehicle for delivering both salvation and civilization. Over three generations the Riggs's message remained constant. In 1895, in an article entitled "A Necessary Use for the Vernacular," published in *Iapi Oaye/The Word Carrier*, Frederick Riggs gave a slightly more elaborate account of the linguistic philosophy his grandfather had outlined and around which his father had organized the Santee school:

> The laying down one language and taking up another is something different from doffing one garment and pulling on another. It is a change of man's inner conditions; of his modes of thought and means of expression. The first language used, the mother-tongue, the vernacular,

has the inner hold. If for any reason it is desirable to bring in another language to supplant the first or to co-ordinate with it, either the first language stands as an obstacle in the way of it or it must be made use of as an assistant.[98]

The Dakota missionaries' determination to recruit the Dakota language "as an assistant" remained unswerving to the end. They had signed on to the federal project when it enabled them to further their own objectives, and although this apparently happy symbiotic relationship between mission and government had been intense, it proved short lived. The mission's work among the Dakota had predated federal support and would continue long after it was withdrawn. In the struggle to make ends meet, however, the Santee school moved beyond its original remit and began to enroll representatives from a wide range of tribes. Although functioning on a reduced scale, the school nevertheless would remain open and operative until 1937. The Riggses never radically altered their curriculum, but the end of federal funding and support ensured that the Santee Normal Training School's halcyon days were over.

As the national, secular system of government Indian schools expanded, it eclipsed not only Santee but also many of the older mission institutions on reservations across Indian Country.[99] Beginning in 1896, the congressional appropriation for church schools was cut by 20 percent every year until 1900, when it ended. According to official figures, the school enrolment of Indian children rose from 12,232 in 1890, to 18,188 in 1895, to 21,568 in 1900.[100] The vast majority of these children were now attending institutions run by the Bureau of Indian Affairs. For Alfred Riggs, this massive expansion of the educational enterprise was not a triumph; it was, rather, a cause for disquiet. That near 22,000 souls were still receiving no missionary attention was a concern, but particularly worrying to Riggs were what he regarded as the consequences of the secular schooling meted out in government schools: "A more dangerous factor than heathenism is the irreligion produced by the government in school. Many good people are engaged in those schools, but all they can effect is to create a semblance of Christianity."

In his review of seventy years of mission work, Riggs supplied what he regarded as telling details of the types of school that Indian children were now attending: 6,000 were in mission schools; 14,000 in tribal schools; and over 28,000 in government schools. For Riggs, the secular schooling offered by government institutions impeded the gradual progress he envisaged for Indians and to which he had dedicated his life. Instead of teaching the fundamental principals of Christianity, Riggs believed the secular curriculum of government schools contributed to dangerous alterations in native belief structures. Syncretic adaptations in native religious practice and belief were outside his comprehension and for Riggs were anathema. On a trip to Oklahoma in 1903, Riggs attended a service of the Native American Church at which he witnessed the Bible and mescal brought together in worship. Predictably, he reacted with abhorrence and was particularly distressed that many of the leading worshipers were returned students:

> Dreams of the new Jerusalem were blended with horse stealing, raids and scalps. The promoters and leaders in these religious orgies are returned students from some of the leading government schools of the country. . . . The condition into which this generation of secularly civilized Indians is coming is that of practical infidelity. They use religion simply to juggle with.[101]

The hybridity of the Native American Church distressed Riggs, prompting him to lament, "they have lost the faith of their fathers and received nothing in its place." Faced with something he classified as "religious orgy," he now elevated to the level of "faith" the traditional Indian beliefs he had previously labeled as "superstition." The Indians' advance into civilization was foundering because it could only take place within a Christian frame, and so Riggs fell back on a fretful demand for "more mission schools" to counteract the ungodly influence of government institutions.[102] But by this time, the days when missions schools supplied the backbone of the educational project had long since past. Even before the Santee school had reached the apex of its fame and power, the federal government had begun funding an Indian educational venture in Virginia that would cast the Indian school system in a quite different mold.

2

Hampton Normal and Agricultural Institute

4. Samuel Chapman Armstrong: Educator of Backward Races

AT THE HAMPTON NORMAL and Agricultural Institute in Virginia, General Samuel Chapman Armstrong organized a groundbreaking educational experiment that combined academic schooling with manual training.[1] It was designed to meet what he identified as the special needs of a "backward race." Although, as he later recalled, "it was not in the original plan of the School that any but Negroes should be received," from the beginning Armstrong firmly believed that Hampton's philosophy and methods could successfully be applied to any "backward" people.[2] Within half-a-dozen years of the school's founding, he had begun exploring the possibility of including Indians in his student population, and so welcomed the opportunity to enroll seventeen of the Fort Marion prisoners.

Hampton was a biracial school. Unique in the United States, its program to educate Indians and exslaves alongside each other reflected Armstrong's distinct racial views:

These people, who are with us and with whom we share a common fate, are a thousand years behind us in moral and mental development. Substantially the two races [Negro and Indian] are in the same condition, and the question as to what education is best for them, and how such education is to be put within their reach, is pressing itself closely upon all thinking men and women.[3]

Ignoring all historical and cultural differences between "the two races," Armstrong instituted his confident answer to "what education is best for them." At the very time the government was making a public commitment to Indian schooling and the absorption of tribes into the body politic, at Hampton, Armstrong was constructing Indians in racial terms, positioning them unequivocally as nonwhite and overtly comparing them and likening them to African Americans.

The first federal showcase institution for Indian education, Hampton was located within easy travel distance of Washington and the school was regularly visited by congressmen and philanthropists. In an era when racial definitions and constructions were fluid, the terms of black citizenship and the possibility of Indian citizenship were being hotly contested. By yoking the education of Indians to the schooling of exslaves and persistently affirming the similarities of the two races, Armstrong ensured that in any discussion of Indian education, the egalitarian assimilative discourse employed by both officials and reformers was constantly shadowed by a racial discourse. At Hampton, he created a connection between blacks and Indians that only made sense when viewed through a racial lens. That lens became increasingly strong and focused in the United States after Rutherford B. Hayes entered the White House and the nation abandoned its commitment to full social, economic, and political equality for exslaves. On the campus in Virginia, in articles in the press, and in photographs, Indians and blacks were seen living and working next to each other. This showcasing of the two races at Hampton meant that visually, philosophically, and racially, as well as pedagogically, a linkage was fostered that would have a profound and lasting impact on the developing Indian school system.

The seventeen Fort Marion ex-prisoners, who arrived at the school in 1878, became the nucleus around which Armstrong expanded Hampton's Indian program, which would continue to operate for over three decades.[4] When the War Department announced the release of the prisoners, after three years incarceration, Richard Henry Pratt had begun searching for educational institutions in the East willing to accept reformed Indian warriors as pupils. He targeted white agricultural colleges, but none was willing to take the risk of accepting students whose pacifism was as doubtful as their academic credentials. "Their case," Pratt complained, "was pre-judged because they were prisoners of war with reputation for atrocities."[5] In desperation, as a last resort, he addressed his request to Armstrong, at Hampton. After ten years spent building up a successful program for freedmen, Armstrong was eager to broaden his experiment to include Indians and accepted the whole group of seventeen.[6] As the day for their arrival drew near, he quipped facetiously, "We expect the Indians next Monday. I want Chinese and New Zealanders next."[7] Although, as far as we know, Armstrong never managed to recruit any Maori, a decade later Hampton's student list did indeed include, "1 China boy" as well as "2 boys from Cuba, 1 from Sandwich Islands and a girl from Africa."[8] Judging the capacities as well as needs of all nonwhite peoples to be akin, Armstrong insisted that "Hampton's work for the "despised races" of our country, while chiefly for the Negro, is really for all who need it."[9]

Armstrong's racial philosophy excited strong feelings and, from its inception in 1878 until its closure in 1912, Hampton's Indian program was subjected to criticism animated by racial anxieties from a variety of different sources. Hampton's trustees were among the first to hear of Armstrong's scheme and also to voice their doubts about his plans. John Marshall recalls how:

> When, in 1878, General Armstrong was asked to receive into his school some of the Indian prisoners who had been confined at Fort Marion, St. Augustine, I was not in favor of the plan. I had little faith in the capacity of the red man for civilization, and felt too that Gen. A. had already as much on his shoulders as he could well carry. I think a majority of the trustees were of the same opinion.[10]

But by this time Armstrong already held the whip hand at the board of trustees and was easily able to use his authority and charm to convince them of the wisdom and efficacy of his plan.[11] Not everyone was so readily reassured. Local white southerners feared racial mixing at the school; northern reformers worried about prejudice against blacks being transferred to Indians; and Hampton's black population was concerned about an Indian takeover of "their" school. Over the years, the initial doubts and anxieties of Hampton's trustees were echoed in different ways by a range of individuals and groups.

Armstrong might have been the most outspoken voice equating Indians with blacks, but he was not alone in his postulation. The prospect of absorbing Indians into United States society prompted many Americans to think in generalized racial terms and to conclude that it would be most appropriate if Indians were schooled alongside blacks. Hampton was the only school where a wide-ranging, self-conscious, biracial program of schooling was ever established, but there were many other intermittent efforts to educate the two peoples together.

At Howard University, Indian Peace Commissioner Samuel Tappan sought to start an Indian program in the early 1870s. Howard enrolled a handful of Indians, but no program was established and Howard remained a black institution.[12] Meanwhile, John Wesley Powell returned from his geological survey work for the government in the west, bringing with him three Ute Indians—Peter Johnson, John Patterson and his interpreter, Richard D. Komas—who he enrolled at Lincoln Institute (later Lincoln University), a black college in Philadelphia. No full-fledged Indian program developed at Lincoln and when Komas died and Patterson returned home, Johnson was sent to Hampton by his sponsor, to become, in 1877, Hampton's first Indian student.[13] But Lincoln continued to enroll small numbers of Indian students. Formerly the Ashmun Institute, a Presbyterian school founded to train black men for religious work in the United States and Liberia, this school had been renamed Lincoln Institute after the Civil War. According to Horace Mann Bond, Lincoln's eighth president and author of *Education for Freedom*, Lincoln was "the first institution found anywhere in the world to provide a higher education in the arts and sciences for male youth of African descent." [14] After the Indian School had been founded in Carlisle, Pennsylvania, many Indian students wishing to continue their education enrolled at this black institution in neighboring Chester County. Cases of Indians attending historically black colleges and universities were sporadic. Nevertheless, they provide strong evidence that many Americans deemed Indians being educated alongside another nonwhite race to be entirely appropriate. Hampton's Indian program fostered such thinking by institutionalizing and showcasing this racial construction of Indians.

The glaring differences between Indians and exslaves, the subjects of his biracial experiment, were never fully acknowledged by Armstrong. Having collapsed Hawaiians, "Negroes," and Indians into a single category he called "child races," he needed to downplay all historical and cultural differences separating the two races at his school in order to sustain both his racial philosophy and the rationale for Hampton. When he first realized that popular attitudes to Indians might enable him to attract money to his school, he wrote an impish letter to his wife, noting that "I am on the track of some more money—it will be necessary to prove that the darky is an Indian in order to get it: but I can easily do that you know. . . . [S]end me your thoughts on the identity of the Indian and the darky—SAME THING, aren't they?"[15] Although his public pronouncements were not couched in this cavalier tone, throughout his career Armstrong was unswerving in his insistence that the "despised races" of the United States needed the benefit of the educational program he had devised at Hampton. The recompense for including Indians far outweighed any drawbacks and also brought financial advantages.

Pratt's "Florida Indians" had all arrived with sponsorship for their education from northern philanthropists.[16] Armstrong immediately exploited the good publicity Indian students could bring his institution. Within just a few months of their arrival, he invited Pratt's star pupil, twenty-four-year-old Etahdleuh, to participate in Hampton's commencement exercises, which were attended by many well-to-do and philanthropic whites. Always in search of funds for his school, Armstrong saw the financial as well as public relations benefits that might accrue to his school by educating Indians, who most Americans judged more interesting and deserving than the exslaves. Aware of the government's shifting agenda for the Plains tribes, he invited President Hayes and Secretary of the Interior Carl Schurtz to Hampton to see the Indian students for themselves. Charming and persuasive, he used this visit to secure federal support for an annual enrollment of 120 Indians at Hampton, each funded by $167 of government money. Armstrong had thus received permission to build a long-term Indian program at Hampton and a guarantee that more than $20,000 of federal money would flow into the school's coffers every year.[17] While he also secured funding from the commonwealth of Virginia, the regular federal contribution for Indians still constituted Hampton's most consistent source of monetary support as well as the largest payment received by the school, after private contributions.[18]

When Hayes endorsed Armstrong's plans for an Indian program at this school for blacks, he was not just supporting education as a pathway into American society; he was also condoning Indian entry through a racial back door. To build, maintain, and expand the Hampton Institute, Samuel Chapman Armstrong needed to satisfy the expectations and convictions of wide-ranging and varied constituencies. White Virginians, northern philanthropists, missionaries, teachers, students, and a growing educated black population all placed different and often conflicting demands on the school. Armstrong's most recent biographer has suggested that to maintain their essential support, he fawned, flattered, equivocated, and even lied.[19] Yet whatever shifting opinions he voiced to satisfy his diverse followers, Armstrong's racial philosophy did not suffer from parallel vacillations; it remained clear and unchanging throughout his life, having been shaped by his childhood and early experiences.

Samuel Chapman Armstrong's Racial Philosophy

Born to missionary parents in Hawaii, in 1839, Armstrong's firm views about the capacities and appropriate education of nonwhite races were strongly influenced by his childhood experiences. His reflections on the history and people of Hawaii hold the key to much of his subsequent racial thinking. In *Lessons from the Hawaiian Islands*, he openly drew on his Hawaiian past to make comparisons between the islanders and America's black population, collapsing these two nonwhite races into a single group and ascribing to them similar characteristics and needs: "The negro and the Polynesian have many striking similarities. Of both it is true that not mere ignorance, but deficiency of character is the chief difficulty, and that to build up character is the true objective point of education."[20]

Armstrong's determination to use education to "build up character" engages with a broader colonial discourse noted by historian R. N. Lebow, who describes the qualities white colonists attribute to their native subjects:

> The characteristics that colonizers have attributed to natives are remarkably uniform. With almost monotonous regularity, colonial natives have been described as indolent and complacent, cowardly but brazenly rash, violent, uncivilized and incapable of hard work. . . . Each image, of course, varied slightly from the other, to include obvious differences in native character or mores, but the panoply of characteristics remained basically the same and effectively differentiated the natives from the white man.[21]

The young Armstrong witnessed his father and fellow white missionaries strive to convert and civilize the people of Hawaii, and this experience not only taught him to "differentiate the native from the white man," but it also shaped his very definite views on nonwhites. Armstrong came to believe that each race was advancing very slowly, at its own individual pace, up a scale of civilization. Notwithstanding the success of single individuals, the progress of each race must necessarily take place over generations. "The real upward movement, the leveling up, not of persons but of people," Armstrong explained in Hampton's newspaper the *Southern Workman*, "will be, as in all history—almost imperceptible, to be measured only by long periods":[22]

> The Indians are grown up children; we are a thousand years ahead of them in the line of progress. Progress is measured by development. Education is not development, but is a means of it. Savages have good memories; they acquire but do not comprehend; they devour but do not digest knowledge. They have no conception of mental discipline.[23]

Progress for Indians, as for all "child races," would take generations, but Armstrong believed it could be hastened by proper training. In order to acquire "mental discipline," the Indians needed to be guided, step-by-step, up the evolutionary ladder, from hunter to herder to farmer. Armstrong's conviction that all races needed to pass through these different stages of civilization was one reason he greeted with delight the gift of a valuable stock and grain farm at Shellbanks, just five miles from campus. This farm, he exulted in his annual report, would give the Indian boys experience of caring for stock and "they will thus be fitted for what is the first step in the civilization of the wild tribes; raising cattle and horses."[24] In *Twenty Two Years' Work at the Hampton Institute*, Armstrong directly acknowledged his debt to his missionary father, who had organized and set up "the five hundred Hawaiian free schools":

> It meant something to the Hampton school, and perhaps to the ex-slaves of America, that from 1820–1860, the distinctively missionary period, there was worked out in the Hawaiian Islands, the problems of emancipation, enfranchisement and Christian civilization of a dark-skinned Polynesian people in many respects like the Negro race.[25]

In particular he noted that on the islands there were two different types of school: at one, "mathematics and other higher branches were taught," while the other was organized "on a simpler basis" and followed a more practical curriculum. In Armstrong's estimation, "the latter turned out less advanced but more solid men," who were able both to build their own home and earn a living. Unhesitatingly, Armstrong chose this as his model for Hampton, making clear that his preferred curriculum was underpinned by his clear racial philosophy and his appreciation of the failings of some of the Hawaiian schools. "The missionary plan in Hawaii had not, I thought, considered enough the real need and weaknesses of the people, whose ignorance alone was not half the trouble. The chief difficulty was, with them [as it is with the Negro], deficient character."[26] Always concerned that the academic syllabus at Hampton might embrace too much, Armstrong was constantly vigilant lest the training of the mind outstrip the training of the heart and the hands, insisting that "over education and lack of personal training are dangers with the weaker races."[27] Vigilance was essential when a group's progress was being accelerated.

Measured according to this social evolutionary scale, blacks had already taken the first essential step towards "civilization" during their enslavement. At Hampton, Armstrong's determination to educate the two peoples alongside each other would expose glaring discrepancies in expected patterns of advancement up this scale. The underlying problem was that the rungs of the social evolutionary scale did not line up with positions ascribed to the different "races" on America's unique racial hierarchy. Indians were popularly as well as scientifically judged to be higher up the scale than blacks and social prejudice against them was also less universal.[28] Yet Plains Indians were not acculturated into white ways. In Hampton's terms, their ignorance of work and Christianity made them decidedly less "civilized." This was the reason Armstrong invited black students to act as models and guides to the Indian students.[29] The most articulate account of how Armstrong recruited one "despised" race to assist in the "uplift" of another comes to us in the writings of Booker T. Washington.

Washington himself was given one of the more elevated positions Hampton accorded its "Negro" students. He was summoned, by Armstrong, from his teaching post in West Virginia to take charge of Hampton's recent intake of Indian students. In his autobiography he skillfully recapitulated Hampton's unorthodox racial hierarchy and went further, presenting blacks as an example for whites as well as Indians: "How often I have wanted to say to white students that they lift themselves up in proportion as they help to lift others, and the more unfortunate the race, the lower in the scale of civilization, the more does one raise one's self by giving the assistance." Yet although blacks roomed with Indian students, coached them in English, drilled them on the parade ground, and tutored them in Hampton's trade shops, once outside the campus the harsh realities of America's racial hierarchy abruptly reversed their ranking. When he accompanied a sick Indian student to Washington DC, Booker T. Washington himself discovered that what he discreetly and euphemistically called "the curious workings of caste in America" dictated that Indians could dine and sleep in white establishments where Jim Crow laws banned all blacks.[30]

The racism of the dominant society was not Armstrong's concern. Instead he focused attention on the process of race elevation and dedicated Hampton to training leaders who could contribute to the gradual advance of their own group. Hampton's Indian graduates, like their black counterparts, were being trained for the painfully slow task of edging their people toward "civilization." "Let us . . . choose the best youth who offer," he suggested, "and send them back (for they will go) to help lift up their people."[31] Armstrong's metaphor is significant; the Indians could not escape their painfully slow progress "up" the ladder of development. He predicted that the elevation of the whole race would take generations, identifying their "lack of character" and "surfeit of freedom" as symptoms of an early stage of development. So while some outstanding Hampton graduates would serve as leaders, he aimed to make the majority of them hardworking and worthy citizens, happy and content to live near the bottom of the social scale. "Three years at Hampton will, I believe," wrote Armstrong, "fit Indians for a simple life of labor in their own homes."[32] He did not openly encourage Hampton students to continue their education, urging them instead to return to work among their own people. Convinced that "a well balanced mind is attained only after generations of improvement," Armstrong doubted that they would be able to compete with whites in the intellectual field.[33]

Armstrong's attitude to the reservation was consistent with his view of Indian aptitude. Properly managed, its segregated environment would, he suggested, "afford the best conditions to prepare the red race for citizenship." So to facilitate their adaptation, and also to create a living exhibit for white visitors, he built a "model reservation" at Hampton. Here neat little cottages and monogamous Indian couples provided an example of how Indians could and should live.[34] The Fort Marion Indians were all from Plains tribes in the Southwest, but when Pratt was enlisted to recruit the first students for Hampton's new Indian program, he was sent out to the Sioux. So Armstrong resolved to build a special relationship with one Sioux agency: Crow Creek. He planned to use the Lower Yanktonai band from the Crow Creek reservation and the Lower Brulé band from the Lower Brulé reservation as "test cases" in his experiment in racial uplift. Both bands were administered by the Crow Creek Agency.[35] "We mean to do everything we can for these two Sioux tribes and watch their course with interest," Armstrong informed the commissioner.[36] By 1887, 104 children from these two reservations were enrolled at the school. "We wish to concentrate on these and show what education can do, co-operating with government work on the ground," Armstrong explained. Hampton's Indian experiment was, therefore, "largely staked on the success of our training Indians from that Agency."[37] By concentrating the school's energies on a single agency with responsibility for two quite different bands, Armstrong wished to monitor as well as demonstrate the gradual uplift of the race.

Hampton and Native Cultures

Armstrong's gradualist, evolutionary approach explains why he sought to nurture the Indian's racial identity as well as organize aspects of Hampton's schooling program to accommodate it. Although he indiscriminately embraced all tribes under the label "Indian," he did not seek to destroy a student's tribal allegiance or, as he put it, "break the race tie and sympathy, and make him a man without a country."[38] Nor did he want to render them inarticulate in their own languages. So although an English-only rule was generally enforced by fines and punishments, it did not apply at all times and students were allowed to speak their own languages before and after the working day and on Sundays.

Intent on teaching white American skills, values, and standards, Armstrong also showed tolerance for many aspects of Indian life. Hampton published a little Indian paper called *Talks and Thoughts* and in a section entitled "Folklore," pupils contributed their own writing, which often included descriptions and details of their native traditions. One Sioux boy's explanation of the significance of war regalia was typical of the many references to native traditions: "The people gave a war-bonnet to the chief, for they said he was a brave man. It was a dangerous thing to wear a war-bonnet during battle. The enemies would shoot first at the man that wore a war-bonnet. They always wanted to kill the most brave man. The war-chiefs were the most brave men and they had to wear war-bonnets."[39] When safely classified as "folklore," Armstrong tolerated discussion of native traditions. Hampton even created a little museum, where both African and Indian materials were exhibited to "stimulate race pride."[40]

While never doubting the absolute superiority of white society, Armstrong sometimes betrayed ambivalent feelings toward the native cultures Hampton's program sought to expunge. The obvious artistic talents of some of the Florida prisoners—Bear's Heart, Koba, Etahdleuh, Ohettoint—gave him pause for thought. During their three years at Fort Marion, the prisoners, as we have seen, had already begun to adapt their traditional art for a white audience. By the time they arrived at Hampton their work looked highly proficient to the white viewer.[41] Armstrong was impressed, and in his first report after their arrival he reflected, "The Indian has the only American art, [and] I believe it to be a duty to preserve and in a wise and natural way to develop [it]."[42] So he encouraged his Indian students to practice and improve their "native art," publishing their sketches and drawings in *Talks and Thoughts* and allowing them to make money by selling their work to white visitors. But recognition of artistic talent in no way changed his assessment of what he judged to be more fundamental deficiencies. Only hard work, accompanied by proper Christian training could, over time, remedy their shortcomings.

Hampton's Curriculum

Hard work always lay at the core of Hampton's curriculum. As an institution with no endowment and an impoverished student body, the school relied on student labor on the school farms and in the shops to support its practical needs. But for Armstrong, the purpose of this student labor was more than fiscal; it was also designed to play a vital pedagogical role by building character. Having commanded "buffalo" troops during the Civil War and then run a district of the Freedman's Bureau from 1866 to 1868, Armstrong was convinced he understood the essential nature and attributes of America's African Americans. He deemed education vital to their future as citizens, but it needed to be a particular kind of education, as Armstrong explained in his first report to Hampton's trustees. The African American's "deficiencies of character are, I believe, worse for him and the world than his ignorance." To remedy these perceived "deficiencies of character"—improvidence, low ideas of honor and morality, and a general lack of directive energy, judgment, and foresight—Armstrong organized Hampton's distinctive curriculum.[43]

When the school first opened, students spent each morning working on the school farm or in the kitchen or laundry. They then went to classes in the afternoon and studied in the evening. When it became clear that such an arrangement was not economically practical, Armstrong was undaunted. "Of course it cannot pay in a *money* way, but it will pay in a *moral* way. . . . It will make them men and women as nothing else will." Armstrong never wavered from this view. He furnished manual training with a clear ideological as well as practical purpose and was utterly convinced that it provided the best education not just for the exslaves, but for all "despised races." "Experience," Armstrong insisted, "has strengthened my conviction of labor as a moral force."[44] So within a day of their arrival, he had the Florida prisoners hoeing onions in the kitchen garden and was delighted with the result. In a letter to his wife he patronizingly announced that the Indians "do as well as our darkies."[45] When the Indians' quite different backgrounds and unfamiliarity with the English language forced Armstrong to make some adjustments to the Hampton curriculum (which had been designed for exslaves who had lived and worked alongside whites for generations), Armstrong remained unshaken in his conviction "that a colored school, on the labor plan, offers better conditions for educating Indians than any other. Both races need similar methods." Just as manual labor was deemed capable of correcting the deficiencies of character of the African American, so too a program of hard work would, Armstrong believed, counteract the Indian's savagery and facilitate the race's rise to civilization. "The idea of work is not in their brains or blood," he wrote in his report of 1879, shortly after the first Indians arrived at Hampton, "they don't see the point of it or its relation to life."[46] Determined that the curriculum at the Hampton Institute would combat this weakness, Armstrong delighted in quoting the words of Secretary of the Interior Henry Teller: "The Indian question will never be settled until you make the Indian blister his hands. No people ever emerged from barbarism that did not emerge through labor."[47]

Labor, whether on the school farms, in the laundry, kitchen, or trade shops, was fundamental to Hampton's mission and curriculum. In the immediate post-Civil War years, Hampton's syllabus was very different from those being developed at other institutions for exslaves, where greater weight was given to academic and professional training.[48] At Hampton, Armstrong developed a pioneering model for the manual training of African Americans in the United States. From its inception, Hampton's curriculum was entangled with thorny and contentious political issues that would become the focus of disagreement and rancor.

Manual education in the United States became a highly controversial subject lying at the center of a heated debate. This debate was not only about the proper function of the school in a democratic society. It had far wider and more fundamental ramifications, because it was also about the different capacities and abilities of the nation's children. As the United States industrialized and public education expanded to provide schooling for a growing immigrant working class, the purpose and function of the traditional little red schoolhouse began to be reassessed. Instead of providing a basic common school education, many now demanded that the school should equip children for employment, by teaching manual skills. Francis Walker, president of the Massachusetts Institute of Technology and eminent statistician, was among the most outspoken in his insistence that schools should prepare the children of the immigrant urban poor for their future as workers. Addressing the issue in a rhetoric that engaged contemporary anxieties by summoning up a past rural idyll, Walker suggested that manual training offered a way to give the city child essential educational opportunities not otherwise open to him: "In the country, the boy finds a hundred opportunities alike at work and at play, for acquiring much that can only be given to the city boy by formal instruction."

One of the most outspoken opponents of this view was William T. Harris. Superintendent of schools in St. Louis and later commissioner of education (1889-1906), Harris was acutely sensitive to the political agenda incorporated in the manual training pedagogy and launched a ferocious attack on the movement. Defending the common school philosophy, which promised equal opportunity for all by offering education as a gateway to upward mobility, Harris condemned the limitations of manual education, which predetermined and restricted a child's social and economic possibilities: "The economic, utilitarian opposition to the spiritual education in our schools comes before us to recommend that we forecast the horoscope of the child, and in view of his future possible life of drudgery make sure of his inability to ascend above manual toil." But Harris's view was being challenged across the United States. Popularized by the Philadelphia Centennial Exposition of 1876, the manual training movement spread rapidly and practical subjects joined reading and writing on many school curricula. By 1890, drawing, wood and metal work, carpentry, sewing, and cooking were being routinely taught to thousands of city children in public schools across the country, while the fight between white educators over how best to educate the poor and disadvantaged continued to rage.

If the issue of manual training for white Americans was contentious, for African Americans it was explosive, because it was entangled with questions of race difference and the legitimate aspirations of the exslaves. Although this type of curriculum was not unique to Hampton and was tried out at many other black colleges, including Howard, Armstrong made it a fundamental element of his school's curriculum. So inevitably, Hampton was seen as directly contributing to the intimate and invidious association that developed between manual training and schooling for second-class citizenship.

Washington and Tuskeegee

When manual training came under attack, the Tuskeegee Institute became a target, because of its principal's high public profile. Having been educated at Hampton, Booker Taliferro Washington made himself the most famous exponent of the Hampton Institute philosophy and always remained in close contact with Armstrong. Armstrong himself had been responsible for Washington's appointment. When invited in 1881 to name the best white candidate to lead the new normal school in Alabama, Armstrong sprung a surprise on the all-white appointment committee when he unhesitatingly put forward the name of his black protégé, Washington.[49] This recommendation might appear to be in direct contradiction to Armstrong's unequivocal racial views about the capacities of exslaves. Yet although convinced that the "Negro race" as a whole could only gradually attain the same level as whites, Armstrong nevertheless believed that unique individuals could rise above and surpass the ascribed racial destiny of their compatriots and identified Washington as one such individual.

The relationship between these two men, of different races and contrasting backgrounds, was intense and intricate.[50] In his autobiographical volume, *Up from Slavery*, Washington writes about Armstrong with admiration and respect blending into veneration:

> I do not hesitate to say that I have never met any man who, in my estimation, is the equal of General Armstrong. . . . I shall always remember that the first time I went into his presence he made the impression upon me of being a perfect man: I was made to feel that there was something about him that was superhuman. It was my privilege to know the General personally from the time I entered Hampton till he died, and the more I saw of him the greater he grew in my estimation.[51]

Having arrived in Virginia penniless and in rags, after a five hundred-mile pilgrimage to an institution he knew of only through hearsay, Washington claims he secured entry to Hampton by demonstrating he could thoroughly clean a room: "The sweeping of that room was my college examination, and never did any youth pass an examination for entrance into Harvard or Yale that gave him more genuine satisfaction. I have passed several examinations since, but I have always felt that this was the best one I ever passed."[52] This memory, published almost thirty years after the event, reflected Washington's lasting respect for the practical aspects of life that he, too, would promote and sustain throughout his career. Washington judged the Hampton curriculum, with its emphasis on hard work, manual training, and practical goals, to be the best way to help educate his people, and he introduced an almost identical curriculum at Tuskeegee.[53]

After building Tuskegee out of a few dilapidated farm buildings with a handful of pupils and turning it into a thriving campus with a black student body of thousands, he won international acclaim as an educator and race leader. This did not quell the growing censure directed at him by well-educated blacks. Washington's most influential and persuasive critic was, of course, W. E. B. Du Bois, the Harvard-educated editor of *Crisis*. In his book, *The Souls of Black Folk* (1903), Du Bois included a chapter entitled "Of Mr. Booker T. Washington and Others" in which he made a critical appraisal of the man and his work. Insisting that "the time is come when one may speak in all sincerity and utter courtesy of the mistakes and shortcomings of Mr. Washington's career, as well as his triumphs, without being thought captious or envious," Du Bois criticized Washington for ignoring black political rights. He attacked his famous "Atlanta Compromise" and specifically condemned manual training as an inferior education, which would always prevent blacks from competing properly with whites. Washington's aspirations had been too low, Du Bois insisted, and had failed to address the needs of what he called the "talented tenth" of the black population, who were essential to lead the masses to social and political equality.[54]

The Hampton Institute was central to this bitter debate about black schooling and manual education, as Du Bois made abundantly clear when he chose Hampton as the venue for his caustic and vitriolic speech damning the manual curriculum. "Take the eyes of the millions off the stars and fasten them in the soil, and if their young men will dream dreams, let them be dreams of corn bread and molasses."[55] When Armstrong set up the first nonmission schooling program for Indians and situated not religion but labor and manual training at its core, he deepened the association between manual education and schooling for inferior peoples and bound not just African Americans but also Indians to a system of schooling freighted with negative associations and outcomes.

Hampton and Manual Training

When Du Bois leveled this acerbic attack against the racial philosophy Armstrong had built into the very foundations of the Hampton Insti-

tute, the General already lay in the central plot of the school's cemetery. After a crippling stroke in November 1891, he had died in May
1893, aged fifty-four, just two weeks before Hampton's twenty-fifth an-
niversary celebration. By this time, the racial mood in the country was
turning sour; legal and de facto segregation was spreading as the black
community became progressively disenfranchised. Across the South, the
American Missionary Association's colleges for blacks were starting to
abandon their more ambitious academic curricula to follow Hampton's
lead, by opening industrial and domestic science departments. Morri-
son Holmes, the principal of the Avery Normal Institute in Charleston,
justified such endeavors as being "in keeping with the tendencies of the
times and the newer education."[56]

Such remarks demonstrate how Armstrong's philosophy and methods
helped create a lasting legacy that would be absorbed into future patterns of black education in the United States.[57] And because Armstrong
had argued so forcefully that Indians required similar methods, and built
an Indian program at Hampton to prove it, his school would also exert
a shaping influence on the developing Indian school system. To the last,
Armstrong never publicly deviated from his claim that the curriculum
at Hampton "would exhaust the best powers of nineteen-twentieths of
those who would for years to come enter the Institute" nor his insistence
that "The Negro and Indian races are especially in need of mechanical
education to fit them for the sphere they shall occupy."[58]

There can be, however, as Ivor F. Goodson reminds us, very wide gaps
between the published curriculum, the taught curriculum and the received
curriculum.[59] Hampton's philosophy and curriculum are relatively easy to
ascertain. What is harder to determine is the way in which its messages were
transmitted by teachers; how judgments about white superiority were reinforced by gesture, word, and action and, more importantly, how the students themselves responded to Hampton's relentless lessons on racial inferiority. A story told by Booker T. Washington is instructive on this point,
providing anecdotal evidence for students' open rejection of Hampton's
racial philosophy.

In an American history class, a white Hampton teacher invited a black
and an Indian student to identify any special contribution that the other
race had made to "civilization." After the Indian student had identified

African American patience, musical aptitude, and desire to learn, and the black student had noted Indian courage, sense of honor, and racial pride, the teacher asked the whole group in what respects the white race was superior. Washington tells us that "no member of the class rose." When the teacher repeated the question, "to his surprise, not one of the class had a word to say." In their silence, the whole class signaled its refusal to accept Hampton's public statements about the inferiority of the "despised races."

For Washington, this incident represented a demonstration of solidarity. Not a solidarity rooted in the two groups' acknowledgment of their shared lowliness, as Hampton encouraged them to believe, but instead a defiant solidarity fostered by white bigotry. Washington describes the incident as illustrating "how all the dark people of this country . . . are being drawn together in sympathy and interest in the presence of the prejudice of the white man against all other people of a different color from his own."[60] Accounts of rebelliousness are hard to find in Hampton's official record for very obvious reasons. Washington's anecdote carries a particularly telling message because it comes to us in the writings of a man who is generally regarded as the greatest exemplar of a Hampton education. His story reveals that, despite his deep and binding relationship to both Armstrong and Hampton, he, along with the other black and Indian students, defiantly refused to sign on to Hampton's demeaning racial philosophy that targeted Indians and blacks with equal ferocity.[61]

Hampton and the Indian School System

Hampton was always a predominantly black institution, yet although the Indian program was much smaller, it acquired widespread, national visibility. For Armstrong and his team of staff, showing visitors around the campus—sometimes as many as twenty thousand a year—became as important and familiar an activity as teaching the students. Local dignitaries, Indian chiefs and parents, teachers, missionaries, benefactors, reformers, ethnologists, senators, congressmen, and presidents all streamed through Hampton's gates to witness Armstrong's racial educational philosophy in action.[62] Armstrong also vigorously promoted his school and ideas in talks and lectures around the country. He became what James M. McPherson describes as "the greatest educational salesman of the nineteenth century," often taking troops of Hampton students on tour with him to provide living examples of what schooling could accomplish for exslaves and Indians.[63]

Courting men in high places as well as the general public, he was also a forceful figure in Indian reform circles, where he spoke out robustly to explain and defend his educational philosophy and program. Although sometimes instrumental in shaping Indian policy, the General became highly critical of the government's increasing hands-on involvement in Indian education.[64] He judged the expanding number of new government schools, run by political appointees, to be unreliable in comparison to the "steady, persistent and increasingly effective" work of independent schools run by missions and, of course, himself at Hampton.[65] Armstrong's criticisms partly stemmed from practical concerns, because he feared a curtailment of Hampton's government financial support. But his disparagement of the projected national school system was also rooted in his fundamental disagreement with Thomas Jefferson Morgan's views.[66]

Armstrong was openly skeptical, as we've seen, about the possibility of "civilizing" Indians in "a single generation." Yet despite the fact that he had tailored Hampton's curriculum to facilitate Indians' unavoidably slow advance, Morgan nevertheless positioned the Hampton Institute, and other similar institutions, at the top of his projected Indian school system. Students would make a staged progression through the reservation day and boarding schools, before gaining entry to one of the off-reservation schools, like Hampton. Morgan was resolved to create a school system where all Indian children could be made to speak, dress, behave, and think like white Americans and was convinced this would assure their entry into mainstream society: "That such a great revolution for these people is possible is becoming more and more evident to those who have watched with an intelligent interest the work which, notwithstanding all its hindrances and discouragements, has been accomplished for them during the last few years."[67]

The rhetoric of rapid assimilation had triumphed. Yet, in their eagerness to embrace an apparently coherent solution to the "Indian Problem," white reformers sidestepped serious debate about the curriculum and the place Indians were destined to find in American society. This is best illustrated in the way Carlisle and Hampton, so often mentioned in the same breath, were seen as providing a harmonious blueprint curriculum for the growing system of government schools, with manual training at its core.

When Pratt founded the Carlisle Indian Industrial School, his inclusion of the word "industrial" in the title of the fledgling institution signaled that he too was placing manual training at the center of Carlisle's curriculum. Before classes even began, he set the Indian students to work mending dilapidated buildings and erecting a hospital, under the supervision of a carpenter, explaining, "Doing that which had to be done to make things better was the inspiration."[68] Manual training was central to Carlisle's curriculum, yet Pratt aggressively eschewed the ideological underpinning so dear to Armstrong's heart. He argued on pragmatic grounds that, vital as it was, manual training was only a necessary short-term measure to bring peace and make young Indians economically self-sufficient. Writing to Senator Dawes of Massachusetts six months after Carlisle opened, he argued: "Education and industrial training for youth, *for all Indian youth* will, in a very short period, end Indian wars and, in a not very long period, end appropriations to feed and clothe them. I don't believe anything else will."[69] As the number of off-reservation boarding schools grew to twenty-five and comparable institutions were opened on almost every reservation in the West, manual training became a generally established component of the syllabus at all Indian schools. Many, like Pratt, ignored the implications for Indians of the furious argument being conducted nationally on the topic of manual education and insisted that this type of schooling was the best way to prepare Indians for citizenship and economic competition. A vital component of Hampton's program had been included in the curricula of all Indian schools from their foundation. Although inevitably manual training was linked to racialized educational practices, Armstrong's racial philosophy had not yet been openly embraced.

Gradually, officials at the Bureau of Indian Affairs openly recognized Hampton as the prime, model institution for Indian schools and accepted not just manual training, but also Armstrong's racial philosophy as their guiding ideology. The clearest sign of this came when Hampton's full curriculum was used as the foundation for a common *Course of Study for Indian Schools*, drawn up by Superintendent of Indian Schools Estelle Reel and published in 1901.[70] Reel openly based the new *Course of Study* on the racial ideas and educational philosophy of Hampton. Reiterating Armstrong's belief that the needs of the young Indian were special and in no way the same as those of the white child, she explicitly legitimated Hampton's philosophy and practice. "The teacher of Indian children," she explained, "must have a general understanding and thorough sympathy with the peculiar circumstances of Indian life, using the articles of the Hampton creed and making her school a school of labor, of love, of life."[71] She sent a draft copy of the *Course of Study*, with a request for comments, to Hollis Burke Frissell, Armstrong's successor, explaining, "I shall appreciate your opinion more than I can say, as most of the ideas embodied in the *Course* were obtained from Hampton."[72]

The racial ideology projected in the new course of study explicitly positioned the Indian as inferior and therefore in need of a special type of education to provide for his special needs. This curriculum was not geared to launch the Indian into competition and integration with Americans but rather designed to help him live a separate and independent life among his own people. In his lessons, therefore, he was to be taught "the history of his forefathers," so that he would continue to identify with his own race. Awareness of his own position on the scale of civilization and his pressing need to advance was to be stimulated by the teachers' endeavors "to arouse in the pupils an interest in the upward struggles of their people in the past, and a determination to do their part towards the progress of their race in the future." Reel was thus openly endorsing Armstrong's ideas on social evolution and the need for separate racial destinies.[73] The publication of the *Course of Study for Indian Schools* was an important step in the pedagogical unification of the Indian School system. It also signaled that in the covert debate about Indian capability, the racial, evolutionary philosophy of Armstrong and Hampton had triumphed, at least in Washington. The negative assessment of Indian capability that had always shadowed the campaign for Indian assimilation had now been openly acknowledged and embraced. Indian educational advance was perceived as being a difficult process, something Armstrong had always insisted.

Hampton-Educated

"The crucial test of our work," Armstrong declared, shortly before the first group of Indian students was about to go home, "will be on their return to their people, where the surrounding current of influences will be as adverse as it has been favorable here."[74] Armstrong's projected goal for both blacks and Indians involved far more than the education of individuals. He envisaged that Hampton would train a nucleus of civilized leaders who would dedicate their lives to working toward the gradual elevation of their own race. All Hampton graduates were given a far-reaching mission: the instruction and moral uplift their own people. So the work of its normal school lay at the core of Hampton's mission.

The vast majority of Hampton's black graduates, almost 90 percent, did indeed follow the path laid down for them and pursued careers in education. By 1880, after little more than a decade, they were teaching almost ten thousand southern black children in schools across the South.[75] In stark contrast, only a handful of Hampton-educated Indians became teachers. Instead, it was white missionaries and employees of the Bureau of Indian Affairs who took on the task of educating Indians and shouldered responsibility for what many considered to be the "white man's burden." From the official perspective, even Indians schooled at Hampton had not gained sufficient education to contribute to the elevation of their people. Judged ill equipped to compete with whites, Indians who found work in schools invariably labored in the laundry, the kitchens, or the trade shops. Hampton's own carefully kept records on its returned students confirm that the vast majority of women became wives and mothers and the majority of men took up subsistence farming. By 1918 out of a total of 359 graduates, Hampton's records show that 268 were farming or raising stock on the reservation and only 11 ex-Hampton students were working as teachers.[76]

That Armstrong himself accepted more modest career goals for Hampton's Indian graduates was made clear when the first intake of Sioux were ready to return home, after three years at Hampton. Armstrong personally accompanied them back to Dakota Territory. His aim was not to help them find work as teachers but instead to use his charm and influence to help secure them agency jobs, so they could live and work like whites and stand as an exemplary group. They could in this way,

Armstrong believed, "act as leaven for the lump." William Parkhurst, the Crow Creek agent, regarded Armstrong's efforts to secure jobs for his students and his hands-on style as a flagrant intrusion on his own authority. Parkhurst used Thomas A. Bland's monthly publication, the *Council Fire*, already known to be fiercely hostile to off-reservation schools, to publish a furious attack on Armstrong's interfering practices and to denigrate the abilities of the returned Hampton students. Armstrong responded in kind. The General's powerful allies in Washington meant that he eventually was able to secure Parkhurst's dismissal, but his relations with subsequent Crow Creek agents remained stormy.[77] Six years later, Crow Creek Agent William W. Anderson sent the first of what would become a run of letters to the commissioner, detailing the poor health, unemployment, arrogance, and backsliding of the Hampton returnees. "As a rule I believe [that] Indian children should be educated on or near the reservation," Anderson concluded, joining a growing chorus of critical voices.[78] By 1887, it was obvious that Armstrong's Crow Creek test-case project had gone awry. He had failed in his goal of "co-operating with government work on the ground," with the result that many of the returnees did not find employment at the agency. Criticism of Hampton's work became national when the Board of Indian Commissioners echoed Anderson's doubts about Hampton returnees' "progress."[79]

Two years earlier, in 1885, Armstrong had witnessed his school openly attacked in Congress. After spending a week visiting the Dakota agencies to investigate the success of eastern schools, a congressional committee, chaired by William Holman of Indiana, reported that the returned students from off-reservation boarding schools habitually lapsed into savagery and went "back to the blanket." He pronounced the schools to be abysmal failures.[80] This was the first salvo in a long-running assault on the schools. Helen Ludlow, Armstrong's right-hand woman and manger of the campus during his absences, defended the school by positioning Hampton at the center of the whole educational project. She insisted that only by upholding this pioneer institution could Indian schools everywhere be safeguarded. "This attack upon the Eastern schools does not concern Hampton alone. . . . It is the whole cause of Indian education that is attacked." Thanks to Hampton's intimate association with the Sioux agencies, Ludlow was able to counter the commission's assertions with facts and figures. She had recently spent several months visiting the same Sioux agencies that were the focus of criticism, and her carefully kept notes, along with classifications of the returnees' "levels of progress," allowed her to pronounce more than half of them (72 students out of a total of 132) to be doing "very well indeed." Only 4 were judged by Ludlow to have retrograded.[81]

Hampton's carefully kept records had allowed the school to fend off this direct attack. The experimental nature of the venture meant that Hampton was keen to measure and chart results, and so staff kept close tabs on all students after they left. Correspondence with returnees, periodical questionnaires, and staff visits to the West were all used to track the returnees and assemble a record of their progress. A file was created for every student, where a record of factual information, such as blood quotient and previous education, was assembled alongside more subjective evaluations of "character" and "home record." The "home record" was an ongoing assessment, made on a five-point scale ranging from "excellent" to "bad," that evaluated each student's relative success in living by the standards of white society. Christian marriage and temperance earned high ranking while at the other extreme marriage "in the Indian way" and participation in traditional dances were judged to spoil an individual's record.[82]

As white criticism of the off-reservation schools grew ever more strident, the Indians at Crow Creek also became increasingly resistant to sending their children away. In 1878, Pratt had persuaded the parents of forty-nine children to allow them to attend a far-away school in Virginia. Just three years later, the tragic consequences of this exodus was sinking in at Crow Creek. Ten of the children, a tragic 20 percent, lay in the Hampton cemetery or had returned home to die very shortly afterwards. Charlie Stone had been one of several Crow Creek children sent back early because of "ill health." Accredited in his Hampton Student File with the doubtful honor of being the "first Indian buried in Church Cemetery at Crow Creek," he was rapidly joined by several of his contemporaries.[83]

Indian opposition to sending young children far from home, linked to the growing number of government reservations schools, meant Hampton increasingly took older students who had already completed several years of schooling on the reservation. In the late 1880s, Armstrong was able to maintain Hampton's student numbers by broadening recruitment beyond this original targeted source. Yet Armstrong's early recruitment policy meant that Crow Creek became home to the largest number of Hampton returnees. This agency remained a test case for the General, and he assiduously cultivated the sympathy and support of the Indians there and encouraged families, like the Little Eagles, to establish and maintain their own "Hampton connection." In *Twenty Years' Work for Hampton*, he reported with satisfaction "that for eleven years Hampton was not without its Little Eagle."

Crow Creek Returnees
Henry Little Eagle (Wambdi-cistina) was the first member of his family to attend Hampton. Arriving in 1881, aged seventeen, he spent four years in Virginia and later returned for two further years of schooling at Hampton, bringing his bride, Lucy Winona, and his brother Edward. After these two years, spent in one of Hampton's cottages for married students, he and Lucy returned to Crow Creek, and Walter Little Eagle, Edward and Henry's brother, came east to Hampton. Walter never went home. He died of tuberculosis in the school hospital and was buried in the school cemetery. But a letter from Walter, published in the *Southern Workman* shortly after his arrival, lays out the educational aspirations that brought members of the Little Eagle family to Hampton:

> I want to go school much so I can get good education and when I be grown be a man I can help my parents and live in houses like white people. As we want to have some grist mills so we can grind our wheats and corn to make flour of. And we want big farms to plant our vegetables and corn, wheat, oats, so the Indians can have large farm and so they can sow plenty of wheat to sell and then can get money for it.[84]

Whether or not the content of Walter Little Eagle's letter was directly or indirectly dictated or shaped by the staff at Hampton does not detract from the basic information it carries. Written in shaky English, clearly a second language, it documents not only the cultural gap between Indian and white but, of equal importance at Hampton, also between Indian and black. This family, considered by the agent as one of the more "progressive" on the reservation, is clearly still learning to farm. Walter expresses a wish for them to grind corn to make flour, so they can make a tentative entry into the market economy. He also plans for them to take a monumental step away from their traditional living habits "and live in houses like white people." His letter encapsulates some of the key differences between Hampton's Indian and black pupils, and these disparities are underscored by the *Southern Workman*'s announcement that, just a few weeks before his death, Walter was baptized by Reverend J. J. Gravatt, the pastor from the local Episcopal church.[85] Unlike the freedmen, many Indians were not Christian. To this should be added the vital fact that Indians also were not U.S. citizens.

Armstrong was always keen to win and sustain the support of reservation leaders. One of the "progressive chiefs" on the Crow Creek reservation, Wizi, who had converted to Christianity but spoke no English, appears to have supported the school through thick and thin. Although his grandson died at the school, immediately after his bereavement Wizi purportedly urged his compatriots to send more children: "If only one of our children returns to teach us the white man's road, it would be worth the loss of all the rest." Armstrong printed Wizi's speech in the *Southern Workman.*[86] A year after the Wounded Knee massacre, Wizi traveled to Washington with a delegation of Sioux who had not participated in the ghost dancing. They followed their official business with a visit to Hampton. By now there was only a handful of Crow Creek students at Hampton, but Armstrong invited Wizi to address the whole student body, and his speech must have been music to the General's ears. Speaking through an interpreter, Wizi told the assembled students of the powerful influence a Hampton education could bring to their lives, if they could learn "enough to get on well, to talk with white people and get on with them." Employing a seminal metaphor with a Biblical ring, he spoke to Hampton's agricultural aspirations for it students and voiced his confidence in the gradual and natural process of Indian schooling: "Looking at our children here, I think how sometimes I put seeds into the ground. If I don['t] see them growing after a time I feel uneasy. Then I look again, and if I see them sprouting, I feel glad. So I feel about our children. I see that seed is growing here now, and by and by it will do good among our people."[87]

To Hampton's student body Wizi expressed his regret that "our fore-fathers didn't know enough to send us to school," and, in a striking inversion of the usual generational hierarchy, he told the Hampton students that he now took his lead from his daughter:

> I have a daughter at home who has been at Hampton to school. I don't know how to keep a house all nice and clean as it ought to be. If it were not all right, I wouldn't know it. But my daughter knows. She comes in and cleans up everywhere, and when I go in the house, I say that's *my child—my daughter*! I didn't even know the house was dirty. She knows it, and she has made everything nice and clean!

His speech, published in the *Southern Workman*, records his parental pride but his exclamation that "I didn't even know the house was dirty" also captures the implicit shame instilled by a Hampton education. Wizi, quite literally, feels the need to strip his house of all signs of Indianness. "There are no Indian trinkets round in my house," he boasts. Instead of using "some of [his] old clothes" to decorate his house he hung "pictures, like you here," he proudly informed the assembly.[88]

Wizi's well-appointed, two-story house was often made the venue for the annual meeting of the Hampton Returned Students and Progressive Association, whose activities were eagerly followed and reported in *Talks and Thoughts*. Assembled from information gleaned from letters sent back to the Hampton teachers, these reports were always upbeat and propagandistic, stressing how the returnees were mindful of their responsibility for racial uplift and the need to "work harmoniously for the benefit of our people." They included information intended to demonstrate the "civilized" character of the meetings: "Guests were not seated on the ground, but at tables. . . . [T]he blessing was asked by the chaplain [a Hampton student] and after the dinner a little time was spent conversing with one another."[89]

But the reports often also carried tiny, telling details, absent from Hampton's more systematized records of student progress, that provide hints of how returned students were blending the legacy of Hampton with facets of their own traditions. In 1897, we learn that the guests were called to their meeting, "not . . . by the beat of an Indian drum, but . . . by a bell, which rang out loud and clear the invitation that brought together the old students who had once been pupils of Hampton." Drawn together by a sound evocative of their days in Virginia, the returnees were, according to the *Southern Workman*, greeted at the gate not by "a lot of blanketed Indians. . . No sir, [but] by a brass band led by the returned Hampton student, Harry Hand."[90] A white observer in Dakota, commenting in the *Southern Workman* on the creation of this band on the reservation, explained that "Harry has made it out of what seemed very unpromising material."[91]

An accomplished musician who played the cornet in a mixed-race band in the local town of Chamberlain, Harry Hand had also set up his own band on the reservation. It is notable that in addition to the instruments the exstudents had learned to play at Hampton, Hand also included the "Indian drum" in the band.[92] The drum, an essential part of traditional dance and ceremony, could not be separated in the minds of most whites from what they perceived to be Indian savagery. It was not deemed by Hampton staff to be an appropriate way to announce the Hampton meeting, yet, thanks to Harry Hand, the Indian drum *did* find its place in the proceedings and provided the percussion in the band that welcomed the returnees. The central yet controversial presence of the drum was summed up in the account of the meeting published in Hampton's *Talks and Thoughts*, "Yes, the old sound of the bass drum was heard in the band, but its tone was softened by the harmony of the other instruments."[93] For teachers at Hampton, the key point was that the drum's "tone was softened by the harmony of the other instruments," which they interpreted as a sure sign that savagery was slowly giving way to civilization. Equally worthy of note, however, is the fact that the Indian drum was still there, being played, and that Harry Hand had incorporated it into his reservation band.

Harry Hand

Harry Hand (Crazy Bull) achieved no fame outside his own small community. Yet at Crow Creek he was a minor local hero. Three years after his death at the age of twenty-eight, his picture was hung alongside those of President McKinley and General Armstrong when the Old Hamptonians once again gathered together.[94] His story gives a glimpse of how one individual used his Hampton education for both himself and his community.

Harry Hand arrived in Virginia at the age of eighteen, after six years of schooling at the Crow Creek Agency School. He joined Hampton's Indian class, and made rapid progress. In less than two years he was writing regular contributions for *Talks and Thoughts*. He started his writing career with a little anecdote about a horse his family had owned—"The Story of a Horse"—but soon he began telling stories he had heard from elders: "A Fox and a Wolf"; "The Brave War Chief and the Ghost"; "A Buffalo Hunt"; "The Spider, the Panther, and the Snake"; "The Adventures of a Strange Family and an Old Sioux Legend."[95] Through Hand's efforts, these stories were, for the first time, presented in the English language, in written form, and illustrated with his own neat drawings. Readers of *Talks and Thoughts* saw pictures of animals talking to one another as well as humans. They also learned about the details of camp life from Hand's meticulous renderings of such activities as tipi construction and beef jerky drying. In March 1893, below a large drawing of "Wo-kda-ke-sa" ("The Story Teller"), Hand described the vital role of storytelling in the education of Indian children:

> In the evening after supper the men would get together, bring their pipes with their long stems and kinnikinick bags, sit in a circle and smoke; while one of the group would tell a story of war or hunting. When they did this, if there are any children present, the old Indian would say, now children, you listen, so that you will know what I ought to have done and what I ought not to have done, so that if you ever meet with the same thing you can remember what I said, so that you can improve on them.

Hand explained the distinction between descriptions of events and stories passed down through generations, as well as the procedures by which these stories would continue to be passed on and retold: "The true stories they tell are free for all, but when they tell fairy stories, the teller has to be given something by some of the listeners. Only those who give something have the right to tell the stories; but they must not tell them unless something is given to them."[96] Such stories were the lifeblood of all Indian societies. Although Hand might be thought to have trivialized them a little here by his use of the term "fairy stories," he nevertheless accorded them a literary standing by his claim that "if the Indian fairy stories were gathered and translated by a good translator and published in book form, they would compare favorably with 'Arabian Nights.'"[97]

Harry Hand provides a hint of why he was publishing the stories. In *Talks and Thoughts*, he expresses his awareness of the limitations of the oral culture that conveyed them when confronted with the disseminating powers of the written word. "We have read of many adventures of white people among Indians, but we never read of adventures told by Indians among white people. Why?" he demanded. Then, answering his own question, he explained, "Because the Indians have no newspaper through which to let the reading public know their side of many stories."[98] In his short life, Harry Hand would work to rectify this situation, furthering his own education in an effort to equip himself to both write and publish.

Hand's time at Hampton ended after five years, due to poor health, but he did not forget the lesson he had learned about literacy. Back at Crow Creek, he was soon appointed instructor in athletics and music at the government school, and it was not long before he capitalized on his school forays into journalism to set up a local newspaper, the *Crow Creek Herald*.[99] Edited by Harry Hand and another Hampton returnee, George Gray Cloud, the little newspaper was a very modest venture, each copy being laboriously written out by hand. Subscriptions cost $6.00 but, as they explained to their friends at Hampton, "The edition is very limited owing to the fact that the printing and illustrating is all done with the lead pencil. A hectograph is in contemplation however."[100] Hand succeeded in his ambition to procure a hectograph and on April 1, 1898, he started a second paper, the *Crow Creek Chief*. This paper was more ambitious in its scope. It published news and information about the Crow Creek Hampton returnees, but it also sought to comment on broader issues that had an impact on Indian affairs in South Dakota. In his first editorial, Hand explained that the paper would aim for political independence on all issues. "The *Chief* desires to be at liberty at all times to express its opinion in regard to political affairs, either Democratic, Republican or Populist." In a letter to his old Hampton teacher, Cora Folsom, he wrote with passion about the need to defend the interests of his people, noting the existence of white people in the local towns "who think that the Indians count for nothing."[101]

Harry Hand was in poor health, but at the age of twenty-seven he wanted to further his education. This aspiration was related to his publishing ambitions: "I need to learn more if I am to make a success of my little paper," he told Cora Folsom.[102] In October 1898, he set out for Haskell to study commercial law, phonography, typewriting, printing, business correspondence, and penmanship. He never completed his studies. By Christmas his health was in serious decline, and he would return home to die that summer. From Haskell Hospital, however, he used his newly learned typing skills to write a letter sending New Year greetings to Cora Folsom and telling her about the fate of the *Chief*. "I had to print that paper with a hectograph and it was too slow and too much work for me, because I had to work in the store too." Optimistically looking forward, he confided in Folsom his plans for the future. "I will try to get a real printing-press and start my paper again, when I get home and get well again."[103] In line with the observations about literacy he had made while still at Hampton, where he had acquired appreciation for the power of the written word as well as the skill to use it, his publishing ventures were perhaps the best way Harry Hand knew "to let the reading public know the Indian side of many stories."

Harry Hand received the blessing and encouragement of the Hampton staff in these ventures, yet surprisingly, the judgment recorded in his Hampton student file under conduct was "good." Only one small entry provides a hint of why his conduct was not judged "excellent." A letter from the Rev. Burt's wife, living on Crow Creek reservation, notes that in 1897, the same year he greeted the returned Hampton students with a full brass band, he was later seen "carrying the Indian drum to the place where the Indians hold their savage dances." This tiny clue alerts us to the fact that Harry Hand, despite his ambitions and educational attainments, as well as his ongoing correspondence with his alma mater, still attended Indian dances and used his musical talents on the Indian drum.

A fragmented outline of Harry Hand's story can be pieced together from records in the archives of Hampton University: snippets gleaned from the *Southern Workman*, official reports on Hand, and letters he wrote to his Hampton teachers. The contact he maintained with the school and the chance preservation of these scraps of information make it possible to assemble this very patchy picture of his life. Most of Hampton's student files, however, contain too little information to construct even a sketchy story of an individual, and even when there is sufficient material, everything in these files constitutes part of the official, white record; if we take it at "face value" we may "risk mistaking what may be a tactic for the whole story."[104] Notwithstanding the biased and curtailed nature of the school's written historical record, it is possible to deduce that Harry Hand lived and operated in two worlds. Living on the reservation, where he was able to secure a good job, he also moved freely in the local off-reservation town and maintained contacts with white musicians. Reading between the lines, it appears that when Hand decided to continue his education, he did so to further a goal not driven by individual ambition but rather by his sense of the need of his own Dakota community for an English-language newspaper. With such a publication, issues and subjects of vital interest to Crow Creek Indians could be aired and discussed and could make whites aware of an Indian viewpoint.[105] His dynamic engagement in this enterprise, inspired and facilitated by his Hampton education, inhibited neither his participation in Indian dances nor his active contribution to these events as a drummer.

Armstrong always planned that Hampton's Indian graduates should return to the reservation and in this there was a happy overlap between the aspirations of the school and those of its Indian pupils and their communities. But in the minds of everyone at Hampton, the white agenda must always prevail. "Education is a means to an end. The end should determine the means." This maxim inscribed on the opening pages of *Education for Life*, a book compiled to honor Armstrong, carries the unspoken assumption that Hampton's white staff would and should "determine" that "end" as well as the "means" by which it would be achieved.[106] They framed their task around the crude polarities of "savage" and "civilized" and worked to guide their pupils toward what they unequivocally regarded as the more elevated and desirable state. So at Hampton, when they doggedly measured and recorded the "progress" of individual students on their self-styled five-point scale—Hampton's own version of the social evolutionary ladder—they gave no credence to native aspirations or to the compromises and agendas created by Hampton-educated individuals and their communities in response to white strength and purposes. All manifestations of Indianness were interpreted as residues of a lower state, which provided evidence to Armstrong and his staff that Indians could not be rushed into civilization. That combined aspects of Indian and white culture might be linked to new, independent, dynamic processes around which both individuals and communities would realign themselves, was, for Armstrong, a prospect as morally offensive as it was intellectually incomprehensible.

Fixated by the notion of linear progress, Hampton's crude system of classification concealed the complexities, struggles, and subtle changes wrought in the individual lives of white-educated Indians. It ignored or brushed over their efforts to reconcile conflicts between the demands of the culture Hampton denigrated as savage and the precepts of civilization and was resistant to any suggestion of hybridity. The label "excellent" that Hampton awarded to a small minority of it exstudents appears unambiguous. Yet it, too, could mask faltering and doubt as well as creative, syncretic adaptations, as we shall discover by exploring the life of one of Hampton's star pupils who merged his own goals and aspirations with those of his alma mater, but, over the course of his life, would gradually redefine and nuance them.

5. Thomas Wildcat Alford:
Shawnee Educated in Two Worlds

GAY-NWAW-PIAH-SI-KA (Thomas Wildcat Alford) was one of Hampton's first students. Neither an ex-prisoner from Fort Marion nor part of the group Pratt recruited to launch Hampton's Indian program, he traveled independently with a fellow tribesman to Virginia from Indian Territory. Both young men shared the explicit intention of acquiring a white education to aid and assist their tribe, the Absentee Shawnee. Alford left behind two separate and very different records of his life. As for many other Hampton students, one is the private, contemporary but fragmented account, which can be pieced together from the letters he wrote to his teachers at Hampton and the pages of the *Southern Workman*.[1] The other, his published autobiography, *Civilization*, is a version of his life he told to a white woman, Florence Drake, in 1936, two years before he died.[2]

The letters provide both factual information and a day-to-day sense of the difficulties of his situation. They cover a selective period of time and, naturally, are tinged by Alford's personal relationship with his teachers. Despite their ostensibly private nature, they often present a highly formalized face; Alford's awareness of Hampton's expectations often led him to blur the usual divide between public and private.[3] Yet although often formal—"semipublic transcripts"—many of these letters display a passion and immediacy that is not present in his autobiography. The published account of his life is shaped by the order, symmetry, calm, and balance available with hindsight. It presents an integrated version of Alford's whole life, but the book is partly structured by the editorial hand of Florence Drake and therefore, as an historical source, is even more complex than the documentary fragments that can be gleaned from the Hampton University Archives. Although ostensibly an Indian story, it has been organized and written down by a white woman, not "exactly in his own words, thus losing much of their beauty and significance."[4] More importantly, as H. David Brumble III reminds us, "to study an Indian's autobiography is not the same as studying his life," and this is particularly true when an Indian author is shadowed by an amanuensis.[5] Yet however problematic a source, *Civilization* does provide rare insights into some of Alford's life choices and motivations. It documents his deep involvement with his people and gives glimpses of his efforts to serve them, as well as hinting at some of the doubts, misgivings, and uncertainties that shadowed him.

On Hampton's scale, Alford's conduct was judged "excellent" and the degree of his apparent acculturation has led some scholars to describe him as a straightforward "accomodationist" who lived his life according to a code and standard learned from whites. But in the Hampton University Archives there is a letter that complicates this clear-cut interpretation and lays bare a more problematical story. Writing to one of his teachers shortly after experiencing the sadness and disappointment of his homecoming, Alford describes his feelings of loneliness, isolation, and confusion, as he tries to find a way forward that will enable him to serve the Shawnee while remaining true to the lessons learned at Hampton. He insists he is determined "to follow the Indian just as far as I think is proper and good, and the white man the same."[6] In the light of this clearly articulated duality, it is possible to read the events of Alford's long life as a creative struggle to fulfill this pledge of double loyalty. Forced to navigate between the polarities of his two worlds, he worked to find a new way of being Shawnee in the United States and to assist his people in an era when the certainties of his childhood were gone and the wisdom of old leaders eroded.

In his autobiography, the reader is often subtly made aware that Alford himself does not always endorse white actions or patterns of labeling. When outlining divisions that developed between the Absentee Shawnee over how best to preserve their land base, he explained: "Those under the leadership of chiefs John Sparney and Joe Ellis—called the progressives—accepted the allotments allowed by the government. . . . Those under chiefs Big Jim and Sam Warrior, numbering nearly half the tribe—known to the government as non-progressive—refused to accept the allotments."[7] Alford both explicitly informs the reader of the proportional strength of those Absentee Shawnee who stood out against allotment and also makes clear that "progressive" is a government-imposed term and concept rather than one of his own. Neither confrontational nor defiant, Alford did not live a life in open resistance, yet aspects of his autobiography suggest a consciousness that was persistently and gently subversive. Alford's story is not a straightforward testimonial to Indian agency, if by agency we mean an oppositional consciousness. As a white-educated, Christian Shawnee, who worked for the betterment of his tribe, Alford's life raises many questions about how we should define leadership and resistance and the processes by which these are enacted.[8]

Alford represents the first generation of Indian youth subjected to the government campaign to school native children and stamp out Indian cultures, and as such his life needs to be examined within the broad framework of this white campaign and the native responses it generated as well as within the more narrowly defined context of Hampton and its special mission. Listening to this bicultural, native voice and paying attention to where Alford positioned himself on contentious issues—allotment, Shawnee language, raising children—allows us to explore the impact of the Hampton Institute on a single individual, who succeeded in leading his people through reciprocity, not opposition, and who helped resist some of the encroachments of the dominant society.

Alford's Generation of White-Educated Indians

Alford was one of thousands subjected to the civilizing program but one of just a few hundred who left a written record. The lives of two of his better-known contemporaries, Charles Alexander Eastman (1858–1939) and Gertrude Bonnin Simmons/Zitkala-Ša (1876–1937), help place his life in a wider context. Alford, Eastman, and Simmons all grew up in traditional homes where no English was spoken, before going on to attend and achieve success in white schools. All three chose to speak to white society by publishing aspects of their story in English, but all negotiated and expressed the complexity of their culturally hybrid identities in different ways.

Eastman was the best-known educated Indians of his generation. One of the very few who went beyond an elementary schooling, he spent seventeen years in white educational institutions and qualified as a doctor, although he only practiced medicine for a short time. Eastman married a white woman, Elaine Goodale and his books, articles, and lectures ensured that he became widely known across America.[9] A beacon of everything the American civilizing campaign aimed to accomplish, nevertheless Eastman himself was conscious that he lived a life straggled between two cultures and was painfully aware of the price he paid for this bifurcation. His writing was partly a romantic vision of both Indian and white worlds, but it became progressively burdened with the many contradictions that increasingly snagged the navigator between them. The apparent comfortable assimilation of his early, golden years gave way to more troubled times.

Charles Eastman wrote that he hoped that learning about his experiences "might help dispel false notions of Indian savagery and strengthen for some readers the conception of our common humanity."[10] His principal aim, he explained, was "not to entertain, but to present the American Indian in his true character before Americans."[11] To ensure that his message would not be rejected by white readers, he always framed his trenchant criticisms of white society obliquely and politely: "I am an Indian, and while I have learned much from civilization, for which I am grateful [,] . . . I am for development and progress along social and spiritual lines, rather than those of commerce, nationalism, or material efficiency.[12]

Eastman's openly voiced misgivings about civilization, spoken so softly in his writing, were to boom ever louder in his life. In his final years, he found himself unable to live fully with either Indians or whites. Now estranged from his wife (and her editorial skills) he found completing his writing projects increasingly difficult. He lived much of the time alone in a cabin on a Canadian island. The most highly educated and renowned Indian of his time ended his days solitary and silent. This was something his biographer Raymond Wilson judged to be his "most symbolic act."[13] Despite this withdrawal, Eastman remained ardent in his support for white education, and while acknowledging their imperfections, he still insisted that "I would give up anything rather than the schools."[14]

His opinion was not shared by Yankton Sioux Gertrude Bonnin Simmons. After more than a dozen years of white schooling and the accolade of a violin scholarship to the Boston Conservatory of Music, Simmons, too, looked like the perfect example of the "civilized" Indian. When in her twenties, however, she suddenly and vehemently rejected both the schools and their mission. While teaching at the Carlisle Indian School she suffered a breakdown, triggered by the realization that she had lost touch with her own beliefs and heritage. "For the white man's papers I had given up my faith in the Great Spirit. For these same papers I had forgotten the healing in trees and brooks."[15] Confused about her identity and struggling to understand how best to use her education, she gradually became convinced that schools like Carlisle were inducing in both the children and herself "long lasting death . . . beneath this semblance of civilization." She made up her mind to leave Carlisle and experienced it as an uplifting decision, "a new way of solving the problem of my inner self. I liked it."[16]

Writing under her self-given Lakota name, Zitkala-Ša (Red Bird), she published a series of autobiographical articles and short stories in *Atlantic Monthly* and *Harper's Weekly*. There she attacked the government's program of assimilation.[17] Mindful of the attitudes and expectations of mainstream America, Zitkala-Ša knew how to make her criticisms hit home. In an autobiographical article entitled "Why I am a Pagan," she juxtaposed a description of the spirituality of her relationship with nature, "where the voice of the Great Spirit is heard in the twittering of birds, the rippling of mighty waters," with a ferocious condemnation of the "doom" and "hell-fire" of Christianity. Identifying Christianity as "the new superstition," she proudly claimed the epithet "pagan" for herself. In this way Zitkala-Ša both underlined and affirmed a category persistently imposed on Indians by whites. She facetiously recapitulated the well-worn, polarizing logic but inverted the traditional pattern of domination and subversion. Celebrating and flaunting her paganism, she affirmed her Indian identity, insisting on the superiority of the Indian side of the binary and challenging white power to define and assign markers and judgments.

In her early twenties Zitkala-Ša claimed an Indian identity that she would continue to develop for the rest of her life. She opted for an Indian name in her public presentation of self rather than the American name she had acquired as a child. She chose an Indian husband, Raymond T. Bonnin, a Yankton Sioux like herself.[18] She collected Sioux legends and stories, transposed native melodies for performance to ensure their preservation and wrote an opera, *The Sun Dance Opera*, based on

native tunes. Working for a number of different Indian societies and organizations, she joined the fight for Indian citizenship, edited the *American Indian Magazine*, and in 1930 founded the National Council of
American Indians, of which she remained president until her death.
Zitkala-Ša used a range of different means to define her own identity
and politically empower Native Americans. She was less well known to
whites than Eastman, partly because her writings were fewer, her message less palatable, and the world she inhabited more intertribal than
white. Yet she, too, believed that she had spent much of her life navigat-
ing between the poles of the binary oppositions she had exposed and rejected.[19] Echoing another binary opposition to make her point, she explained in "The School Days of an Indian Girl" that she was "neither a
wild Indian, nor a tame one."[20]

Eastman and Zitkala-Ša used their white education to tell not only
their own stories but also to become conscious spokespeople for all Native Americans. Visible and active on a national stage, they were the in-
tellectuals of a generation whose white education had determined the
contours and predicaments of their subsequent lives. The majority of
Indians who attended boarding school returned to live among their
own people, having gained only a smattering of white education. Alford, with just six years of schooling in total and no aspiration to supply a voice for all Indian people, typified more nearly the general pattern. His experience was nonetheless colored by the fact that he was
being groomed for Shawnee leadership and was sent to Hampton with
a specific and sacred mission.

Alford and the Hampton Institute

As the sun sank below the horizon of Indian Territory on a balmy October evening in 1879, two chiefs of the Absentee Shawnee tribe visited Alford, their nineteen-year-old kinsman. They arrived in silence
and "in single file, from the west," and so Alford was instantly alerted
to the gravity of the occasion. Just two days before he and his compatriot, John King, planned to set out for Virginia, the chiefs had come to
entrust them with a weighty task. They were to go east to Hampton as
tribal representatives: "Very solemnly the chiefs spoke to us. They reminded us of the responsibility we had assumed for our people when

we consented to the mission. We were not to go as individuals, but as representatives of the Shawnee tribe. The honor, the dignity, and the integrity of the tribe was placed in our hands."[21]

The young men's Hampton schooling, one of the chiefs explained, would "enable us to use the club of white man's wisdom against him in defense of our customs and Mee-saw-mi, as given us by the Great Spirit." The chiefs' plan, Alford later recalled, was motivated by their fear "that a crisis was near in the life of the Indian race. . . . A change of some kind was inevitable," and "a tribe should get some of their men educated so they might understand the treaties and messages sent from Washington." Neither chief spoke English, but both felt a new and desperate need for their people to learn from the white man so as to enable them to negotiate effectively and defend their interests.[22]

The great-grandson of the famous war chief and pantribal political leader, Tecumseh, Alford was eager to lead his people. The chiefs promised him that when he and John King returned, they "would be able to direct the affairs of [the] tribe and . . . assume the duties and position of chiefs at the death of the present chiefs." This promise was made with one, strict condition attached to it: that they "should not accept the white man's religion. [They] must remain true to the Shawnee faith." Fully mindful of the high-risk strategy in which they were engaging, the chiefs spent all night discussing with their young emissaries the "life that was before [them], its dangers and possibilities." Their agenda was clear: the youths should enroll at the white school, learn "the white man's wisdom," then return home to help their people retain their lands and identity.[23] This is exactly what Alford would do, but in terms powerfully shaped by his Hampton education and not in a manner the old chiefs had planned or could ever support.

At age twelve, after several years of attending the Quaker mission school, Alford realized that:

> I no longer had any fear of white people, but had a great desire to learn their ways. . . . I loved my people and I liked their ways; I had a profound respect for and confidence in those men who were my father's friends, who had such a bitter hatred against the white race, or rather against those things that the white race represented. There were

some warm friendships between Indians and white men, but generally the Indians hated the thought of civilization. Deep down in my nature however, there was a yearning desire for things which civilization represented.[24]

Seven years later, traveling east from Indian Territory to Virginia full of enthusiasm, he was ready to acquiesce in Hampton's regime. Dressed in a cadet's uniform, he marched daily to the rhythm of the school band. In the morning he studied basic reading, writing, and arithmetic and in the afternoon learned practical skills and farming. Already demonstrating his personal determination and initiative, in his spare time he began to compile a Shawnee dictionary. The *Southern Workman* reported his painful progress, noting "he has not gotten through with the 'A's yet," but commended his dedication to this arduous task, explaining, "his tribe has no such book and one is greatly needed."[25] In just three years, Alford attained the level required by Hampton for graduation.[26]

In his younger years, at the mission school in Indian Territory, he had adopted the first name of the missionary, Thomas H. Stanley, who was his father's friend. Later at Hampton, he awarded himself a full, three-part American-style name: Thomas Wildcat Alford. But his three years at Hampton had induced changes far more fundamental than this new name. Whites had confronted him with knowledge, choices, and dilemmas that complicated and transformed his life. The chiefs' apparently simple directive to "use white man's wisdom against him in defense of our customs" was less straightforward now he had acquired some of that wisdom.

Hampton was suffused with Christian teaching and slowly, after much spiritual agonizing, Alford responded to the "continual pressure and interests of . . . friends and teachers" and took the decision to convert to Christianity. He made his choice, fully aware that "when [he] accepted this faith, [he] renounced virtually all hope to be a ruler, a chief of [his] people." But although he had converted and was thoroughly convinced that his years at Hampton had "opened [his] mind and heart to a broader understanding of the human race and a greater love and appreciation of [his] own people," Alford had renounced neither his Shawnee past nor his people.[27] Returning home eager to tell them all he had learned, he was devastated when instead of being welcomed, he found himself spurned and rejected. To the Shawnee chiefs and many of his people, his schooling represented a bitter failure, a betrayal that disqualified him for leadership.[28] Disappointed but not daunted, Alford used the skills he had acquired at Hampton to change course by taking work as a teacher on another reservation. When eventually he succeeded in returning home, it was to the post of Absentee Shawnee School principal. Later in life he would work as a surveyor and a farmer. Sometimes shunned, regularly criticized, but always active in the affairs of his tribe, Alford lived the rest of his life among his own people. He remained a devout Christian and when he died, aged seventy-eight, he was buried at the Shawnee Mission. This was an emblematic final resting place, because it was at the mission school that, aged twelve, he had innocently set out on the educational path that would change his life. The Shawnee Mission aptly embodied both the continuity of a life lived almost entirely in one place and the centrality of an alien religion that had so definitively altered its course.

During his years at Hampton, Alford often accompanied Armstrong on speaking tours. The General exploited white notions of Indian exoticism to titillate audiences into contributing to his school. On such occasions Alford would appear in his Shawnee regalia, prompting the Philadelphia *Inquirer* to note that "an interesting feature of the occasion was the appearance of the Indian students in the really tasteful and beautiful dresses of their respective tribes."[29] More often, Alford was asked to be a walking, speaking example of a "civilized" Indian. At his graduation, he was given the honor of making an address. His words conveyed a renewed sense of mission, but a sense of purpose very different from the one he had brought to Hampton just three years before. "It will be a great pleasure to meet my people whom I left nearly three years ago in the West," Alford told the assembly, "and to lead them out from the darkness of barbarism and ignorance into the path of peace and prosperity."[30] Couched in Armstrong's social evolutionary language, his speech appears to convey a total inversion of his original plan and suggests that Hampton had co-opted his sense of mission and diverted it toward its own quite different goals. Encouraging the young man in his loyalty to his people, the teachers at Hampton worked to convince him that he should serve them in ways very different from those envisaged by the chiefs and that he could reconcile duty and faithfulness to the Shawnee tribe with the message of its own teachings and loyalty to the United States.

While Thomas Wildcat Alford came to endorse the idea that his own tribe had a shared destiny with the United States and sometimes used the social evolutionary language and categories taught by Hampton, he refused to acknowledge the conceptual and racial implications embedded within them. In his graduation address, he linked "the darkness of barbarism" to ignorance rather than any inherent incapacity and insisted that the Indian only lacked opportunities and education. Later in his life, he was made painfully aware that despite his own competence and ability, he was himself constantly excluded from white society. He could not compete on equal terms and he attributed this not to any racial hierarchy but explicitly to white racism. "Although I was a pretty good workman at several different kinds of labor, no one seemed to want to hire an Indian, when there were white men to do the work."[31] Despite such personal disappointments and affronts, he nevertheless continued to endorse Armstrong's belief that the Indian's future lay within the United States.

For Alford, attending Hampton marked the major turning point of his life. "Three years in an Eastern school brought about a great change in both my feelings and my personal appearance," he recalls in his autobiography.[32] This mild statement and the sixteen pages he devotes to his school years, only hint at the profound impact the Hampton Institute had on every aspect of his life. His religious conversion transformed his relations with his own people, effectively disempowering him. "What did it matter if I knew ever so much that would be good for my people," he reflected, "if I never was allowed to guide or lead them?"[33] It was ironic that Hampton wanted to send back educated Indians who could command respect and authority in their tribes and yet that it hobbled Alford in his ability to play this role. As a descendant of Tecumseh and a member of one of the principal clans—as well as the chosen representative of the Shawnee chiefs—Alford had been set on a path that was certain to lead to power and authority in his tribe. Although always billed as "Shawnee Chief-elect" when on tour with Armstrong, Hampton could not endorse the passage to power the Shawnee chiefs had laid down. Hampton demanded that its graduates secure and hold power exclusively on its own terms. The Indian's prime loyalty had to be diverted from his tribe and their traditions to the United States and its values. This was something the Shawnee chiefs had anticipated and feared.

When Alford made his promise to the Shawnee chiefs, squatting in the dusk under the "spreading branches of a great oak tree," it had not occurred to him that he would ever be tempted to break it; its implications for his political future were unimagined.[34] Likewise, when he took his decision to convert to Christianity, he had an inkling of how this would impact on his future with the tribe but no sense of the effect it would also have on his personal future. While he was at Hampton, Alford met and planned to marry a young Dakota woman. He returned to Indian Territory with plans for the important work they might do together.[35] At first ostracized and unable to find work, when he eventually secured a permanent teaching post he believed he was now in a position to marry his Dakota fiancée. At this point, however, he received a letter from his fiancée's pastor, which, he writes, made "a strong objection to our marriage on denominational grounds. It seemed that the pastor had the idea that if the young lady separated herself from his particular church that her soul's salvation would be forfeited." Both at the time and later Alford could not accept the position of this man, "but Religion and church doctrines were so new to me that I did not feel myself capable of arguing the question with the reverend gentleman." He felt obliged to accept the man's decision, "although it was a terrible blow to all [his] plans and hopes."[36] Alford's years at Hampton and his conversion to the white man's religion thus stymied his personal as well as his political life.

Shawnee and American

On his return home, the shift in Alford's values forced a change in the people with whom he associated. The impact was instantaneous: "My people received me coldly and with suspicion. Almost at once they suspected that I had taken up the white man's religion, along with his habits and manner of conduct. There was no happy gathering of family and friends, as I had so fondly dreamed there might be. Instead of being eager to learn the new ideas I had to teach them, they gave me to understand very plainly that they did not approve of me. I had no home to go to, and my relatives did not welcome my presence."[37]

No longer able to mix freely with his people, he spent time with the missionary, the school employees and the white traders. When his need for a job became desperate, it was the missionary who took him on as an interpreter. Symbolically, the only work now available to him was as an intermediary between the peoples of the two worlds he straddled. The job was poorly paid, but Alford found it very gratifying, "for it gave [him] an opportunity to talk to the Indians about the religious life [he] had found so satisfying. It also gave [him] an opportunity to tell them something about the ways of civilization, and most of all," he explained, "it really did bring me into contact with them."[38] This passage from his autobiography pinpoints the sad irony of his situation. Sent to Hampton as a representative of the Shawnee being groomed for leadership, he now had to search for ways to meet with his own people.

Yet he was keen to serve his tribe whatever the obstacles. In a letter to the *Southern Workman*, he laid out his hopes for his people. In language and terms he had learned at Hampton, he described his ambition: "To uplift them from their blindness of barbarism, and low state of human life, into a life of peace, prosperity and self-supporting."[39] Although Hampton specifically encouraged its pupils to become teachers, Alford was more ambitious and felt shocked when the only permanent employment he was able to procure with his people was as principal of the government school.[40] Despite his acute disappointment, Alford quickly adjusted his sights and justified his position. "I realized that I would not have the influence with the older people that I coveted, but wouldn't it be far better to direct the education of the young? Would I not be able to instill into their plastic young minds and hearts some of the good things I had learned while at Hampton? I believed that I would."[41]

During Alford's early childhood, the pressure of white expansion brought troubled times to Indian Territory and consternation to the Shawnee. The traditional chiefs' support for Alford's Hampton schooling was just one sign of the anxiety they experienced. The Shawnee were searching desperately for the best way to hold onto their lands, and within Alford's band, as we have seen, there were fierce divisions centering on the issue of allotment. One group believed that accepting allotments would provide the best way to protect their spiritual and cultural independence; a second group bitterly opposed white society in all its guises and pinpointed resistance to land allotment as the Shawnee's best means to defend tribal strength and integrity. Like many leaders in other tribes, this group was convinced that the loss of a communal land base would undermine and destroy their tribal community. The issue of allotment remained central to the fight between the Shawnee and the United States government for over thirty years. When the land boom began in Oklahoma, Alford became convinced that his kinsmen now risked losing all their land to the whites and so undertook to persuade all members of his tribe to accept their allotments. Working as a surveyor for the government, he assisted in allotting Shawnee Indian lands, and when one group refused to co-operate, he secretly collected the names of all heads of family and allotted them land against their wishes.[42] Believing fervently that allotment was the only way to protect Shawnee land ownership, Alford used his inner knowledge of the tribe simultaneously to protect Shawnee rights and enforce the government's allotment program. His undercover actions earned him the hatred and ire of the more traditional Shawnee and their chiefs.

Disqualified from playing the role of a traditional leader alongside these chiefs, Alford instead chose to serve his people from within the U.S. government. First as teacher, then surveyor and allotment officer, he worked for the Indian Service on and off for many years. It became, as he noted in his autobiography, his life work, providing him with many opportunities to help his people. One extraordinary irony of his life lies in the fact that he did, in the end, achieve his original ambition and became a Shawnee chief, although not in the traditional way. His appointment was not made by the elders but by a U.S. government agent, and it came about through an alphabetical accident. In 1893, he was made a member of the tribe's newly formed business committee. "As my name was first on the list," reports the story, "I was chairman automatically and was in reality at last in the position of chief or principal advisor of my people, recognized as such by the government at Washington."[43] Taking his responsibilities seriously, Alford saw no contradiction in working for the interests of his people in this way. He even came to criticize the old chiefs and their traditional power structures, complaining that "many otherwise intelligent agents prefer to deal with the Indians through the old tribal system of recognition, to the detriment of the younger generation every year attaining manhood." He thus endorsed the values of the Indian Service and chose to recognize the younger, so-called progressive leaders.[44] Paradoxically, it was the traditional chiefs, whose authority was rooted in the old tribal system he now criticized, who had given their blessing for him to go to Hampton.

The dual loyalty with which Alford lived—to his own people, the Shawnee, and to his adopted nation, the United States—is mirrored in the correspondingly fractured historical perspective of his autobiography. Covering the period before he was born, he gives a short history of his tribe. Told from a Shawnee perspective, it no doubt echoed the stories he heard told repeatedly when he was a child. Significantly, this version of Shawnee history is not incorporated into the main text. Instead, it stands alone in a discrete, four-page appendix to the book. Well informed about his people's history, Alford did not or could not integrate it into his own story. The problems inherent in any attempt to combine a traditional history with that of the United States are openly acknowledged by scholars.[45] Reflecting on the history of her own people, the Cheyenne, Henrietta Whiteman suggests that "Indian History, in a all probability will never be incorporated into American history, because it is holistic, human, personal, and sacred."[46] For the same reasons Alford presented the history of the Shawnee separately; it could not be fitted into the master narrative of the United States, which provided the structure for his chronicle.

From the time of his own birth, the narrative frame of his autobiography changes and Alford assesses all-important political events in terms of U.S., not tribal, history. This becomes an exceedingly delicate exercise when he arrives at the moment at which Indian Territory is forcibly merged with Oklahoma; an event which cost many tribes their autonomy and provoked passionate feelings. Alford assiduously avoids any reference to those feelings while at the same time carefully absenting Indian people from the celebrations. "The two states were admitted as one state amid great rejoicing and celebrating by the white people."[47] The separate responses of Indian people, although covertly alluded to, are not presented. Superficially, it appears as if Alford has allowed his American personality to prevail over his Shawnee identity. Yet his position, like his identity, is ambivalent. He chose to present his own life, as well as Shawnee history, from the dominant people's viewpoint, yet he still placed the Indian center stage. If he welcomed the merger of the Shawnee with the United States, it was because it provided an opportunity for the Indian to become "a really great factor in the commonwealth."[48] In his heart, Alford admitted, he always remained essentially Shawnee. "The people we know and love make up our world, be they great or simple," he explained. "The Shawnee Indians are my people, they make up my world."[49]

Alford's Life and Autobiography: Essays in Biculturalism

Alford's world was complex and his was not an easy life. He suffered periods of unemployment and financial hardship and his wife died young, leaving him with three small boys to raise. Throughout, he appears to have demonstrated remarkable resilience and resourcefulness. During his adult years, when Indian Territory was being rapidly taken over by whites, he fought hard to help the Shawnee hold onto their land rights, yet he also participated in the "run" that opened up the Shawnee reservation for settlement, securing a plot of land for himself.[50] In this, as in most things, he appeared to demonstrate a pragmatic capacity for adjustment. When his conversion had made it impossible for him to become a chief, he had realigned his political ambitions. When thwarted in his desire to marry his Dakota friend from Hampton, he had redirected his emotional energy and married a white woman, the sister-in-law of the Quaker missionary.[51] Caught in the uncomfortable intersection between two cultures, Alford was nevertheless usually able to find a modus vivendi. Even at one of the most stressful times of his life, when he was fighting to prevent the Shawnee from being dispossessed and removed to Mexico, his son wrote a letter describing the "wholesome, happy life the family lived socially and at home on the farm," making clear that the fraught political situation had not destabilized Alford's home life.[52] Alford ended his days living in the midst of his community at Shawnee. When he was sixty-six the *Southern Workman* reported:

> The many friends of Thomas Wildcat Alford, of Shawnee, Oklahoma, will be glad to hear that he is still running his farm at Shawnee. Mr. Alford has had an active life as a leader of the absentee Shawnee tribe. He has been surveyor, government teacher, interpreter, real-estate agent and farmer, and is one of the most influential Indians among the Shawnees.[53]

In these final years he took the opportunity to "speak out" and tell his story publicly. *Civilization* ends on a similar calm, melodious note. "Since leaving the Indian service," Alford tells us, "I have lived quietly at my old home. . . . Here I shall remain until the end."[54] The tranquil tone of these sentences, backed by the information carried in the *Southern Workman*, suggests that unlike many others, Thomas Wildcat Alford had succeeded in reconciling the multiple conflicts and contradictions of his Shawnee-American identity.

Alford's is one of a cluster of published Indian autobiographies that chart the impact of white civilization on an individual Indian and his community.[55] Focusing on the daily detail of life, his book does not invite his reader to reflect on the psychological dimensions of the issues he is discussing. Yet for the modern reader, it is impossible not to think about the many hidden psychological processes that must have been at work. In this context, it is enlightening to remember that *Civilization* was published the same year as F. Scott Fitzgerald's famous essay "The Crack-Up" in which he described his nervous breakdown, a personal collapse that paralleled America's swing from prosperity to depression. Lying in a hospital, acutely aware of the fragility of the human mind, Fitzgerald observed that "the test of a first-rate intelligence is the ability to hold two opposed ideas in the mind at the same time, and still retain the ability to function."[56] The first generation of Indian youth who were sent away to white schools were forced to learn another culture in its entirety, from the profundity of a new religion to the inanity of the correct way to comb their hair. They were compelled to hold not just two competing ideas in their minds, but two competing cultures. The glib "before" and "after" photographs, used by the schools as visual propaganda, contrast with the experience of many students, who underwent an ongoing and multifaceted process of identity transformation. Reconciling a white education with a workable Indian identity meant realigning multiple and often conflicting loyalties as well as negotiating the shifting boundaries of religion, community, nationality, race, and politics throughout an entire lifetime.

Alford was just one of thousands of nineteenth-century Indians who was taught traditional ways before being sent to white schools. Those who successfully managed the continuous backward-and–forward transitions this demanded have sometimes been described as bicultural. In an effort to convey the full dimensions of such an expanded identity, Malcolm McFee entitled his study of one educated, acculturated Blackfeet

Indian "The 150% Man."[57] Scholars in all disciplines now recognize the challenge, creativity, and variety embraced by such cultural syncretism, which both complicates and expands the experience of being and becoming Indian.[58] Not everyone could accomplish this demanding feat. Some, tragically, did not cope at all, and those who did managed in many different ways.[59] Only a few went on to write or tell their bicultural life stories.

The dual authorship of Alford's autobiography is built into the title, *Civilization, as Told to Florence Drake*. It alerts us to the fact that this is a "bicultural document": a creation not just of two individuals but of two cultures.[60] In fact, some of the interest and significance of this book resides in the particular nature of its biculturalism. *Civilization* was just one of dozens of Native American life stories that appeared in the 1930s, a consequence of the reading public's new interest in Indians. There was now a correlation in the public mind between Indians and both tragedy and exoticism rather than threat. With the acculturation policies of the previous half century now under fierce attack, white Americans were suddenly keen to hear from survivors of the exotic cultures in their midst. Many of the native life stories written at this time were ethnographic. White anthropologists, who solicited the stories of ordinary Indians, used them to authenticate their studies of primitive peoples, and the role played by these professional amanuenses was often highly interventionist. It shaped not only the material they gathered but also the thought processes and presentation styles of their subjects.[61]

Contemporaneous with these collaborative personal narratives, a small number of Indians wrote and published their stories with much less white intervention.[62] The first generation of American-educated Indians had now come of age with both a need and an ability to tell their own stories, but even when a white hand did not wield the pen, white traditions, language, and epistemological concerns still shaped and colored these narratives. Alford's story most obviously falls into this second category of autobiography, but with one or two significant nods towards the first. Like the ethnographic studies it was a collaboration, although on this occasion the story was told not by an illiterate Indian, but by one who was white-educated. Although Alford spoke and wrote English well, he nevertheless chose to tell his story orally, the Indian way. He spoke his life with his voice, but he left it to posterity as a silent, written text, between the covers of a book, an American document. This record of his life echoes its deepest paradox: Indian in content but American in form, his autobiography recapitulates the tension and hybridity he lived with.

The autobiography gives us one, full version of his life, but its tenor is very different from the fragments we can garner from earlier articles, speeches and letters. His letters, as noted at the beginning of this chapter, read more like "public transcripts" than private documents. Sporadically, however, a more "hidden transcript" is revealed, where Alford expresses indignation and anger. His graduation address was made at the moment when he was most wholeheartedly committed both to Hampton and American society. Eagerly anticipating his return home to initiate his people into the blessings of civilization, he used the address as an occasion to condemn publicly the destructive power of "civilization, which was raging and approaching on the Indian with strong irresistible force and would soon sweep over his reservation like prairie fire that consumes everything which comes in contact."[63] Five years later, he would write bitterly to one of his ex-teachers to describe the pain and misery being inflicted on his people by the government's allotment policy: "It is a blessed thing that the Indian does not know what is coming to him when he accepts land in severalty and thus becomes a citizen of the United States or else he would hold on with more tenacity to his old way of life, until the doctrine of extermination put him out of his misery."[64]

Very little of this passion and fury are evident in *Civilization*. It is hard to know how much of its measure and control was exerted by Florence Drake and how much was a reflection of Alford's advanced years and a desire to gloss over contention. When he compares the Shawnee and Christian religions, and describes some of the difficulties he had comprehending miracles, he explains how he consciously avoided confronting this problematic aspect of Christianity:

> I was taught while in school to avoid the superstitions of my people, and I was convinced that it was the thing to do when I came back among them. ... But why is a miracle predicted by an Indian a superstition while that by a white man or a Jew is not a superstition but a prophesy? ... During those years that my wife and I attended the little mission church, I had a class in Sabbath school. I tried to teach the beauties and importance

of the life of our Savior, Jesus Christ, as contained in His Gospels, but I avoided discussion of the miracles.[65]

Just occasionally in his autobiography, however, Alford does not "avoid discussion" of the thornier issues. Observing the decline in health suffered by so many of his people since they had been surrounded by whites, Alford is incited to a rare moment of anger: "Little Indian children of that day and time were as healthy and generally as happy as little animals. It remained for civilization and the white man's system of living to breed discontent and to make invalids of a large number of our people."[66]

Yet this condemnation of the white man's system is not without ambiguity; he refers to the healthy Indian children as "little animals." Drawing on the evolutionary scale he learned at Hampton, he implicitly places the Indian on the lower rungs of civilization while simultaneously condemning that same civilization. This contained, unresolved tension embedded in the writing intermittently breaks through to become as overt in the autobiography as it is in the letters.[67] "After only minimal contact with whites," Alford laments, "the Indians' needs had multiplied, and even their living expenses had begun to mount. Our people were no longer satisfied with the meager necessities of existence. . . . It seemed that civilization was nothing more or less than a multiplication of man's needs and wants."[68]

Both his autobiography and his letters reflect the strains in Alford's life; together they give us a sense of how this tension was experienced differently at different times over an entire life. This is most poignantly demonstrated in his children's upbringing. Another boarding school graduate, Luther Standing Bear (1868–1919), who wrote a series of autobiographical books, resolved in 1933 that if he had the task of educating a child and found himself "faced with the duty of choosing between the natural way of my forefathers and that of the white man's present way of civilization" that he would "unhesitatingly set that child's feet in the path of my forefathers. I would raise him to be an Indian!"[69] This was perhaps more easily written in 1933 than 1885, the year Thomas Wildcat Alford's first son was born. It is clear that over the years, events and experiences modified Alford's views. He brought up his children (who were half white) to be Christians. He sent them to Hampton, a school with a mission to transform the traditional Indian into an American citizen. He insisted that they speak only English and not learn Shawnee. Yet by the time he wrote his autobiography, he had reached the conclusion that his most important achievement had not been giving them a white education but rather "instill[ing] in their hearts and minds some of the principles of [his] people."[70] When assessing his own life and what he had to offer his children, he confessed that he wanted to pass on to them what he saw as the advantages of being Indian: "Surely strength of character is a commendable trait and our white friends would very well profit by some of our tribal teachings, such as loyalty, perseverance, and self-reliance."[71]

As a youth, Alford had chosen to adopt American values and live his life according to the doctrines of Christianity. When he returned to his people he wanted to help them understand white ways. But by the time he published his autobiography, he was able, despite his own life choices, to voice stronger appreciation of Shawnee values and traditions and his tribe's attempts to preserve them. Times had changed as much as he had and this opinion was more readily acceptable among whites than when he had first set out for Hampton: "My people were among those who once owned this vast country, they were strong and brave and virtuous, according to their knowledge. If I have failed to live up to the standards of the whole race, they at least have fought for their convictions."[72]

When judged by Hampton's standards, Alford's was a success story meriting the accolade "excellent" on his record; he had returned to the reservation to work for his people's uplift, played an active leadership role, and lived a Christian life. Within his own heart, however, Alford nevertheless continued to believe that he remained essentially a Shawnee, who represented and defended the interests of his people. This dual loyalty was condoned by the lessons in racial destiny he had learned at Hampton. If he had failed to keep his promise to the traditional chiefs, he had nonetheless used the "white man's wisdom" to lead his people and defend their interests while also working at creating a lasting and personal legacy that bound together his two worlds.

For Alford, the most important text he produced was not his autobiography but his Shawnee translation of the Gospels. "The more that I read and studied the English language," Alford disclosed in his autobiography, "the more my admiration grew for my own Shawnee language and I was anxious to preserve it in all its purity and beauty." So on his return from

Hampton, he began his translation work, convinced that "in the description of nature and things natural, and in the idea of things intangible, the
inner man, the soul, the Spirit and God, the Shawnee language is peculiarly
sweet and full, and seems to stand alone."[73] It would take him most of his
life, but in 1929 *The Four Gospels of Our Lord Jesus Christ, in Shawnee
Indian Language*, was published.[74] Thomas Wildcat Alford, the Shawnee
Indian who had worked so hard to bring American values, religion, and
civilization to his people and who had insisted that "I desire my children
not to know any Indian language, for it breeds superstition" came to feel
that his own mother tongue was the language best suited to convey the
subtleties of nature's secrets, God's word, and man's spirituality.[75] From
one perspective, this attempt to preserve his native tongue by translating
the Christian Gospels into Shawnee represents the supreme irony of Alford's life: he was seeking to protect the Shawnee language through the
prime text of the white man's religion, the same religion that had, by its
adoption, robbed him of his political birthright and estranged him from his
own people. From another perspective, the "tedious hours of hard mental
labor" spent translating the Christian Gospels into Shawnee over many
years was an inspired and therapeutic task for Alford to have chosen: it
gave him the opportunity to convey the values and truths of his manhood
in the language of his infancy; it brought together his past and his present; it allowed him to heal the breach caused by his Christian conversion;
it united all the conflicting parts of his bi-cultural identity. Like all Indians
whose American education forced them to live in the margin where two
cultures over-lapped, Alford relied on his own capacity to find creative so-
lutions to the psychological and practical problems of biculturalism. Acknowledging that under the American system of commercialism such a
long-term endeavor to save a language might be judged "foolishness. . . .
[E]gotism or selfishness," Alford concluded, "Be it so." His private act of
salvage was executed for his own "joy and satisfaction" and also to ensure that the "majesty and sweetness" of the Shawnee tongue would not
be lost to "future generations."[76] If Alford could not erase the long-established oppositions between "savagery" and "civilization" he had been
taught at Hampton, through the creation of his Shawnee Bible he was able
in some small measure to blur this binary. His prodigious work of translation stands as a unique monument to the abiding contradictions of his
life as well as his own creative capacity to reconcile them.

Carlisle Indian Industrial School

3

6. Richard Henry Pratt: National Universalist

RICHARD HENRY PRATT judged any effort to translate the Bible into an Indian language to be seriously misguided. The complex motivations driving Alford's project were of no consequence to Pratt, who believed white-educated Indians should look forward to their American future rather than hanker after their Indian past. Harsh in his condemnation of white missionary translations—be they the contemporary endeavors of the Riggs' at the Dakota Mission or the historical work of John Eliot—he was adamant that "Indians could learn to read and understand English just as quickly as their own language." Vernacular translations were redundant, because they encouraged Indians to live in "communities by themselves."[1] Pratt's aspiration for all Indians was that they should abandon their tribal communities and integrate into mainstream white society. He was convinced that Indians only needed a "broad and enlarged liberty of opportunity and training to make them, within the short space of a few years, a perfectly acceptable part of our population."[2] Triumphant when he secured official permission to conduct an educational experiment to prove this theory, he dedicated the Carlisle Indian School to a dual mission. First, to eradicate native tribal cultures and instruct Indians in white ways to equip them for citizenship in the United States; second, to demonstrate to white Americans that this transformation was both possible and desirable. Pratt spent the next twenty-five years shaping, nurturing, expanding and commanding the Carlisle Indian School as well as defending its program and philosophy. The school was a living experiment, which became a monument to him and the mission he championed.

The experiment, as we have seen, had begun in St. Augustine. Those three years at the old Spanish fort had given Pratt the confidence of his convictions and would also have a powerful formative impact on the program as well as campus design of the Carlisle Indian School (more on this in chapter 7). The year Pratt spent at Hampton also proved decisive. Witnessing the organization of Armstrong's school, as well as the daily activities of its dynamic, college-educated, senior-ranking principal, was very instructive to an army captain who had benefited from only a few years of elementary schooling. This Pratt openly acknowledged: "I had obtained many practical ideas in regard to industrial training during my boyhood days and in my experience in Florida, and to these I had added much from being at Hampton a year."[3]

Ambitious and with a taste for command, Pratt had rejected Armstrong's invitation to run Hampton's Indian program. "I plainly told the General that I could not bring myself to become satisfied with such a detail."[4] He had instead set himself the task of winning government support for his own institution, exclusively for Indians and located in the midst of an industrious white community. The character of the host white community was paramount to Pratt's scheme, because he was concerned that Armstrong's Indian program was fatally compromised by its location: "I pointed out that the woods were full of degraded Negroes . . . and that the remoteness from the observation of our best people was a fatal drawback." More fundamentally, Pratt was dubious about Armstrong's tenacious commitment to "racial education."[5]

As a young army officer in the Tenth Cavalry on the Plains, Pratt had commanded both African American soldiers and Indian scouts. These close personal contacts, as well as encounters with friendly and warring tribes in the West, led him to "pondering much over the race question."[6] Early on he arrived at the unequivocal conclusion that the apparently glaring differences between the races were the product of environmental factors, not innate differences. Observing how a clutch of wild turkey eggs, which he carried home and placed under a barnyard hen, hatched and became "in all respects" just as amenable as the best domesticated members of the turkey tribe, he concluded that a direct analogy could be drawn with Indian tribes, all of whom needed only "the environment and kind treatment of domestic civilized life to become a very part of it."[7] Pratt fought any suggestion that Americanizing the Indian would be a long and arduous process. Dismissive of the social evolutionary ideas of his day, he insisted that "my deductions are from practical and not theoretical knowledge."[8]

Pratt's reasoning might have been uncomplicated. However, it, too, sprang from robust "theoretical" roots, which lay deep in America's eighteenth-century traditions of universalism. Pratt embraced this tradition of political thinking in its purist form and gave his own simplified restatement of John Locke's environmentalist doctrine. "It is a great mistake to think that the Indian is born an inevitable savage. He is born a blank slate like the rest of us."[9] For Pratt, no inborn deficit disqualified the Indian from full citizenship. "The Indian is a man like other men," he held. "He has no innate or inherent qualities that condemn him to separation from other men or to generations of slow development."[10] Believing that just as the barnyard environment had domesticated wild turkeys, so, too, with parallel ease, the school could tame and train young savages to assure their equality and fitness for citizenship. It was Pratt's passionate conviction that "Equal ability comes when the same training is given during association."[11] His determination to integrate Indians into mainstream American society meant he embraced for them the possibilities and optimism inherent in universalism, along with its associated tyrannies. This was social transformation through education and all aspects of Indian traditions and culture were to be given very short shrift: "There must be no holding onto Indianism in this transformation." Directly tying the creation of Carlisle to the universalist founding principles of the United States, Pratt made the immigrant experience his working model for Indian assimilation.

The Immigrant Model

The millions of immigrants who had relinquished language and traditions to join the American republic set a pattern Pratt believed Indians could and should follow. He facetiously informed Secretary of the Interior Carl Schurz, who had emigrated to the United States as a young man, that "You yourself sir, are one of the very best examples of what we ought to do for the Indians. . . .[They] need the chances of participation you have had and they will just as easily become useful citizens. They can only reach this prosperous condition through living among our people."[12] Like most of his countrymen, Pratt found it hard to grasp that, once offered the benefits of the American republic, Indians might still choose their own traditions and culture. Viewed from his consistently environmentalist perspective, only exclusion from the benefits of American society could account for what he saw as the Indians' "backward state."

This rejection of a race paradigm lay at the core of Pratt's thinking. Toward the end of his life he expressed his racial views with trenchant ferocity. Tackling the taboo subject of race rape, he heartily condemned the blind eye always turned toward white men who committed the same "heinous offense" for which black men were lynched. Lifting the lid on another sensitive topic, he questioned the faulty fractional logic of the one-drop rule. This pattern of racial inheritance was so deeply embedded in American society that to his Philadelphia audience, in 1913, Pratt's speech must have sounded radical to the point of folly: "We consign every person with any tinge of negro blood to the negro race. Where is our equity in this? If the white blood is of such immaculate excellence, should not half or more of white blood carry the individual over to the white race?"[13] Never one to mince his words, after his retirement Pratt claimed a license to expound on sensitive race issues that he necessarily treated with more sagacity during his active years.

While Carlisle's superintendent, he had done all in his power to keep discussion of Indian education totally separate from the "negro problem." Fully conscious of the prejudice and hatred directed at blacks, Pratt fervently believed Indians could escape the same fate if their social and educational destiny was never paired with that of the "negro." Critical of Hampton's race education because it collapsed the two peoples into a single race category, Pratt was always reluctant to see Indians mixing openly with African Americans; he did not want the two races to become linked in the public mind. Indians were not, in his view, being educated to assimilate into a segregated, broad-based, racially tinged, American society; rather, they were being trained to join white society on equal terms.

Although he obdurately refused to employ a racial discourse, Pratt was fully conscious that in late nineteenth-century America, Indians occupied an ambiguous racial position. Being neither white nor black, they had a dubious in-between status. There was therefore an ever-present danger that they might be placed in the nonwhite category. Indeed, in the commonwealth of Virginia, the high level of African American–Native American intermarriage fostered anxiety among whites concerned to protect clear racial categories and, in 1920, would prompt a drastic legal response, when Virginia reclassified all its Indian population as "black." Pratt's determination to protect his experiment from accusations of racial taint is evidenced

on the student cards of a group of youths belonging to the Shinnecock nation, who arrived at Carlisle from the Southampton Agency in New York
State on September 4, 1882. Four days later all of them were sent home
unceremoniously. On their Carlisle record cards the reason for discharge
was given as "too much Negro."[14] Despite the fact that these young men
were legally defined as Indians, Pratt clearly feared his aspirations for the
whole race might be jeopardized by their presence at his school. Indians
presenting as black were obviously positioned on the wrong side of the
black/white binary and so directly compromised Carlisle's mission to integrate its pupils into mainstream white society.

The Indians' irrefutable nonwhite appearance carried the grave risk that
as they were absorbed into mainstream society, America's racial undertow
would drag them toward a shared classification with blacks. This process
of racialization was likely to be actively aided and abetted by their integration and Americanization. Pratt's forceful views and belligerent personality prompted him sometimes to deny and challenge the harsher racial designations of the wider society (as chapter 9 forcefully illustrates),
but they could not insulate him from an acute awareness of the "in-between" status of Indians. Faced with the stark polarizing power of America's black/white racial binary, Pratt had no doubts about how he wanted
Indians to be classed.

So at Carlisle, Americanization of clothes, values, language and deportment were linked to a "whitening" process that was sometimes openly acknowledged at the institution. A cryptic joke in the school newspaper accentuated this point in the school's second year:

> The whole of the fence surrounding the school domain has been white-
> washed by the boys during the past month and judging by the number of
> requests received from the boys who wished to participate, or as they put
> it "learn the whitewash trade," the work is quite popular, perhaps ow-
> ing to the fact that in this way they can become *white men* in the short-
> est possible time.[15]

More subtly, J. N. Choate's "before" and "after" photographs cleverly
demonstrated that a Carlisle education brought not just crisp clothes, short
hair, and a manly gaze but also whiter skin. Through the careful use of
front lighting and white powder, this local photographer became skilled

at presenting a subtle message of racial bleaching that was evident in his photographs of groups as well as those of individuals. Yet even if studio pictures could lighten skin and round features to dramatize the before/after, out on the street, their subjects were still marked by their distinctive physiognomy. When measured on the absolutist scale of America's color chart, they were nonwhite.

The racial dynamic of American society generated a tricky conundrum for Pratt. If fully successful, his Americanizing campaign would destroy the one thing that could protect the Indian from racialization and all its consequences: "Indianness." The Indians' status as original Americans combined with their exotic past, for which white fascination waxed as Indian potency waned, stood as semiprotective markers of their difference from other nonwhite groups; it distinguished them from and elevated them above African Americans and other nonwhites. The passage of the Chinese Exclusion Act, when Carlisle was only in its third year, was just one of the more glaring demonstrations of rising public doubts about the inclusion of groups categorized as nonwhite. This kind of race prejudice directly threatened the essential goal of Carlisle's experiment, and so it is not surprising that the Chinese were given sympathetic coverage in Carlisle's *Indian Helper*: "All the Chinese workmen in a flour mill, a woollen mill and a laundry in Sacramento, California, were discharged last Monday and 300 white men will be employed in their places. The Chinese are having great trouble in this country now. Some white people don't like the Chinese, and are trying to make them leave the United States and go back to China."[16]

No such return was possible for Indians, but this might also constitute an advantage. Pratt was instinctively aware that a carefully packaged, white-led version of "Indianness" could be used to supply a reminder of the Indian's uniqueness. This might serve to balance the racial-gravitational pull toward the downside of the binary.

In Florida, Pratt had already staged shows of archery and Indian dancing as well as a mock "buffalo" hunt, and in his memoir he boasted that, had he been so minded, he could have "out Buffalo Billed Mr. Cody in his line."[17] Omitted from his memoir, no doubt because it seriously compromised his later entrenched position, is the information that during Carlisle's early days, Pratt used the children at Carlisle to stage similar shows.

One of these took place just three months after the school opened, in the unlikely venue of a Presbyterian women's college, where dancing was normally strictly banned. In January 1880, the local paper reported that "fourteen little redskins" were transported by train from Carlisle to Chambersburg. Here, in the Wilson College chapel, in front of an audience of "fair students, stern teachers, and favored townspeople," Sioux and Cheyenne children gave "a performance consisting of dances and singing." Afterward, the children returned to their school, and there is no written record left behind to tell us if, like the dancers at Fort Marion, providing a spectacle for whites also offered an opportunity to share dance techniques and pursue an agenda of their own. A journalist from the Chambersburg *Herald* judged the show a mediocre event, "not in the highest manner artistic" and sounding "very peculiar to the Caucasian audience."[18]

Pratt's reasons for arranging such a performance must have been complex: to show off "his" Indians, to gain publicity and perhaps revenue for his fledgling school, and to titillate and beguile a white audience. Evident in all of these motivations was the associated desire to put the children's "Indianness" on public display. In a circumscribed, sanitized, protected Christian environment, reminders of their Indian past—their racial etymology—would, Pratt hoped, serve to protect them from a future that merged them with other nonwhite groups. For Pratt, advocating the immigrant model of assimilation, while signaling the Indians' unique status as "first Americans," gave Indian citizenship a legitimacy unavailable to other nonwhite groups. Public performances of Indian dances were, however, a dicey undertaking to be associated with, for a man so outspokenly committed to quashing Indian cultures. The opportunities for misinterpretation of Pratt's desired message were legion and multiplied dangerously once Bill Cody's extravaganza was in full swing. It is not clear from the record when Pratt stopped organizing such displays locally, but by the time Cody had achieved international prominence he had taken a strong stand against all Wild West shows and actively condemned the employment of Indians in any such reenactments of their savage past. By now convinced that the shows undermined everything for which he worked, he concluded in his memoirs that "they were not calculated to promote any advantage to interracial respect."[19]

So Pratt turned to other less volatile means to foster "interracial re-spect" and dramatize the Indian's special status. The infamous before/after paired photographs, reproduced by the hundred in J. N. Choate's local studio, supplied a less risky and more manageable way to communicate a similar message as the live performances. These twinned pictures served a variety of purposes for the school. Their most obvious message, repeated over and over using different subjects, was one of transformation, and it was a lesson that could be conveyed and received in varying degrees of intensity. Readers of the *Indian Helper* who signed up ten new subscribers for the paper were rewarded with a choice in the level of contrast they wished to view in their forty cent "prize": "Two photographs, one showing a group of Pueblos as they arrived in wild dress, and another of the same pupils three years after, or, for the same number of names, we give two photographs showing still more marked contrast between a Navajoe as he arrived in native dress, and as he now looks, worth 20 cents a piece."[20]

Pratt selected carefully from among these numerous records of individual renovation for images to use in Carlisle publications. Although the paired pictures of the Navaho young man, Tom Torlino, show the most "marked contrast" and are among the most sensational, this was not the diad he chose for the front cover of a photographic pamphlet published to advertise the school and exhibit its fifteen-year history.

Relying on the now familiar before/after theme, Pratt selected a duo of pictures that did not display the glaring disparities of the Tom Torlino pair. When integrated into a front-cover pictorial collage, the two inset, circular photographs of Chauncey Yellow Robe present a clear chronicle of Indian progress, yet there is no trace here of a narrative of Indian savagery or wildness (fig. 6). Tropes of Indianness are instead utilized to signal nobility and peace.[21] The "before" picture of Yellow Robe uses a skillfully doctored Choate studio portrait to represent "Indianness." Behind his calmly, seated figure, tipi seams have been superimposed on the interior backdrop, to create the impression of an authentic, plains location. Encircled by a representational Indian shield, with feathers decorating its rim, he is nestled into the words of the cover's title, the tip of his feather visually fused into the first word of *United States Indian School, Carlisle, Pennsylvania*. His gaze looks out from the picture, meeting the viewer's eye directly, and his hair, though long, is clean and kempt. His appearance is

6. Catalog cover of Carlisle Indian School, 1895. Courtesy of Archives
and Special Collections, Dickinson College, Carlisle PA.

neat, handsome, and noble. His clothes are not Indian buckskin but cloth
with a row of large jacket buttons plainly visible and a tied neckerchief
at his throat, giving a suggestion of refinement. Although an Indian blanket is slung over his arm, his moccasined feet (along with his companions)
have been cropped from the picture.[22] It is mainly the large, signifying eagle feather (and tell-tale dark skin) that indicates this is an Indian boy. Beneath him, a tipi encampment illustrates where he has come from. In this
scene, a lone Indian is carrying a bow, but he is seated and neither fierce
nor warrior-like. The scene, accompanied by a wandering dog, is harmonious, almost domestic.

From the photograph of the young Yellow Robe, the eye is drawn from
left to right and up the page to a matching circle displaying a larger-scale,
mature Yellow Robe. Clean-cut features, short hair, and wing collar with
tie accentuate his dignified, sideways gaze. An elaborate picture frame, contrasting with the primitive shield containing his boyhood picture, and a
giant, semifurled American flag underpin this dominant image of the collage. Beneath it, a three-story frame house with porch and chapel alongside depict the home he was sent to live in on arrival. Printed in red, white,

and blue, the collage has a patriotic flavor. Its prevailing mood, however, is one of domesticity, accented by the incongruous wallpaper-design background on which the pictures have been mounted, which surrounds not only house and flag but also tipi and quiver. As suggested by Yellow Robe's inclusion in the "Seventh Class of Graduates" on page 22 of the pamphlet, this schematized construction of Chauncey Yellow Robe's history serves to exhibit the progress of a real, live individual Indian.[23] Just as importantly, it presents a peaceable, romanticized, usable Indian past from which Pratt sought to persuade whites that the Plains Indians were merely awaiting the opportunities offered by Carlisle to claim their place in the republic.

That the images of Chauncey Yellow Robe were openly being used for the school's propagandistic purposes is undeniable, and this lays Pratt open to the accusation of exploitation. Yet certain details of Yellow Robe's life work to problematize this accusation. The deep level of affection Pratt engendered in many of his past pupils, as well as their loyalty both to him and his cause, which they embraced as their own, contribute to a judgment of the superintendent that is multifaceted. If Chauncey Yellow Robe's was definitely the face that fit the story in 1895, he himself proved to be much more than just Pratt's poster boy.

Rising to become superintendent of the government Indian School in Rapid City, South Dakota, Yellow Robe fulfilled all Pratt's hopes for a Carlisle graduate and remained in regular contact with the man he wrote to as "General" and called his friend. He expressed open affection for Pratt and his family, remembering fondly that, "as a boy in Carlisle," Pratt's daughter Nina always treated him "like a brother."[24] When in 1913 Carlos Montezuma proposed that the aging Pratt should make a return to Carlisle, Yellow Robe enthusiastically supported the move. Confident that many others would do so too, he sent the Apache doctor a list of "the Carlisle graduates that were under General Pratt" for him to contact to ensure that Pratt's return to the alma mater would be properly feted.[25] Although we do not know what Chauncey Yellow Robe felt about the before/after cover in which he featured, we do know that later in life he wrote "a short article on my boyhood days on the plains . . . up to my school days."[26] This article can be seen as a literary version of the "before" picture and thus indicates his own collusion in this bifurcated presentation of his life.

Equally as determined as Pratt to see the tribes fully integrated into American society, Yellow Robe, unlike Pratt, had also clearly come to think of himself and others as belonging to a distinct racial group. He praised Charles Eastman for his lectures and work to bring "public opinion . . . more in favor of the Indians," telling Pratt he felt that the Santee Sioux was "doing great credit to his race."[27] In a similar vein, when he wrote to thank Carlos Montezuma for sending his article "The Indian of Tomorrow, the Indian of Yesterday"—Montezuma's title giving a buoyant inversion to the usual progress chronology—Yellow Robe told him, "You are certainly the pride of our race and always will be."[28]

Race had become a category with general currency among white-educated Indians. When they joined forces in 1911 to found a national organization, they wielded it with confidence, demanding "that a just opportunity be given whereby the race as a whole may develop and demonstrate its capacity for enlightenment and progress . . . as an American people in America."[29] Four years before Horace Kallen made his classic case for cultural pluralism, the Society of the American Indian was making a similar appeal on behalf of the Indian race: assimilation without loss of Indian identity.[30] Yellow Robe, although unable to attend the first meeting, was keen to support the association and dismayed when he heard of the divisions among the delegates. Despite his loyalty to Pratt and the assimilation model, he told Montezuma he thought Indians needed to be united, that they needed to "put our best efforts that we preach about into action." Without the power of solidarity, he feared Indians would be kept "silent behind the fence."[31] Finding strength and a voice through race unity was a compelling prospect for Yellow Robe and many other Carlisle-educated Indians. Perhaps unsurprisingly, eleven of the eighteen founding members had connections to Hampton and Carlisle, as did the majority of delegates at the society's first conference.[32] Pratt cheered on some of his most successful students as they struggled to build a national Indian association. He could not, however, condone racial clustering and, in his early years, had never envisaged that it would be necessary. Now eight years into his retirement, he continued to rail against anything that smacked of racial separation, remaining convinced such tactics were always certain to fail "through ignoring the individual as a unit and binding him in masses to race destiny."[33]

Pratt and the Indian School System

"Race destiny" was anathema to Pratt, so it was profoundly ironic that he should have founded an Indian school where Indian children were educated apart from other Americans. Fully aware of this contradiction, Pratt always insisted Carlisle was a temporary measure. He prescribed a short and intense period of activity for all Indian schools, before the work of educating Indians was handed over to American public schools and colleges. The Carlisle Indian School, Pratt maintained, was an institution with a short life expectancy:

> No thought was further from the mind of its founder than that the Carlisle school should live to have a history. Its plan for making American citizens out of the Indians appeared so clear, so practical, and so easy to carry out that only the demonstration seemed necessary in order to commend it to the public and so lead the way for all Indian youth to be developed to a point where we could do away with special Indian schools by admitting the Indians to the established schools and industries of the country.[34]

Carlisle's task was to demonstrate the feasibility of educating Indians for citizenship. For Pratt, Carlisle and similar schools were only a temporary measure to educate the last generation of Indian children. After that, Indians, just like immigrants, would enter the mainstream of American life. In Pratt's eyes, Carlisle's educational program represented an absolute break with all previous efforts to educate Indians because of its insistence on training for work, quashing Indian cultures, and rapid integration with the white population. As we've seen, he was quick to criticize the work of missionaries, being impatient of their long timescale, lenient attitudes to native cultures, and paternalistic approach: "The churches had missions and mission schools among the Indians, but [they] . . . never wanted to lose their converts from tribal living into wider opportunities."[35] Pratt regarded Carlisle's zero tolerance of all aspects of Indian culture and insistence that Indians should be launched into mainstream society as a new departure as well as "a healthy criticism upon the years of religious failure [i.e., of the missionaries]."[36] Whereas missionaries had gone to live alongside the Indians in their own communities and toiled for generations to convert and school them, Pratt's approach was abrupt: severance from the home environment and transportation into "the midst of civilization." Both were fundamental to the Carlisle Indian School's endeavor, encapsulated in the slogan, "To civilize the Indian place him in the midst of civilization; to keep him civilized make him stay."

Having formulated his uncompromising, personal racial philosophy during his soldiering years and then instituted it at Carlisle, Pratt defended it unaltered to his dying day. During his twenty-five years as Carlisle's superintendent, he was unremitting in his efforts to demonstrate the validity of his beliefs and, even in old age, never halted his public crusade nor relinquished his inner certainty. Writing to his daughter from his home in California in 1917, after having just read a swinging attack on his philosophy and methods in the *Reminiscences* of Lyman Abbott, he confided to her how he felt his views and actions had been misrepresented by the book, which accused him of "railroading the Indian into civilization." Unrepentant, he reiterated his continuing confidence in everything he had done and confessed that "It is impossible for me to divorce myself from the conviction that my method is the only Christian, American, common sense and feasible method."[37]

Pratt's method, like the man, was straightforward and unbending. During his year at Hampton supervising the ex-prisoners, at a time when the experiment in Indian schooling was still young, he and Armstrong had talked "much about the future of these young men and the need for them to become Americanized."[38] They had agreed about the need for education but openly embraced very different models of Americanization. Yet if Hampton and Carlisle had become bound up with the racial and pedagogical thinking of their respective founders, they also possessed much in common.

The "eastern" schools shared purpose and public profile as living showcases for the experiment in Indian education. As flagship institutions with intertwined origins and histories, they were frequently referred to in the same breath and developed a pattern of schooling rooted in a general view of what was needed to convert wild Indians into American citizens. At both schools work was of the essence. Discipline was seen as imperative and a necessary antidote to tribal indigence. The army background of both founders lent a military atmosphere to these schools. Children at both Hampton and Carlisle wore uniforms; they marched and drilled; they lined up for inspection; they responded obediently to the bells that ruled and punctuated their daily lives. This regime was considered not only essential to the smooth running of the institutions but a vital form of discipline intended to civilize young savages. In part as a result of Pratt's sojourn at Hampton, the curricula of the two institutions also appeared very similar. At both, the day was divided into two halves; one for study and the other for practical work and training. Those paying a visit to both schools might have spotted few differences in the training being offered. Impressed by the sight of Indian youth marching on the parade ground, sitting quietly in rows of desks, or busy in the industrial shops, the small, telling details that revealed the quite different racial philosophies underpinning the programs were less remarkable. For example, at Hampton, Indian students lived in dormitories given names that supplied obvious reminders of their membership of a specific group—Winona Hall, the Wigwam—while at Carlisle the buildings were designated with less colorful, more descriptive terms—"the girls' building," "the small boys' building." More notable, and of special interest to white visitors, was the "model reservation" at Hampton, where Indian couples played house like white people, in preparation for their return home. This was tied into the home building scheme, supported by the ethnologist Alice Fletcher, as well as to Armstrong's plans to see his students return to their reservations. Quite deliberately, Pratt had built no equivalent "model reservation" on the Carlisle campus. Instead he looked to the local community to provide training in white ways through his "outing" program.

Probably the purest working example of Pratt's philosophy, the "outing" system involved sending Indian students to live and work with American families and was, as he saw it, the "right arm" of the Carlisle School. He had developed the system while in charge of the Indians at Hampton. With the cooperation of his "model" Kiowa student, Etadleah, and the help of Deacon Hyde, he had succeeded in placing the young men on individual farms in Berkshire County, Massachusetts, for the summer months of 1878.[39] Hampton continued to follow the practice, but Pratt was very jealous of his part in setting up the scheme. When an article in the *Southern Workman* claimed "outing" to be a Hampton invention, Pratt sent a curt letter explaining his part in developing the idea of "outing":

I began your Indian feature at Hampton and inaugurated the Indian outing system for you. . . . I did it upon a principle for which I had argued
long before, claiming that the Indian should be brought out from the
reservations and permitted to live among us and associate with us. . . .
Right is right and wrong is wrong, and I am led to this expose by your
constant habit at Hampton of gobbling everything, which occasionally
becomes nauseous.[40]

His petulance notwithstanding, "outing" was indeed utterly consistent
with Pratt's broad philosophy and at Carlisle he quickly involved the surrounding white population in his educational experiment. A summer outing program was begun the school's first year, with twenty-four boys and
girls being "sent out into individual homes in the country contiguous to
the school to work for pay, live in and be treated as members of the family, and to generally conform to the habits and customs of the home life of
our best agricultural population." The program grew rapidly, with 109
being placed out the following summer and 29 staying out. The program
continued to develop until some students were spending periods of up to
two years on "outing."

As the first outing officer, Miss Annie Ely carefully vetted local families and collected character references to ensure they would provide the
correct moral environment. At the end of the year, white patrons were required to write a conduct report on each Indian student. Pratt set out the
aims and purpose of the venture in his report to the commissioner: "Our
object in placing pupils in families is to advance them in English and the
customs of civilized life. We send out as many as we can spare toward the
end of the school term, then visit them before our school opens in September, and if everything is satisfactory and persons wish to keep them,
arrange for them to stay one or two years. Pupils remaining out over the
winter must attend school at least four months continuously, and their labor out of hours must pay their keep."[41]

Most male students worked on farms, helping with a range of activities,
and females assisted with household and childcare tasks. Despite teething
problems the first year, when half the students returned or were sent back,
local residents quickly developed an enthusiasm for this cheap form of labor. Demand rapidly exceeded supply, allowing Pratt's scheme to expand
until nearly half the students enrolled were not on campus but instead liv-

ing on farms and villages across Pennsylvania and beyond. This diaspora was heartily welcomed by Pratt because association with upstanding representatives of the white population was integral to his educational program. Nevertheless, despite rubbing shoulders with honest toiling folk, Indian youths were also becoming familiar with drudgery and being schooled into acceptance of a lowly place in white society.

With such an extensive outing operation, it was impossible to ensure the proper treatment and safety of all pupils (as chapter 10 demonstrates). Problems connected with running the program, linked to changing attitudes to the reservation, meant that some years after Pratt left Carlisle his successor followed Hampton's lead and in 1912 built a "model home" on the Carlisle campus for students to learn and practice domestic skills.[42] This change in Carlisle's traditional approach was noted and fiercely criticized by a past student who had been at Carlisle during Pratt's time. She extolled the virtues of outing and condemned the new "cottage plan":

> When I was a student at Carlisle, we were taught and constantly reminded to hitch our ambition to a star; and in a measure to train us to pursue such ambition, we were placed every summer under the outing system in refined and cultured homes where we were trained in the management of refined home life. Most every Indian girl gets a real taste of home life by cooking over a cook stove and taking care of kerosene lamps long before she goes to Carlisle. . . . Your cottage plan merely duplicates this experience. . . . I think Carlisle is making a mistake in training her girls to believe that they have no future other than the dreary and unappealing life of an Indian reservation. Teach the girls to . . . hitch their ambitions to a star and not a kerosene lamp.[43]

Her approval of the "outing" program and Indian ambition would have won Pratt's hearty approval.

He himself seized every opportunity to launch students into white society. In 1910, the school was able to report that more than half of Carlisle's graduates were making their living away from the reservation and that out of a total of 514, only 54 were engaged in farming.[44] These figures might seem to provide evidence to support Carlisle's claim that it fit its students for mainstream society, but, backed by photographs of the graduating classes, they also provide a salutary reminder that only small numbers of students gained enough schooling to achieve graduation or the skills to find well-paid work. Despite Pratt's educational ambitions for his students, it is notable that not a single one graduated before 1889. The first group numbered just fourteen and over the following years numbers fluctuated but were never high, dipping as low as six in 1893.[45] Carlisle supplied no more than a basic primary education, a fact that places Pratt's aspirations in sharp perspective.

Nevertheless, even when no longer Carlisle's superintendent, Pratt continued to trumpet the socially transforming powers of the nonreservation schools. To a military audience in Philadelphia in 1913, he described how "Hundreds of educated Indians have escaped the thralldom of reservation life through non-reservation schools, and have successfully gone into professional and industrial occupations in our civilized communities: Lawyers, doctors, preachers, literary pursuits, bookkeepers, engineering and all industrial life, and have abundantly established their competitive equality."[46] Undeterred by the absence of professionals to match his claim, he brought seven men from different tribes onto the platform "as samples to prove [his] contention:

> One has been employed in the Disston Saw Works for nine years; one is in the locomotive repair shops of the Reading Road for the last five years; one is a plumber for eight years; one is an automotive painter in a repair shop on Market Street; one is a traveling salesman for a wholesale house for seven years; another is a printer with the Lippincott Company; and the last is a blacksmith."[47]

What was important for Pratt was that firstly, they had achieved economic equality in a white world and "their pay is the same as that of the white men by whose side they work." Secondly, that they were independently integrated into white communities, "scattered and individually in happy contact with our people, instead of living together in a race mass, nursing and plotting prejudice to their own hurt." Thirdly, and here Pratt openly unleashed a controversial weapon from his amalgamation arsenal, that "five of them are happily married to white wives."

The contentiousness of the issue of miscegenation was not lost even on the thick-skinned Pratt, who immediately backed his observation with the simple yet provocative and racially barbed observations that "Through all the years white men have taken Indian wives and made their homes with the Indians." So, he asked, "Why should not Indian men take white wives and live with the whites?"[48] Although Jefferson himself had been in favor of this method of removing Indians from the body politic, even in the City of Brotherly Love genetic integration as a solution to the Indian Problem would have provoked unease. The union of a white woman with an Indian man excited particular disquiet.[49] Pratt was fully aware of this, because he had witnessed firsthand the everyday racism found in the local communities. When a Seneca boy, Jack Johnson, had been expelled from the local public school, Carlisle's outing agent had reported back to Carlisle that Jack was not fully to blame, because "his teacher . . . showed a disposition of dislike for the Indian race and seemed to forget that she was dealing with an individual."[50] Pratt opposed all such racist behavior, but miscegenation was a more complex issue. Vehemently opposed by many whites because of their racist fears of blood contamination, it was supported by Pratt for motives many today find equally suspect—as part of his broad campaign to integrate Indians and obliterate all aspects of their societies. During his time at the Carlisle Indian School, however, he was careful not to broach head-on the sensitive issue of Carlisle students marrying into the local population. But as time passed, and he became increasingly maverick, he was less inhibited.

In his early years, Pratt had been fully in step with the mood of the government. Within a year of Carlisle's founding, he had suggested to Senator Henry Dawes that "there could be a system of industrial boarding schools on the reservations, from which the most competent should be taken for final training in the schools in the midst of civilization."[51] Over the following two decades, twenty-three off-reservation boarding schools were established, bearing many resemblances to Carlisle, and similar institutions were set up on almost every reservation. When Thomas Jefferson Morgan laid out his plans to integrate Indian schools into a system, he placed Hampton and Carlisle at its summit. These two pioneer institutions would no longer take students directly from the reservation but instead supply the final years of schooling for the most able.

By now Carlisle was the biggest, most celebrated Indian school and Pratt the most renowned Indian educator in the nation. Always a maverick, he did not readily comply with the demands and strictures of the Bureau of Indian Affairs and as the years passed, he quarreled with everyone and fell out of step with government policy. Feeling alienated from other Indian educators, he stopped attending their annual school conventions.[52] At Lake

Mohonk in 1896, having spoken out peevishly against Civil Service appointments, he openly rounded on the Indian Rights Association:

CAPTAIN PRATT: "I never joined this 'Indian Rights Association.'"

MR. SMILEY: "You had better do it."

CAPTAIN PRATT: "No, I am not in sympathy with their methods, and I can stand alone."[53]

But he was soon to find he could not "stand alone," and three years later wrote to Commissioner Jones to complain: "I am tired of contending with my brother superintendents of the agency and the other non-reservation schools near the Indians. They have opposing views and purposes in part begotten of their environment and which I think are encouraged from your office, and they are largely banded against Carlisle. There are so many of them and so few of me that they carry the day."[54]

Jones quickly assured Pratt of his support and invited him to share his views at the next meeting of the National Education Association. By the end of his administration, however, the commissioner himself was questioning the efficacy of institutions like Carlisle, having become convinced that reservation schools were better suited to providing Indian children with the most appropriate industrial and agricultural education. Pratt found himself and his work at Carlisle increasingly marginalized, and his obstructive criticism and direct attacks on the bureau led to his being abruptly "relieved of his post" in June 1904. Characteristically, he went down fighting. Until his dying day, aged eighty-three, he continued, undisturbed by self-doubt, to make speeches and write letters advocating his own uncompromising ideas about Indian education.

While he was still superintendent of Carlisle, Pratt secured military promotion, thanks to the enactment of a new law conferring promotion on retired officers who had served during the Civil War. He had arrived at Carlisle Barracks a mere captain, had risen to the rank of colonel, and, after nearly twenty-five years "of special duty with reference to Indian education," he left the school a brigadier general. It was an extraordinary achievement for a man who had not seen active service since 1875 and a reminder that, in his own eyes especially, he always remained a military man. When he died, he was buried with full military honors in Arlington Cemetery, even though this necessitated his body being transported across the country, from California to Washington DC.

Pratt's status as an army officer was fundamental, and close scrutiny of the military elements of the Indian educational experiment reveals some of the complexities of the venture. At Fort Marion, schooling of the younger prisoners began alongside their induction as quasi-army recruits, visually dramatized by their attendance at class clad in the Civil War Union-blue uniforms Pratt had procured from army surplus. As their tongues were trained to enunciate the unfamiliar sounds of the English language, their bodies were simultaneously disciplined to obey orders, stand to attention, and march in step. This regimentation, more fitting for cadets than civilians, was deemed as necessary for their bodies as for their minds. Pratt paid close attention not only to what they wore but how they wore it. When some of the prisoners converted their trousers into leggings, "this called for immediate correction" and a strict reminder "that the clothing belonged to the United States Government and was only loaned to them so they might dress themselves becomingly." They were made to "crease their trousers, keep the brass buttons on their coats and caps bright, and polish their shoes."[55] Marching and drilling had multiple functions at Fort Marion, and Pratt used it for the same purposes at Carlisle, where girls, too, were included in the exercises. Marching taught subservience to the command of a "superior" and brought rigor and rectitude to supposedly undisciplined "savage" bodies. Pratt quickly learned that a well-ordered, uniformed squad represented the antithesis of the wildness, slovenliness, and indomitable spirit generally associated with Indians and that it excited widespread white interest. He seized every opportunity available to demonstrate and show off the Indians' marching skills. At Fort Marion, "daily drills had been resorted to early" for the prisoners and soon "the drill hour became the favorite period for visitors."[56] Pratt capitalized on this experience, and at Carlisle he regularly invited the townspeople to view the students, marching in tight, straight ranks, breaking by fours, forming platoons, and wheeling to the right and left as a single body on the school's parade ground. He sent them out to march in the town's parades and further afield, too, to New York and Chicago for the Columbian quadricentennial. In New York the *Recorder* pronounced the "comely maidens" and "young braves, divided into four companies of twenty-five," to be "unquestionably the most interesting feature of the whole pageant." Pratt must have felt triumphant when the local paper pronounced that "but for their straight black hair and swarthy coloring, they might easily have passed for a battalion of West Pointers."[57] Yet this proviso, which openly drew attention to indelible racial markers, was of far greater significance to Pratt's venture and the campaign to assimilate Indians than he could ever admit. The New York *Recorder* lauded the students' skills, but the nub of its message was clear: Carlisle's Indians provided an impressive spectacle, but for whites, their essential defining characteristic continued to be their racial difference.

When the 1893 World's Columbian Exposition opened in Chicago, Pratt clashed openly with officials about how Indians should be represented. Scornful of displays showing the primitive conditions of indigenous life organized by Frederick Putnam on the Midway, Pratt countered by taking a battalion of Carlisle boys to Chicago. He quite literally put them through their paces, ensuring that on every occasion they were linked not to scenes of barbarism but to enactments of order, industry, and civilization. The students quartered with units of the regular army and marched behind them through the White City. Instead of guns, they carried representations of the various paths to civilization taught at Carlisle, mounted on top of short poles: books, slates, agricultural implements, printing paraphernalia, and tools of a range of other trades. Yet despite all this, they remained inescapably marked by visible physical traits that linked them to the "brown bodies" exhibited on the opposite side of the river, in the ethnographic exhibitions of the Midway.[58] For Pratt, this synchronized marching offered a kinetic demonstration of the students' discipline and submission to authority. While no doubt, as he noted, "it was a memorable thing for the boys and girls to have marched through the streets of our greatest city"—and in the months afterwards, "the spirit of the school was greatly energized by these experiences"—nevertheless, drilling and marching could be engaged in and enjoyed for quite different reasons.[59] The centrality of military exercise to the school's daily life meant that it could also provide a potent site of resistance for the students. White militarism could be claimed, toyed with, adapted, and subverted (a topic further explored in chapter 8) while remaining for Pratt a straightforward and vital part of his educational experiment.

It was at Fort Marion that he had first drilled the Indians and also set up the military chain of command that introduced a pattern of surveil-

lance demanding the Indians' collusion. They were organized into companies with sergeants and corporals, taught how to march, issued with guns,
and then commanded to guard themselves. Although at Fort Marion the
Kiowa escape plot almost scotched the whole scheme, Pratt perpetuated
this pattern of self-surveillance and self-command at Carlisle and enlisted
the Indians in the school's disciplinary command structure:

> Our 185 boys are divided into three companies, having a first sergeant,
> three sergeants, and four corporals for each company. In suitable weather,
> they are instructed in the primary movements and setting up process of
> army tactics. This is invaluable on account of health and discipline. A
> sergeant, a corporal, and four boys are detailed in their order daily for
> guard duty, but during the night they watch over our grounds as protec-
> tion against fire and improper coming and going.[60]

Indian boys making a bid for freedom thus had to evade an Indian-stu-
dent guard. Girls were less likely to runaway, but it was not long before
they, too, were included in military exercises on the parade grounds. While
drilling imposed the rhythm and pattern of white discipline, it also conferred power and could act as a source of respect and satisfaction. Maggie
Tarbell (Mohawk, St. Regis) still remembered, at the age of ninety-nine,
how she was, "Captain of Division A."[61] In the school's early years, during a local parade through the town, Samuel Townsend (a Pawnee) noticed with delight how a local boy "Looked at our shiny boots and polished buttons with envy" and mused, "He was probably surprised to see
an Indian looking like that." Drilling and marching, although the epit-
ome of regimentation and obedience to authority, was multifaceted. For
this Pawnee boy, the envious glance of a white resident was the source
of a flash of racial pride. For Pratt, military exercise lay at the core of his
curriculum for Indian transformation and the school's participation in local parades was integral to his determined effort to court the good opinion and support of the Carlisle community. Local hostility to the school
would be tantamount to failure.

Carlisle School and the Local Community

In his memoirs, Pratt reports that before the founding of the school, he
instigated the drawing up of a petition, signed by every Carlisle resident,

calling for the conversion of the abandoned Carlisle Barracks into an Indian school.[62] Seeking to replicate his happy relationship with the town of St. Augustine, he worked to involve the Carlisle community in the school's activities, starting with the local churches. Although the first new building he ordered constructed on the campus was a chapel, located close to the entrance and visible immediately on entry to the grounds, Pratt also assigned all the boys "to the different Sunday schools in the town of Carlisle, who cordially and effectively co-operate with us in their moral training."[63] In later years the girls were also sent to local churches to receive Christian instruction and further the school's links with the local white community.

Pratt was also keen to make contact with the faculty of the oldest and most prestigious educational institution in town, Dickinson College (founded in 1763). He arranged for Dickinson's Professor Lippincott to pay weekly visits to the Indian School to hold a Sunday service in chapel and took groups of students to the Dickinson campus for occasional lessons.[64] Pratt held up Dickinson's prestigious preparatory school as a beacon for aspiring students. During Pratt's years, more than a score of Indians enrolled there and some went on to graduate from Dickinson College.[65] Pratt's experiment in Indian education was being conducted for white purposes, and the town of Carlisle was both its host community and its first witness. He needed the support of the townspeople and he heeded their views.

When the first students had arrived in town dressed in their native clothes, it triggered a frisson of excitement. Pratt felt obliged to bring the train carrying the children into town at midnight, to protect them from the jostling and ogling stares of the crowd that had assembled to greet them. The high fence he hastily built around the campus was to control the townspeople as well as the Indians. Pratt wanted his experiment conducted according to his own strict rules. Yet, eager for the Indians' transformation to be watched and witnessed, he issued an open invitation to visitors to tour the school grounds at set times, to listen to the twelve-man Indian brass band playing on the bandstand at weekends, and to attend the end-of-year commencement exercises. The Indians would, Pratt hoped, become a familiar and accepted part of the community; the first step in their passage toward full integration into mainstream American society.

Pratt's ethnocentric vision invariably blinded him to the depths of

Indian attachment to their own cultures and societies. Yet the historical record carries evidence of a series of incidents, unmentioned in his
memoirs, that also signals the powerful resistance of the local white
community to full Indian integration. Always a place of fascination,
the Indian School was welcomed as a source of employment and con-
tracts and came to be seen as a supplier of cheap labor for local farmers. Yet from the start, even in this carefully selected town with a tradition of racial tolerance and a pride in having hosted a station on the
Underground Railroad, the specter of racism had not been exorcized.
One of the early signs that Indians could never be ordinary members
of the Carlisle community came when the first child died. It rapidly became clear that it was unacceptable for Indian children to be buried in
the local cemetery and Pratt had to open a cemetery at the school. Carlisle had traditionally been segregationist in its burial habits, with blacks
laid to rest separately from whites (we explore this issue in full in chapter 9). Primeval fears linked to death are often cited to explain and justify the segregation of graveyards, but the school's commonplace industrial program also generated alarm.

In 1880 a local manufacturer wrote to the Carlisle *Sentinel*, stating that
"We hear the Indians are no longer making bows and arrows, but have
taken to building wagons and fashioning harness. Can Indians compete
with craftsmen? There are some in this town with wives and children to
feed."[66] Whether the writer of this letter was doubtful about the quality
of these items or fearful they might flood the local market is left ambiguous. Either way, Pratt addressed the problem. As the Indian wagon makers,
blacksmiths, cobblers, tailors, bakers, harness makers, and tinners churned
out ever more goods, he stridently insisted that "All this work we without
hesitation place side by side with the productions of the shops of our white
brothers anywhere." Yet he did not place them for sale on the open market. Instead he negotiated with the Bureau of Indian Affairs to buy all the
items that could not be used at the school for distribution at Indian agencies in the West.[67] To allay local anxieties about economic competition,
Pratt chose to supply the small, protected market of the Bureau of Indian
Affairs. This represented something of a contradiction, because competition in all its guises was always fundamental to Pratt's philosophy.

Competition was his major motivation for creating the famous Carlisle football team. To begin with, Pratt strongly resisted the students' demands for a team. Eventually he gave in, making two conditions: firstly, that the Indians would "never under any circumstances, slug," for then people would say "they are savages and you can't get it out of them"; secondly, that in the course of three or four years they would "whip the biggest football team in the country."[68] Pratt was demanding that the Indians, quite literally, beat the Americans at their own game, and they did. He brought in a top-notch coach, "Pop" Warner, to ensure his demand was fulfilled, and the Carlisle team's success not only brought Jim Thorpe to national attention, but it also facilitated the growth of pride and confidence among Indian supporters across the nation.[69]

Determined to see Indians compete and win in the white world, Pratt nevertheless harbored his own internalized ghosts of racial thinking. We can see this revealed in his long-standing fascination with measurable differences in Indian bodies. He invited Marion T. Meagher, an artist in the department of anthropology at the American Museum of Natural History in New York to visit Carlisle and make a series of drawings of four of the students "as models of the type of their respective tribes."[70] It was in a similar spirit that, while at Fort Marion, he had allowed a Smithsonian sculptor to make plaster casts of all the prisoners' heads, to go on display as representative specimens of their race in Washington. Measurement of this kind, as Stephen Jay Gould has cogently demonstrated, always treads a thin, sometimes nonexistent line between the physical and intellectual: different shape implies different capacity. Although Pratt himself never yielded openly to the rising tide of scientific racism, nevertheless he was not impervious to the thinking of the broader society nor to the pressures exerted on Carlisle. This pressure was felt not just as the racial climate changed but from the very start. At a school ostensibly dedicated to integrating Indians and committed to universalist principles, there were implicit and even explicit accommodations to a society unwilling to grant equality to Indians. The execution of Pratt's philosophy was far more nuanced and compromised than his direct and often blustering rhetoric. Often undetectable in the written record, these inconsistencies are more readily revealed through interrogation of the Carlisle campus.

7. Carlisle Campus: Landscape of Race and Erasure

PRATT INHERITED THE disused Carlisle Barracks. Over twenty-five years, he renovated, adapted, and augmented these buildings to meet the goals and purposes he had set for the Carlisle Indian School. From the start, the design and layout of the campus was an important element in Pratt's pedagogical program. The dual mission to which he had dedicated Carlisle—training Indian children for American citizenship and demonstrating to white Americans that this planned cultural transformation was indeed possible—determined all planning and building decisions. Carlisle's curriculum was founded on a rejection of any overt reference to the Indian's racial heritage and premised on the Indian's capacity to enter American society on equal terms. Yet Pratt was engaged in a radical social experiment. When applied to Indians, his universalist philosophy challenged political, social, and, most importantly, racial boundaries.

Although the rhetoric of Pratt's campaign was always unwaveringly universalist, on the Carlisle campus, where encounters between whites and Indians were orchestrated and relationships with the local community coordinated, the straightforward luxury of linguistic assertion was gone. The delicate task in which Pratt was engaged required negotiation and accommodation with the values of the local community and broader society and these would be recapitulated spatially on the Carlisle campus (fig. 8). Analysis of the physical layout of the campus—position and size of buildings, siting of gateways, entrances, pathways, and conduits, and social-spatial relationship between town and campus—reveals telling details about the covert purpose of the school and its day-to-day workings, which are entirely absent from the official written record. Interweaving traditional archival research with interrogation of this spatial record reveals a multifaceted story, exposing compromises, denials, evasions

7. Carlisle Indian School students, March 1892. Photograph by
J. N. Choate. Reproduced with permission of Cumberland
County Historical Society, Carlisle PA. PA-CH2041–2.

and subtle day-to-day forms of racial segregation and domination that
belie the simplicity of Carlisle's stated mission. It enables us to perceive
some aspects of white rule that could not be openly admitted. Pratt's
pronouncements, speeches, and reports persistently asserted that once
educated, Indians could readily compete with white Americans and find
their place at all levels of society. The Carlisle campus silently delivered
a very different set of powerful visual messages, both to Indian children
who lived and worked at the school, and to white visitors who went to
tour and inspect. Carlisle's dual purpose dictated that the campus was
organized for a dual function: both physical apparatus, where the experiment to transform Indians was being conducted, and living showcase, where the results of this experiment were displayed to the white
public. The message communicated to those living on the campus was
different from the one conveyed to those visiting. Students, who were
ostensibly being trained to step out as equals, experienced in the physical organization of the campus confinement, surveillance and a militaristic rule that unremittingly asserted the patterns of white power that
would attend their absorption into white society. Simultaneously, how-

CAMPUS AND TENNIS COURT, INDIA SCHOOL, CARLISLE, PA.

8. Carlisle Indian School campus and tennis court, 1908. Photograph by John Leslie. Reproduced with permission of Cumberland County Historical Society, Carlisle PA. PC46002–2.

ever, the message conveyed to white visitors was designed to reassure them that educated Indians could be rendered compliant and that the terms of Indian assimilation would not threaten the social, economic, or racial norms and proprieties of the dominant society.

When Pratt took over the Carlisle Barracks, the buildings had been unoccupied for eight years and were physically run down and neglected. He immediately embarked on a program of renovation and began reshaping and molding the barracks to his own special purposes. His background and training meant that he did not look to traditional missionary models of schooling but instead planned and organized a military institution. The parade ground at the center of the campus was retained and quickly put to use for drilling and marching. Existing buildings were assigned new functions, and these carried a powerful set of visual messages for both pupils and visitors. In his reallocation of space, Pratt identified all buildings linked to white purpose and occupied by whites and located them together, and as more were constructed they joined this assemblage. So schoolrooms, administration block, staff housing, and chapel were located near the entrance, at the south end of the campus. To the north and furthest from the entrance was the Indian section: the boys' and girls' quarters, the disciplinarian's house, the laundry, the hospital and workshops, and, eventually, the school cemetery. A map of the barracks made shortly before Pratt took over shows an ordered quadrangle of buildings (fig. 9). By the time Pratt left Carlisle many more had been constructed, but these did not disrupt the basic regularity of the barracks' layout (fig. 10).[1] This neat visual symmetry, however, masked a racially asymmetrical attribution of space. A symbolic dividing axis, marked by the superintendent's quarters, bandstand, and dining hall (erected by Pratt) separated one half of the campus from the other. At Carlisle (unlike at the Santee School), Indian children lived and dined separately from whites and if they died, they were buried in a segregated cemetery. A clear and strict separation of whites and Indians had been systematically and progressively inscribed on the buildings and landscape of a school whose professed goal was to bring these two groups together.

Operating under time pressure when he first organized the school, it is possible that the design of existing buildings dictated their new uses. But this appears unlikely because the buildings that ran down the two sides of the compound had been officers' quarters and were nearly identical.[2] Whether this racial division of space was deliberate and conscious is not revealed in the record. But whether deliberate or not, it is significant—given his professed desire that Carlisle should be a living demonstration of his belief that Indians could live in the midst of American society—that in organizing the school's spaces he incorporated patterns of racial segregation already familiar and entrenched in the broader society. Each new building etched these separations deeper into the face of the campus: the chapel, constructed in the school's first months, was located close to the entrance, in the white "quarter," as was the assembly hall. The replacement hospital and new boys' dormitory were built at the opposite end, in the Indian section. White teachers and staff who did not supervise in the trade shops had few reasons to visit this section. Indian students moved around the campus, on the strictly laid-out paths and walkways, to attend lessons in the school building and services in the chapel, but their manual training took place in the converted sta-

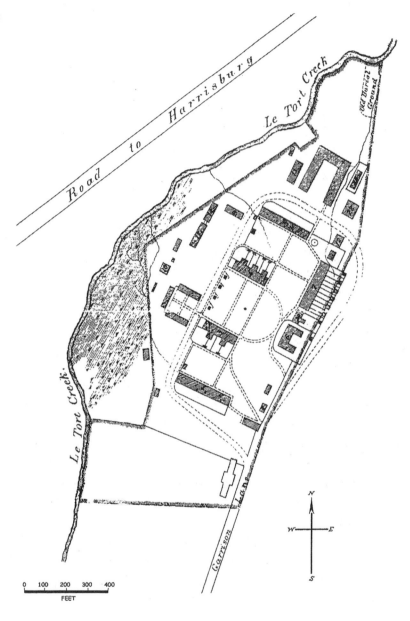

9. Map of buildings of Carlisle barracks at the foundation of the Indian school, 1879. Rescaled and adapted by the author from an 1870 map of Carlisle barracks.

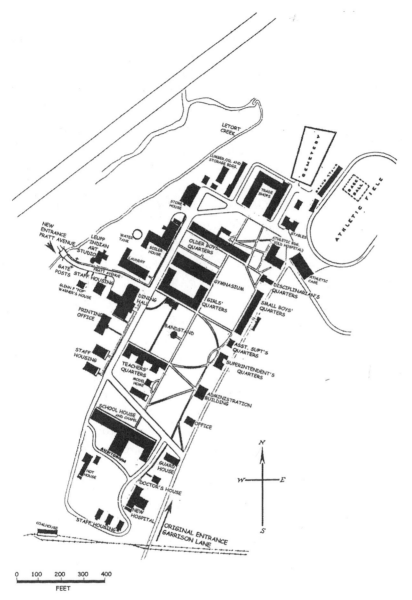

10. Map of buildings of Carlisle Indian School at closure from "Map of General Hospital No. 31," U.S. Army Military History Institute, Carlisle PA. Rescaled and adapted by the author, with cemetery superimposed to scale.

bles at the north of the campus, and they slept in dormitories near-by. Carlisle was a spatially segregated campus.

The location of specific buildings governed encounters between whites and Indians. So, too, did the seven-foot-high fence Pratt ordered to be built around the whole campus during the school's first week (clearly visible in fig. 8). Fully aware of local fascination with the exotic children in their midst and keen to manage personally any inspection or viewing of his living experiment, he was equally determined that the spatial organization of the school should guarantee the confinement, control, and surveillance of the students. In St. Augustine, where he had initiated his educational experiment, the architecture of the fort had confined the prisoners and communicated a powerful message of coercion. The interior space of Fort Marion had been controlled and patterned not just by its soaring ramparts but by the design of its entrance. This not only provided sole access to the fort; it also, as noted in the prologue, was not visible from the interior as an exit owing to its oblique angle of construction.

When Pratt took over the Carlisle Barracks, he immediately remodeled the entrance so that it replicated that of the old fort. This minor structural change achieved major reorientation of the spatial organization of the whole school. Entry to the Carlisle Barracks had always been via Garrison Lane. The lane led up hill from town. It joined the grounds of the post at the southern corner, then ran past the old guardhouse and through the entrance gate before it veered east, behind the commanding officer's and officers' quarters, and then round to the stables at the northern end of the post. However when Pratt took over the barracks, a second road also led onto the post (fig. 9). This one branched off Garrison Lane to the left, well before the guardhouse, and swept west down the hill, before turning to parallel the first road and eventually join it. These two roads inscribed a rough rectangle around the post. They allowed for a double point of entry and a free flow of traffic around and through the grounds. One of Pratt's first moves was to interrupt this free flow by blocking off the second entrance and forcing all traffic through the gateway beside the guardhouse (fig 10). This enforcement of a single prescribed route can be interpreted as a bid to control the admission of white visitors to the post. It was also, very clearly,

11. Garrison Lane entrance to Carlisle Indian School, showing guard house, 1885. Photograph by Frances Benjamin Johnston. Reproduced with permission of Cumberland County Historical Society, Carlisle PA. J00304-2.

a way to monitor the movement of all Indian students. From inside the school grounds, not only was the exit totally invisible (fig. 8), but the single entrance/exit meant all arrivals and departures of students could be watched and controlled. Anyone entering or leaving the school had to pass the guardhouse, with its sentries and often, too, within feet of unseen Indian students, locked in one of its four, stone cells, as punishment for breaking rules (fig. 11). Both the surveillance and penal dimensions of the school's program served as a reminder to every one of the power relations at work.

While Pratt quite deliberately altered well-established transit routes in and out of the grounds, he never changed or enhanced the appearance of the main entrance (fig. 11), even though throughout the whole of his time at Carlisle, Pratt was constantly planning, building, and rebuilding the structures and thoroughfares of the campus. The school gates were simply a rough, hinged continuation of the white fence that surrounded the campus and ran down Garrison Lane; there was no arresting institutional sign, no imposing gateway.[3] The huge, carved, wooden gate from the post's former days (fig. 12) had been burned in 1863 by

12. Gate of Carlisle barracks at Garrison Lane, 1845. From Thomas G.
Tousey, *Military History of Carlisle and Carlisle Barracks* (Richmond VA:
Dietz, 1939), 195.

the departing Confederate army, and its successor, while functional, was
simple and unprepossessing.[4] Everything about the entrance to the Carlisle Indian School was plain and understated; it neither proclaimed itself nor demanded viewing attention.

This was the physical site where thousands of Indian children crossed
from one world to another. It was a locus of change, as Luther Standing Bear, Lakota author and ex-Carlisle student, later observed. A member of the first group of students to arrive at Carlisle, he, along with the
other children, disembarked from the train and walked up Garrison
Lane. When they arrived at the barracks, "The gate was locked, but after quite a long wait it was unlocked and we marched in through it. I
was the first boy inside. At that time I thought nothing of it, but now I
realize that I was the first Indian boy to step inside the Carlisle Indian
School grounds."[5]

Retrospectively, Standing Bear became acutely aware of the symbolic significance of this gate. Crossing that threshold brought with it a new world, a new life, a new identity; few who passed through it would leave unchanged. This was the message trumpeted by Pratt and consistently publicized in the dramatic "before" and "after" photographs he published. There were no half measures and all in-between stages were denied and judged as failure, a cultural version of the "one-drop rule."

So for Pratt, it might seem that the gateway of the Carlisle Indian School was symbolically fundamental to all he was attempting to accomplish. Thresholds and gateways, anthropologists have shown us, carry exactly the symbolic message Pratt wanted to purvey.[6] They are marginal zones that both separate and link two distinct worlds. Gates, through their opening and closing functions, are twice symbolical in linking two worlds.[7] When thought of in these terms, the gateway to the Carlisle School appears an ideal candidate to have been enlisted for Pratt's publicity purposes, to proclaim the message Luther Standing Bear understood it to carry. Yet Pratt never exploited the powerful symbolic potential of the Garrison Lane gate. From the beginning, he was acutely conscious of the Carlisle Indian School's historic destiny and employed local photographer, J. N. Choate, to take hundreds of photographs of buildings, grounds, pupils, visitors, and all activities at the school.[8] Yet among all these photographs there is not a single picture looking *in* through this main access, which for more than twenty-five years was safeguarded as the school's principal entrance (fig. 11).

Pratt's failure to build an imposing gateway for the Carlisle Indian Industrial School and his resolute maintenance of the Garrison Lane entrance was almost certainly deliberate, reflecting his sensitivity to the public image of his school and its relationship to the community. The entrance to the Carlisle Indian School was not planned to impress Indians. It was intended primarily for white viewing and Pratt wanted the message it relayed to be read as neither challenging nor threatening. He chose to focus attention on the students themselves and their individual transformations, because this raised fewer fundamental questions about how they might impose themselves on the community and U.S. society. A remarkable entrance would solicit remarks; any change to the old gateway could be interpreted as a statement. It was far safer to leave the old gates standing at the crossing point between school and community. So for nearly thirty years, visitors, students and staff slipped in and out through the southern-most corner of the campus, past the guardhouse, and through the designated, unadorned main gate of the school.[9]

The location of this entrance in relation to the town was also significant. White visitors to the school gained few glimpses of the campus before their arrival. Nevertheless their journey there was important to the impression they gained of the school. They traveled first through the industrial landscape of the eastern section of town, with its warehouses, factories, and chimneys. Just fifty yards before reaching the gate, they were forcibly reminded that the school was on the "wrong side of the tracks" when they physically had to cross the freight train tracks (laid in 1884) or wait for a long line of coal trucks to rumble past. Although Pratt argued forcefully for Indian equality, the school's location in the industrial section of town made an oblique reference to the place educated Indians might find in American society; Pratt's constant reference to the importance of work was reiterated by the school's surrounding industrial landscape. Visitors approached the school up the paved sidewalk of Garrison Lane, which guided them toward the entrance through half-a-mile of coarse, white, wooden fencing, running both sides of the lane. They had no view of any building except the guardhouse or even of a sign until they turned the last corner and passed though the gate. The panoramic view of the campus, with which they were rewarded on arrival, was not visible from outside the campus.[10] The Carlisle Indian School did not visually assert or proclaim its presence in the town and was fully visible only to those who chose to visit.

When puzzling over the school's discreet inscription on the landscape and humble and self-effacing entrance, it helps to remember that there was already a clearly defined visual and architectural context in which visitors and local townspeople would read and interpret its message. To understand this context, it is instructive to look at another Carlisle educational establishment with a much longer and more secure history.

Dickinson College
Just two miles southwest of the Indian School, close to the center of Carlisle, stood Dickinson College. Established to educate sons of well-

to-do members of the white majority, Dickinson was the social opposite of an experimental Indian school like Carlisle whose mission was to incorporate an excluded minority. A brief comparative interrogation of these two different campuses exposes the two quite different discourses of race and power embedded in their respective architectures and facilitates interpretation of the message Pratt was working to convey through his unchanged entrance and allocation of space and buildings at the Carlisle Barracks. The built environment reflects the means, confidence, and intentions of those who plan and finance its building, so that relations of power are inscribed in individual edifices and also, of particular importance here, in their spatial relationship to one another and to the surrounding environment.[11]

When the Indian School came to Carlisle, Dickinson College was already starting to plan its imminent centenary celebrations. Chartered the year the revolutionary struggle ended and the colonies won independence from England (1783), this embryonic school had been located one hundred miles further west than any other college in the new United States. Its foundation symbolized a powerful faith in the continuing vitality of the westward movement and national expansion.[12] Although its fortunes had fluctuated, by 1879 Dickinson College could boast a "long, unbroken line of Alumni," which included cabinet officers, congressmen, senators, judges, a chief justice, and a president of the United States—James Buchanan (1857–61). The college regarded itself as a strong participant in the history and fate of the nation. When fire had destroyed Dickinson's grand, newly completed main building in 1803, no less then seventeen members of Congress, including Jefferson, joined townsfolk from Carlisle to contribute funds for its rebuilding; the burning of Dickinson was regarded as a national as well as local calamity.[13] In 1879, the college pronounced itself "more firmly established than at any previous period of its history" and looked forward to its centennial year and an ambitious program of "projected improvements."[14]

This ambitious building program of "projected improvements" would expand, enhance, and reconfigure the campus. The main Dickinson building and "jewel" of the campus, funded by congressmen and now fondly known as Old West, had been designed by government architect Benjamin Latrobe from plans submitted by the trustees. Latrobe is often considered America's first professional architect, and he had definite ideas about the proper appearance of public buildings. Instead of brick, as suggested by the trustees, Latrobe had insisted the college building should be constructed in "stone, proper for a large edifice, giving it the appearance of strength."[15] Old West's four limestone stories, trimmed with brownstone, its huge, central, arched doorway, echoed in eight, smaller, arched first-floor windows, and its soaring cupola crowned with a mermaid weather vane gave to Dickinson a classic, imposing, edifice around which future campus buildings would be organized. Measuring 150 feet long and 45 wide, with "all the dimensions and altitudes of the different stories and basement . . . carefully planned, with a view to harmonious architectural effect," Old West was as impressive in size as it was in design.[16] Set back from the road on which it looked directly out, its building line exactly paralleled Carlisle's Main Street, because it was from Main Street that its imposing bilateral symmetry was oriented for viewing (fig. 13). A gateway, cut in the low perimeter wall opposite Old West's massive door, was framed by twin posts. From here, a double avenue of campus trees led the eye straight up the ten brownstone steps to the arched door, pediment roof, and sky-reaching mermaid. Old West set the tone for all subsequent Dickinson edifices. Beside it, East College (completed 1835), a more modest construction but built to the same proportions and in the same limestone, toed the same building line at the back of the campus, allowing the leafy grounds to continue enhancing the scale of the campus and reinforcing the message of Old West. Everything about the Dickinson campus was organized to accentuate its tasteful eminence and high purpose.

Care was taken to ensure that no building ever obscured any of the others when viewed from Main Street and that all could be seen to best advantage thereby enabling the design of the campus to work continuously to publicize the glories of the college.[17] Bosler Library went up in 1885. Constructed in the same brownstone as the trim of Old West and to the same monumental proportions, it was built on an L-shaped footprint that framed the college grounds but blocked none of the views. The library building faced onto campus, with an extra structure set in its eastern wall to allow its main entrance to be turned toward the street, its arched doorway linking it visually to Old West. Here was yet another

13. Dickinson College campus from across Main Street, as it looked in 1880.
Courtesy of Archives and Special Collections, Dickinson College, Carlisle, PA.

building deliberately and ostentatiously offering the activities of the college for public viewing. Dickinson's first scientific building, which was completed the following year, was designed "exclusively for scientific purposes, in preference to large monumental buildings for all purposes," but it, too, was integrated into the campus very creatively.[18] The available lot, between West and East College, measured 90 by 240 feet. To preserve as much of the grounds as possible as well as prevent this more modest, serviceable building from detracting from the grander edifices, the new scientific building was positioned behind West and East College. Sitting on the northern boundary of the college, it extended east and west behind the older, taller buildings, but like every other building on the campus, it, too, looked out to Main Street.

The location of the Dickinson campus was crucial to this public display. Although, ironically for our purposes, Benjamin Rush had toyed with the idea of situating his college in the temporarily disused Carlisle Barracks, its eventual home, two blocks west of Carlisle's central courthouse square, served its historic aspirations well. The college was seen by many people who never set foot in Carlisle. The railroad tracks of the

Cumberland Valley Railroad, which linked Harrisburg, Pennsylvania, to Hagerstown, Maryland, ran right down Main Street. When the first great engine smoked and clanked its way west, past the town's central square in 1837, passengers looking out the window would have been instantly aware of the contrast between the small-scale wooden houses and shops of the town and the imposing limestone structures and leafy vistas of Dickinson. Passengers traveling east, who had become familiar with the rich grasslands and scattered white wooden farmsteads of the Cumberland Valley, would have been struck by the panoramic sweep and stone buildings of the college. The pillared gates and straight path leading to Old West would momentarily line up, allowing them a snapshot-framed view of Old West.

Situated more than ten miles from the great Susquehanna River, in its early days the town of Carlisle had been totally dependent on stagecoach links to the rest of the nation. Once eighteen miles of railroad track connected Carlisle to Harrisburg, not only were Philadelphia and Baltimore easily accessed but also new routes opening to the southwest. That same railroad network would later transport thousands of Indian children from their homes in the West to the Indian school in Carlisle, and it was a crucial component in Pratt's decision to locate his school at the barracks. By the time the Carlisle Indian School was established, between six and eight passenger trains passed each way every day, and Dickinson College could use its strategic position to great advantage.[19]

Integration as well as separation of college and town were marked in several ways by the Dickinson campus layout. Walls and entrances were key. The perimeter wall enclosing the rectangular campus was only three-foot high (contrasting with Carlisle's seven-foot fence) and allowed easy viewing into the leafy interior from all points. At various times an iron or wooden fence was added, but these never obstructed the view into the campus. The angular corners, where the wall turned through ninety degrees, were softened by being cut off diagonally and made into entrances. Further gateways were cut in the wall to allow admission to the college at convenient spots. The wall marked the limits of the college grounds yet never obstructed visual access, and the many gateways and entrances invited physical admittance. The main gateway might appear at first glance to be in an unusual position—on a corner

14. Dickinson College main gateway at the corner of Main and West streets, ca. 1900. Courtesy of Archives and Special Collections, Dickinson College, Carlisle PA.

of the campus—but this was no accident. It, too, was designed to display the college's lofty presence in the town while simultaneously signaling its integration into the community. Situated on the angle of the southeast corner of the campus at the point closest to the town's center, the wrought iron, lamp-lit, main college gate faced directly down Main Street to the square (fig. 14). It confidently and tastefully marked the border between town and college while making each readily accessible to the other.

In the context of Dickinson's main gateway and its many minor entries, we can more easily read the statement made by the Indian School's guardhouse entrance. Here we find unobtrusive, plain markers, limited and difficult flow between town and school, and an invisibility of both buildings and school activities of the school from the exterior. While Dickinson looked boldly outward, Carlisle looked diffidently inward. And this was not because Pratt did not want the school's work noticed— far from it. He enthusiastically publicized its work, issued a constant stream of invitations to townspeople and national dignitaries, and took care to ensure that the Carlisle Indian School was included in ceremonies and parades across the country. The understatement of the school's entrance carried an implicit part of the message Pratt wanted visitors to take home with them: Indian assimilation into mainstream society would be as unthreatening as it was unobtrusive.

Potential Entrance for the Carlisle Indian School
The corporeality of buildings often creates an illusion of inevitability; the way things are can suggest this is the only way they could have been. When we look at the topography and layout of the Carlisle School in its early days, it openly presented the possibility of a quite different entrance from the one Pratt determinedly maintained at Garrison Lane (see fig. 9). The original army post Pratt inherited only gave room for expansion westward, so all new buildings pulled the school's center of gravity in that direction. The farmland Pratt leased for the school also lay to the northwest. It was a long walk there and back for pupils who spent half a day on farm work and half a day at their desks. To shorten this journey time, Pratt ordered the little foot bridge across the Le Tort creek to be widened and strengthened for farm vehicles, having secured permission from Judge Henderson for Carlisle pupils to use the well-trodden track, which ran straight across his land to the Harrisburg road.[20] The school now had a second entrance, and it was one that offered great potential.

The road across the Le Tort Bridge lay on a straight line with the bandstand, the flagpole, and the superintendent's house (fig. 10). In 1884, there was a sweeping view from the east up the hill from the bridge that took in almost all the buildings. The remains of a circular drive from the old cavalry school days, just to the left of the bridge, was partially visible. If Pratt had been interested in creating an imposing entrance for his school, with open vistas, sweeping driveways, and arresting gateway, this was his moment. But within the year, he began laying the foundations of a huge dining hall, which would serve the school and later U.S. General Hospital Number 31, until it burned down in 1923. The effect of this building was decisive. It ruled out the possibility of an entrance road leading directly onto campus from the main Harrisburg road and necessitated a more circuitous curved roadway from this direction; it blocked the view of the superintendent's house (the most impressive building on campus) from both bridge and Harrisburg road; and, for anyone looking out of the campus, it screened all but momentary glimpses of this exit.[21]

This dining hall is critical to our understanding of the visual grammar of the campus Pratt was working to build. He used its triple, brick-built stories to enclose the space of the school and shield if from outside view. Positioning the dining hall opposite the superintendent's quarters, he completed the enclosure of the central area of the school, blocking off views of both road and exit from inside the campus. (In later years the laundry [1895] and boiler house [1890] would similarly block views from the pupils' quarters.) The space where the children lived was now entirely enclosed.[22] Due to the dining hall, the school had to be approached from the Harrisburg road at an oblique angle, along a track leading past the laundry building at the corner of the campus. The dining hall both physically and visually served Pratt's double agenda. It completed the enclosure of the campus, thus intensifying both the confinement of students and the possibility for surveillance, and it also definitively prevented the creation of a grandiose entrance that might trigger hostility by challenging popular expectations of an Indian school.

Throughout Pratt's time at Carlisle, the Garrison Lane gate was referred to as the main entrance. Additional buildings and roadways on the campus and developments in the town of Carlisle meant that the new entrance gradually superseded the original one at Garrison Lane. The most influential event in this process was the arrival of the trolley. Built in fits and starts, the final section of the north-running line finally reached the end of North Hanover Street, close to the Indian School, at the end of 1898. With Pratt's approval, an extra spur was added, using Indian labor to run the trolley lines across government land, bringing the terminus right into the school, beside the laundry building.[23] Townspeople could more easily visit the school, enabling Pratt to continue fostering the support and interest of the local community. After a few years, a double cottage was built by students beside this new entrance, relieving the back-end view of the dining hall that greeted visitors at their arrival on campus and, in the unfailing upbeat words of the *Redman and Helper*, improving "the appearance of that part of the

15. New Entrance of Indian School onto Harrisburg Road, 1908.
Photographer unknown. Reproduced with permission of
Cumberland County Historical Society, Carlisle PA.

grounds."[24] But despite its increased use, this was not yet referred to as the main entrance.

It was not until after Pratt's peremptory dismissal in 1904 that the four-posted brick entrance (which still exists today) built by his successor, William Mercer, on the west side of the campus, became acknowledged as the main gate of the school (fig. 15). Facing down what was now called Pratt Avenue toward the Harrisburg road, its quadruple, brick, orb-topped pillars, on occasions flanked by two Indian guards, heralded vehicular and pedestrian entry to the Carlisle Indian School. This was a very different kind of gateway. Its construction signaled acknowledgment of the primacy of the new western entrance, a reconstellation of the campus, and also overt rejection of the assimilationist philosophy Pratt had so resolutely espoused.

The new gate faced away from the town and out toward the farmlands of North Middleton County. While the philosophical and geographic center of gravity of the school had been progressively pulling in that direction, Pratt's departure and the erection of this gate marked the end of an era. Just a few years later, the construction of the Leupp Indian Art Studio, beside the new entrance gate, clarified for visitors the Carlisle Indian Industrial School's redefined mission.[25] In this studio, Indian students were taught traditional arts and crafts. Visitors were allowed to watch the classes and invited to buy Indian-made crafts and trinkets. The campaign to "transform" Indians into equal citizens, always so controversial and compromised, had now been abandoned in favor of a strategy of "improvement" and acceptance of separate levels of development. This was a scheme that was neither worrying nor threatening and allowed the school openly to proclaim its existence and inscribe its doorway on the landscape. The double gate, with two pathways leading from it into the campus, stood as a brick and iron statement of this new policy.[26]

A Cherokee student, graduating from Carlisle in 1912, obliquely reveals that she had read the subtext inscribed in this new school gate. Anna Melton's article, published in the *Carlisle Arrow*, conforms to the prescribed upbeat tone of all the school's publications. Yet her romanticized description of the campus incorporates a veiled critical appraisal of Carlisle's purpose and an indirect acknowledgment of the compromised nature of its mission:

> At first glance this picture seems composed of little else than imposing entrances, colonial buildings, winding paths, velvet grass, flower beds everywhere. . . . Viewing it more in detail, one sees that there are two entrances to the campus, one on the south and the other on the west side; the latter is the main entrance marked by two imposing pillars of brick and limestone, each finished with a wrought iron bracket upon which is fastened a handsome black lantern. From this entrance branch two paths, the one to the right is a beautiful road made especially for the sightseers who come to look at the beauties of the campus; while the one at the left is a plain concrete walk which leads up to the buildings. . . . The [former] of the two roads winds up through the campus; and, on each side of it is an avenue of trees, conspicuous among which is an aged walnut tree which stands more stately than the others and a little apart from them as though it thought itself better than they.[27]

When "viewed in more detail," not only do we learn from Melton about the Carlisle campus' two entrances, but also that anyone entering by the new main gate is made to choose between two alternative paths.[28] In describing the two paths, Melton informs us of the separation of Indians and non-Indians that occurs at the school's entrance and also introduces the notion of assumed superiority. She describes the "walnut tree, which stands . . . a little apart from [the others] as though it thought itself better than they" and then explicitly locates it on the "beautiful road." Her writing is rosy in tone, and she paints "a gorgeous picture never to be forgotten." Yet Anna Melton obliquely reveals that she has read the subtext inscribed on the landscape and layout of the school: Indians and non-Indians were expected to travel two different paths. Leading the reader up the concrete path toward the buildings of the campus, on reaching "the long, low building which attracts attention," she hastily retreats from her acute descriptive metaphor into the language of romanticism. She insists that "this ivy-covered building reminds one of a picture of an old English church" and neglects altogether to tell the reader that underneath this ivy cladding lies the plain, functional Carlisle laundry building.[29] As Anna Melton attempted to negotiate her own passageway between personal truth and prescribed doctrine, the conspicuous rupture between her expressive style and her message means that her pointed commentary constantly undercuts her sentimental writing. Her short piece allows us a rare, momentary glimpse of one student's pointed evaluation of the racial division of space on the Carlisle campus and her cogent understanding of how this reflected concealed white purposes.

Anna Melton was just one of a handful of students who left behind a firsthand record of how she felt about her school experience. A few white-educated Indians published accounts of their school days that provide invaluable insights, but these were the most articulate and confident and almost all wrote with the perspective of hindsight.[30] Recently, interviews with survivors have shed new light on how white-educated Indians lived and subsequently came to view their school years, but representatives from the first generations of children sent away to school are no longer with us to tell their stories.[31] A written response, such as the one left behind by Anna Melton, gives a rare glimpse of one individual's assessment of Carlisle. From later reports in Carlisle's paper it appears that she made good use of her Carlisle education and returned to Oklahoma to become a teacher in a rural school.[32] But thousands of other children who passed through the Carlisle campus returned to their reservation homes leaving no written trace of their stay or their subsequent lives. Only occasionally can the raw and immediate experience of Carlisle's children and young adults be unearthed and extracted from the propaganda of the school's publications, which were so vital an element in Carlisle's publicity machine.

8. Man-on-the-Bandstand:
Surveillance, Concealment, and Resistance

WINNING AND HOLDING the support of white Americans was always essential to the survival of Carlisle. Just three months after the school was founded, under a succession of different names, a school newspaper began rolling off the Indian school presses in a continuous stream: *Eadle Keatah Toh*, the *Morning Star*, the *Red Man*, the *Red Man and Helper*, the *Arrow*, the *Carlisle Arrow*, and ultimately the *Carlisle Arrow and Red Man*. Between 1909 and 1917, there was also a monthly periodical that initially called itself the *Indian Craftsman* but then changed its name to the *Red Man* in 1910—this merged with the *Carlisle Arrow* in 1917. These periodicals were the public voice of Carlisle, which sought to inform whites about the goals, activities and achievements of the school.

Beginning in 1885, a second, smaller, weekly four-page newspaper also began production at the school. Published every week until 1900, in the guise of a school magazine, the *Indian Helper* reported events, handed out admonitions and advice, printed letters, and documented the activities of staff and students. Although strictly censored, the pages of the *Indian Helper* carry a detailed record of everyday life at the school. They provide the fullest available documentation of the minutiae of daily interactions at Carlisle between white educators and the children they sought to transform. When the propagandized version of events relayed by the *Indian Helper* is closely interrogated within the physical context of the school, it reveals a previously indiscernible narrative, with telling details about how the "civilizing" campaign was conducted and also evidence that deepens our understanding of the children's responses.

Indian Helper
The *Indian Helper* was a more modest publication than Carlisle's main newspaper, and it made clear in both its title and subtitle, the *Indian*

Helper: FOR OUR INDIAN BOYS AND GIRLS, that its targeted audience was the Indian children themselves. Students at the school, children who had gone "out" to work for families in the Pennsylvania area, and a growing body of Carlisle-educated Indians who had returned to their reservation homes were the paper's main readers. White supporters of the Carlisle Indian School, including many children, were also eagerly courted and added to the list. Readers paid twenty-five cents for an annual subscription, and their numbers peaked at twelve thousand in 1898.

Articles and stories carried in the *Indian Helper* were slanted, sanitized, and clearly subjected to strict editorial control. Information about the paper's editor is therefore essential to any understanding of how to read *it* as an historical source. But the identity of its editor was the *Indian Helper*'s most baffling characteristic. Each week a notice on the second page announced: "The INDIAN HELPER is PRINTED by Indian boys, but EDITED by The-man-on-the-band-stand, who is NOT an Indian."[1]

This anonymous, invisible, white, male persona brazenly located himself on the school bandstand, claiming it as both home and editorial site. From here he watched the children and commented on their activities. To understand his purpose and the relationship he tried to cultivate with the children through the pages of the *Indian Helper*, it is necessary, once again, to look closely at the buildings and grounds of the Carlisle campus and at the bandstand in particular.

The *Indian Helper* was consciously woven into the very fabric of the Carlisle Indian School. Analysis of the interplay that was fostered between this publication and the physical environment of the campus lays bare some of the daily detail of Carlisle's oppressive program as well as the covert responses of some of the children. It allows us to witness the intense level of scrutiny to which the children were subjected as they went about their daily lives. This mimicked and parodied a system of surveillance pioneered in prisons and was intrinsic to Carlisle's mission to destroy native cultures. The Man-on-the-bandstand, who combined characteristics of God, Uncle Sam, and grandfather with those of prison officer, spy, and dirty old man, was created as an active component in Carlisle's program, working to substitute *his* creed and code for values and beliefs the children had learned at home. When interrogated within the physical context of its production, the pages of the *Indian Helper* disclose some of the ploys and strategies the children used on a day-to-day basis to withstand the force of Carlisle's mission.

For fifteen years, no one besides the Man-on-the-bandstand claimed editorship of the *Indian Helper*. From his bandstand in the middle of the school grounds, this "man" supposedly watched the children, eavesdropped on their conversations, and then reported and spoke out in the pages of the *Indian Helper*. Sometimes he would analyze or critique an issue, but he did not restrict himself to a traditional editorial column. His preferred style was to interject his comments and opinions all through the paper, briefly but unexpectedly, in little homilies and asides: "How nicely the girls go through with their gymnastic drill!! They must not forget to stand as erect when out of class as they do when exercising."[2]

His attention focused always on the children. Few things about their dress, deportment, manners, physical appearance, or behavior escaped his comment. Interspersed among commonplace school news, the minutiae of their lives were described and placed on public display. The children were his subjects, observed and reported on, as well as his exhibits demonstrating the success of the educational experiment. All-seeing, all-hearing but selectively revealing, in the columns of the *Indian Helper* this imaginary persona strutted across the pages that allowed for his construction: a commanding, authoritative, omnipotent, but illusory presence. Powerful but illusive, nothing about the Man-on-the-bandstand was straightforward or stable. Every week in the *Indian Helper* there was a "Puzzle Corner," with conundrums, enigma, and riddles for readers to solve. Placed at the end of the paper, it appeared to be the Man-on-the-bandstand's signature, because the biggest, ongoing mystery was the question of his identity.

The Man-on-the-Bandstand

Who was this invisible, ubiquitous, unnamed, and secretive Man-on-the-bandstand, and what was his function in a school ostensibly committed to helping Indian children find a place in American society? For readers living far from Carlisle or with few links to the school, the identity of the Man-on-the-bandstand remained a perpetual puzzle and their letters, printed in the *Indian Helper*, were used to further this sense of mystery. Reporting that "a little girl in Iowa would like to know what we mean by the Man-on-the-band-stand," he confided, "That is what a great many people would like to know, but that is the Man-on-the-band-stand's own secret."[3] Ten years later he was a little more forthcoming but equally cryptic in answer to the same question, explaining, "The Man-on-the-band-stand is the NEWS personified."[4] But anyone who lived and worked at the school or spoke to the Indian boys who worked at the Print Shop was well aware that for twenty-five years supervision of all school publications lay in the hands of the white woman who ran the print shop and lived in the teachers' building, which stood just fifteen yards from the bandstand: Miss Marianna Burgess. So was Marianna Burgess the Man-on-the-bandstand? This question was posed directly one week and then answered negatively, in a section of the *Indian Helper* called "Question Box":

Q. Who is the Man-on-the-band-stand? Is it Miss Burgess? L. D.

ANS. The Man-on-the-band-stand is the editor of the INDIAN HELPER, who sees *everything*, but does not print all he sees. The Man-on-the-band-stand is not Miss Burgess.[5]

This answer was confusing, but it contains a truth. One week, when Burgess was away from the school, she teasingly revealed to readers of the *Indian Helper* the part she regularly played in the production of the paper as well as her intimate association with the Man-on-the-bandstand: "the Indian printer boys received many deserved compliments on last week's HELPER which they issued in the absence of the Man-on-the-bandstand's chief. The old man *thought* they would do well if they tried."[6]

Marianna Burgess shared his initials, M. B., and she played on this in the paper. Her relationship to the M.O.T.B.S., as he was often called in the *Indian Helper*, was intense, complicated, and shifting. She generally described herself as his chief clerk. On occasions, however, a Mrs. M.O.T.B.S. was mentioned, with the suggestive implication that this was Burgess. It was certainly she who constructed his multiple personalities and developed his voice. He was her creature. In the pages of the *Indian Helper*, where she created, paraded, operated, played, and flirted with him, we find her delighting in his power, ambiguity, and numerous roles. Through him she attempted to control, intimidate, and manipulate the children, and from behind the safety of his undetectable façade, she claimed the freedom to report, uncensored, her own version of all that went on in the school. He allowed her to live a secret, vicarious life. But although she might wield the editorial hand, call herself his chief clerk, and constantly energized the mystery surrounding his identity, Burgess and the Man-on-the-bandstand were not one and the same person. The Man-on-the-bandstand was a constructed persona, claiming more ubiquity and power than Marianna Burgess could ever hope for.

The *Indian Helper*, like the Carlisle Indian School, was under Pratt's authority. Pratt's army uniform, which he often sported going about his duties at Carlisle, was a constant reminder of the source of his authority.[7] On occasions, Pratt would position himself on the bandstand in the middle of the campus, where he could see and be seen (fig. 16). Although he was not the Man-on-the-bandstand, Pratt's imposing six-foot high figure, silhouetted on the bandstand, gave a shadowy reality to this imaginary man, and Pratt's presence at Carlisle was essential to the Man-on-the-bandstand's existence. Pratt had been seconded from the U.S. Army and War Department, and behind him and the campaign to expunge native cultures stood the full apparatus of the American state.

Pratt's so-called Florida boys were ex-prisoners, and some of the other children enrolled at Carlisle—those from Geronimo's band and individuals such as Kesetta Roosevelt—were officially classified as prisoners-of-war during their time at the school. The majority might not strictly have been prisoners, but they were hostages to their parents' good behavior out west, subjects of an educational experiment approved, bolstered, and financed by the federal government. It is within this power structure that the *Indian Helper* and the persona of the Man-on-the-bandstand have to be configured. This constellation of power transformed what might have been only an imaginary, laughable, chameleon-like editorial voice into a sinister and threatening force.

The Man-on-the-bandstand's traffic in enigmas, evasions, and secrecy cloaked a monstrous power game. He claimed, as he frequently reminded his readers, to be unknowable (like God!) and chided them for believing otherwise. "How smart some people think they are when

16. Richard Henry Pratt on the bandstand with newly arrived Navaho students. Photograph by J. N. Choate. Reproduced with permission of Cumberland County Historical Society, Carlisle PA. BS-CH-009a.

they are sure they know all about the Man-on-the-band-stand!" "The fact is," he continued, "no one but the old man himself knows anything about him, except that he tells the truth."[8] Reveling in his own mystery, he gave away tantalizing hints and tips about his identity, teasing and tormenting his readers. Perhaps the most bizarre was a small diagrammatic drawing of a face, published under the heading:

THE MAN ON THE BAND-STAND

WOULD LIKE TO KNOW

Who took this picture of him.[9]

The picture was meaningless, an apparently harmless enigmatic joke. But within the context of the Carlisle Indian School it carried a hidden, ominous message about power and visibility. This supposed "photograph" of the Man-on-the-bandstand divulged nothing about its alleged subject. The mocking request, "The Man-on-the-band-stand would like to know who took this picture of him," suggests indignation that someone might have caught a glimpse of him and even had the audacity to take a photograph. The sketched lines of this diagrammatic cipher, however, teasingly confirmed his identity as both unknowable and invisible. By contrast, every feature of the children and their new American identities were regularly exhibited in the many photographs taken by local photographer J. N. Choate.

Photographs were one of the main weapons in the armory of the Indian School.[10] The *Indian Helper* was one of the vehicles by which they reached the outside world. Repeatedly offered for sale or handed out to readers in exchange for securing subscriptions to the paper, these photographs of the children presented them scrubbed, dressed, arranged and displayed for the public eye. While close-up photographic images of the Indian children, the products of Carlisle's civilization program, were paraded for all to examine, an enigmatic drawing was all that was seen of the Man-on-the-bandstand. It was a mask for his shifting and multiple personalities and a mocking boast about his invisible and indecipherable power. In the pages of the *Indian Helper*, the Man-on-the-bandstand repeatedly bragged that he could see all that went on. Indeed, a short-lived publication called the *Indian Boys' and Girls' Friend*, which predated the *Indian Helper* and can be seen as its precursor, was allegedly edited by a Mr. SeeAll. Alongside his editorial name, Mr. SeeAll's picture depicts the full-length profile of a diminutive, bald man, dressed in a dark suit and peering though a telescope. He is standing on one set of giant binoculars while beside him a second set, positioned like a pair of cannons, is trained on his line of vision. Readers are informed: "Mr. SeeAll is old and not pretty, but when he looks through his glass, Oh My! He can even look into the minds of people and tell what they are thinking about!"[11] But the *Indian Boys' and Girls' Friend* only survived for two issues. When the *Indian Helper* took its place, it is significant that Mr. SeeAll had disappeared from the front cover. From the less visible recesses of the second page and with no accompanying portrait, the Man-on-the-bandstand now claimed the editorial role.[12]

The Bandstand

The layout of the school buildings provides an important key to understanding the purposes of the Man-on-the-bandstand, who was always referring to his physical presence on the Carlisle campus. When one Indian subscriber allegedly asked, "Will you please explain why you are called the 'Man-on-the-band-stand?'," the answer came back: "If the questioner were at Carlisle, he would know why. The Band-stand commands the whole situation. From it he can see all the quarters, the printing office, the chapel, the grounds, everything and everybody, all the girls and the boys on the walks, at the windows, everywhere. Nothing escapes the Man-on-the-band-stand. . . . Already he sees into the homes of the boys and girls who go out upon the farms."[13]

Situated at the symbolic as well as architectural hub of Carlisle, the bandstand commanded panoramic views of the whole school, but its full potential for voyeurism was realized only when it was made the permanent "home" of an invisible, vigilant observer.

When Pratt took over the Carlisle Barracks the bandstand already stood in the middle of the parade ground, overgrown with bushes and in a dilapidated state.[14] Pratt ordered it renovated and painted, making it a feature that commanded not just the parade ground, but the whole school.[15] As chapter 7 shows, in the early years the Carlisle buildings lay along three sides of a quadrangle surrounding the bandstand. To the east side, the two-storied, double-verandahed house of the superintendent faced in a straight line across the parade ground, past the flagpole, looking directly up the bandstand steps.[16] To the north lay the girls' dormitory, the boys' quarters, and the industrial shops. On the southern side of the quadrangle stood the teachers' house and the school building, and in the far southeast corner, the low, stone guardhouse, with its four, dank, prison cells. Only the western boundary of the quadrangle lay open when the Carlisle Indian School was first established and, as we have seen, Pratt sealed this off by constructing the school's three-story dining hall.[17] The high school buildings and the seven-foot fence surrounding the whole campus meant that the children could not look out, but any one standing on the bandstand's raised, covered platform was afforded a panoramic view of the whole school. He could as easily oversee the children at meal times, gaze through the windows of the girls' rooms, or stare at the heavy, grilled door, behind which Indian boys suffered their punishments in solitary confinement.[18]

When not stationed at his post, the Man-on-the-bandstand led his readers to believe that he moved unseen among the children, observing their activities and eavesdropping on their conversations. He could drop in, undetected on any event, innocent or otherwise. In fact the more apparently innocent his visitations the more menacing they feel: "The Man-on-the-band-stand pricked up his ears when he heard strains of music on Friday evening. Then looking toward the sewing room, and seeing a bright light shining through the window, he stepped over to see what might be going on. . . . He stole in so quietly that no-one saw or heard him."[19]

Sometimes he singled out individual children, although he did not always name them. On these occasions, he described his view from the bandstand and movements around the grounds in such minutiae that they could be tied to specific people and events: "The Man-on-the-bandstand sometimes looks right over the dining-hall. If he should tell the girls' names who do some very silly things back there, they might be ashamed."[20] Not only was he spying and eavesdropping, he also recruited the children as informants: "Some one whispered in the ear of the Man-on-the-band-stand that if he had taken a peep into the Teacher's Club kitchen he would have seen Carrie Cornelius working faithfully."[21]

When good behavior was reported, the implication was that bad would be too. From his privileged vantage point, the Man-on-the-bandstand observed, reported, and discussed the lives of Indian children while they attended the school, and then, when they left Carlisle, using the *Indian Helper* and the U.S. postal services, he followed them back to their reservation homes. His location at the center of the school transformed an innocent bandstand into an inspection tower. Had he been a silent observer, his presence might have been disturbing but unthreatening. His ability to publish his sightings made the Man-on-the-bandstand menacing.

Today it is impossible to imagine the Man-on-the-bandstand stationed at his post without being reminded of both the design and purpose of Jeremy Bentham's panopticon.[22] Bentham envisioned a radical new method for simultaneously punishing and reforming prisoners and went further, suggesting that asylums, factories, workhouses, and even schools could also be successfully run using the same plan and principle. In *Panopticon* (1791), he presented his design for this innovative penitentiary, where order would be maintained without resort to physical violence, surveillance and recorded evidence being substituted for force.

Fundamental to Bentham's design was the inspection tower, constructed at the center, from where the subduing gaze of authority would look out and observe the prisoners in the tiered cells organized around it. The prisoner could not see into the tower, but under the ever-vigilant eye of a superior power that watched and recorded his every move, he was compelled to examine his conscience, acknowledge his guilt, and mend his ways.[23] This was a surveillance more intrusive than mere policing. It regulated, but it also demanded an inner change in the prisoner, enlisting him in the enactment of his own transformation. Although the tower might not be occupied full-time, its physical presence would create the impression of continuous surveillance.[24] For Bentham, the beauty of his panopticon lay in the multipurpose potential of its design: "Morals reformed," "health preserved," "industry invigorated," and "instruction diffused": "public burdens lightened . . . all by a simple idea of Architecture."[25] In England, Bentham's twenty-year campaign to construct a panopticon penitentiary failed, but he had provided prison architects with a design deemed capable of promoting discipline through surveillance.

In the United States, when the Eastern State Penitentiary opened on the outskirts of Philadelphia in 1821, its debt to Bentham was obvious, and it became internationally acknowledged as a landmark experiment in reform, building technology, and prison architecture. Here Bentham's concept of surveillance as an instrument to induce order and penitence merged with Quaker ideas about institutional reform and criminal behavior, a merger represented in the rows of cells that radiated out from the central tower at Eastern State Pentitentiary. Alexis de Toqueville in 1831 and Charles Dickens in 1842 were just two among thousands of tourists (peaking at ten thousand in 1858) who felt drawn to climb the inspection tower to witness "the Pennsylvania System" at work. Toward the end of the century, between 1877 and 1894, an expanding prison population prompted a series of additions to be made to the original construction. By this time, the system was foundering and had been subjected to widespread condemnation for its inhumanity. But over a million people had visited the central tower, and many more knew what it looked like from the photographs of William and Frederick Langenheim.[26] Bentham's' panopticon had become a commonly known and widely understood mechanism.[27]

Two hundred miles from Philadelphia's pioneering prison, the Indian School in Carlisle represented a later and more circumscribed reform movement than the one that inspired the penitentiary. The movement to educate the Indian was a more modest, low-profile experiment in social change, accompanied by no grand architectural scheme. Although Carlisle supplied the blueprint for a system of government Indian schools, the school was set up in a dilapidated, disused barracks, not a special, tailor-built edifice. Yet the task of civilizing Indian children, as projected by reformers, shared something in common with earlier schemes to reform prisoners: both relied for their success on the subject imbibing a new morality. To experience the demanded inner transformation, Indian students, like prisoners, were required to participate in the process of their own correction and consciously reject their previous lifestyle and behavior. At Carlisle, no carefully crafted inspection tower looked out over the pupils, but in the pages of the *Indian Helper* the bandstand was commandeered to perform this function.

Before the Carlisle Barracks were handed over to Pratt, they had been used by the U. S. Army to train young cavalry recruits to fight Indian tribes out west. At this time, the bandstand seemed a commonplace, innocuous structure and a far cry from the inspection tower we have been discussing.[28] Its location in the middle of the parade ground reflected its social and musical functions and carried no ominous connotations. When the Indian School took over the barracks, the bandstand retained its innocent demeanor. But, by a series of ingenious strategies, this inoffensive gazebo was converted into an inspection tower, claiming greater potency than Bentham ever dreamed of and powers more diverse than those enforced at Eastern State Penitentiary. The invention of an invisible man, who made the bandstand his home and watched the children continuously from its raised platform, turned this roofed structure into a quasi-inspection tower. Unlike Bentham's panopticon, the bandstand's architecture did not immediately declare its purpose. To the uninformed eye, it still looked like a pretty, pagoda-shaped bandstand. To anyone made aware of its unseen resident and his reports in the *Indian Helper*, its open-sided, octagonal shape and elevated platform could never look the same again.

This "inhabited" bandstand was perfectly equipped for both visual and auditory surveillance. Bentham, in his first version of the panopticon, had planned to supplement visual surveillance with a parallel system of acoustic surveillance that would be made possible by a system of pipes leading from the prisoners' cells to the central tower. The difficulties of ensuring that sound only traveled in one direction, thereby preventing the prisoners from listening to the inspectors, had forced Bentham to abandon this part of his scheme.[29] Bentham, when designing his panopticon, was bound by the constraints of real life. For the Man-on-the-bandstand, who resided in a world of fantasy and make-believe, issues of feasibility imposed no such limits. Capable of single-handedly maintaining his constant vigil from the center of the school, he also claimed the power to *listen* to the children. In him the voyeuristic, eavesdropping powers of the panopticon reached new phantasmagoric heights, which he flagged and indulged in the *Indian Helper* in a column entitled, "What I See and Hear." Although supposedly living on the bandstand in the center of the school, he also trumpeted his ability to step down from his home to spy on the children wherever they might be. He could mingle unseen among them on the grounds, prowl through the classrooms and dormitories, or gatecrash a school picnic undetected. To understand the Man-on-the-bandstand's claim to possess special powers, we need to turn our attention both to the particular historical and social circumstances that allowed for his creation and to ongoing life at Carlisle. Here it is the differences between Bentham's prisoners and Carlisle's Indian children that is instructive.

While neither Bentham nor the Philadelphia Quakers ever doubted that the gaze of authority, directed from the panopticon onto the prisoner, possessed the power to induce guilt and contrition, this was a supposition rooted in a Christian notion of conscience and the individual soul. Many Indian children did not share this Christian cosmology. Despite wide differences in their separate tribal cultures, they had grown up in societies where community and kinship lay at the core of all definitions of good. For them, the concept of individual salvation or damnation was completely alien because their lives were inseparable from those of family and kin. The gaze of authority, as envisaged by Bentham, might be able to intimidate them, but it would fail to trigger the personal remorse and guilt deemed essential for inner transformation. At the Carlisle Indian School, therefore, inspection would have little effect unless it was accompanied by an interpretive voice that was able to furnish this inner narrative for Indian children. In the pages of the *Indian Helper*, the Man-on-the-bandstand labored to outline and impose this narrative in its daily detail and nurture the values and guilt of Christian conscience.

The Voice of the Man-on-the-Bandstand

For the Man-on-the-bandstand to command genuine authority, it was necessary not only that he speak from a position of power but also that the Indian children concede him that power when they responded to his voice in the pages of the *Indian Helper*. Although he worked to furnish the children with an inner voice of conscience, he could never be sure that this would not be drowned out by older, deeper, Indian voices. To understand this process, it is helpful to consider Louis Althusser's doctrine of interpellation. Althusser proposes that a subject can come into being as a consequence of language and that his existence is always shaped by that language. To demonstrate his theory he stages a social scene in which a subject is hailed by an officer of the law with the words "Hey, you!" The subject turns around and in so doing, accepts the terms by which he or she is hailed. For our purposes, the officer of the law should be taken to be our old friend, the Man-on-the-bandstand, who hails his subjects in the pages of the *Indian Helper*. Althusser, to illustrate the power of ideology to constitute subjects, has recourse to the example of the divine voice that names, and in naming, brings its subject into being. The "voice" of interpellation is figured as a voice almost impossible to refuse because it is derived from God's voice. It is here that we find the weakness in Althusser's theory, which is also the key to understanding the compromised power of this "voice" of interpellation and therefore of the Man-on-the-bandstand. Althusser presupposes an unelaborated doctrine of conscience, which accounts for the subject's readiness to accept guilt to gain a purchase on identity. Althusser's subject is both open and vulnerable and feels compelled to turn when hailed by the voice of interpellation. But what of the subject who carried within him/her no such predisposition? What of Indian School children who, despite their Christian baptisms at Carlisle churches, still knew and answered to different gods? One of the fundamental tasks of the Man-on-the-bandstand was to work to instill in each and every Carlisle pupil that inner voice of conscience.

In the aching silence experienced by every far-from-home child, where the voices of grandfathers and elders should have been heard, the Man-on-the-bandstand sought to make his own voice resound. He wanted to subvert loyalties as well as values. Through innumerable references to the school, to staff, to individual children, and to the activities of Carlisle alumni, he strove to create a new "imagined community" of educated Indians, with Carlisle at its center.[30] He tried to draw the children into a world no longer shared by elders and relations. Reading the *Indian Helper*, whether at school, on "outing," or back home on the reservation was meant to provide a link between each subscriber, Carlisle, the Man-on-the-bandstand, and a broad-based Indian world very different from the one embraced by tribal affiliation. At this level, the Man-on-the-bandstand struggled ingeniously and consistently to further the goals of the Carlisle Indian School. To achieve his purpose, his voice was as vital as his gaze.

Voice, of course, was the Man-on-the-bandstand's only tangible feature. Or to be more accurate, voices, because his shifting personality was echoed in the numerous different voices he used to address the children in the pages of the *Indian Helper*. He would abandon his posture of authority, step down from his bandstand, and assume a variety of different persona as he moved among the children, matching these identities with the range of styles and voices that simultaneously created them. But where a subject stands, what identity it there assumes and by what values it is marked, makes a political difference, and for this reason the Man-on-the-bandstand always made clear that at the drop of a hat he could climb back into his stand and reclaim the voice of authority.[31]

When not asserting his authority, he claimed the right to a dizzying array of personalities and voices.

Sometimes he gave counsel, like a wise grandfather, pointing out the children's frailties as Indians and suggesting the best way for them to live their lives: "Horace Greeley's advice to the young white man was, 'Go west, young man!' but the advice of the Man-on-the-bandstand to all *Indian* young men who have had but little experience in caring for themselves, is 'Stay *east*, young man,' till you get *strong* in experience."[32]

Often sounding like a Horatio Alger novel, he lectured them from his podium about the proper conduct and manners necessary for achieving success in America: "The Man-on-the-band-stand would like to hear the pupils say, 'Yes, sir,' and 'No, sir,' every time when they answer a gentleman. Politeness goes a long way with a person wishing to make a success in life."[33] Employing instructive and slightly threatening tones, he could assume the role of school monitor and outline or reiterate the school rules: "The Man-on-the-band-stand would like to see all our workers present at morning services."[34] When giving praise and approval to reinforce the lessons of "civilization" taught at Carlisle, he could sound like a patronizing uncle: "The girls are buying rugs for their rooms when they have a little spare cash and the Man-on-the-band-stand is pleased to see the bright, cheery and home like effect it has upon their rooms."[35] Just as easily, in the semblance of a disappointed parent, he could single out students for humiliation or embarrassment. On one occasion it was one of "his" own printer boys who was the focus of his attention and "his" bandstand that was used as the site of punishment: "The Man-on-the-band-stand felt so disgraced and ashamed when one of his clerks was placed on the band-stand for punishment last Sabath [*sic*] that he could not hold his head up."[36] Using wheedling and insinuating tones, he also invited the children to inform on their compatriots when they left Carlisle and returned to their reservation homes: "Let the boys and girls who go home, write to the Man-on-the-band-stand something about what our other pupils are doing who returned before."[37] He could become sulky, petulant, and sorry for himself over small, banal incidents and sound like a spoiled child excluded from the party or a demanding geriatric denied his whim: "Miss Phillips gave each of her friends a beautiful colored Easter egg on Sunday. The Man-on-the-band-stand was left out again, but he doesn't like eggs anyhow."[38]

When speaking in this voice, he would attempt to solicit the children's sympathy instead of admonishing them. Indulging in an exploitative, obvious reversal of the balance of power, he demanded that they nurture and care for him, bring him presents, and acknowledge his stoicism in staying on his bandstand in all weathers.[39] An equally dramatic change of style took place when the Man-on-the-bandstand moved openly into fantasy. Always located in a realm of semi-make-believe, when he became privy to the thoughts of Father Christmas or struck up conversations with fairies, the world of whimsy he inhabited progressed one stage further in its mix of the weird and infantile: "The Man-on-the-band-stand stood for a few moments with closed eyes, one warm day this week, and as he was thus apparently in deep thought, a little fairy came along and called out to him, 'Grandpa, what are you thinking about?'"[40]

In soft, intimate tones a world apart from his booming voice of authority, the Man-on-the-bandstand told the fairy a story, a fable of Christian morality. Whether cajoling, persuading, hectoring, or instructing, he incessantly alerted the children to how they should behave and what they should become. He was almost always indefatigably upbeat, particularly when his focus moved from the children to their physical environment and his delight in improvements and physical changes to the campus. He detailed the construction of buildings, the laying of paths, and the introduction of modern conveniences such as lighting and steam central heating.

But in all his portrayals of the Carlisle campus, the Man-on-the-bandstand assiduously avoided any description of the cemetery and its extending lines of gravestones.[41] Nearly a hundred children died at the school during its first decade. Single-line reports of their deaths appear in the *Indian Helper*, disconcertingly intermingled with news about the social activities of staff and pupils. During a period when children were dying weekly and a large number were lying sick in the school hospital, the Man-on-the-bandstand took the unprecedented step of addressing the subject directly.[42] In buoyant tones he recommended willpower as a means of recovery, instructing the children to:

Will yourself to get well!

Many people cure themselves of sickness now by using their WILL power. It is easy to die if we just give up to all our pains and aches and think we are more sick than we really are.[43]

Even sickness and death were converted into grist for his moralizing, educational mill.

The Man-on-the-bandstand could, as we have seen, veer between different moods and voices: from congratulatory to instructional, from teasing to critical, from open to secretive, and from friendly to sinister. When much of the *Indian Helper*'s readership was in the process of acquiring both literacy and the English language, the Man-on-the-bandstand's antics inevitably generated some bewilderment. It was hardly surprising to learn that, "Somebody asks, 'Is the man-on-the-bandstand you speak of a real person?'" Predictably, the answer given was both unenlightening and enigmatic. "Perhaps he is, perhaps he is not, we will leave you to guess that conundrum."[44]

The Children and the Man-on-the-Bandstand

During the years when the Man-on-the-bandstand was up to his tricks, approximately five thousand children passed through the Carlisle Indian School. It is difficult to assess how the majority responded when so much in their lives was new and terrifying. Was the Man-on-the-bandstand an intimidating presence haunting the campus? Did they find him menacing? Were they confused by his various guises? Or could they disregard him and dismiss his games as the silly pastime of a batty white woman? On one occasion Marianna Burgess published a letter that clearly titillated her. An Apache girl, Nellie Carey, had been savvy enough to join Burgess in her game and addressed a letter to her as "Mrs. M.O.T.B.S." before quickly and jokingly correcting herself and referring to "the Man-on-the-band-stand's Chief Clerk."[45] Examples of sophisticated engagements with the Man-on-the-bandstand such as this are rare. Nevertheless, his antics in the *Indian Helper* furnish us with a wealth of covert information about the children's response to Carlisle and its program.

Often this is reported as wrangles between him and the children. For a number of weeks these focused on the children's marching and their refusal to keep time with the piano as they left the school chapel. Although an apparently small thing, in the pages of the *Indian Helper* the Man-on-the-bandstand returns to it again and again, while at the chapel the children persist in their rebellion. The boys are worse than the girls, the Man-on-the-bandstand notes disdainfully, reminding them that it is the boys who benefit from the most drilling! Week after week he mocks and tut-tuts, giving verbal tuition. "We can't learn to be soldiers till we learn to march to music. Right foot on accentuated note looks rather funny."[46] The boys were clearly having fun; their public show of insubordination gave them a small opportunity for revolt in an area deemed of key importance in a military school.

A similar wrangle erupted over the children's refusal to keep off the grass and stay on the straight paths that crisscrossed the campus. Sometimes he tried to put the frighteners on them, warning how wet feet would lead to pneumonia and death.[47] More often, he gave a detailed description of the "crime." On this occasion, it is the lines of desire and defiance the children had, quite literally, stamped onto the face of the campus: "The attention of the Man-on-the-band-stand has been called by one in authority to two paths that are being worn across the grass plot in the shop court, by people who are too indifferent to go around. One is across the center from center door to center door, and the other is a short cut to the dining room and town. Come! Come!"[48]

Encapsulated in his constant complaints and lists of infractions is a revealing record of the many different ways the children found to flout the rules or oppose the school. Marching out of time, walking on the grass, going barefoot, stealing apples, spilling whitewash on the croquet lawn, or chipping paint off the bandstand were fairly minor infractions. "Talking Indian" was considered more serious. The habitual Saturday ritual of uncovering and identifying those who had offended was designed to shame the so-called offenders. Regularly reported by the Man-on-the-bandstand, it also provides a detailed record both of the children's determination to speak their own languages and the failure of Carlisle's boasted English-only policy.

In the pages of the *Indian Helper*, one of the schools most serious and persistent problems, runaways, went almost unmentioned. Runaways plagued the authorities at Carlisle. If students were caught and brought back, they were punished by being locked in the guardhouse.[49] The gravity of the problem was such that the Man-on-the-bandstand only dared approach this problem indirectly. One week he told, "A True Story of Three Indians Lads Who Tried Running Away from School." Although he named the boys—Ben Stumpfoot, Harry Shortneck, and Ed Buffalo Horn—he reassured readers that they were not from Carlisle. They had attended a western school in a previous decade. The story was told for a moral rather than informative purpose, because these boys reportedly ended up not in the guardhouse, but with frostbite.[50] At many different levels, individuals, as well as groups of children, challenged the proprieties of the school and actively as well as passively resisted the program of civilization. The most serious of their offenses were ignored or referred to obliquely, but nevertheless, in the pages of the *Indian Helper*, we are given dozens of details about the many tiny and ingenious ways the children invented to thwart school authority.

On occasions, the children's acts of resistance and rebellion engaged the American legal system. We learn, for example, that "Disciplinarian Thompson spent Tuesday in Harrisburg attending Federal court in the settling of liquor cases." This makes it plain that Carlisle pupils have been in trouble with the law, having gone several stages further than pilfering apples. Serious crimes, like theft and arson, brought trials and prison sentences, accompanied by detailed coverage in the local press. When two girls, Fanny Eaglehorn (Oglala Lakota) and Lizzie Flanders (Menominee), tried to burn down the girls' building twice in the same evening, they were caught, put on trial, convicted of arson, and sentenced to eighteen months in the famous Eastern State Penitentiary in Philadelphia. The Man-on-the-bandstand could not turn a blind eye to such a public offense and the *Indian Helper* gave a full description of their crime. Readers learned how the two girls had first set fire to papers in the reading room after supper on a dark Sunday evening in November.[51] Then, after this blaze was discovered, they secretly climbed to the top floor of the girls' building and lit a second fire in a clothes closet, while the rest of the school attended chapel. This fire was also detected, and the girls were caught. In relating a story that so obviously reflected badly on Carlisle, the Man-on-the-bandstand focused not on the crime, but on the speed and efficiency of the school's firefighting force. Yet in detailing their actions, he had also inadvertently exposed the planning and determination that accompanied Fanny Eaglehorn and Lizzie Flanders's attempt to burn down their dormitory. Rarely discussed publicly, arson was a common occurrence at all Indian Schools and one of the most dramatic ways the children found to express their resistance.[52] The Man-on-the-bandstand condemned the girls, insisting they "had a bad record before they came and have been stubborn and ugly ever since they arrived, no amount of kindness shown them having any effect." For this, he blamed the depravity of their home life.[53]

Always at his harshest when discussing the children's traditional histories and cultures, the Man-on-the-bandstand missed few opportunities to teach the master narrative of U.S. history. At a school debate on the motion "Whether or not the treatment of the Indians by the early settlers caused King Philip to war," Marianna Burgess was one of the three judges who, predictably, decided that "the best argument was on the negative side."[54] In the pages of the *Indian Helper*, all aspects of the children's home lives were constantly vilified. After a trip to Dakota, Burgess even felt qualified to stage a conversation with the Man-on-the-bandstand to discuss the filth she saw and infer the immorality lying behind it:

M.O.T.B.S: "Did you really find the Indians so filthy as you would have us believe from you last letter?"

M.B. "Yes, indeed! Why if I should describe the worst things I saw you would not allow such a letter to be published in your little paper."[55]

Yet despite all efforts to quash the children's cultures and denigrate their home lives, it was clear these could be expunged from neither their memories nor their hearts. Their letters, poems, and stories printed in the *Indian Helper* often reveal a message quite different from the one the Man-on the-bandstand wished to convey. Published to demonstrate how they profited from and endorsed Carlisle's program, they often carried another, covert message. In an English class a Lakota boy, Frank Lock, wrote a letter that the Man-on-the-bandstand entitled "Exchanging Books for Ponies." While ostensibly about his new aptitude with books, the boy's memories of his life in Dakota as well as his respect for the elders whose values he is supposed to be rejecting, shine through in his letter to a friend back home:

> I am enjoying the fair weather here and the good time, but often thought of the old places, where we have had lots of fun in training and lasso-ing young ponies and how we were often unhorsed, and how we used to set traps to catch foxes and wolves and how we would go to fish and search bird nests and how we used to come home with big hearts, having plenty of game and how we made old folks happy, how I used to try to have my ponies run faster than yours, and how we tried to have fat ponies; but I have now adopted the school books as my po-nies, and so if I desire to have my books run fast, I study them harder and there is no doubt that you can't beat me in that race.[56]

The energy and detail of the early writing belies the message carried in the last two lines. Despite rigorous policing and the watchful eye of the Man-on-the-bandstand, the children's pleasure and attachment to their home lives and values could not be totally suppressed, even in the pages of the *Indian Helper*.

Indian schools faced their greatest challenge when the children returned to their reservations. Critics of the educational experiment spearheaded by Carlisle constantly reported that when students went home, they re-verted to traditional ways and "went back to the blanket." Although Carlisle encouraged its students to stay in the east, the vast majority re-turned to their reservation homes. In an attempt to maintain a hold over these returnees, remind them of the standards and values taught by Car-lisle, and counteract the influence of their families and communities, the *Indian Helper* was sent west to thousands of reservation homes. Going one step further, in 1891 Marianna Burgess published a little book en-titled, *Stiya: A Carlisle Indian Girl at Home*.[57]

The Portable Bandstand

Written in the first person, *Stiya* is ostensibly the story of a Pueblo girl's return home and her courageous efforts to live the lessons learned at Carlisle. Burgess had been on an extensive visit to the Pueblo Indians and utilized the information and observations she had collected on this trip to denigrate the homes, dress, and all aspects of Pueblo life. Burgess portrays Stiya as disgusted by the meanness of her home and the filth and superstition that pervaded it and describes her homecoming as traumatic, not joyful:

> Was I as glad to see them as I thought I would be?
> I must confess that instead I was shocked and surprised at the sight that met my eyes.
> "*My* father? *My* mother?" cried I desperately within. "No, never!" I thought, and I actually turned my back upon them.
> I had forgotten that home Indians had such grimy faces.
> I had forgotten that my mother's hair always looked as though it had never seen a comb . . . .
> I rushed frantically into the arms of my *school*-mother, who had taken me home.[58]

Burgess anticipated the situations a returning student would encounter and then wrote the script for how they should respond. She appropriated their experiences and emotions in a deliberate attempt to manage and direct them both. The voice of the Man-on-the-bandstand might be able to command and even commiserate, but his was the male voice of white authority, emanating always from his bandstand and located far away in Carlisle. In the voice of Stiya, female, intimate, guileless, and fresh, Burgess sought a way to bring the Carlisle message closer to home using a very different messenger. By purportedly identifying and empathizing with a Pueblo girl, she claimed the opportunity to speak as an Indian, from inside Pueblo society.

The story told in *Stiya* first appeared in the *Indian Helper*. Beginning in September 1889, a weekly article entitled "How an Indian Girl Might Tell Her Own Story if She Had the Chance" was given the Man-on-the-bandstand's "signature of veracity": "The facts as given below are known by the Man-on-the-band-stand to be true, the experience is similar to that of many an Indian girl whom he knows about."[59]

In this serialized version, the Pueblo girl is called Mollie. When Burgess published the same story as a book, she decided to change her heroine's name to something more unusual, explaining, "We have a little Stiya with us at present and use her name because it strikes our fancy."[60] The photographic studio portrait on the frontispiece shows a young woman who is clearly Indian, but she is presented wearing a long sleeved, waisted, buttoned-to-the-neck dress, typical of the times, and she is leaning on the back of an ornate Victorian chair. Depicted as indistinguishable from a respectable lady, the caption reads "STIYA, CARLISLE INDIAN GIRL." It is a familiar depiction of transformation, but in this case, "Stiya" has been robbed of more than her tribal identity. The picture shown is not of Stiya Kowacura, the Pueblo girl whose name Burgess had fancied and taken. It is a photograph of an Apache woman, Lucy Tsinah, who also happened to be one of the few married students at Carlisle.[61] So, in the first two pages of her book, Burgess demonstrated a total disregard for the separate identities as well as tribal distinctiveness of the two girls she amalgamated and collapsed the identities of two individual women from two different tribes. Sold for fifty cents through the pages of the *Indian Helper, Stiya* was carried home by many returning students and sent out to reservations across the United States. This was the closest Burgess could come to creating a portable bandstand, capable of carrying Carlisle's message back to the children's homes.

Stiya, Laguna Pueblo author Leslie Marmon Silko tells us, provoked "the only big quarrel my great grandmother ever had with her daughter-in-law, Aunt Susie." These two Pueblo women were in complete agreement about the offensive nature of the book's contents. Their intense feelings centered instead on what its fate should be. Aunt Susie thought the defamatory text should be preserved as "important evidence of the lies, racism, and bad faith of the U.S. Government with the Pueblo people." Grandma A'mooh thought the book should be burned, "just as witchcraft paraphernalia is destroyed." The story of this family row was passed down orally through three generations of Silko's family. Written down and first published in 1994, it gives us a unique glimpse of two Pueblo women's impassioned response to Marianna Burgess's written words in her "portable bandstand" and to the campaign to crush Indian cultures.[62]

Pratt always claimed that his school would accomplish its task in a single generation. After twenty years, with thousands of Indian children corralled in boarding schools and the "Indian Problem" apparently unsolved, both government and public began to question the rationale and expense of this experiment. In response, on July 13, 1900,

Pratt absorbed the *Indian Helper* into the *Red Man*. This larger, widely distributed, weekly publication did not include the day-to-day detail of school life the *Indian Helper* had contained but instead took on the task of publicly defending Carlisle. The Man-on-the-bandstand did not disappear, but he was restricted to a single column, "The Man-on-the-band-stand's Domain." Denied the freedom to strut and roam all over the paper, he became less expansive, speaking in short paragraphs and terse one-liners.[63]

Changing Indian policy, combined with Pratt's cavalier attitude to the Bureau of Indian Affairs in Washington, soon provoked a crisis at Carlisle. On June 11, 1904, the War Department sent a letter relieving Pratt of his duties as superintendent of the Carlisle Indian School and appointing William A. Mercer of the Seventh Cavalry to take his place, effective June 30. The extent of the disaster was signaled in the diminished size and thickness of the *Red Man and Helper* published on June 17, which measured less than half its normal dimensions and printed Pratt's letter of dismissal on the front page. That week, on page 3 of this shrunken paper, the Man-on-the-bandstand filled a column with insignificant news. It was his final appearance. Without farewells, he unceremoniously vanished. The next two editions of the *Red Man and Helper* were merged in a bumper edition, publishing a full account of Pratt's defense of his position. The following week, the *Red Man and Helper* announced the arrival of Captain William A. Mercer and a section entitled "Miscellaneous" took the place of "The Man-on-the-band-stand's Domain." The Carlisle Indian School was very obviously "under new management" and this was the last *Red Man and Helper*; a notice informed readers the paper would resume publication as the *Arrow*, after taking "a vacation for a brief period."[64] The *Arrow* was a very far cry from the old *Indian Helper*. Commercially funded, its huge pages were peppered throughout with local advertisements.[65] The contrived intimacy of Burgess's "imagined community" of Carlisle-educated Indians had entirely disappeared and with it, all the mundane details of everyday life at Carlisle.

Nevertheless, archival copies of the *Indian Helper* carry an enduring record of fifteen years of life at the Carlisle Indian School. If we focus our gaze beyond the paper's propaganda and read it within the physical context of Carlisle, it is possible to reconstruct aspects of day-to-day life and uncover fragments that tell us about the children who lived and worked at the school. The paper carries a slanted but living record, whereas at the Carlisle Barracks, only names on gravestones in the cemetery furnish surviving physical evidence of the children's erstwhile presence at the Indian School.

9. Indian School Cemetery: Telling Remains

IT IS STILL POSSIBLE TO visit the school cemetery and read the names on nearly two hundred identical markers standing in six, neat rows. The small, well-kept, rectangular graveyard faces out onto the main road, beside the back entrance to the U.S. Army War College in Carlisle. A metal plaque, screwed onto a boulder standing beside the little wrought iron entrance gate, informs visitors that this is an "Indian Cemetery." Smaller writing underneath gives a fragment of the cemetery's history: "Buried here are the Indians who died while attending the Carlisle Indian School (1879–1918). The original Indian Cemetery was located to the rear of the grandstand on Indian Field. In 1931 the graves were transferred to this site."

This snippet of the cemetery's history makes clear that the original graves have been moved. Interrogation of the history of the site reveals not only removal but hidden patterns and reverberations of racial exclusion, segregation, erasure, and appropriation. These echo and amplify those we have already seen in the organization and layout of the school campus.

In his stringent analysis of how history is inscribed on the landscape by plaques and monuments, *Lies Across America*, James W. Loewen admits to avoiding cemeteries, because he believes that although tombstones can convey biography they rarely reflect civic discourse.[1] At Carlisle, the mute record carried by the school cemetery reaches beyond the realm of both biography and civic discourse. This surviving remnant of the campus bears witness to the thousands of Indian children, from nations across the United States, who were enrolled in Carlisle's assimilation program and stands as a tangible link to individual children who lived at the school but never went home. At the same time, it is also the surviving physical manifestation of a white discourse about race and dispossession. Exploration of the racial politics that governed burial patterns at the Carlisle Indian School lays bare the processes by which dead Indian children, and the land they occupied, became indivisible from the construction and inscription of a national, racial identity.

The Carlisle cemetery carries an account of the school's history not found in the official record but that can be pieced together from a range of sources. Among the hundreds of photographs commissioned by Pratt to publicize the children's advance from savagery to civilization and chart the growth and improvement of the campus, there is no single surviving photograph of the old cemetery, and it is likely that none was ever taken.[2] It is only possible to discover where it was sited on the campus by scrutinizing surveys (drawn up to facilitate the laying of the borough sewer) and engineering maps made by the U.S. Army. From these it is possible to locate the cemetery at the northern extremity of the campus and chart its expansion, from a small triangular shape to a large rhombus. Such white-made records were created for practical not public purposes, yet if they are closely examined, they reveal previously undisclosed evidence not only about the cemetery's location but also about the school's burial practices.[3] Shrouded from public view, the history of the cemetery is central to understanding the history of the school and its contribution to national racial definition.

Not all the children who died while in the East are buried in the cemetery. Those who died while working on local farms during the summer, or on longer "outing" placements, were often not brought back for burial at the school. Although little research has been done on this topic, we can assume that across Pennsylvania and beyond, small local cemeteries hold the remains of children from the Indian School (we trace the story of one such child in chapter 10). Many more children were sent home to die. Indeed, as the high death rate at Carlisle became a subject of fierce criticism, Pratt very deliberately started to send sick and dying children back to die in their communities. In 1881, fourteen were "returned to homes on account of sickness," and in 1885 thirty-six "on account of failing health or mental weakness."[4] Yet the lengthening lines of gravestones in the school cemetery to the north of the campus provide evidence of far more than the tragically high death rate among Carlisle's Indian children. The very existence of this cemetery contradicts the school's declared mission to assimilate Indian children into white society.

Spatial Politics of Burial

The dead Indian is and has always been an alluring trope. Spirits of dead Indians haunt the literature as well as psyches of white Americans.[5] Decisions about where dead Indians should be laid to rest, what ceremonies should accompany their burial, how and whether they should be memorialized, and whether they had a right to "rest in peace" were inseparable from the ongoing geopolitical campaign to seize Indians lands and expunge Indian cultures. Interrogation of these processes exposes the dynamic and interconnected role played by white land claims and constructions of race in the creation, demarcation, segregation, obliteration, and reorganization of spaces for the dead. Such analyses make it possible to understand patterns of burial, as well as disputes over interment, as physical and symbolic contests about property, power, racial privileges, and status. The spaces that are given to the dead are, as Philippe Ariès reminds us, "the identifying mark of a culture."[6]

Land lies at the hub of Indian-white relations. In the United States, Pennsylvania holds a lustrous reputation for having treated the colony's Indian tribes fairly and commendably in land negotiations. Yet even in this apparently exemplary state, all Indian lands had been progressively and systematically incorporated into the white body politic by the end of the eighteenth century, and Indian negotiators' pleas that the Indians be allowed to hold onto diminutive tracts had been overridden. By the mid-eighteenth century, whites controlled both government and lands. Then suddenly and unexpectedly, in nineteenth-century Pennsylvania, a new Indian "demand" for land was asserted: children who died at the Carlisle Indian School required burial.

Through interment, the dead make claims on the land. The need to lay a body to rest in a small plot has a quotidian familiarity that often veils its political and historical specificity. The United States came into being at a time of significant change in social and political consciousness. This was matched by a critical shift in attitudes toward personal mortality in both Europe and America. The new individualism brought "an enhancement of the sense of self-value" and a new emphasis on commemoration and memorialization of the dead. A prosperous and self-confident wealthy class that surrounded itself in the trappings of luxurious domesticity in life also sought to stretch its power and influence beyond the grave. France, sharing republican ideological roots with the United States, was at the forefront of the movement. In 1784 all the ancient city graveyards in Paris were closed and the accumulated bones of centuries removed to outlying quarries, which became catacombs. The clear link between contemporary politics and burial practices was made obvious when, "the year following this mass clearance of the human debris of the ancien régime, the storming of the Bastille signaled a start to clearing away the ancien régime itself." Three, new, extensive landscaped cemeteries were built outside the city walls to offer burial space for the recent dead. The most famous was Père Lachaise, where grand avenues and serpentine walks offered the Parisian bourgeoisie a consciously Elysian setting in which to purchase plots for family monuments and mausolea. This cemetery's success rested on its economics as much as its aesthetics. For the first time, burial was not in the control of church authorities; anyone with money could invest in a plot of land for perpetual memorialization. Though the property owner might be mortal, the fact as well as the display of ownership was eternal.[7]

Père Lachaise gradually became the economic and aesthetic model for cemeteries across Europe and America. Many American towns opened new leafy, landscaped cemeteries on their perimeters, the most famous being Mount Auburn outside Boston. Americans had no need to contest the powers of an established church, but these privately owned premises offered a welcome solution to the problems of overcrowding and public health. Simultaneously, and significantly for the argument here, they provided a site where prominent local families and individuals could purchase plots on which to build imposing monuments to undyingly confirm their wealth, status, and racial exclusivity.

In Carlisle, Pennsylvania, the new Ashland Cemetery on the eastern perimeter of the town was one such site. Ashland gave the Boslers, the Hendersons, and other prominent families the opportunity to invest in well-situated burial plots. Through the economics, and, as we shall see, the racial politics of interment, their social and political identities became strengthened and, quite literally, permanently built into the landscape. Death became a potent means to assert physical and symbolic property rights, as well as to legitimate spatially and visually personhood and power. Poorer members of the white community were not excluded, but they had to satisfy themselves with smaller, less prominent plots. African Americans were specifically banned from Ashland. To the north of the city, Carlisle's small black population continued to bury its dead in a diminutive, intensely used area.[8] Well-entrenched social-racial hierarchies thus determined not only who should be buried where and how, but they also ensured acceptance of these class- and race-determined practices. In Carlisle, Indians were not yet included in this racial division of space. The founding of an Indian School in the midst of this confident and well-established town presented an interment problem no one had anticipated. Its solution would expose and confirm firmly established patterns of racial segregation, openly position Indians on the nation's chromatic scale, and physically inscribe on the landscape their nonwhite status.

Racial Politics of Burial

Less than seven weeks after the initial group of Indian students had been brought to Carlisle, the first child died at the school.[9] Local press accounts and records of St. John's Episcopal church confirm that before the body of Amos LaFromboise, a thirteen-year old Sioux Indian boy from Sisseton Agency, Dakota, was taken to Ashland Cemetery there was a service at the Indian school. Following prayers at the graveside with the Rev. W. C. Leverett officiating, he was buried in the government-owned plot.[10]

To school superintendent Captain Richard Henry Pratt, Ashland must have appeared an obvious and convenient place to inter the child. The cemetery lay in Carlisle's East Ward, just a mile south of the school.[11] The government had purchased a 540-by-32-foot plot in December 1865. It lay along the western perimeter of the cemetery on what became known as United States Avenue. Here, five hundred unknown veterans of the Battle of Gettysburg had been buried in a huge trench grave.[12] A dozen veterans lay under individual stones at the opposite end of the government site. In the central area, over fifty burial sites remained vacant.[13]

Possibly there were murmurings and disquiet among the local population about this Indian burial on a site used by Carlisle's elite. Certainly, Pratt was very keen to gain official endorsement for his action. The day after the Sioux boy was laid to rest in Ashland Cemetery, Pratt wrote to the War Department requesting "to be informed whether the Burial Ground at that place is available for the interment of Indian youth who may die while attending that school." His enquiry initiated a flurry of correspondence between the quartermaster general, the adjutant general, the judge advocate general, and the secretary of war, all of who displayed some confusion and, between them, took more than two months to arrive at a decision. To begin with, the adjutant general was not sure whether Indian children *could* be buried at Ashland Cemetery and wrote to the quartermaster general: "It seems not to be allowed in the deed. Whether interment of red men would violate the grant or no, I am not able to decide. Possibly the Executive would make a new deed covering the case. The War Department should not object, unless it endangers its property rights."[14]

Adjutant General Townsend's initial wavering and unsteadiness points to the high degree of ambiguity surrounding this issue and the need for interpretation of existing legal documents. He airs the possibility of drawing up a new deed but is quite explicit that the property rights of the War Department should not be endangered, thus signaling that property ownership was an important factor in the decision-making process. Ultimately, however, the judgment handed down rested on a clear racial designation and a positive answer to the question of "whether interment of red men would violate the grant or no." The judge advocate general was called on to make the final decision, and he informed the War Department that "The deed in this case conveys to the United States the 'exclusive and entire right of interment and sepulture' in a certain burial lot of the Ashland Cemetery in said Carlisle, 'to have and to hold'—as it is added—'for the burial of such *White persons*' as the grantee may admit to be buried there: In my judgment these last words constitute a *condition* annexed to the grant, that the premises shall be used for the burial of White persons only; and I have therefore to express the opinion that the interment therein of an Indian would not be legally authorized."[15]

This judge's definitive interpretation of a preexisting deed reflected and furthered a racial definition of Indians. In the judgment he handed down, not only were Indians constructed as nonwhite, but even in death they were forced into segregation. This recapitulated existing black/white patterns of cemetery spatial use and embraced Indians in an all-too-familiar racial attribution of space. While the adjutant general had raised the possibility of creating "a new deed," the judge advocate general chose instead to rule out this possibility and focus his decision on a clause added to the original deed, limiting burial in Ashland to "White persons." Indian children, who had been brought to Carlisle to be instructed how to live like whites, were now legally barred from lying alongside them in death and were openly categorized as nonwhite.

History of the School Cemetery
In Washington, government discussions of this case had been dragging on for more than two months, when, in Carlisle, a second Indian boy at the school died. This time, Pratt did not organize a burial in Ashland Cemetery. Instead, the Cheyenne boy (who had been renamed Abe Lincoln) was buried in a plot of open farmland to the north of the campus, close to an area marked "Old Burial Ground" on historic maps of Carlisle Barracks. When Pratt later received word that "under the grant the U.S. cannot inter *Indians* in . . . Ashland Cemetery," it seems clear that he had the body of the Sioux boy buried in Ashland disinterred and then reburied at the school because records of the cemetery include his name.[16] On the cemetery plot map, Amos LaFromboise lies alongside the Cheyenne boy, Abe Lincoln. The Carlisle Indian School now had its own discrete, segregated cemetery. A judgment about the Indian's nonwhite racial identity had been built into the contours of an institution dedicated to educating Indian children to join white society. Nevertheless, Pratt used burials and the design and layout of this cemetery to further his Americanizing program, subsuming the bodies of the dead within the school's purposes.

The children were all interred with Christian prayers and laid to rest in an east-west position, according to Christian tradition. While it could never match the landscaped glories of Ashland, efforts were made to beautify the school cemetery, and the school children were recruited into American practices of mourning and commemoration. The *Indian Helper* noted that "girls are raising funds for the decoration of school graves . . . and are contemplating buying rosebushes and other growing plants for the school cemetery."[17] There is no evidence that any Indian families or community members were ever present at interments or that they were allowed to carry out their own traditional ceremonies. The extensive range of nations on Carlisle's enrollment list meant that practices surrounding death in the children's home communities varied enormously. To Pratt this was irrelevant. He signed a contract with Ewings, a local firm of undertakers, to deal with all the practicalities of death, according to white values.[18]

The graves of the children were made to resemble those of whites. Identical rectangular headstones extended in an ever-growing line, scoring the landscape with a sad record of the Native American diaspora Carlisle had precipitated. Eight stones the first year, ten more the next, and ninety-six within the first decade.[19] Each stone gave name, nation, and age. Its location in the cemetery recorded the chronology of death—Lakota lay beside Cheyenne, Ponca next to Pueblo, Kiowa alongside Wichita, in an intertribal pattern that scrambled the children's geographies, histories, and backgrounds. The cemetery stood as the physical manifestation of a composite, monolithic white-created Indian identity. Yet it also accurately bore witness to the children's recent pasts: their multitribal schooling at Carlisle and, in death, their exclusion, as Indians from the white society they were being trained to emulate and join.

Eight surviving stones from the cemetery, which together span burials between 1883 and 1900, suggest that during the Pratt years the children were all memorialized with identical markers.[20] Only one stone was different. No marker in this cemetery more powerfully conveyed the complex racial anomaly represented by this site and the intensification of an individual's social and racial status in death than "the stone of gray granite . . . erected by the Young Men's Christian Association" at the grave of Thomas Marshall, a little more than a year after his death.[21] This stone will be examined in closer detail below, but fully to appreciate its significance, we need to know more about the life of Thomas Marshall.

Thomas Marshall

A talented Lakota from Pine Ridge, Marshall arrived in Carlisle in 1895, not to become a student of the Indian School but to join Dickinson Preparatory School. From here he would progress even further, matriculating as an undergraduate in Latin and Science at Dickinson College and winning an entrance prize in his freshman year. To support himself at Dickinson, he lived at the Indian School where he worked in the storehouse as janitor and then, in his junior year, as tutor in charge of the small boys' dormitory.[22] His intellectual and personal qualities had been evident to white teachers from his early years. After he graduated in 1894 from White's Manual Labor Institute in Wabash, Indiana, the superintendent of this Quaker institution, O. H. Bales, immediately began to seek funds to enable Thomas Marshall to continue his education. This was no easy task, because a deepening resistance to giving any support to Indians who sought education beyond the elementary level was developing among officials in Washington. In a letter to Superintendent of Indian Schools William Hailman, Bales detailed Marshall's academic and personal qualities and talents:

> He will have completed Rhetoric, Algebra, and three books of Caesar's Commentaries by the last of June, having taken in thoroughly the lower branches in their order. At odd times he has acquired a useful proficiency in shorthand and type-writing. He studied Book-keeping, and showed, during two months of responsible charge of our Account Books and office work, a remarkable aptness and application of the principles. He is a good bass singer, performs well on various brass instruments, and renders organ voluntaries with fine effect.

Bales went out of his way to convince the superintendent that his own support for Marshall was less to do with the young man's Indian status than "on account of his worthiness, superior natural ability, integrity, and attainments." The school superintendent concluded by noting that, even though "all his early associations were among the Sioux Indians. . . . He is however, to all appearance, Caucasian."[23] Bales deemed Marshall's supposed non-Indian, or "white," physiognomy not only worthy of mention, but as an additional attribute, likely to qualify him for educational funding from the superintendent of Indian schools. In short, he suggested that Marshall should be given support because his combined abilities and looks meant that he could successfully "pass" in the white world.

Thomas Marshall's Carlisle student card records his Indian blood quotient as one quarter.[24] Whatever the accuracy of this information, it is clear that while at Dickinson, Marshall chose not to accentuate his Indian looks.[25] Yet he apparently carried his Indian identity with both ease and humor. In the Dickinson compilation of "Junior Statistics," individual undergraduates published pithy answers in response to a set of five questions. In his entry, Marshall playfully claimed and subverted white stereotypes of Indians: "Name: Thomas P. Marshall; Forte: Reserve; Past: In a Wigwam; Present: At the Indian School; Future: With his Squaw; Greatest Need: Less Modesty." The joke about "his squaw" had specific resonance, because Marshall was engaged to the Yankton Sioux writer and musician Zitkala-Ša (known also as Gertrude Simmons) who from 1897 to 1899 was a teacher at the Indian School.[26] Like Simmons, Thomas Marshall functioned effectively in the white world, although unlike her, he was a committed Christian. A leading light of the Indian School's YMCA, he acted as president and represented the school at national meetings. Marshall appears to have moved easily between the white-run Indian world of the Carlisle School and the white world of Dickinson College. In a photograph of the Dickinson class of 1900, he blends in unremarkably with his white classmates. But it was alongside Indian students that he would lie in death.

Thomas Marshall never graduated from Dickinson College. He died suddenly, on April 23, 1899, from a disease diagnosed as "malignant" or "black measles." Tellingly, it was his Indian home in Dakota that officials at the Indian School immediately identified as the source of the illness. Flying in the face of contemporary medical knowledge about the transmission of infectious diseases, an announcement in the *Indian Helper* was adamant that "He got the disease through a letter from home where two of his family have died recently of measles. The case is completely isolated, and we do not fear any epidemic." [27] The Indian School blamed a contaminated letter from Indian Country. The Dickinson College community was stunned by Thomas Marshall's sudden death. His class met to issue formal resolutions to express their grief and at a memorial service on the campus, Dickinson's president gave a eulogistic address.[28] Yet there was never any suggestion that he should be buried anywhere but in the Indian School cemetery. The serendipity of Thomas Marshall's date of death placed him beside an eighteen-year-old Cheyenne boy, in the second line of stones now extending across the graveyard.

The following year, however, the YMCA broke with Indian School practice when they erected a huge, granite headstone to memorialize Thomas Marshall, and in so doing signaled his special status, in a manner with which we have become familiar at Ashland. In height and mass this stone dwarfed the others, setting Marshall apart from his "Indian" neighbors. On it, the intertwined letters of "YMCA" publicized and commemorated the organization as well as Thomas Marshall's life. Unlike all the other stones in the cemetery, this one was graced with a year of birth as well as a year of death. But no mention was made of Marshall's Lakota origins; through this omission, the commemorations on his stone erased his Indian identity. Thomas Marshall's grave might easily have been mistaken for that of a white man, apart from its telltale location. In death, as in life, he had been made to "pass." On the side of the hillside that sloped northward from the blacksmith shop and other utilities toward the refuse dump, this huge granite boulder stood as both a commemorator of Thomas Marshall's life and as a monument to white insistence that Indians should resemble but remain separate from whites.[29]

The Indian Cemetery after the Closure of the School

In 1918, when the Carlisle Indian School was closed by the government, the buildings of the Carlisle Barracks were handed back to the U.S Army for wartime medical service as U.S. General Hospital Number 31. Two years later, an Army Medical Field Service School was opened at the post. Many of the buildings now occupied by the military had been constructed using Indian labor, some even paid for by the children's earnings. Now only the names, engraved on the surviving headstones in the school cemetery, provided a cryptic record of over ten thousand Indian children from across the United States who had lived, studied, and worked there for nearly forty years.

The medical school officially rejected this cemetery as a burial site because in the field medical school quartermaster's judgment, it was "solely an Indian Burial Ground."[30] Arrangements were therefore made for the post to use Ashland, where it was estimated that there was "sufficient room on the [government] plot to take care of the requirement of this station for years to come."[31] So the Indian cemetery rapidly fell into a state of disrepair.[32] Then, as the medical school grew, the graves were seen as an obstacle to the development of the post. In 1926, the commandant at the Carlisle Barracks, General Ireland, made an unofficial request to have "the Indian interments, now in the middle of Carlisle Reservation, gotten out of the way." Clearly unaware of the Indian cemetery's history, he suggested "the Government plot in Ashland Cemetery" as his site of preference to receive the remains.[33] His proposal stands as a reminder that, unlike those buried in Ashland, the Indians did not own the land on which they were interred; they had not bought permanence. Once again, forty-six years after the first denial, Indian children were refused burial in Ashland. This time the reasons had shifted: the decedents could not be buried in the government plot at Ashland because they had no "military, naval Marine Crop or Coast Guard Service," and more practically, it was noted that with only fifty unused burial sites available in the government plot, there was insufficient space to accommodate all the children's remains.[34] Insistent that "the future development of the post will require the site now used for the interment of the Indian dead," General Ireland secured permission to have the cemetery razed and "removed from the present site to the north-east limits of the reservation, or elsewhere."[35]

The "New" Indian Cemetery

The last student buried had not been in his grave a decade when work began to relocate the school cemetery to a small, rectangular plot, measuring 180 feet by 55 feet on the outer perimeter of the post.[36] Removal began as soon as permission was granted, in the July heat of 1927. The local newspaper gave an account of the work under a headline that highlighted not the Indian children but the unpleasantness of the task: "Removing Bodies of Carlisle Indians: Men at Army Post have Gruesome Job." Inaccurate facts about the cemetery were given. The first burial was erroneously dated 1882 and the cemetery's existence was attributed to Indian parents' absence of concern for their dead children. "When an Indian would die, he was buried in the Indian School graveyard, unless the remains of the student were claimed by relatives." The Indians' presence in Carlisle was given a benign explanation. "At one period there were 1,000 Indians here, wards of the nation, receiving an education." Only a few lines were given over to an erroneous, potted history of the school, with the bulk of the article, in a narrative of mystery and horror, supplying titillating details alongside ghoulish particulars about the state of the bodies:

> The excavators found a skull with a bullet hole in it. It was the skull of
> an Indian who committed suicide years ago while in Carlisle. He had
> been in poor health and it is believed grew despondent. Only a bit of
> flesh was found on one side of his body. All of the bodies disinterred
> so far are skeletons. Some of the clothing worn was found to be in a
> remarkably good state of preservation. Coffins crumbled when handled to any extent. A necktie and a pair of shoes were still in excellent
> condition. In one of the coffins was found a diamond ring. In one casket, which contained the body of a girl, the hair was separated from
> the skull, but it was of luxuriant growth and in good condition.[37]

In place of the old cemetery, a "building for officers' use and occupancy" was constructed.[38] The cemetery's relocation thus repeated an age-old pattern of Indian dispossession and the assertive inscription of white ownership on the landscape.

The transfer of the cemetery scrambled and erased part of the history of the school as well as a painful chapter in Indian-white relations shared by every tribe in the United States.[39] The original cemetery had grown up slowly, over forty years. Lying in five uneven-length rows, most of the deceased children had a standard headstone, although some of the later ones were given only wooden markers and a few were left unmarked.[40] Despite the absence of any photographs of the cemetery, studying a plot map drawn up at the time of removal in conjunction with the students' Carlisle record cards discloses the sequential pattern by which the cemetery grew from the middle. Four, long, parallel lines of graves stood on lands belonging to the original army post site that Pratt took over. A fifth short line of eight stones was added, at an acute angle to the first line. These were the last interments, standing on farm-land deeded to the school in 1887.[41]

When the cemetery was relocated, the chronology of the children's deaths was lost. Their remains were reburied in random order, to fit the neat, symmetrical pattern of the new space. None of the original standard-issue headstones accompanied the children. Instead, their new graves were marked with soldiers' stones. Two miles down the road, at Ash-land Cemetery, two different styles of stone had been used to mark the graves of Civil War veterans: one with a shield embossed on it and the other with a cross.[42] The Indian children were all given the stone with a cross. Standing in six, tight, even rows, these new, white, army-issue stones simultaneously cleansed, standardized, militarized and Christianized them. Only Thomas Marshall, his stone transported from the old cemetery to stand splendidly alone in the central plot, was permitted continuity in his memorialization. His stone proclaimed, in its grey granite and privileged position, the special status reconferred on him, although its cryptic engravings continued to pose perplexing questions about his identity and the basis for his interment in an Indian cemetery. Ironically, Marshall's unique stone was, and still remains, the single surviving visible feature connecting the new Indian cemetery to the original school burial ground.

Erasure and Appropriation

At the time of their deaths, none of the Indian children was a citizen of the United States, yet in burial most lost their Indian designations and were memorialized under recently acquired American names—Abe Lincoln, Henry Jones—or sometimes new "Christian" names coupled to translations of a parental name—Charles White Shield, James Fox-catcher. In the process of removing and remarking the cemetery, more of their fragile and changing identities was expunged and lost. The age of each individual, which had been etched on these stones, was omitted from the new markers. One effect of this was to reduce the poignant impact of so many young deaths. Nations, dates of death, and even new American names were often mistranscribed. A Lipan Apache boy (whose story we return to in chapter 10) was known at the school as Jack Mather, but his stone in the new cemetery reads "Jack Martha."[43] On the original stone of John Bull, who died of tuberculosis, aged fifteen, after spending little more than a year at Carlisle, his nation is spelled the traditional way, Gros Ventre; on his new marker the stone mason has carved "Grosvontre."[44] Margaret Edgar, from Acoma Pueblo, who died in August 1885 after just one year at the school, has no details at all on her stone, apart from her name.[45] Some of the dead children were "lost" altogether, so thirteen graves in the new cemetery were marked "unknown."[46] When the cemetery was removed, "several graves containing bodies but unmarked were found and this accounts for unknown interments."[47]

The removal of the cemetery instigated other losses and confusions. The child listed as being buried in plot D12, on the chart of the old cemetery drawn up at the time of removal, is Sanson Novan, a Chiricahua Apache who was one of the children from Geronimo's band. Brought to Carlisle from Fort Marion in 1888, he died the following year, on March 9. Yet there is no stone for Sanson Novan in the new cemetery, and in plot D12, where the chart indicates he should have been buried, stands a stone marked with the single word "Earnest." Only one child named Ernest/Earnest is recorded as having been buried in the school cemetery. This was Earnest Knocks Off, son of Lakota chief White Thunder, of Rosebud Agency and one of the first children to arrive at the school. Earnest White Thunder begged to go home with Spotted Tail when the chief visited Carlisle. The chief was outraged by what he saw. He condemned Carlisle's military regime—the children's drilling, their "soldier uniforms," and his youngest son's incarceration in the guardhouse—and took all his children away.[48] Spotted Tail wanted to remove all the Sioux children, but was forbidden by officials in Washington. While his train was standing in the Carlisle station, the thirteen-year-old son of the other Brulé chief, White Thunder, stowed away, but he was discovered and forcibly taken back to the school. Prevented from leaving, he subsequently fell ill. According to a letter Pratt wrote to his father, Earnest was sent to the hospital, where he refused all medicine and food. He died on December 1880, at the age of thirteen, after just two months at Carlisle and was buried in plot D29 in the recently created school cemetery. The chart for the new cemetery records that Earnest was reinterred in plot C12 and indeed, on this site stands a stone, which reads, "Ernest, Son of Chief White Thunder, Sioux, December 14, 1880." It appears that Ernest White Thunder is memorialized twice in the new cemetery and, if this is the case, it is grimly ironic, because Luther Standing Bear, in his first autobiographical text, *My People, the Sioux*, writes that the boy's father made a specific request for a headstone, which Standing Bear claims was refused:

> Of course his father, Chief White Thunder, was very angry that he had not been notified that his son was even sick, and he stopped off at the school, en route to Washington, where he was going with the expectation of being appointed head chief at Rosebud Agency. White Thunder said he wanted the body of his son sent home, but if the authorities would not do that, they might at least place a headstone over his grave. Neither request was ever granted.[49]

That two headstones might have been erected for the same child reflects the disorder that must have accompanied the cemetery's removal.

In its new location, facing out onto Poorhouse Road, the school cemetery was far from the main site and unconnected even by a path to the Medical Field Service School. Conveniently out of the way, it could be ignored, until a row broke out between the Department of the Interior (holding jurisdiction over the Indians) and the War Department (holding jurisdiction over the Carlisle Barracks) over who was responsible for its maintenance. The dispute revolved around the issue of whether the Indian cemetery could be defined as a post cemetery by Army regulations because it contained no military personnel.[50] Once it had been officially determined that the military was indeed responsible for the cemetery's upkeep, it became the subject of a facelift and was reclaimed by the army. Wooden posts and a woven wire fence, used to mark the cemetery's boundary, were torn down and replaced by a concrete curb and wrought iron railings. Spare capacity was also identified, and the cemetery was now officially determined to be able to accommodate 229 bodies.[51] On January 21, 1935, the first non-Indian was buried in the new Indian cemetery; the infant son of an officer serving at the post.[52] Over the next thirty years, all burials were of whites. Their graves were marked with the same plain, white, cross-embossed, veteran-style stones that had been given to the dead Indian children. The transfigured Carlisle Indian School cemetery had been claimed and occupied by the U.S. Army.

Gradually, the remaining plots were filled, generally by infants and children of officers serving at the post, but occasionally a white adult was also given space. Staff Sergeant Bruno Verano from Pennsylvania, serving in the medical department, buried two sons in the cemetery in less than two years. When a few years later, in 1945, he, too, died, aged forty-two, he was buried in row F, close to his two sons. By this time, an arrangement had been made for military personnel who died at the Carlisle Barracks to be buried in Ashland Cemetery. But for Bruce Verano, the Indian Cemetery offered a way to perpetuate patriarchal family ties. The Veranos have the privilege of being the only family with two generations interred in the cemetery.

When, in 1951, the Carlisle Barracks became home to the U.S. Army War College, the campus rapidly expanded to fill the vacant lands of the whole military reservation and engulfed the Indian cemetery. A new road, linking the main campus to Poorhouse Road, meant that the cemetery now stood beside the busy back-gate entrance of the War College. To the outsider, it did not look out of place here because at first glance it so thoroughly resembled a military cemetery. Occasionally, Indian people who knew about Carlisle came to pay their respects.[53] But as the Indian children's presence in Carlisle receded into history, the cemetery became incorporated into a romanticized, sanitized, white version of events.

It became a site to commemorate Indian nobility and mourn tribal disappearance without confronting the problematic mission of the Carlisle Indian School. Staff and children from the barracks, as well as locals who visited the cemetery, often left trinkets and coins on the graves. On May 19, 1983, an eighty-one year old retired master sergeant, living in nearby Mechanicsburg, went one step further. He paid a visit to the adjutant at the barracks to gain permission to be buried in the cemetery. Clarence F. Barr who retired in 1946, had worked at the barracks for eighteen years doing a variety of jobs, including serving as a cook and working in the military police office. In his early years, he had been among the group of workers who assisted in moving the graves to their new site.[54] During the remainder of his time at Carlisle Barracks, he must have noted white burials taking place in the relocated cemetery. The last interment in the Indian cemetery had been in 1957. After that, for almost thirty years, all military personnel and their families had been buried at Ashland. Nevertheless, Clarence Barr was granted his wish. He died on August 23, 1984, and five days later the front page of the Harrisburg *Patriot* reported, "Retired Master Sgt. Clarence F. Barr was laid to rest with full military honors in the Indian Cemetery at Carlisle Barracks."[55] With this burial, the new Indian cemetery was declared closed. In August 2005, however, June Wagner Barr claimed her right to be buried alongside her husband, and her inscription was added to his stone. Clarence Barr's gravestone stood as a final marker of appropriation, a white, military man and his wife taking the last space.[56]

In one of history's symmetric ironies, a white man had chosen burial in an Indian cemetery originally established because an Indian could not be buried alongside whites. Barr's motivations for choosing an Indian cemetery as his final resting place must have been complex. Although he helped move the bodies of dead Indians, he had no connection with living Indians, having arrived at the Carlisle Barracks too late to see the Indian School in operation. His wife, however, is reported to have explained that, "He always liked Indians. He studied their ways. He read a lot about them." One of the local papers echoed this rationalization in its headline to the account of his funeral, which celebrated the fulfillment of his desire to be interred in the cemetery: "His Wish: Old Soldier Buried Among Friends."[57] By portraying the dead Indian children as Barr's "friends," the copywriter at the Harrisburg *Patriot* implied that Barr had established a connection, not with any of the real Indian children who had died while attending the government boarding school but rather with a noble and romantic notion of Indians. The journalist catalogued a dozen tribes—Apache, Sioux, Cheyenne, Paiute, Oneida, Washoe, Commanche, Shawnee, Seneca, Pawnee, Chippewa, Arapahoe—and copied some of the most "Indian-sounding" names from the headstones—Friend Bear, Dora Morning, Charles Whiteshield, Titus Deerhead, Herbert Littlehawk, Young Eagle, Percy Whitebear, Almeda Heavyhair, Nannie Little Robe. He used this exotic "evidence" to demonstrate how, through burial in the Indian cemetery, Barr had, quite literally, found his place among children whose "markers provid[ed] a directory of noble Indian heritage." This ultimate appropriation of Indian land, accompanied by a narrative of "playing Indian" at its most macabre, was of keen interest to the local community and Barr's funeral was given extensive coverage in the local press. It was the front-page story in the Harrisburg *Patriot* and a major news item inside the Carlisle *Sentinel*. The *Sentinel* published a page-wide photograph showing solemn and tearful relatives, sitting on fold-up chairs beside the open grave in the cemetery with the armed honor guard standing to attention behind. This spectacle of military esteem and family sorrow provided an unthreatening way for the local community to integrate the history of the Indian School into its own narrative. It served to displace attention from the Indian children and what had happened at the Carlisle Indian School and relocate it within the white community. It allowed an alleviating narrative, in which whites were seen to be the principle sufferers of grief and an old soldier's burial alongside his "comrades" was both a triumph for one man and a solemn but safe connection, across the years, to the days of the Indian School:

> Then taps sounded.
> The mournful notes sounded across the barracks grounds—all the way back to 1879.
> "It's what he always wanted," Mrs. Barr said.[58]

The significance of this funeral to Indian-white relations within the community was emphasized again fifteen years later. Plans for an Indian powwow, organized to honor the children who had been brought to Carlisle, prompted a past president of the Pennsylvania Poetry Society to suggest that the "festival," as he called it, might wish to use a poem he had written about the Barr funeral. The words of his poem made no reference to the assault on Indian cultures that the Indian School had championed but instead painted a rosy picture of unity between the two races. For many whites, the cemetery was not a place that encouraged grappling with a problematic past or acknowledgment of the existence of living descendants of the schoolchildren but instead provoked mournful nostalgia and a romanticizing of dead Indians.[59]

Unsurprising, therefore, an Indian ghost story emerged, with links to the cemetery. It offered whites a way to deal with the complex emotions and questions raised by the legacy of the Indian School and the existence of an Indian cemetery in their midst.[60] As Barbara Landis has shown, stories about the mischievous activities of an errant spirit started circulating in the 1970s. A Halloween-style haunting in one of the school's surviving buildings was persistently linked to Lucy Pretty Eagle, a Sioux girl who died at the school in 1884. Landis exposes many of the invented and inaccurate facts on which the story is based and tracks how it has been repeated and elaborated. She suggests that the Lucy Pretty Eagle ghost story continues to be retold because it offers a gripping yet trite way to address the existence of the Indian School while at the same time facilitating evasion of the many difficult aspects of its history. American literature is replete with spectral Native Americans and Renée Bergland has argued that they "function both as representations of national guilt and as triumphant agents of Americanization."[61] The Lucy Pretty Eagle ghost story can be seen to fulfill both these purposes with the added frisson that it is substantiated by the physical evidence of her grave. Entering the cemetery through its small gate and walking to the front so as to view the stones, Lucy Pretty Eagle's grave, located in the first row at the very front of the cemetery, is the first one the visitor sees, (row C, plot 21). The mass uniformity of all the stones means that, unlike in Ashland Cemetery, the eye is not drawn to any particular monument. In the Indian cemetery, it is location and wording that make individual markers conspicuous and with her prime site and sweet name, Lucy Pretty Eagle's is one of the most arresting; invariably, it has the most gifts of sweets and money laid on it and also a pair of sneakers.

Lucy Pretty Eagle might have been singled out for minor notoriety, but in the plot immediately behind her grave (row C, plot 1) stands a much less noticed stone adorned with few tokens of mourning. It marks the grave of Jack Mather (misengraved Jack Martha), whose connection to Carlisle was far more real and enduring than the one fabricated for Lucy Pretty Eagle. A Lipan Apache, who arrived at the school in 1880, Jack Mather died in February 1888, but his nephew would also attend the Carlisle Indian School from the age of four and then go on to live the whole of his life in the local Carlisle community (unaware that his uncle lay buried in the cemetery). Jack Mather's sister, Kesetta, also attended the school and became Carlisle's longest-enrolled student. The two children, Jack and Kesetta, had arrived at the school together, in 1880. While the cemetery's silent and telling exposure of the school's history cannot reveal the detail of their stories, an exploration of Kesetta's life carries an account of the Carlisle program and the federal campaign for Indian assimilation at its most extreme.

Modes of Cultural Survival

4

10. Kesetta: Memory and Recovery

KESETTA AND JACK SPENT their early days on the Texas-Mexico border. In 1877, their Lipan Apache band was attacked by Colonel Ranald Mackenzie's Fourth U.S. Cavalry, and almost everyone was massacred. But the two children hid and were afterward found by soldiers, who took them prisoner. From that moment, Kesetta and Jack lost contact with their people, and all links to their culture and their past were abruptly and permanently severed. Classified as "prisoners of war," they lived for a while with a military family, traveling between different forts in the West. When the Carlisle Indian School opened, Mackenzie sent the two Lipan Apache children to Pennsylvania to be enrolled as students. Neither of them ever returned home. Jack died of tuberculosis after seven years and, as already noted, was buried in the school cemetery. Kesetta, classified as a "prisoner of war" for the rest of her life, remained on Carlisle's student register until shortly before she died, at the age of thirty-nine.[1]

Kesetta appeared ideal material for Carlisle's experiment. She was already completely cut off from the influence of family and community; her culturally unencumbered status offered a perfect test case for a school intent on obliterating all traces of tribal past and training individual Indian children for absorption into mainstream America. Kesetta, however, did not shine nor achieve the high goals Pratt had set. Although she lived and worked in white society, her short life embodied the impact of Carlisle's program and the government's campaign of assimilation at its most total and brutal.

After her capture, Kesetta lived entirely within parameters defined by whites. The series of white-assigned last names she carried during her life—Smith, Lipan, Roosevelt—reflected and matched the deracinated existence forced on her. After just a few years in Carlisle's classrooms, she was sent on "outing" and spent her adult years working in a succession of white homes as a paid servant. She lived a larger proportion of her life in Pennsylvania and the surrounding area than in her native Southwest.[2] The Carlisle Indian School represented the most enduring continuity in her life. All ties to her Apache people had been forcibly cut, yet her continuing links to the Indian School signaled her uninterrupted white designation as Indian; this designation would persist down the generations, to be reinscribed on her half-white son. The trauma and rupture that characterized Kesetta's life meant that for her no resistance and only minimal autonomy was possible.

Yet on the other side of the continent, fighting for their physical and cultural survival, her people defied and withstood the fracture initiated by the U.S. Army when they had captured Kesetta and taken her east. Deliberately and secretly, down four generations, they kept her memory alive. For whites, the erasure of Kesetta's Indian identity was never complete. For the Lipan Apache, it never began.

From the moment their children were taken by the U.S. Army, the Lipan people desperately sought news and information about them, but they never heard from the children again and never found out where they had been taken.[3] During all the years Kesetta was registered at Carlisle, her people were in crisis. For decades they had struggled to confront the devastating power of the U.S. Army and defend their lands and lifestyle. Raids up and down the border and relentless assaults by troops meant that Lipan Apache numbers and power rapidly dwindled. Numbering several thousand at the beginning of the century, by the 1880s they had been reduced to a handful of bands with a few dozen members. Some clusters of Lipan pulled back over the border and merged with the populations of Texas and Mexico, and a small group moved onto the Mescalero Reservation in New Mexico. Shrunken in number, defeated, and subjugated, the Lipan Apache reluctantly adapted to the dominant power of the United States, but Jack and Kesetta's people had not forgotten their stolen children. The intensity of their loss, and the silence that followed, only served to deepen the memory.

Collusion between violence and silence can nurture the will to contest grand patterns and overall schemes of history, as Helena Pohlandt-McCormick has argued in her work on South Africa. In such cases, Poh-

landt-McCormick suggests, acts of speaking, or doing, can actively create what she describes as "landmarks of memory."[4] In the nineteenth
century, the Lipan Apache had neither the strength nor the will publicly to correct the larger American grand pattern of history, but they
did have the motivation and means to protect and secure their own. At
secret annual remembrances, they retold events surrounding the kid-
napping of their children, who became known as the "lost ones." Creating and progressively enforcing a "landmark of memory," they ensured that their people's knowledge of the children was kept alive and
passed down orally through four generations.[5] Among the Apache, the
only place it is believed appropriate to mention a lost family member's
name is family reunions. Secret and utterly private, the "hidden transcripts" of these family gatherings ensured that Jack and Kesetta, although never again seen by their own people, maintained their place
within Lipan collective memory.

Inevitably, the Lipan story of the children's lives ends at the moment
of their capture, yet fragments of their later years can be pieced together
from an assortment of disparate sources. Carlisle Indian School newspapers, supplemented by Carlisle records in the National Archives, yield
a patchy, brittle account, with little to suggest the children's feelings or
reactions. A letter that Jack sent to the school from his new home in
Florida gives a welcome human touch, but nowhere is there a record of
any words that Kesetta wrote or spoke. Kesetta is utterly silent. Yet despite this, her story can be recovered.[6] Although she left no written record of her life, she did leave a three-year-old son.

The birth of Kesetta's son ensured that the official and bureaucratic
record had to continue. It can be tracked through the Orphan's Court,
the accountant's rendering of her estate, and in her son's school reports
lodged at the Indian School. Kesetta's student file in the National Archives is thin, containing only her enrollment cards, but her son's file is
much bulkier and carries a wealth of information about both him and
his mother. Inevitably, the story it holds ends abruptly in 1918, when
the Carlisle Indian School was closed.

But Kesetta's son continued to live in the town of Carlisle. Oral histories, recorded in the 1980s, as well as recent interviews with townspeople, made it possible for her story to be carried forward into the pres-

ent day. Kesetta's great-niece was traced to Philadelphia and an internet search, to establish links with the Lipan Apache, led to the discovery of her great-great-nephew in Texas. The story they helped recover not only connected the bifurcated Texan and Pennsylvanian elements of Kesetta's life but also reunited the Lipan Apache with a kinswoman who had been lost to her people for 125 years.

Kesetta was born in about 1867 shortly after her small band, led by her father, Ramon Castro, had been forcibly moved to the newly established Fort Griffin, near Albany in Texas.[7] The Lipan Apache, or n'de tindi as they called themselves, were a small group of Easter Apache bands roaming across Texas and Mexico. Their numbers were by this time greatly reduced, after defending their lands and lifestyle against Spaniards, Mexicans, and Comanches. By the 1870s, their principal enemies had become American settlers, backed by cavalry stationed at numerous forts across the region. Fort Griffin was part of this new line of defense. Built to protect stage and mail lines as well as settlers, it provided a base for troops fighting to subdue the tribes of the southern plains.[8] The Lipan Apache based at the fort were considered prisoners of war, but, like the Kiowa and Comanche, they persisted in raiding the Texas frontier. A larger band, led by Juan Castro, had moved over the border into Mexico, from where they could raid with greater security.[9]

Colonel Ranald Slidell Mackenzie, who had earned a formidable reputation commanding cavalry during the Civil War, arrived on the Texas frontier in 1869 and took command of the Fourth Cavalry. Mackenzie would play a decisive role in the history of many Indian people, including Kesetta and her band. Ordered by President Grant to ignore Mexican sovereignty and strike the Indian villages lying south of the border at Remolino, on May 17, 1873, Mackenzie crossed the Rio Grande and attacked three villages under cover of darkness. Military historian Robert Wooster writes that "the action at Remolino was more akin to a massacre than a battle as the Indian warriors were away hunting when the attack occurred."[10] It was judged a bold success by the army.[11] By the Lipan Apache it was remembered forever as "the day of screams." Stories of the horrors of that night were passed down from generation to generation.[12] The screaming did not end there. Mackenzie and his troops crossed the Rio Grande repeatedly.[13] On one occasion, they followed Ramon Castro's small band. Having located his camp, they attacked, killing many Lipan Apache. After the assault, Castro discovered that his two young children had been taken prisoner by the soldiers.[14] For many years, desperate at this loss and what he interpreted as the deliberate theft of his children by the U.S. government to test his loyalty, his band continued to fight American troops ferociously. He never saw his children again.[15]

The children, a girl of about ten and a boy a few years younger, began a life with whites that was characterized by progressive rupture, loss, and movement. Now named Kesetta and Jack, for four years they traveled around with the cavalry, from Fort Clark to Fort Duncan back to Fort Clark in Texas and then on to Fort Hays in Kansas. It appears that they were "adopted" by a member of the Fourth Cavalry who played in the band, Charles Smith, and his wife Mollie. Their itinerant lives can be traced by following the movements of the Fourth Cavalry band, listed meticulously on a commissioner of pensions record card.[16] A report in Carlisle's *Morning Star* confirms this part of their history, stating that "they became children of the regiment, and for four years lived with it, moving from post to post as the regiment changed stations." In the personal archives of the Smith's granddaughter, a photograph of the children has a handwritten description on the back reading, "Kesetta and Jack Smith, taken in Hays City, Kansas, February '80" and an added, "We get a school report and a letter from them every month and they always address Mollie (my wife) as dear 'Mama.'" The picture shows the children blank-faced and dressed for the occasion in their Sunday best.[17] It may have been made as a memento for the Smith family before Jack and Kesetta were transported from the Southwest forever, on the orders of Colonel Mackenzie.[18]

Identified on the back of their Hays City photograph as "Jack and Kesetta Smith," just one month later, in March 1880, they were enrolled at the Carlisle Indian School as Jack and Kesetta Lipan. Their changed name signaled a further disruption of their identities. But when laid alongside later photographs taken of the children at the Carlisle Indian School, the February 1880 picture provides clear visual evidence of who they were (fig. 17). At Carlisle, however, the progressive erasure of their past continued when even their sibling relationship was disregarded, and Kesetta became known officially at the school as Kesetta Roosevelt. It is unclear where the name Roosevelt came from, but it is easy to track the origin of Jack's new name. He was "adopted" by Pratt's old friend from St. Augustine, Miss Sarah Mather, and became known at Carlisle as Jack Mather.[19] "Roosevelt" and "Mather" severed the children's connection to each other as well as to their own people, the Lipan Apache. Their new names also wiped clean the bureaucratic slate; in administrative terms, their lives had "started again" when they were sent to Carlisle. On her student card, Kesetta is recorded as having been born in Kansas. She had traveled to Carlisle from Fort Hays in Kansas, and so Kansas was recorded as her official place of origin, not Mexico or Texas, where she had grown up and witnessed the killing of her mother and many of her people.[20]

Three years later, Kesetta still bore the marks of that physical attack on her body. Conducting a full medical examination of Kesetta on her arrival, staff discovered three large scars: one on her forehead and two on the front and back of her shoulder. When questioned, Kesetta reportedly told them these were left from wounds inflicted by a stone her mother had used to try to kill her, "so as to keep the white men from getting me in the fight." Full details of this story were published in the school paper to exemplify not the desperation and fear of a Lipan mother when confronting the U.S. Cavalry with memories of the "day of screams" but rather as evidence of Indian savagery on realizing the "result of the battle would be against them."[21]

When Kesetta arrived in Carlisle she was about thirteen years old. If she had remained with her Lipan Apache people, this would have been a very important time for her. An elaborate feast would have been given as part of a ceremony to celebrate her womanhood in a sacred way. Kesetta never wore the clothes specifically made for an Apache girl's puberty ceremony or listened to the women's wisdom passed down to her by elders. Instead, she donned the regulation girls' uniform of Carlisle and learned to drill and march.[22]

Jack

The little we know about Kesetta and Jack's lives at the school is garnered from snippets of information appearing in Carlisle's publications. Colonel Mackenzie apparently took an interest in Jack and wrote him

17. Kesetta Roosevelt and Jack Mather. Photograph by J. N. Choate.
Reproduced with permission of Cumberland County Historical Society,
Carlisle PA. CS-CH 47.

letters, but this connection to the officer who had ordered the massacre of his people did not last long. In a Carlisle publication we learn how "the great calamity that has befallen General Mackenzie, in the loss of his mind, deprives Jack of his friend and guardian." From the Indian school newspaper we also learn that when playing with his friends, making and using bows and arrows, Jack seriously injured his right index finger; seven months later it was amputated by the school doctor.[23]

After four and a half years at the school, now a young man of about sixteen, Jack was sent on the long journey by land and sea, via Philadelphia, New York, and Savannah, to make his home in St. Augustine with Miss Mather. His own account of his first days in St. Augustine, written in a letter to Pratt, was published in the *Indian Helper*. He writes how he found the town strange, the Florida oranges tasty, and the flies troublesome. The highlight of his day, however, must have stirred memories of his old life: he describes with pride how "this morning I went out riding with Miss Mather."[24]

Sarah Mather was by this time a woman of nearly seventy. Originally from New England, she attended Mount Holyoke for a year, where she earned a Teaching Certificate. With her lifetime companion, Miss Rebecca Perrit, she then moved to St. Augustine, Florida, and in the 1850s they built a house in the center of town, on King Street, and opened a boarding school for young ladies.[25] Their school closed down during the Civil War. So when Pratt arrived in town, in 1875, he enlisted these two experienced teachers, along with half a dozen others, to instruct the Indian prisoners at the fort and participate in the first stage of his educational experiment. Four years later, when Secretary of the Interior Schurtz gave Pratt authority to establish the Carlisle Indian School, Sarah Mather, at the age of sixty-three, enthusiastically accompanied Pratt on his trip to Dakota to help enroll Sioux girls. The experiment in Carlisle had been approved in Washington, "provided both boys and girls are educated in said school." They returned together to Carlisle with eighty-four pupils, including twenty-five girls.[26] After helping the school in its early days, Sarah Mather returned to Florida, but she continued to retain a close interest in developments at Carlisle and made frequent visits to the school. She took a shine to Jack and, as he had been removed from his own family and community, nothing stood in the way of her making him her adoptive son.

When Jack moved to Florida, Sarah Mather found him local jobs. St. Augustine was a tourist town for northerners seeking winter sun and for a time he was employed in a local hotel, receiving a wage of $1.25. Later his pay went up when he became apprenticed to a carpenter.[27] But for Jack, the most momentous event of his three years in St. Augustine must have been the arrival in town of nearly five hundred Apache prisoners of war. The U.S. Cavalry was gaining the upper hand in the Southwest, subduing and capturing the raiding Apache bands whites regarded as the scourge of the region and transporting them to Florida. So once again, the old fort in St. Augustine became a prison for Indians. This time, not just warriors but women and children too were classified as prisoners of war and incarcerated in the old Spanish fort. The first group of seventy-seven—fourteen men, thirty-three women, and twenty-nine children—were escorted into Fort Marion, in April 1886. In September, four hundred more were brought to Florida, including Chatto's band.[28] That same month, Geronimo, the famous Chiracahua Apache chief, was also captured.

For both Apaches and Americans this was a major event. Geronimo had escaped from federal custody four years earlier and had been fighting continuously on the Mexican border. His capture broke the spirit of his shrinking band of followers and effectively ended the last major Indian war, allowing the Southwest to be claimed for American settlement. Geronimo and sixteen other chiefs and warriors were transported east and imprisoned separately at Fort Pickens in Pensacola, Florida. The Chiracahua women and children were taken on to St. Augustine. Their arrival brought the number of prisoners incarcerated in the fort to 492. Originally built for defense, not habitation, Fort Marion could be made to accommodate a maximum of 150 people in its casemates. Eleven years earlier, Pratt had discovered that these damp rooms, built of porous cocquenelle, wreaked havoc on Indian prisoners' health and he had moved his group of 78 prisoners up onto the four-sided terreplein that surrounded the fort's central courtyard. The terreplein was again used to house this much larger group of prisoners. Once again the skyline of the old fort was transformed, this time by 130 cone-shaped, army Sibley tents. These canvas and wood structures provided basic shelter for the Apache, although space was so restricted there was no room for beds of any kind.[29] Conditions at the fort were crowded and unsanitary, so that during the year, twenty-four prisoners died: one man, seven women, and sixteen children.[30]

For the local community, the makeshift canvas village on the roof of the old fort was a constant visual reminder of the Indian presence in St. Augustine. Many townspeople considered them prisoners and criminals and did not associate with them, but the children were eager to acquire Apache-made bows and arrows, and tourists bought baskets, moccasins and model cradleboards sold by the women.[31] In the streets of St. Augustine, the Apache language was regularly heard as the Indians walked about the town in groups, sold their wares, or visited the photographic studio on St. George Street to have their portraits taken.

The Chiricahua Apache prisoners were in St. Augustine for a year. Living in the center of town on King Street, Jack Mather would certainly have encountered them. For the first time since his own capture more than a decade before, he would have heard a language that closely resembled his mother tongue. From gossip in the town and perhaps discussion in his own home, he would have learned that 108 of the Chiricahua Apache children, classified as prisoners of war like himself, would also share his destiny and be taken to Pennsylvania, to be enrolled at the Carlisle Indian School.[32] In November 1886, shortly before the last ten Apache prisoners were brought to Fort Marion, the first group of Chiricahua Apache children, aged twelve to twenty-two, were selected for transport to Carlisle. A second group followed them a month later. On April 27, 1887, when all the remaining Apache prisoners had been packed into a special twelve-car train for transportation to Mount Vernon Barracks in Alabama, a third group of children was selected. Instead of accompanying their parents to Alabama, they, too, were separated from their families and sent north to Carlisle.[33]

Nine months later, Jack Mather himself would make the same, long journey north to Carlisle, leaving behind the balmy climes of Florida for the freezing temperatures of a Pennsylvania January. He had been diagnosed with consumption. In the school hospital he joined a sizeable group of sickly children of all ages.[34] Two weeks after his return, on Sunday, February 5, 1888, Jack Mather died and was buried in the school cemetery.[35] Evidence confirming the end of his short life is misleading: his present-day marker is incorrectly inscribed with the name "Jack Martha," and the map, drawn up in 1927 before the cemetery's removal, calls him by the same misspelled name.[36] Only the brief notice in the *Indian Helper* the week following his death—"Died of consumption Jack Mather, an old pupil of Carlisle, for two years past in Florida"—confirms that this is the same Lipan Apache boy who was brought to the school as a prisoner in 1880.

Kesetta

At the time of Jack's death, Kesetta Roosevelt was not in Carlisle but in Norfolk, Virginia, where she had been living with and working for a white family, the Paxtons, for almost five years. Kesetta's registration at Carlisle was the longest of any student. Apart from a short, three-year break, between 1892 and 1895, she was named on the Carlisle enrollment list from March 1880 until April 1903: a period of over twenty-three years. Most of those years were not spent in Carlisle's classrooms but working for white families in the region. After two years at the school, Kesetta spent the summer with a family in Lancaster, Pennsylvania, as part of the "outing" system.[37] The following year when her school term finished, now about sixteen years old, she was sent to live with the Paxton family in Schuylkill County, Pennsylvania.[38] This placement was more permanent and, instead of returning to Carlisle in the fall, she attended the local public school in Schuylkill Haven. Such arrangements were common. At any one time, a good proportion of the children enrolled at the school were not living in Carlisle. So, for example, at the start of one school year, the *Indian Helper* reported that: "On Friday, 142 Indian boys and girls returned from farm homes to attend school here this winter, while 216 others have remained out to go to public school with white children."[39]

In mid-November, after almost three years with the Paxtons, Kesetta returned to the school. That week, in the *Indian Helper*, there was a cryptic comment suggesting that she was not considered one of Carlisle's star pupils. "Kesetta Roosevelt is with us again. She stayed at her place nearly three years, and SOME of the time she did well."[40] Yet the

Paxton family was clearly pleased with her. The following April she returned to Schuylkill Haven to look after their growing family. Six months
later, when the family moved to Virginia, they took Kesetta with them.
Pratt had to give his permission for this move; not only was Kesetta a
charge of the school, she was also still regarded as a prisoner of war of
the War Department.[41]

In 1892, after twelve years on the enrollment list, Kesetta was officially discharged from the school for the first time. She was now a young
woman of about twenty-five and she continued to work for the Paxton
household. Had nothing changed, there would have been no record of
her later life and all trace of her might have been lost. Like so many other
ex-Carlisle students, she might have disappeared untraceably into the local population. But Kesetta decided not to spend the rest of her days in
Norfolk, Virginia. With no known community to return to in the West,
her only home base was the Indian School and in 1895 she returned
to Carlisle. In 1916, twenty years after Kesetta left the Paxton family,
the father of that household, Joseph Paxton, would make an attempt
to reestablish contact with Kesetta, and his letter gives a suggestion of
why she might have left the family. Explaining that Kesetta's last letter
to his family had been sent in 1901, from a Baltimore address, Paxton
wrote to the school requesting more recent details of her whereabouts.
He recalled with affection how she had been "very fond of [his] children when they were smaller." Reflecting on the reason for her leaving
his household, he concluded that it was because the circumstances had
changed and explained that his "family was quite large and as the children grew up and left home, she became dissatisfied and wanted to go
back to Carlisle."[42]

Kesetta left the Paxtons in December 1896. She arrived back at the
Carlisle Indian School just two weeks before Christmas, on the cold-
est day of the season. The thermometer registered one degree above
zero and the first snow covered the ground.[43] Once again she was for-
mally reenrolled as a pupil, for the usual period of five years. Her registration card looked no different from any other, despite her advancing
years, but the *Indian Helper* used her return as an opportunity to publicize one of Carlisle's policies of encouraging students to remain in the
East to live independent lives: "Miss Kessetta Roosevelt, who has been

her own woman in the East for the past ten years, independent of the school, is now visiting with us."[44]

Kesetta was now almost thirty. After the relative stability of twelve years spent with the Paxton family her life now became less secure and more itinerant. She had no family of her own to return to and no means to provide for herself besides working as a domestic. Three years working for a Pennsylvania family in Willow Grove was followed by a placement further afield with the Bishops, in Columbus, New Jersey. When the Bishop family moved from Columbus to Trenton the following year, they took Kesetta with them.[45] A month later, however, Kesetta left their household and returned to Carlisle. This time she was sent out to work in Delaware, with a Mrs. A. W. Powell, but she stayed only a year before being sent to her fateful placement with a Mrs. Bishop, in Baltimore, Maryland. It looked as if this was to be Kesetta's last official "outing" placement from Carlisle. Noted as being "self supporting," she was again discharged from the school in June 1902. Three months later, just one year after going to live with the Bishop family in Baltimore, Kesetta was back at Carlisle. The record is unclear as to whether this was the same Bishop family she had left two years previously, but indisputable was the fact that when Kesetta left Baltimore and returned to Carlisle in October 1902, she was nearly three months pregnant.

No named individual is identified as the father in the record, but he is recorded as being "white."[46] Her condition was not yet noticeable and the *Redman and Helper* unsuspectingly reported her presence on campus: "Kesetta Roosevelt, one of our Apache students who has been living in a country home for years, is with us on a visit." In November, the outing officer sent her back to the Powells, the family in Delaware for whom she had worked before she went to Baltimore.[47] She was not with them for long. When her predicament became obvious, Kesetta was sent to the Rosine Home in Philadelphia, an institution run by the Quakers for those who were described at the time as "fallen women."

On Kesetta's Carlisle student card, the reason for her discharge was falsely recorded as "Time out." This was a phrase generally applied to children who left Carlisle after the prescribed five-year period. Kesetta's story, as we have seen, was quite different. When she was signed up for the third and final time at the school in October 1902, she was thirty-five years of age, but her original status was still not forgotten: on her card she continued to be designated as "prisoner." For Kesetta, ever since she had been taken from her Texas home, Carlisle Indian School had represented the single continuity in her life, the place to which she had always returned. But on April 1, 1903, she was discharged from Carlisle for the last time; it looked as if Kesetta Roosevelt's lengthy association with the school had finally come to an end. On May 22, 1903, in the Rosine Home, Philadelphia, Kesetta Roosevelt gave birth to a boy. Helped by the ladies of the Rosine Home, she found work in Lahaska, a town just north of Philadelphia, and moved there with her infant son, Richard. In 1905, while she was living in Lahaska, twenty surviving members of the Lipan Apache Band of Texas were moved onto the Mescalero Indian Reservation, although another small group of Lipan Apache that included Ramon Castro's family remained at large.

In the winter of 1906, Kesetta fell fatally ill with consumption. During the last five weeks of her life, she was nursed by the wife of a local accountant, Elizabeth Slotter. For Slotter, this was a business arrangement. She presented her bill for caring for Kesetta, and a separate bill for looking after and boarding her son, to the accountant of Kesetta's estate, who was also her own husband. The monies were paid. Between them, J. Titus Slotter and Elizabeth Slotter received $75 dollars from Kesetta's small estate for their services rendered at the end of Kesatta's life. The sum represented a quarter of the money in the estate. Kesetta had worked until the last week of her life, and when she died $15 was still due to her in wages. A further $283.68 was also still held in her account at the Indian School from her previous earnings.[48] So she left behind a diminutive estate for her son, which also constitutes a financial strand by which to track her story in the archival record.

Kesetta Roosevelt ended her days in a town where she would have been known only as an Indian woman with an illegitimate child; the complexity and intricacies of her early life, in Mexico, Texas, Kansas, and then her later years in Virginia, New Jersey, Delaware and, of course, Pennsylvania, had been completely obscured. At the Carlisle Indian School, which had been Kesetta's home base for most of her life, her "disgrace" inevitably imposed a total silence about her death. Ironically, in the edition of the school newspaper where her death should normally have been reported, a story about another "dead Indian" was published. An anonymous donor had offered a $1,000 award to locate the gravesite of the Indian chief after whom his city, Kokomo, Indiana, had been named, in order that he could to erect a monument to commemorate him. Chief Kokomo, whose true story was unknown and who had been dead for over sixty years, could safely be appropriated to enhance and romanticize the narrative of a booming U.S. city: "W. F. Mann, the city civil engineer, has been instructed to find the grave of the dead chieftain and is making a thorough search of the early records of Howard county. He has not yet found anything in the way of accurate information. Chief Kokoma died about sixty years ago and his story is not well known. . . . [T]here seems to be no record of the precise location of his grave."[49]

Kesetta Roosevelt, whose story was known only too well, had been dropped from Carlisle's record. The school newspaper did not report her death or the location of her burial nor did it give details of the $6.00 gravestone, funded out of her own estate, that marked her lonely burial place in Lahaska, Pennsylvania.[50] Only through her son are we able to follow her story. His existence, together with the funds Kesetta had accumulated in her school bank account from years of hard work, meant that despite the obscurity of her life, she had left behind a record. When her life ended, her story continued.

Richard

Richard was a little over three and a half years old when his mother died. After her death, he was returned to his place of birth, the Rosine Home in Philadelphia.[51] Six months later, Melosina Diamant, the president of the Rosine Home, filed an application for Richard Roosevelt to be enrolled at the Carlisle Indian School. In the space where the form enquired why no "adequate education" could be provided at the child's home, Rosine's matron, Margaret Rich wrote, "Not a proper Institution for a boy his age." She also confirmed Richard's identity as "Indian," verifying that he was "known and recognized in the community in which he lives as an Indian."[52] Richard was being sent back to where his mother had come from. Even though Richard had never enjoyed contact with any native community and was officially acknowledged on his application form to be half white, he was nevertheless categorized as "Indian." On August 13, 1907, he was enrolled at the Indian School.

Richard Roosevelt had no legal guardian and the cost of appointing one was judged too prohibitive by the attorney responsible for administering his mother's estate. So the sum of $111.73, due to him as her "only heir," was passed directly to Moses Friedman, the superintendent of the Carlisle Indian School, and, like his mother, Richard became a ward of both the government and the Indian School. Though all Kesseta's links to the people of the Lipan Apache nation had been deliberately severed after her capture in Mexico, on his Carlisle student card, her son was recorded as being a member of the Lipan nation.[53]

Richard Roosevelt was too young to be listed among the new students entering Carlisle in August 1907. But the week after his arrival on campus this four-year-old had caused enough excitement for the school paper to note that "Richard H. Roosevelt is very popular among the large girls."[54] Having been enrolled as "Richard Roosevelt" and also publicly referred to by this name, inexplicably Richard's name was changed. On his student card, in all correspondence relating to his mother's estate, and later in progress reports from the school, he is called "Richard Kasetta" (or different spellings of this name: Kesetta, Kasetti, Kasitti, Kissitti).[55] At this time, Indians were not citizens and so were not included on the white register of births, deaths, and marriages, so Richard's changed name appears not to have been accompanied by any legal formalities. Whether consciously or not, the white official who decided to alter his name from Roosevelt to Kasetta had coupled Richard to the single unchanging element of his mother's designation: her first name.[56] But in so doing, they had also dislocated the obvious last name link between mother and son, made the connection between the two of them more obtuse, and ensured that her story and his ancestry were made harder to track. This might have been a deliberate attempt to veil the stigma that was attached to illegitimacy at this time. Nevertheless, when researching this story, because Kasetta in any of its spelled forms is a distinctive name, it signaled a possible relationship between Kesetta Roosevelt and Richard Kasetta. The connection needed to be established and verified, and for this the photographic records of the Indian School provided a lead.

18. Dress Parade, Indian School, Carlisle, Pennsylvania, c. 1907. Photograph by Maynard J. Hoover. Reproduced with permission of Cumberland County Historical Society, Carlisle PA. 323b #01.

A color-tinted photograph, showing uniformed pupils assembled in tight ranks on the school parade ground, is one among dozens of similar shots, printed cheaply as picture postcards and sold to bring Carlisle both publicity and revenue. When studied carefully, this photograph reveals an unusual element, because barely discernible in the center of the card, a diminutive figure can be seen (fig. 18).[57] Standing to attention on the top step of the bandstand, he is apparently "reviewing the troops." His uniform suggests that he is a pupil at the school, although he looks like an infant, and at this time Carlisle was only admitting older students already equipped with several years of schooling. A clue to this boy's identity is supplied by another photograph from the same era: a studio-portrait of a small boy, standing dressed in Carlisle's dark, military jacket and cap. It has the following words hand-written across the front in white ink: "Richard Kissitti. Age 4 years. Tribe Apache. Baby of Indian School, Carlisle, Pa." (fig. 19). Further documents in Richard Kasetta's Carlisle student file at the National Archives confirm beyond any doubt that "Richard Kissitti" was indeed Kesetta Roosevelt's son.

19. Richard Kissitti [*sic*], age four, the Carlisle Baby, c. 1907. Photograph by Leupp Studio. Reproduced with permission of Cumberland County Historical Society, Carlisle PA. 13-25-03.

Young, orphaned, with no links to any Indian nation but powerful links to the Indian School, Richard Kasetta's status at Carlisle was, from the beginning, out of the ordinary. Within five months of arriving at the school he was no longer residing in the dormitories with other students, but had been taken home to live with a white family in town, Mrs. Martha Sharp, who was at this time sixty-seven, and her daughter and son-in-law, Mary and Jack Culbertson.

Martha Sharp had lived in Carlisle for over thirty years. A member of the prestigious Second Presbyterian Church, she knew and mixed with the powerful and influential families of the town, like the Boslers and Hendersons.[58] Her late husband had owned a hotel, Franklin House, and after she was widowed, Martha Sharp set up a boarding house near the center of town, at 14 West High Street, to provide lodgings for students at nearby Dickinson College. Martha Sharp's daughter, Mary, was still single and in her late twenties in 1897, when she took up the post of matron of the Teachers' Club at the Indian School. She chose not to return to her post after the summer vacation of 1897 and, although the school paper reported she was contemplating moving to Chicago, in November 1898, Mary Sharp's wedding announcement appeared.[59] On Thanksgiving evening that same year she married John Purviance Culbertson (known as Jack).[60] This union was to be of critical importance to the future life of Richard Kasetta.

On her wedding day, Mary Culbertson's continuing attachment to children at the Indian School was made clear when "a number of the girls were remembered . . . with wedding cake."[61] The man she married, Jack Culbertson, also had friendly links to the school. He often accompanied the young boys on walks or demonstrated some of the magician's tricks for which he had become widely renowned locally.[62] Jack Culbertson had grown up in the neighboring town of Chambersburg and came from a well-established family. His grandfather had built up a straw board manufacturing business in Chambersburg. His father inherited it and went on to engage in a variety of other local business enterprises as well as to serve as a director of the National Bank of Chambersburg and the Baltimore and Cumberland Valley Railroad.[63] John Purviance Culbertson Jr. acquired not only his father's name but also his business acumen. In Carlisle he bought a substantial plot of land to the north of the town, bordering the Conodoguinet Creek. Here he would develop Bellaire Park. As Americans across the nation began to discover the delights of leisure pursuits, Culbertson provided a pleasure park for the residents of Carlisle. He built rafts, water slides, and bathing huts for swimming, supplied canoes for boating, constructed a huge hall for dancing, and organized the cutting of winter ice from the creek to chill the drinks and freeze the ice cream of his summer visitors. Townsfolk made the short trolley ride from the center of town, to a well-established picnic site at Cave Hill, where they boarded one of the Bellaire Park motor launches to take them upstream for a day of entertainment. When little Richard Roosevelt arrived at the Carlisle Indian School in 1907, this venture was still in its infancy.

The most obvious explanation for why Richard ending up living with Martha Sharp and the Culbertsons lies in Jack and Mary Culbertson's links to the Indian School. After her marriage, Mary had resumed her post as matron of the Teachers' Club, and she would have been working there when the field agent brought the little boy from Philadelphia to Carlisle. When he joined the family, Martha Sharp and Jack and Mary Culbertson had recently moved from the boarding house on West High Street to a sizeable townhouse nearby. Richard was given his own room on the second floor and from then on, 133 West Pomfret Street became his home. When old enough, he started in the kindergarten class at the local Hamilton elementary school, just two blocks away, and later went on to attend the Carlisle High School. Family snap shots show him swimming in the creek at Bellaire Park, playing outside his house and standing in posed groups with Martha Sharp in the Pomfret Street yard.[64] They reveal a childhood very different from the institutionalized life of other children at the Indian School.

Yet Richard Kasetta continued to live under the auspices of the Indian School. After nine months in his new home, when he fell ill, he returned there to be nursed in the school hospital.[65] Once back on Pomfret Street, he was visited by school officials, who regularly reported his situation and progress to the superintendent. When the 1910 Census was filed, Richard Kasetta was included on the list of Indian School students, described as a "ration Indian." This was a pattern that was to characterize the whole of his life. Living with many of the trappings and benefits of white society, his identity was nevertheless consistently inscribed as "Indian."

At the school he was claimed as a mascot from the very beginning. Paraded in his miniature uniform, when he was sick he was described as "our Carlisle baby": "Little Richard Kissitti, our Carlisle 'baby,' is confined to the hospital with an attack of grip. We all wish him a speedy recovery."[66]

His mascot role became more pronounced as the school's football team rose to prominence on the national gridiron. The year 1912, when Richard was nine, was a triumphant one for the school. The Carlisle Indians beat West Point, Louis Tewanima brought back an Olympic bronze for running at the Stockholm Olympics, and Jim Thorpe also won his infamous gold medals for the Biathlon and Triathlon. These were Indians the town of Carlisle could own and honor and a huge reception was organized for the returning heroes. Richard Kasetta's special role at the school allowed him to share vicariously in this glory. "I called Thorpe, Uncle Jim," he reminisced years later in an interview with a journalist, "He used to carry me around on his shoulders."[67] When Thorpe married his first wife, in 1913, at St. Patrick's Catholic Church in the center of town, ten-year-old Kasetta was among the guests. Perhaps his semi-celebrity lifestyle influenced his behavior because by the following year Jack Culbertson was growing impatient with the boy and wrote to tell the school superintendent that Richard was "too mischievous" and required "better discipline." Martha Sharp, however, was clearly of a different opinion and, as her son-in-law explained, did "not want to give him up." For two years her feelings prevailed.

Then, when he was fourteen, Richard was removed from the white Carlisle High School. He was sent away to work for the Buchholz family in Philadelphia, as part of the Indian School's "outing" program. This placement was not a success and after a year, Arthur E. Buchholz, an inspector for the Bureau of Health, recommended to the school superintendent that on his return "The very best thing for him for two years would be strict military discipline in such a school as you have, and the less he visits his former surroundings the better it will be for him."[68]

It looked as if Richard Kasetta was going to spend several years training and drilling as an Indian student. But by this time, Carlisle's mission to assimilate Indian children was facing fierce criticism nationwide, and the school itself had already been made the subject of a Senate investigation. Precipitously, in the summer of 1918, the Carlisle Indian Industrial School was closed. The Indian students were hurriedly sent home or dispersed to other schools. The auditor responsible for winding down the affairs of the Indian School wrote to the commissioner of Indian affairs to explain the special situation of Richard Kasetta and to enquire what should become of him. Commissioner Cato Sells replied, "I consider it advisable to allow Mrs. Martha Sharp custody of the child."[69] So from the age of fifteen, young Dick Kasetta officially ceased to be a charge of both the Indian School and the federal government. Instead, he became the responsibility of a seventy-eight-year-old white woman and her family. It appeared that he had found a place for himself in this predominantly white, eastern colonial town. But that place would always be inseparable from his ascribed identity as "Indian."

Although the Carlisle Indian School no longer existed, exstudents and graduates still made return visits to the town. Generally, they dropped in at Moses Blumenthal's store in the center of town, on North Hanover Street, where the Indian School teams had always bought their kit. With the school gone, Blumenthal's became the main meeting point for Indians returning to Carlisle. When Muck Wardecker bought the premises, he maintained this Carlisle connection. The walls of the store displayed a growing collection of Carlisle memorabilia, mostly focusing on Thorpe and his successes. When visiting Indians arrived, the proprietor would send for Dick Kasetta, to share stories and reminisce with them.[70] For the returnees, Kasetta provided a welcome, living link to their days at the Carlisle Indian School. For the local white population, his connection to the now-gone school and his dark skin continued to define his identity, and he was often referred to locally as the "Indian." Living his whole life in Carlisle, he became the town's totemic Indian. In 1963, at a Civil War Centenary celebration, he was persuaded to play this role in all its stereotypical glory and wore a full, dress-up Indian costume for the parade through town.

After the Carlisle Indian School's closure, Dick Kasetta was the only Indian living in town, apart from Montreville Yuda. Yuda's links to his tribe were almost as murky as Kasetta's. His father was an Oneida from New York State, but Montreville had grown up and attended public school in Los Angeles. At the age of twenty-two, he enrolled himself at

Carlisle, having left home and totally lost contact with his own family. Yuda became a strong personality on campus and a driving force behind the initiative that led to the Senate investigating Carlisle. As a student, he was also a frequent visitor to the pie shop owned and run by a white family, the Flickingers, on Garrison Avenue. Here, pupils from the school would gather round the piano to sing and play their instruments, and here, too, Montreville Yuda met Helen Flickinger. Their developing romance was vehemently opposed by Helen's father, who "did not want his daughter to marry an Indian." In the face of his opposition, they eloped to New Jersey and married. Later, they returned to Carlisle, where they raised George, their only son. Born in 1924, George Yuda still lives in Carlisle and knew Dick Kasetta. Unprompted, in a 2002 interview he enquired what tribe Dick Kasetta belonged to and said his father had always thought Kasetta was Crow. Yuda still has memories of the stigma attached to his parents' union and can remember overhearing Carlisle townsfolk pointing and whispering to each other, "Look, she's the one who married an Indian."[71]

Dick Kasetta would, no doubt, have been subjected to similar pressures and prejudices. This may be one reason he did not marry until very late in life. After his guardian, Mrs. Sharp, died in 1927, he continued to live with the Culbertsons at the house on West Pomfret Street. He worked locally and often frequented the bars in town where he was known for his ability to shoot pool. Kasetta helped manage the park at Bellaire, but by this time the pleasures of the park were competing with other sources of entertainment made accessible by the newly acquired automobile. Bellaire Park did not close, but its activities declined, and slowly the Culbertsons sold off the holiday cabins they had built along the Conodoguinet, although they never sold their own summer home in Bellaire Park. Jack and Mary Culbertson had no children and when they died, Jack in 1929 and Mary later, in 1947, they left their cabin and the remaining grounds of Bellaire Park to Dick Kasetta.

One year after inheriting this substantial property, Kasetta married a local white woman, Helen Rice, who he had known for many years. At this time he also, inexplicably, changed the spelling of his name to Kaseeta.[72] According to a story remembered by Rice's niece and nephew, he had taught Helen to dance in the Bellaire dance hall by allowing her to stand on his feet. When they married and moved into the Bellaire cabin, Kaseeta was already in his mid-forties and Rice herself a few years his senior. It was clear there would be no children. To what degree the sale of Kaseeta's childhood home, the loss of the last member of his adoptive family, and the acquisition of his own property prompted and enabled his decision to marry is unclear. He was marrying a local white woman, but from a social background far more modest than the one in which he had grown up on Pomfret Street. The degree to which his own racial marking impeded him from marrying within the social circles he frequented is hard to ascertain but warrants notice.

Helen Rice had earned her living as a domestic servant. Her marriage and move into the house in Bellaire Park allowed her to recreate a lifestyle she had not enjoyed since her family lost their farm in her childhood. The eldest of eleven children, Rice was sixteen when her mother died and she brought up all her younger brothers and sisters. At Bellaire, Helen's siblings visited frequently with their children and when her sister, Sarah, died suddenly, her niece, Tess, came to live with the Kaseetas. Tess remembers Helen Rice as warm and loving and well able to nurture her extended family. By marrying Helen, Dick Kaseeta had enabled her to recreate the home environment in which she grew up and also allowed himself to be embraced by a new, ready-made white family.

But in Carlisle his Indian roots were not forgotten. When Jim Thorpe was in the news or when the Washington Redskins decided to locate their summer training camp at Dickinson College, Kaseeta was interviewed as Carlisle's "authentic Indian." Willing to give personal details of Thorpe's sporting prowess in the days of the Indian School, Kaseeta was much vaguer when talking about his own background. He informed one journalist that he was a Chiricahua Apache orphan who had been brought to the Carlisle Indian School from Oklahoma. This version of events made some sense—Kaseeta was after all an orphan and an Apache—but it also glamorized and sanitized his story. It inaccurately linked Kasetta to the famous Chiricahua Apache and Geronimo rather than the little-known Lipan Apache, allowing him to embrace the romance of a known Apache past, and it left out the stigma of his illegitimacy. A vital component of Dick Kaseeta's life had been omitted: his mother.

It is unlikely that Dick Kaseeta ever knew who his mother was or had enough information to be able to piece together his own story. When he died of cancer in 1970, he was buried in Memorial Gardens Cemetery, on the western outskirts of Carlisle, the opposite side of town from where his uncle lay in the Indian School cemetery.[73] Twenty-nine years later, his wife was laid to rest beside him. Nothing about the Kaseeta plot gives any hint that one of its occupants was half Apache. Richard Kaseeta had lived his whole life with a white-inscribed "Indian identity." Although enjoying no tribal specificity or cultural contact, he was nevertheless racially marked and assumed the role of Carlisle's totemic Indian, unaware of his own parenthood and history. While his Indian identity was recognized by everyone, his gravestone gives no hint of this; it is engraved with just his name and dates. His Lipan Apache connection, which had shaped and defined his whole life, had been totally erased.

By this time, the Lipan Apache people had also lost much of their history and almost all their population. Reduced to a handful of individuals living on the Mescalero reservation or dispersed around the Texas-Mexico border, they are mentioned most often in historical accounts focusing on the eighteenth or nineteenth century. No history of the Lipan Apache has ever been published and lacking the renown of the Chiricahua, it is hard to find out about this once numerous group.[74]

In an attempt to uncover more information about Kesetta's band as well as details of her capture, I decided to search the Internet. A short, Web site history of the Lipan Apache included the following paragraph: "In 1861 Ramon Castro and some followers were forced to settled at Fort Belknap, Texas, as a condition of their allegiance to the U.S. Government. It was also an attempt to exterminate the Lipan Apache. The U.S. Government moved the Lipan Apache people as prisoners of war and in 1867 they transferred the Lipan to Fort Griffin near Albany, Texas. By 1885 less than 20 Lipan Apache Band members were alive."[75]

This seemed to offer a possible link to Kesetta's people, so I emailed the author to tell him about the two Lipan children who had been captured by Colonel Mackenzie and taken to the Carlisle Indian School and to ask if he knew anything about them or their band. I received a reply the next day:

It's my understanding that the children were never to be seen or heard from. I would be very interested in knowing the name and location of where they are buried, so that I, and our people, can visit them to give them a Lipan Apache blessing.

Ramon Castro was my great great great uncle and it is said that the children taken were his children. They were taken from him to test his allegiance to the U.S. Government. One of the main reasons why they continued to fight so hard was his sadness over the incident.

Question, how did you find out about this? It's my understanding that only family members know about this story.

Daniel Castro Romero Jr. had sent me evidence that 125 years after their capture by Mackenzie's cavalry, the Lipan children were still remembered by their own people. I learned, too, that their story had been told and retold through four generations. On the second Saturday in August every year, the Castro family holds a reunion where they recount their family history and hold a ceremony of remembrance for all the Lipan killed at Remolino and lost in other tragedies.

In answer to Romero's request for information about the two children's burial places, I was able to email a photograph of the Indian School Cemetery and details of the location of Jack Mather's stone. But for Kesetta, the only information I had about her final resting place was encapsulated in a line added to her last Carlisle Student Record Card: "Died in Lahaska, PA, December 24, 1906." For the Indian School this closed Kasetta's record and allowed her cards to be moved to the "dead" file.

For Kesetta's niece, Tess, ninety-six years later, this information offered the possibility of a different kind of closure. Knowing now that Kesetta had been cared for by Quakers and had died in Lahaska, she made contact with the Quaker community in the town and was told that Kesetta had indeed been buried in the Quaker cemetery. Visiting the pretty, rustic cemetery in Lahaska, Tess found the plain grave with a simple inscription, "Kesetta," and laid a wreath on it.

As yet no Lipan people have been able to make the long cross-country journey from Texas to Pennsylvania, but photographs of Kesetta were sent to Daniel Castro Romero Jr:

> On the day I received the photographs, I was standing in line waiting to buy postage stamps when I opened your envelope. For a moment, I could see into my daughter's eyes, as my eyes watered at the picture

of Kesetta. She looks exactly like my daughter. She has the same eyes, facial features, you name it she has it. I was very moved, I could only think of what her parents went through. My ancestors must have been at a loss not knowing where their daughter had gone, never to see her again. She has [finally] made the journey back home.

Ironically, Kesetta "made the journey back home" thanks to photographs created as part of the Carlisle Indian School's propaganda to publicize its program of cultural obliteration. Across the generations, these pictures provided a link to confirm and bear witness to her story and substantiate the "landmark of memory" that had been laid down repeatedly for her by her people over the years.

Kesetta's story is tragic. For her, Carlisle represented exile, associated with a series of ruptures. The education she received there equipped her to do no more than hold down a series of menial jobs. She joined white society but only at the very lowest level, as a live-in servant to a succession of white families. The split in her life that was created when all links to her Indian childhood were suddenly and utterly severed matched the bifurcation that was integral to the ideology of the Indian civilization program. Totally alone in the world, without family or community, it seems likely that in her last "outing" home she suffered sexual exploitation or abuse by a white man. She spent her final three years separated from everyone she had known in the white world she had been forced to live in before meeting an early death.

Kesetta's life encompasses some of the harshest aspects of a campaign designed systematically to strip native children of their cultures. Such programs were not confined to the United States. Everywhere they carry with them a long and cruel legacy, which only recently has begun to be addressed. In Canada, some survivors found the strength to tell their stories. Harrowing evidence in a series of court cases focused public attention on the painful bequest left by Indian boarding schools. Irwin Cotler, the Canadian justice minister, described the abuse suffered by native children as "the single most disgraceful, racist and harmful act" in Canadian history. On November 20, 2005 an agreement in principle was approved by the Canadian Federal Cabinet and on May 10, 2006, the final Residential Schools Settlement Agreement was approved. About eighty thousand members of Canadian First Nations now qualify for a share of $2 million dollars that has been made available as compensation for physical and emotional abuse sustained while enrolled in government schools. Phil Fontaine, the national chief of the Assembly of First Nations, said this agreement represented "the first step towards closure on a terrible, tragic legacy for thousands of First Nations individuals who suffered physical, sexual or psychological abuse." Financial payments cannot address the suffering that has been inflicted, and so a five-year, community-based Truth and Reconciliation Commission has been set up to offer former students the opportunity to tell their stories in a safe and supportive context. The Aboriginal Healing Foundation will also be remandated and funded, enabling it to continue its support for local healing programs.[76] In the United States, the destructive power of schools like Carlisle, and their impact on succeeding generations, has not been fully and openly confronted in the court system. Yet it is becoming widely accepted that many boarding school students lived their lives hobbled and haunted by their white schooling and that their suffering affected succeeding generations.

Despite the many traumas inflicted on Indian children at white-run schools, a few Carlisle students claimed for themselves an equal place in mainstream society; these were the minority.[77] Some lived divided lives, unable to find a place in either white society or in the homes they had left. The majority returned to their reservations and found a way to cobble together lives that incorporated elements of what they had learned in school. There were some survivors, however, who succeeded in using their education to benefit their communities and/or enhance their own lives. For them, the legacy of their white schooling was complex and multifaceted. Having surmounted many of the difficulties associated with white education, they claimed their schooling as a means of resistance and self-preservation. This enabled them, in different ways, to meld their newly acquired skills with the values and patterns of their old lives and remake traditional priorities to ensure their survival. The life of Kesetta, preserved in fragments in the written and photographic archives as well as the living memory of her people, is an example of and testament to one extreme consequence of the white educational campaign. The life of Susan Rayos Marmon is representative of the other.

11. Susan Rayos Marmon: Storytelling and Teaching

SUSAN RAYOS ARRIVED AT Carlisle in August 1896, a little over fifteen years after Kesetta. She too was thirteen when she made the long, two thousand-mile journey from Paguate in the Southwest. The personal context in which she would receive her education, however, was very different from that of the Lipan Apache girl. Susie's father, Rayos A-you-teee-ya, had died, but she set out on her venture into the white world with the firm support of her mother, Maria Angela Tsi-wa-ca. The home and community she left behind, although changing, was not shattered and would still be there for her to return to a decade later. Susie had already spent four years at the Albuquerque Mission School when she enrolled at Carlisle for the standard five-year stint. Over half a century later, she recalled that she must have been "about nine years old [when] they came out to Paguate [her native village] and offered the chance to come to the Presbyterian Mission School. My mother had just one daughter, but she wanted me to go because she wanted me to have an education."

Over the next ten years, Susie would "have an education." When she left home she only spoke Keres. Four years later, when she set out for Carlisle, she had learned English.[1] Already she had become familiar with alien patterns of knowledge and belief and the rudiments of a quite different "regime of truth."[2] For Susie Rayos, as for all Indian children who were the first in their communities to undertake white schooling, the demands it imposed brought many challenges. But Susie would claim as her own the new skills it brought and with them the power to define new truths for herself, her family, and her community.

Her Carlisle student record card shows that Susie Rayos followed Pratt's well-established academic and practical regime, and each summer she was sent on "outing." She worked for seven different families in New Jersey and Pennsylvania before graduating from Carlisle in 1903. That final summer, after seven years in the East, she went home but soon returned, to enroll first at Dickinson College and then in the teachers' course at Bloomsburg State Normal School (now Bloomsburg University). Her teacher's training qualified her for a job in the Indian Service and she worked at Carlisle for a year.[3] Then, after more than a decade away, she returned to live and work in the Southwest as teacher at the Isleta Pueblo school. A short time later, she married Walter B. Marmon and moved to Laguna Pueblo, where she spent the rest of her life. Her marriage tied Susie to a powerful Laguna family with strong links to Carlisle.

Walter had spent three years at the school, from 1897 to 1900, and many of his siblings—Agnes, Annie Bell, Maria, Effie, Robert—had also been Carlisle students.[4] The Marmon children were half white. Their father, Robert Gunn Marmon, had arrived in the West as a surveyor for the government. Living at Laguna, he learned the language, married a local woman, Sarah Annallo/Anaya (who spoke no English), and made his home in the town.[5] He never returned to Ohio and lived the rest of his life at Laguna, even serving as governor of the Pueblo for a year.[6] When his first wife died, he was left with a young family. Early in 1893, Walter and his brothers and sisters gained a stepmother when their father married his wife's sister, Maria Anaya.[7] Sarah had not attended Carlisle, but Maria had spent five years at the school, from 1884 to 1889. Although she had arrived unable to speak or read any English, she proved an outstanding student and was reported in the *Indian Helper* to have "received perfect marks for lessons and conduct in the school-room."[8]

So Susie and her mother-in-law shared the experience of this militaristic, white-run boarding school, located nearly two thousand miles from their home. Although they did not attend Carlisle at the same time, the two girls were both students during the Pratt years, so would have undergone similar educational programs and even known some of the same long-serving teachers, such as Marianna Burgess. Maria, however, returned home after the standard five-year period, having reaching the fourth grade level. Susie stayed longer and was one of a minority of Carlisle students who attained the required level to graduate. She

then went even further down the white education route, becoming the
first Laguna woman to graduate from a white college. Her enrolment at
Bloomsburg represented a momentous step. She moved from a school
founded and run explicitly to instruct a racial minority in the skills and
values of mainstream society to a white institution embedded in the
dominant culture, which taught its students how to pass on these skills
and values. Qualifying as a teacher in 1906, Susie held true to this vo-
cation for the rest of her life.

Back at Laguna, once her own five children (Miriam, Josephine, Walter, Fred, and Harry) were old enough, she returned to teaching. In the
one-roomed Laguna day school behind her house, she held classes for
the children of the pueblo as well as her own and some of her many
nephews and nieces. Her nephew, Lee Marmon, spoke of her as being
"a strict but wonderful teacher."[9] Determined that all her pupils should
use education as a route to success, she urged them to stay in school as
long as possible. When John Pino dropped out after sixth grade, he recalls that Susie came after him: "Anyway, she talked me into going back
to school, and it helped to get a good job with the railroad. Back in the
Pueblo, I have held a number of offices." In 1977, when he recollected
the impact of her persuasion, Pino was head of Pueblo Housing and attributed his ability to do this work to the fact that he had returned to his
studies.[10] To Laguna, Susie Rayos Marmon brought a heart-felt commitment to schooling, but her definition of education was far more comprehensive than the one taught at the Bloomsburg Normal School.

Brought up in the old ways, Susie never stopped telling the stories
that for generations had preserved and disseminated Laguna culture
and maintained its fundamental truths. Her great-niece, Leslie Marmon Silko, explains how:

> The ancient Pueblo people depended upon collective memory
> through successive generations to maintain and transmit an en-
> tire culture, a worldview complete with proven strategies for
> survival. . . . The ancient Pueblo vision of the world was inclu-
> sive. The impulse was to leave nothing out. Pueblo oral tradi-
> tion necessarily embraced all levels of human experience. Oth-
> erwise, the collective knowledge and beliefs comprising ancient

Pueblo culture would have been incomplete. . . . The Pueblo oral tradition knew no boundaries. Accounts of the appearance of the first Europeans (Spanish) in Pueblo country or the tragic encounters between Pueblo people and Apache raiders were no more and no less important than stories about the biggest mule deer ever taken or adulterous couples surprised in cornfields and chicken coops.[11]

Susie's pedagogy embraced and furthered this inclusive "vision of the world." For her, instructing the children of Laguna to read and write and to speak English, and continuing her own historical studies and writing, were vital activities and fully compatible with the more holistic, personal, and sacred patterns of learning and communication invoked when telling stories to maintain the complex of Pueblo knowledge and belief. What a community "accepts and makes function as true" is, inevitably, changeable over time and can be manipulated by those with the power to do so.[12] Susie knew this. She regarded education, in its narrow sense as defined by white schooling, as a way for individuals to develop and for the community to gain new skills to defend and protect itself. She also knew how, in its broader, more inclusive meaning, the educational processes of the Pueblo carried with them the power for self-definition and survival, made possible through the reiteration of stories that linked generation to generation and past to future. In her own life, Susie experienced, furthered, and entwined these two very different systems of education and truth, white and Indian. Her legacy and her memory have been honored and preserved within both.

As with Kesetta, it is possible to piece together a rudimentary, flat and fragmentary account of Susie Rayos's school life from the archival records of the Carlisle Indian School and Bloomsburg Normal School. But her school days represented just a beginning for Susie. Her long and distinguished career as a teacher and educator meant that she earned appreciation and public recognition for her many years of teaching the children of the pueblo as well as for her role as a proponent for schooling in the state. During the 1960s, she served on the first Commission of Indian Affairs for New Mexico and in 1971 was named "Outstanding Indian Woman in the Field of Education" by the North American

Indian Women's Association. At a banquet held for her at the Albuquerque Indian School, she received her award and other honors, including
a letter from the president's wife, Mrs. Pat Nixon, who described the
award as a "living tribute to your tireless devotion to the better education of the youthful descendants of the first inhabitants and cultivators
of our Nation's soil."[13] Susie's fame and recognition extended well beyond the bounds of Albuquerque and Laguna, and on July 4, 1976, as
part of New Mexico's bicentennial celebrations, thousands more heard
about her story and her work when an interview with her was transmitted on KGGM-TV The most visible, physical endorsement of her educational work came when a school in Albuquerque was named the Susie
Rayos Marmon Elementary School. When she reached her one hun-
dredth birthday, on April 24, 1987, Governor Gary Carruthers declared
April 24 to be "Susie Marmon Day in New Mexico." A birthday gathering, organized at the Laguna Tribal Building, brought more tributes:
a recognition letter from the National Organization for Native American Women; a plaque and congratulations from the All Indian Pueblo
Council; happy birthday greetings and a Certificate of Recognition of
Service from Governor Chester T. Fernando of Laguna; happy birthday
wishes and congratulations from President and Nancy Reagan, Senator Pete Dominici, and Representative Manuel Lujan. These were the
public trappings of success and recognition that singled Susie out as an
individual who had lived and worked in her community and made a
unique contribution to the world of education, which was so important
an element of white society. Americans of all backgrounds who came to
know her in this public context learned about her prowess in the classroom and her determined commitment to education.

But readers of Leslie Marmon Silko's *Storyteller* are given far more
intimate and private insights into the woman they come to know as
Aunt Susie. She is introduced here, in her later years, as a gentle, powerful, and resourceful woman who "had come to believe very much in
books / and in schooling" yet who also, "cherished the Laguna stories / all her life" and told them repeatedly. To Silko, her great-niece,
who "grew up right there at Laguna, next door to Susie," she was an
educator of a different order; she "told me a lot of the stories, and in
some sense trained me."[14] Silko recalls her soft voice and rich vocabu-

lary: "I write when I still hear / her voice as she tells the story," she informs the reader. The portrait of Aunt Susie painted in *Storyteller*, by one of America's foremost native writers, is respectful, warm, and personal. It shows the Susie who had been to Carlisle and who is publicly honored in the world of education: "From the time I can remember her / she worked on her kitchen table / with her books and papers spread over the oil cloth." But, more crucially, it reveals the Aunt Susie who, in response to a young child's questions, "would put down her fountain pen / and lift her glasses to wipe her eyes with her handkerchief / before she spoke . . . to tell me all she knew on a subject."[15] Silko lays her Aunt Susie's love of books and her links to Laguna's oral traditions lovingly alongside each other, but it is Aunt Susie's authority as a storyteller that is important here:

> She was of a generation,
> The last generation here at Laguna,
> that passed down an entire culture
> by word of mouth
> an entire history
> an entire vision of the world
> which depended upon memory
> and retelling by subsequent generations.[16]

Among other familial voices in this polyphonic text—Grandmother Maria Anaya Marmon, Aunt Alice Little—Aunt Susie's is the first the reader hears. Silko positions her as both teacher and teller: "This is the way Aunt Susie told the story." And she is also credited with prescience for her resolve to keep telling the stories:

> She must have realized
> that the atmosphere and conditions
> which had maintained this oral tradition in Laguna culture
> had been irrevocably altered by the European intrusion—
> principally by the practice of taking the children
> away from Laguna to Indian schools,
> taking the children away from the tellers who had
> in all past generations
> told the children an entire culture, an entire identity of a people.[17]

Aunt Susie, in Silko's account, understood the rupture that had been inflicted on Laguna culture and the associated disadvantages that would be suffered by her people unremittingly if they were unable to sustain their own links to the past and basis of truth.

In *Silencing the Past*, Haitian historian Michel-Rolph Trouillot examines how the dominant impose their own account of history and warns how "forces . . . less visible than gunfire, class property, or political crusades . . . are no less powerful."[18] He shows how, by laying down the historical narrative, those in power shape and determine the pattern of the future for everyone unless they are actively challenged. They select and protect the facts, regulate their analysis, and vigorously silence alternative versions or interpretations.[19] His book is about history and power. It deals with the many ways in which the production of historical narratives involves the uneven contribution of competing groups and individuals who have unequal access to the means for such production.[20]

Aunt Susie understood that unceasing access to Pueblo stories safeguarded "the means for such production" and protected "an entire history" as well as the future and survival of the people. This was potently illustrated when, in a fight for their land rights, the people of Laguna Pueblo enlisted the memories embedded in tales and anecdotes passed down through the generations. To prove that six million acres had been granted to Laguna by the king of Spain "hundreds of years before the United States even existed," they turned to the stories. "The old folks were up against the state of New Mexico with only the stories." After twenty years, Laguna would win the legal fight, but they received no land, only payment (twenty-five cents an acre with no interest), and most of this would go to the lawyers. During the early days of this trial, in a difficult task of cultural translation, Aunt Susie played an active role shaping and preparing the accepted truths of Laguna society to pass muster and stand as evidence in a white court of law. She met with the old folk "twice a week after supper at our house to go over the testimony" and "interpret English" in a community struggle organized to regain the lost land. Aunt Susie's determination to fight for Laguna land, her knowledge of white systems of logic, and her intimate acquaintance with English meant that she was well equipped to help the Laguna old folk organize their information—about childhood outings and visits to the contested land to haul wood or gather pinions—for presentation as factual proof in court. She worked closely with them to "prepare their testimony, that from time immemorial the Kawakemeh, the people of the Pueblo of Laguna, had been sustained from hunting and planting on this land stolen by the state of New Mexico."[21] Presented here as "spry when compared" to the old folk, Aunt Susie is competent to mediate the white world for them because her unswerving loyalty combined powerfully with her hybrid knowledge.

For Silko, it is this potent intermingling that is key. In her Laguna kitchen, Aunt Susie is presented as being as devoted to her books as to the stories; her commitment to the two lends both authenticity and authority to Silko's own bringing together of text and traditional oral stories. In *Yellow Woman and a Beauty of the Spirit*, Silko describes this as a quite natural progression: "From the spoken word, or storytelling, comes the written word, as well as the visual image."[22] All stumbling blocks separating oral from literary are here flattened, with Aunt Susie not just authenticating the stories but also validating the rival "regime of truth" of the white world.

This "truth" is "centered on the form of scientific discourse and the institutions that produce it." That is to say, that "facts" here are only accepted as true once they have been announced as such by "those who are charged with saying what counts as true"; usually those in the scientific community.[23] Silko describes how, when she was a student, she deliberately chose the topic of "race" for one of her college papers and then felt compelled to go to the library of the University of New Mexico, to search for the fact, the "truth" about race. "My parents and the people of Laguna Pueblo community who raised me taught me that we are all one family. . . . I had to test what I had been taught as a child because I had also been taught that the truth matters more than anything."[24] It is ambiguous which "truth" Silko is here referring to, but the implication is that it is the white "truth" of scientific enquiry, made available in books in the library. This personal story sheds light on a family story Silko tells, about the quarrel between Aunt Susie and Grandma A'mooh over how Marianna Burgess's offensive book, *Stiya*, should be dealt with.

Both women, having been sent away to Carlisle, had "returned with a profound sense of the power of books."[25] Yet they held very different views about how the destructive power of *Stiya* should be combated. Grandma A'mooh (as we heard in chapter 8) was adamant that it should, quite simply, be burned, like witchcraft paraphernalia, and she "lifted the lid on her cookstove to drop in the book." Aunt Susie intervened and argued that the text provided evidence of the racism and bad faith of the government and so, at all costs, should be preserved as a vital part of the historical record of the Laguna people. A fight such as this was almost unheard of in a society where confrontations between mother-in-law and daughter-in-law were always scrupulously avoided. Both its occurrence and its resolution are illuminating, because the fight oscillates around not just the *Stiya* book, but more fundamentally around the potency and acceptability of two quite separate "regimes of truth." Aunt Susie's desperate determination to safeguard the book, demonstrated by her willingness openly to challenge her mother-in-law's wishes, stemmed from her awareness that it could stand as evidence of the government's destructive treatment of Pueblo people. When finally, having totally failed to persuade Grandma A'mooh of the rightness of this "regime of truth," Aunt Susie requested that she herself should be the one to carry out the act of incineration. Having lost her fight to protect the book as future scientific evidence, she spiritedly demanded her own rights within the traditional Pueblo system of values, because, as Silko explains, "According to Pueblo etiquette, it would have been unthinkable for my great grandmother to refuse her daughter-in-law's request for the book."[26] Aunt Susie dutifully burned *Stiya* herself, but she remained unconvinced that as a means to protect the truth, the book's destruction by fire was more efficacious than its preservation as a written text. For her, the truth that could be found in books was linked to a strategy for survival.[27]

More than a decade of white schooling had given Aunt Susie a reverence for the written word, and she married into a family who shared this respect. Robert Marmon chose to leave his Ohio home behind and live his life at Laguna, but he brought his books with him and kept them in a tall bookcase, where they remained even after his death, under the care of his second wife, Maria Anaya, Silko's paternal grandmother.[28] She looked after the young Silko while her mother was at work, and the child called her Grandma A'mooh. In adulthood, she realized this was because she "had been hearing her say/ "a'moo'ooh" / which is the Laguna expression of endearment / for a young child." Maria Anaya had been alerted to the power of the written word not just because of her time at Carlisle but because she, too, understood, like all her generation, how the authority of the word, written down in land grant documents, defined the legal rights by which the Laguna people held their homelands. Silko recalls that "she spoke and wrote English beautifully." Also, that she read to them, "over and over, from a tattered little book called *Brownie the Bear*," and Silko suspected that this might have been "because she feared we'd prefer listening to reading," adding in parentheses, "(who wouldn't?)."[29] For the Marmons, the literary and the oral lived side-by-side; stories that were read and stories that were told could coexist and complement each other. In Silko's account, both Aunt Susie and Grandma A'mooh, strong women in a matriarchal society, understood the intensification of knowledge and power brought through this hybridity.

Steeped in the oral tradition, Aunt Susie repeatedly told stories to all the children around her. For Harriett Marmon, one of her grandchildren, "the book the *Storyteller* is Susie 'all the way.' Her stories bring her right back to this world."[30] Stories were a potent way of reaching across the generations to impart information and values to the young and remembering ancestors long since dead. "When Aunt Susie told her stories, she would tell a younger child to go open the door so that our esteemed predecessors might bring their gifts to us. 'They are out there,' Aunt Susie would say. 'Let them come in. They're here, they're here with us *within* the stories.'"[31] When Aunt Susie passed on these ancient stories, however, Silko makes it clear that sometimes she told them in English, using a vocabulary—including "words like *precipitous*"—inflected by the experience of her years at Carlisle:[32]

> She is one of the first generation of people at Laguna who began experimenting with English—who began working to make English speak for us, that is, to speak from the heart. (I come from a family intent on getting the stories told.) As you read the story, I think you will hear that. And here and there, I think, you will hear the influence of the In-

dian School at Carlisle, Pennsylvania, where my Aunt Susie was sent
(like being sent to prison) for six years.[33]

The Indian School could be "heard" in the stories, but Silko presents
the Carlisle experience with ambivalence; the source of a rich vocabulary yet also entailing incarceration. Carlisle was integral to Aunt Susie's
life, and Josephine, her second daughter, also remembers how aspects
of her mother's Carlisle experience became part of the ebb and flow of
daily life. When she sang to them as children, she included songs she had
learned while on "outing" in Pennsylvania, and the ones they all loved
best, Josephine recalled, were about the seashore, because they evoked
a landscape so very different from their homeland.[34]

Aunt Susie brought elements from an alien and different world with
her to Laguna. The melding of these two worlds was not straightforward.
Silko remembers how as a child she herself "understood very early that
there were two distinct ways of interpreting the world. There was the
white people's ways and the Laguna way." She became conscious that
her mixed ancestry meant that she "belonged on the outer edge of the
circle, between the world of the pueblo and the outside world."[35] Aunt
Susie was not of mixed ancestry, but her white education had determined that she, too, carried within her aspects of this "outside world,"
and her marriage to Walter Marmon functioned as a centrifugal force
pulling her toward it.

Robert Gunn Marmon, Aunt Susie's father-in-law, and his brother
Walter Gunn Marmon, had been the first to live on this "outer edge."
Delineated not only culturally but also racially, it would have an impact on all their descendants at Laguna. Susie's own children, while embraced within the Pueblo community, also occupied an ambiguous position. They were the same generation as Lee Marmon, Silko's father,
for whom "the Indian School and the taunts of the children did not sit
well. . . . It had been difficult in those days to be part Laguna and part
white, or *amedicana*."[36] This uncertainty within Laguna was reiterated far more harshly in the "outside world" where overt racism was
never far from the surface. Silko tells how Robert Marmon was made
aware of America's uncompromising, one-drop racial rule when he was
called "Squaw Man," and white society denied his own sons the privileges that he enjoyed:

> Once when he and two of his young sons walked through the lobby of Albuquerque's only hotel to reach the café inside, the hotel manager stopped my great-grandfather. He told my great-grandfather that he was welcome to walk through the lobby, but when he had Indians with him, he should use the back door. My great-grandfather informed him that the Indians were his sons, and then he left and never went into the hotel again.[37]

Contemporaneous with this incident, when the Marmons were being judged racially tainted as whites, they were also being judged culturally tainted as Indians by a white anthropologist, Elsie Clews Parsons. Parsons made field trips to Acoma, Zuni, and Laguna pueblos in 1917. Framing her study within the parameters laid down by Franz Boas—focusing on culture elements, diffusion, and culture history—she found that "at Laguna, ceremonialism or sacerdotalism is disintegrated and the social organization is considerably Americanized." She attributed much of what she interpreted as cultural contamination due to the presence of Walter G. and Robert G. Marmon and their marriages to local women, which at Laguna, she believed, had interrupted ritual practice and disrupted community cohesion.[38] For Parsons, with her ethnographically constructed notions of cultural purity, all evidence of hybridity was interpreted as contamination, and the arrival of the Marmons, and the introduction of white cultural practices and familial relations, was blamed for the controversy that arose between "conservatives" and "progressives."[39] Aunt Susie Marmon, by extension, was implicated in the subsequent Americanization and divisions within the pueblo.

Despite the narrative crafted by Silko, in which Aunt Susie is depicted as a powerful, sustaining, and creative influence, carrying forward Laguna traditions and finding new ways to pass them on, her role and memory do not go uncontested, even within her own family. Her granddaughter, Marietta Padilla, the daughter of her son Harry W. Marmon, like Aunt Susie herself, trained as a teacher. Attending a Summer Institute at the University of New Mexico, in 2001, Padilla wrote a paper exploring how the revitalization of an indigenous language, such as Keres, might contribute to increasing literacy rates among native children. She went on to voice her determination "to help [her] people recover their loss

of the Keres language." Identifying her own family's history as pivotal
in the undermining of Keres at Laguna, she explicitly named her grandmother and Carlisle as the key culprits:

> Our family had a sense of culture taken away when my father's mother,
> Susie Rayos Marmon, was taken to the Carlisle Indian School in Penn-
> sylvania. When she returned home, she used the English language a
> majority of the time because she was a day school teacher. She no lon-
> ger relied on her native Keres language to communicate. Carlisle had
> restricted her use of the Keres language because if was thought that by
> restricting the use of native tongues that [*sic*] Native Americans would
> be stripped of their "Indianness." She went on to become a day school
> teacher and left her "Indianness" behind.[40]

In a short, two thousand-word paper, Padilla obviously was not able
to explore the issue in full. But notably, although she wrote that she
"never really understood [her] family history until [she] read about it in
Ceremony," she did not endorse Silko's view of Aunt Susie, as outlined
in *Storyteller*. Padilla's appreciation of her grandmother is not linked to
her role as a storyteller but instead to the practical action she took, "to
make sure her children learned the [Keres] language" by having "them
stay with their grandmother in Paguate during their early years, before
they were of school age."[41] When Silko recalls Aunt Susie's voice telling the stories, she remembers, "She had certain phrases, certain distinctive words /she used in her telling." For Silko, these words were in-
dicators of her great-aunt's impressive vocabulary and the fact that she
was "a brilliant woman, a scholar / of her own making."[42] For Padilla,
however, we can presume that these English words and phrases signaled
the demise of the Keres language. Rather than being judged an innovative linguistic tactic to preserve the stories and maintain the old truths,
they were instead seen as unwelcome markers of linguistic and cultural
loss at Laguna.

The very first story Silko tells her readers, in *Storyteller* is "a story that
Aunt Susie liked to tell"—the one "about the little girl who ran away"—
and she tells it "the way Aunt Susie told the story." As was customary
for all Aunt Susie's stories, this one gets repeated in *Yellow Woman and
a Beauty of the Spirit*, as part of Silko's explication of "Language and

Literature from a Pueblo Perspective."[43] Here, she uses it to explain how in Pueblo culture, stories provide a way to heal and assuage pain. If an individual suffers a personal crisis or catastrophe, stories are told about others who have also suffered. So the story of the little girl is a story that "may be told at a time of sadness or loss."[44] Focused on the child's suicide, in response to her mother's refusal to cook for her the food—*yashtoah*—that she wants, it revolves around one of the most intense experiences of personal loss and pain it is possible to imagine.[45] Yet the outcome is not utterly sad. After the child has drowned, the mother "stood on the edge of the mesa and scattered her daughter's clothing, the little moccasins, the *yashtoah*. She scattered them to the east, to the west, to the north, to the south. And the pieces of clothing and the moccasins and the *yashtoah* all turned into butterflies. And today they say that Acoma has more beautiful butterflies: red ones, white ones, blue ones, yellow ones. They came from this little girl's clothing."[46]

In the context of Aunt Susie's contested legacy and the pain associated with cultural loss that she is charged with instigating, it seems appropriate that through one of her favorite and most-told stories, Aunt Susie should have bequeathed to her family a means to bring healing. The story of a mother who inadvertently brought on herself the deepest loss imaginable yet who lived to see beauty and life develop out of her own bereavement is a story that offers hope and restoration in the midst of anguish and grief.

Susie Rayos Marmon contributed personally to the seismic changes that took place at Laguna. The extent of her influence was acknowledged by Francis Smith, chairman of the Laguna school board in the 1970s, when he named education "as one of the things that makes Laguna progressive," before going on to list the natural resources enjoyed by Laguna: "Mrs. Marmon, along with uranium, pink marble and red rock."[47] By connecting her to beautiful, strong, as well as potentially explosive materials, he implicitly acknowledged the extent of Susie Marmon's awe-inspiring powers.

Widely accredited and honored by the white educational world she had been schooled into and had actively claimed as her own, Susie Rayos Marmon became better known to an extensive public as Aunt Susie through intimate and private memories of her published in the writings of her great- niece, Leslie Marmon Silko. Aunt Susie had used her Carlisle education and her excellent command of the English language to ensure that the Laguna stories, which embraced "the whole of creation and the whole of history and time," were passed down. She knew that they carried within them recipes and maps as well as information about the weather, geography, and resources of the local landscape. And besides this, they also offered a source of spiritual and psychological support for succeeding generations. Aunt Susie was a survivor par excellence. She melded together the workable truths of two societies, although neither in her own life nor in those of her family was she able to evade the painful inconsistencies and conflicts this entailed.[48] In both her teaching and story telling, she worked to claim the power of the white man's wisdom, to combat the corrosive forces it introduced into her own community, and to preserve and protect "an entire history / an entire vision of the world."[49]

Epilogue

Cultural Survival as Performance, Powwow 2000

> Wherever our drums are, and our elders pray for the ground to be a
> sacred center for singers and dancers, there we stay alive. The songs
> remember where we have been and tell us the good way to go on. Our
> steps are prayers that we will go on in a good way. Every beautiful thing
> we make and wear, as we dance, speaks of our hope and prayers—and
> when we powwow, we have a good time.
>
> —Carter Revard, Osage

ON MEMORIAL DAY WEEKEND in 2000, for the first time since the
Carlisle Indian School closed its doors in 1918, hundreds of Native Americans from across the United States journeyed to the small Pennsylvania
town for "Powwow 2000: Remembering the Carlisle Indian School."
From California, New York, Florida, New Mexico, South Dakota, Maryland, and as far away as Alaska they came, their car and camper license
plates in the campground north of the town reading like a geography
of the United States. Most had never before visited the town of Carlisle or the school; many had a relative who had been a Carlisle student;
all came to pay tribute to the children who had been taken from their
homes and brought to Carlisle to learn the white man's ways.

The Powwow venue was the Carlisle Barracks, now the home of
the U.S. Army War College and a training ground for top military personnel. The event's unusual setting matched its exceptional character.
Brant Philips, a forty-nine-year-old Nez Perce from California who has
attended hundreds of powwows countrywide, felt that "The location,
and all the stories behind it, are what make this celebration all the more
joyous and sad at the same time."[1] The hay bales and bleachers for the
powwow arbor were set up in a field on the perimeter of the military in-
stallation, a few hundred yards from remnants of the old school build-

ings, which have been incorporated into the day-to-day activities of the War College.

Over the course of the weekend, small groups of Indian people broke away from the powwow to visit the quadrangle of buildings and parade ground where Indian children had marched a century before. Much of the former school has been torn down or obliterated by the expansion of the military post, but a significant clutch of buildings still remain. The present-day guest house, Washington Hall, standing on the corner of the old campus, was the school hospital. Built when Carlisle was only five years old, it was later adapted to house the famous athletic teams. That weekend, many Native American visitors climbing the stairs to see where Jim Thorpe had stayed were surprised to find, beside the printed plaque, "Jim Thorpe Room," a handwritten note reading, "Scott Momaday." The Pulitzer Prize winning author was the Powwow's keynote speaker. He had asked to stay in Thorpe's room and his temporary nameplate was just one among many visible reminders that live Indians were physically repossessing Carlisle.

Native American visitors stepping out of the guesthouse found themselves at the corner of what had been the main quadrangle of the Indian School, standing on a straight path whose route had not altered since Indian children trod it. This path passed in front of several of the original buildings—the old superintendent's house and large administrative office built by the students as part of their vocational training—and led down to the old campus entrance.[2] The original entrance is long gone, but its position is still marked by the old stone guardhouse that supported the original gates and that is now the post museum.

Inside this cool, damp, eighteenth-century powder house, with six-foot-thick walls and no windows, the long and varied history of the Carlisle Barracks is on display. One small corner is dedicated to the post's Indian School days; a brief perfunctory account is illustrated by four photographs. No mention is made of the fact that just a few yards away, visitors could peer past the glass barrier and NO EXIT sign and still see four, small, heavy doors, hiding cells where recalcitrant Indian runaways were incarcerated. The bars of these cells lend a chilling immediacy to the school's history.

Other traces of the Indian School are still visible. Walking back across the quadrangle, visitors past staff houses constructed by students and the little model home where, in the school's later days, Indian girls were educated in American homemaking skills. The Coren Apartments, where teachers lived, gives an impression of what the girls' dormitory opposite would have looked like, before this building burned down in 1924.[3] Today, it has been replaced by tennis courts, but the gymnasium nearby looks exactly as it did in nineteenth-century photographs. Inside, the oval running track still hugs the brick wall, fifteen feet above the hall where local dignitaries gathered for commencement day ceremonies and Indian children were schooled in calisthenics.

In the middle of campus stands a replica bandstand, built in 1980. Many of the Native American visitors instinctively climbed its steps to gain a commanding view of the surrounding buildings and grounds. Most were unaware of the imaginary man-on-the-bandstand who had once resided there, but returning to the powwow grounds, everyone understood the special importance of the Carlisle sports field they passed.

Visitors to the grounds of the school gained a tangible sense of the lives that had been lived there by their ancestors, but many left with a range of complicated emotions. Donna Herne (Mohawk) commented later that for her it felt as if the children had been prisoners. For others, the connection to Carlisle was more joyous. Two weeks after the powwow, Anne Wheelock Gonzales (Oneida) was certain she would return to Carlisle. "I never imagined I would ever visit Carlisle Indian School," she emailed, "Now I can't wait to go back. . . . You can't imagine how I felt when I ran across the football field where Grandpa played. I could just feel his presence all over campus."[4]

In the town, too, there are still many visible reminders of the Indian School. Most of these focus on Jim Thorpe who, for both Indians and whites, is the happiest reminder of Carlisle's history. There's a wall of framed photographs in one of the local truck stops; a backroom "shrine" full of Thorpe memorabilia at the men's clothing store Wardecker's, where the Indian School athletes were offered a special line of credit; and a three-foot-high stone that pays tribute to Jim Thorpe's achievements and stands in the central square. While Thorpe is Carlisle's best-known denizen, there are many other less trumpeted links between the town and the Indian school.

Diagonally across the main square from the Jim Thorpe stone stands St. John's Episcopal Church. Here, in the early days of the Indian School, the children attended a special, segregated, Sunday school class. Many were baptized at St John's, including the children of the famous Brulé Sioux chief, Spotted Tail. One hundred and twenty years later, some of the "survivors," who are descendants of over ten thousand young Indian people who attended the Carlisle Indian School, gathered at St. John's Episcopal church for an evening reception to open the Memorial Day powwow weekend. Names in the guest book include those whose links to Carlisle are strong and famous, like Eastman and Wheelock. But others were there whose connection to the school is equally deep, like Jim West, who had come to honor his Cheyenne grandmother, Rena Flying Coyote. Included among the guests were many representatives from different bands of the Sioux nation, because Sioux children, from the Rosebud and Pine Ridge Agencies, had been the first to arrive and their people were always strongly represented at Carlisle. Large photographs, mounted on the walls, displayed the history of the school as recorded by the white-directed camera. The "arrival" pictures, showing the children lined up in front of the school buildings or bandstand, wearing buckskin, blankets, feathers and beads, supplied the only glimpse of Indian culture. These pictures had been taken and used for propaganda purposes, before their clothing and adornments were confiscated to be burned, sold, or sent away to museums. The expressions of the children who stared out displayed a complicated fusion of shock and sullen defiance. But, more than a century on, within a mile of where these pictures had been taken to excite white interest in the extinguishing of their "savagery," their stare was now returned by the sympathetic gaze of their twenty-first century descendants, many of them clad in ribbon shirts, beaded jackets, and shawls.

That evening, many, whose knowledge of Carlisle had come to them from stories passed down within their own communities, consciously came together and met with strangers from other tribes and nations to talk about the lives of their relatives who had attended the school. As with any reunion, those who chose to come to Carlisle were a self-selecting group. Others deliberately stayed away, too disinterested, lost, bitter, or angry to face the return. Nora McGee, a fifty-five-year-old Oneida from New York State, vividly remembered her grandparents and great-grandparents talking about Carlisle with scorn and anger. She understood why several of her older relatives had refused to attend the weekend's events. "They just couldn't let go," she said.[5] The intensity of the school's legacy meant that a decision to return was tied to deep emotions and long-standing agendas.

Not all those attending came from far away. Karen Troupe lives in the Bloserville area, just outside Carlisle. She knows she is part Cheyenne, but has lost contact with this part of her heritage. After conversations with local farmers, she has come to the conclusion that her family from the Great Plains must have formed part of a large community of Native Americans who settled in the area after they left Carlisle and did not return home. For Troupe, the story of the Indian school is associated with a painful sense of loss, and her attendance at the powwow was part of her endeavor to forge a connection to help ease that pain.[6]

The longest journey to the powwow was made by a family whose home is in America's furthest-flung state. From Alaska, Mary Jones had visited Carlisle for the first time sixteen years earlier in search of information about her mother's sister, Mary Kininnook. All her life she had known that her namesake aunt had gone to Carlisle and had died when her own mother was eight. On her first visit, Mary Jones's husband and daughter helped her sift through the Carlisle files kept by the Military History Institute. But they could find no record of Mary Kininnook. Later, medical cards she obtained from the National Archives revealed that Mary Kininnook had died of tuberculosis or pneumonia in the school's hospital, aged fourteen, on December 28, 1908. Yet when the family searched in the school cemetery, there was no marker for Mary Kininnook. After continuing their research, they were forced to the distressing realization that Mary Kininnook's headstone must be one of the fourteen engraved with the single word, "Unknown." Mary and Willard Jones, accompanied by their daughter Eleanor Hadden, returned to Pennsylvania for the Memorial Day weekend powwow as part of their continuing search for Mary Kininnook and their desire to honor her.

In South Dakota, as soon as news of the pending powwow had reached the Dubray family, they knew they had to go. Jimmie Dubray began preparations for a Lakota spirit-releasing ceremony for the children in

304

20. Indian School cemetery at Powwow 2000. Photograph by
Chip Fox, © 2000 *Philadelphia Inquirer.*

the school cemetery. Nineteen were known to be Sioux. Sadly, in November 1999, he suffered a heart attack. Before he died, he insisted that it was imperative that his family go to Carlisle. Passing responsibility for the spiritual events of the powwow to his son-in-law, Aaron DeSersa and Aaron's adopted son, Wayne Cave, he instructed them to prepare for and perform the spirit-releasing ceremony for the children who had been buried far from home with no traditional rites. For the Dubray family and their community, the return to Carlisle was vital, and its pain was made more intense by their recent personal loss.

The reception at St. John's in the center of Carlisle brought Native American visitors and local townspeople together for the first time, but the main events of the powwow took place over two days on the grounds of the old Indian School north of the town. A key focus for the Dubray and Jones families, as well as many others, were the traditional ceremonies held for the children in the cemetery (fig. 20).

Facing out onto the main road beside the back entrance to the U.S. Army War College, the school cemetery had been spruced up and smartened for the weekend. All Friday morning the grass-cutting tractor had moved slowly up and down between the rows, while gardeners trimmed hedges, laid down fresh, dark soil around each stone and buffed the imposing "Indian Cemetery" brass plaque beside the little wrought iron entrance gate. Despite past insensitivities and cruelties, in the classic traditions of the army, the War College was doing its bit for the occasion. When the work was finished, the school cemetery resembled a military burial ground even more than it usually did.

At all times, the sight of an Indian graveyard on an active military post is bizarre. On the grounds of the Carlisle Barracks on Memorial Day weekend 2000, an even more incongruous scene emerged. The conical outline and jutting poles of three tipis now broke the skyline, standing more than fifteen feet high. Their entrances faced out toward the cemetery, due east, according to traditional custom, to catch the first rays of the rising sun. Erected to provide changing areas for the powwow dancers, they, and the recently constructed, round, hay-bale powwow arbor provided the first visible sign that Indian people had returned to Carlisle and that the proceedings would be run on their terms.

For the first time ever, on the morning of May 28, 2000, sacred Native American rites were practiced openly on the grounds of the Carlisle Barracks.[7] The day dawned damp and overcast and the buzz of Saturday traffic was only intermittent when a group of about fifty people assembled near the gate of the Indian cemetery. Inside the railed enclosure, several rows of chairs had been set up for elders and those with a relative buried in the cemetery, but no one ventured through the gate. There was a mood of reverence and community, and people spoke easily and quietly to each other. But there was also a general feeling of diffidence. No one was quite certain what was going to happen. The names carved on the headstones indicated that different tribes had representatives buried in the cemetery, and each had their own rites and rituals for mourning the dead. Nowhere else did Sioux lie alongside Crow, Navaho beside Pueblo, Apache flank Chippewa.[8] Their presence together scrambled separate cultures and histories as well as geography. In death as in life these children had been forced together and to make contacts at odds with their past. As a result, their descendants were now all powerfully connected by their shared links to the Carlisle Indian School, which had forced itself into their respective histories. The order and symmetry of the stones masked a story of rupture and disarray. Yet the cemetery is the school's most poignant as well as vital surviving remnant.

Not only does it provide evidence of the tragic toll the school exacted on young Native American lives, but it is also the one place where any visible trace of the children survives. All the informative plaques on the remaining school buildings employ the depersonalized label "Indian." In the cemetery, despite its sanitized appearance and the garbled history affected by its layout and inscriptions, the stones carry the names and tribal affiliation of real children who lived and died at the school: Samuel Flying Horse, Sioux; Charles Fisher, Crow; Abe Lincoln; Cheyenne. The graves stand as a physical connection to an effaced and painful chapter of Native American history, sacred because of the sacrifice the children had been forced to make.

Standing beside the ceremonial pit, where the fire of cedar and hemlock burned strongly near the entrance to the cemetery, Wayne Cave informed the mourners that some of the "lost ones" were not buried here but "over there," and he pointed west, toward the location of the original school cemetery. His gesture was a sharp reminder of the harsh pattern of events that had made this Memorial Day weekend ceremony so late in its enactment. He explained to the group that he was going to conduct a spirit- releasing ceremony. This was a Lakota rite, to help the spirits pass to the other side; it had never been performed for these children. When the drummer began his steady beat, it was the first time this sound had ever been heard at the Carlisle Barracks.

The ceremony was for all the children, but the buffalo meat offered to the spirits gave it both a cultural and regional character, so it seemed appropriate that Thomas Marshall's outsized stone at the central plot should be made a representative grave for much of the ceremony. Tobacco leaves, carried round the cemetery and placed on every stone, with a larger amount to bless the "unknowns," served as a reminder of a cultural tradition shared by all tribes. The air was heavy from burning sage when the family from Alaska stepped forward to continue the ceremony. Willard Jones made clear that the Tlingit also shared the tradition of "feeding the spirits." But, he explained, "We are people of the sea, so the offerings we have brought are dried salmon, haddock and seaweed." As he explained the traditions of the people of Alaska to an attentive assembly from far-flung homes and diverse backgrounds, the noise of the traffic on the adjacent road grew to an incessant rumble.

Above it, the strident voices of military personnel could be heard, diverting cars and refusing entry to all vehicles. Ironically, the U.S. Army was working to give Native American mourners a moment of respectful peace to remember their dead.

For the Alaskan family, the events of the Memorial Day weekend represented an important punctuation point in their long search. They came dressed in their finest attire; Eleanor had made a new headdress and wore a Tlingit blanket. Willard, speaking in an open and direct way, explained to the mourners that they knew his wife's aunt was buried in the cemetery, but that there was no known marker. She was one of the "unknowns." Everyone present was there to mourn lost children, and Willard invited them all to join the ceremonial. One by one the mourners took a small handful of the sea products from the proffered bag and dropped them onto the fire of cedar and hemlock boughs, slowly forming a close circle around it. Gathered together to honor and grieve, the occasion was, as Scott Momaday observed later, something like a "giveaway": generous, inclusive, and encompassing.

As a thin rain began to fall, the people moved into the cemetery and talked quietly among themselves. Throughout the weekend, although all the subsequent powwow events took place on the adjoining field, the cemetery remained a central focal point. Many, like Donna Herne, had not known of its existence before their visit to Carlisle. But no one left without paying their respects. Throughout both days, individuals and groups would drift away from the stalls and dancing to walk between the little white stones and read the names engraved on them. For many it was a shock to recognize some of the names of the dead or to see their tribal label chiseled onto a marker. N. Scott Momaday paused to honor Zonekeuh, a fellow Kiowa, perhaps aware that his kinsman had been one of the original Fort Marion prisoners. By the end of the weekend, gifts of coins, toys, candy, beadwork, and sweetgrass had been left on many of the graves. Beside the stone of a Pawnee boy, a long, severed plait of hair and pair of scissors indicated that someone was in deepest mourning.

By 10 o'clock, the powwow had become a public event and a crowd of more than two thousand people began to assemble, wandering round the stalls and fry-bread stands and finding themselves places on the bleachers and bales of straw in time for the grand entry at noon. As is common at powwows, a guard of honor of Native veterans led the procession of dancers in full regalia into the arbor. On the grounds of Carlisle Barracks, where previously school boys and girls from many nations had been endlessly drilled, paraded, and marched, these modern-day Indian soldiers signaled a complicated message. Their medals, neat uniforms, and polished boots declared them proud members of the U.S. Army, but as they carried the flag and led the dancers into the powwow arbor, they did not march. Their feet moved instead in an interrupted step to the steady heartbeat-rhythm of the Indian drum.

The drizzle had by now become a downpour, and the rain would fall almost incessantly throughout the weekend, soaking but not deterring the dancers. For many, the history of the school became much clearer after the keynote address. Scott Momaday explained how although some had benefited from skills learned at Carlisle, many more had been destroyed by the experience. He did not flinch from repeating the chilling Carlisle motto, "Kill the Indian and save the man," but then gave voice to what he deemed the correct equation: save the Indian and save the man.

But as Jim West (Cheyenne) explained, "most of the Indian people there . . . had come to celebrate a relative, a family member, not a school." When they called for a memorial dance, all those with grandparents and great-grandparents at Carlisle entered the arbor. Some had never danced before; others were old hands. For all of them it was an important moment, and they wore their best regalia. On his breastplate, Jim West pinned a photograph of his grandmother, Rena Flying Coyote (fig. 21). As he later confided to his niece, "I had brought my eagle feather bustle 2,000 miles for that dance and I put it on, rain or no rain. I could hear Pops telling me to 'dance proud.'"[9] The drums beat all weekend. Their pulse accompanied music, singing, and dancers' swaying regalia that came from the length and breadth of America. Grass dancers, traditional dancers, jingle-dress dancers, shawl dancers: men, women, and children all danced to honor the children who were taken from their homes and brought to Carlisle to learn the white man's ways.

Few local residents had ever witnessed an Indian powwow. The drenching rain ensured that those whose curiosity might have persuaded them

21. Jim West (Cheyenne) with photograph of his grandmother, Powwow 2000. Photograph by Chip Fox, © 2000 *Philadelphia Inquirer*.

to view the event as a colorful spectacle stayed away. Some went up to the barracks that weekend because powwow publicity had alerted them to a previously unknown chapter of Carlisle history; they were stunned to discover there had been an Indian School on their doorstep. For others, whose ancestors had attended the school and then remained in the region, the powwow represented their first opportunity to reconnect with a lost past. The feeling of rupture experienced by those who had never gone home was repeated in those who had returned. Many found their years away from the nurture of family and community had left them emotionally scarred and unready for the responsibilities of adulthood. Jim West paid tribute to his grandmother: "Rena's heart is not 'on the ground' and her strength is a great legacy to us all." But to his niece he also acknowledged the "chasm that has made it difficult for your Father and I to know how to be an extended family with our cousins." He identified "Rena's experience at Carlisle" as "another link in the chain of dysfunctionality that runs through my family."[10]

West was prompted to write an honest, open letter to his niece while returning to New Mexico after spending the weekend at Carlisle. The powwow had been organized to honor the children and to help promote the truth and knowledge that are always a prerequisite of healing and reconciliation. For many it brought a new awareness of what had taken place at Carlisle, but this was not always accompanied by closure.

Carlisle and its many look-alikes still exert a profound influence on the whole native population of the United States. Benjamin Washington, a Seminole, was not yet one year old when Carlisle was closed, but stories about the school reverberated through his Florida childhood. For him, Carlisle was part of "a scary bedtime story your parents would tell you before you went to sleep. 'Be good and stay out of trouble or you will be shipped off to the school in Carlisle, or some place like it.'" He confessed that his fear of being sent away had often kept him out of trouble as a young child. At age eighty-three, when he heard there was going to be a powwow at Carlisle, he knew he had to go.[11] Returning to the site of the school was for many a profound experience. Brent Michael Davies, a forty-year-old Mohican composer who performed at the powwow and wrote the song, "Dawn," to honor the alumni, felt the significance of this physicality very keenly. "I can hold a spear point in my hand," he explained, "Someone in my clan made it 6,000 years ago. I feel connected when I touch it. I can feel my inheritance and know who I am." For him, returning to Carlisle was associated with the same task of understanding his history and identity. "Now that it's dead, Carlisle Indian School is a far greater touch stone for Native Americans than when it lived. Now we can return to touch Carlisle as brothers, sisters, fathers, mothers, grandfathers and grandmothers. We can return to grasp Carlisle as 'The People' and carry the remnant in our hands . . . and know who we are."[12]

William Herne and his twin sisters Diane and Donna drove together to Carlisle as a family team to represent their grandmother, Maggie Tarbell Lazore. At ninety-nine she was one of only two surviving alumni of Carlisle.[13] Several other members of their family had also gone to the school and over the weekend the Hernes all felt they had suddenly discovered a lost piece of their past. Diane took photographs of the town, the school, the cemetery, and the powwow in equal numbers. They returned to St. Regis, New York, conscious of their need to talk more about a story that had never been told in its entirety. William and Donna are both trained counselors and acutely aware of the problems of many young people in their community. They left Carlisle with new empathetic knowledge of the experiences of children who attended the school. William reflected wryly on his own brief brush with a comparable pedagogy, remembering how at kindergarten he had been told off for speaking Mohawk. He wondered how the experiences of the Carlisle children might have been modified if they had been able to go and talk to someone like Donna. He realized there had been nothing in the dominant society to help them process what was being demanded of them: they had simply been "ordered to march in step." The Hernes, along with many who attended the powwow, feel very strongly that what happened at the government Indian schools needs to be known and discussed, that the "survivors," as well as those who have been made dysfunctional by this history, need the whole story to be told.

After the powwow, William, Diane, and Donna Herne returned to the Mohawk reservation in St Regis to recount and reflect on the events at Carlisle with three generations of their family. For many, the native diaspora precipitated by the schools have robbed them of any such community where memories can be discussed and revived.

Dorreen Yellow Bird was forcefully reminded of this fact and the "roots of change and disruption that Native People come from" the moment she heard about the powwow. She likened the jump her mind made to touching a bookmark on her computer, making a "whole new view, different from today, pop up." When she received the e-mail about the Memorial Day weekend powwow at Carlisle, she instantly remembered her grandfather, Louis Felix, a Santee Sioux sent to Carlisle in 1893. He was trained to be a "disciplinarian" or matron, Yellow Bird recalls, and "went on to be a boys' matron at a boarding school in Arizona." Some time later he was moved to Minnesota, to work at the Leech Lake Indian School, for another tribe, the Ojibway or Chippewa. His career in the Indian Service furthered the rupture and separation initiated by Carlisle. Yet his granddaughter survives him. Prompted by news of the Carlisle powwow, she is able to write his story for worldwide electronic distribution in the online version of the Grand Forks *Herald*. "It is those roots of change and disruption that Native people come from," Yellow Bird explains, "and it is the seeds of tenacity that have allowed us to survive."[14]

Many traditions have been compromised or lost, but for Juanita Neconie (Pawnee) recognition of the tenacity of native people's endless capacity to adapt was reinforced when she saw the northern drummer hold his cell phone to his drum, so that a friend could hear the beat, hundreds of miles away back home. Despite the pain intrinsic to the event, Powwow 2000 was a triumphant moment. Native American people had returned to reclaim the grounds of the Carlisle Barracks. As Jim West wrote to his niece: "We prayed that day in languages that had been forbidden. We wore buckskins covered in beadwork, shawls, and all forms of traditional regalia, which had been taken from the students of Carlisle, our Grandparents and Great Grandparents. We were still dancing that day on the grounds of the school that was going to 'kill the Indian and save the man' and had long since disappeared. It was a good day."[15]

Notes

Introduction

Thomas Wildcat Alford, *Civilization, as Told to Florence Drake* (Norman: University of Oklahoma Press, 1936; repr., *Civilization and the Story of the Absentee Shawnees* [Norman: University of Oklahoma Press, 1979]), 73. Citations are to the 1979 edition.

1. Colin Gordon, ed., *Michel Foucault, Power/Knowledge: Selected Interviews and Other Writings, 1972–1977* (Harlow UK: Longman, 1980), 97.

2. Joel Spring, *The Cultural Transformation of a Native American Family, 1763–1995* (Mahwah NJ: Lawrence Erlbaum Associates, 1996); for Canada see J. R. Miller, *Shingwauk's Vision: a History of Native Residential Schools* (Toronto: University of Toronto Press, 1996).

3. Norman Hampson, *The Enlightenment: An Evaluation of Its Assumptions, Attitudes and Values* (London: Penguin, 1990); Henry F. May, *The Enlightenment in America* (New York: Oxford University Press, 1976).

4. Mike Hawkins, *Social Darwinism in European and American Thought, 1860–1945: Nature as Model and Nature as Threat* (Cambridge UK: Cambridge University Press, 1997); J. D. Y. Peel, ed., *Herbert Spencer on Social Evolution: Selected Writings* (Chicago: University of Chicago Press, 1972); George W. Stocking Jr., *Race, Culture, and Evolution: Essays in the History of Anthropology* (New York: Free Press, 1968).

5. Peggy Pascoe, "Miscegnation Law, Court Cases, and Ideologies of Race in Twentieth-Century America," *Journal of American History* 83.1 (June 1996): 44–69. Pascoe provides an excellent examination of the historical development of the concept of race in this essay.

6. Frederick Hoxie, *The Final Promise: The Campaign to Assimilate the Indian, 1880–1920* (Lincoln: University of Nebraska Press, 1983).

7. Robert A. Trennert Jr.'s *The Phoenix Indian School: Forced Acculturation in Arizona, 1891–1935* (Norman: University of Oklahoma Press, 1988) is the first study of an individual institution and begins in 1891; Sally Hyer, *One House, One Voice, One Heart: Native American Education at the Santa Fe Indian School, 1890–1990* (Santa Fe: Museum of New Mexico Press, 1990), starts her book in 1890; K. Tsianina Lomawaima, *They Called it Prairie Light: The*

Story of Chilocco School (Lincoln: University of Nebraska Press, 1994) focuses on the 1920s and 30s; Clyde Ellis, *To Change Them Forever: Indian Education at the Rainy Mountain Boarding School, 1893–1920* (Norman: University of Oklahoma Press, 1996), studies a school that opened in 1893; Brenda Child, *Boarding School Seasons: American Indian Families, 1900–1940* (Lincoln: University of Nebraska Press, 1998), looks at the first part of twentieth century; Scott Riney, *The Rapid City Indian School, 1898–1933* (Norman: University of Oklahoma Press, 1999), begins his book in 1898.

8. For a collection of primary documents detailing this campaign, see Francis Paul Prucha, *Americanizing the American Indians: Writings by the "Friends of the Indian," 1880–1900* (Cambridge MA: Harvard University Press, 1973; repr., Lincoln: University of Nebraska, 1978).

9. The racist philosophy that accompanied Indian schooling is addressed briefly and perceptively in Donal Lindsey, *Indians at Hampton Institute, 1877–1923* (Urbana: University of Illinois Press, 1995), 180–84.

10. For scientific racism, see Thomas F. Gossett, *Race: The History of an Idea in America* (Dallas TX: Southern Methodist University Press, 1963); George W. Stocking Jr., *Race, Culture and Evolution*; John. S. Haller Jr., *Outcasts from Evolution: Scientific Attitudes to Racial Inferiority, 1859–1900*, new ed. (Carbondale: Southern Illinois University Press, 1995). On the social construction of race ideologies, see Reginald Horsman, *Race and Manifest Destiny: The Origins of American Racial Anglo-Saxonism* (Cambridge MA: Harvard University Press, 1981); Alexander Saxton, *The Rise and Fall of the White Republic: Class Politics and Mass Culture in Nineteenth-Century America* (London: Verso, 1990); Audrey Smedley, *Race in North America: Origins and Evolution of a Worldview* (Boulder CO: Westview, 1993); Barbara J. Fields, "Ideology and Race in American History," in *Region, Race and Reconstruction: Essays in Honor of C. Vann Woodward*, ed. J. Morgan Kousser and James M. McPherson (New York: Oxford University Press, 1982), 143–78; Thomas C. Holt, "Marking: Race, Race-making, and the Writing of History," *American Historical Review* 100.1 (February 1995).

11. This political program claimed the attention of contemporary "Friends of the Indian" and, until recently, has dominated historical scholarship. The most comprehensive studies are by Francis Paul Prucha—in particular, vols. 1 and 2 of *The Great Father: The United States Government and the American Indians* (Lincoln: University of Nebraska Press, 1984). Michael Omi and Howard Winant, *Racial Formation in the United States* (New York: Routledge, 1994), focuses on the decades after 1960 but supplies a conceptual frame for addressing the broader issue of racial formation. Matthew Frye Jacobson, *Whiteness of a Different Color: European Immigrants and the Alchemy of Race* (Cambridge MA: Harvard University Press, 1999), examines the instability of the concept of race and documents how immigrant groups were engaged in a struggle to embrace "whiteness."

12. See Cheryl Walker, *Indian Nation: Native American Literature and Nineteenth-Century Nationalisms* (Durham NC: Duke University Press, 1997), especially chap. 1, "The Subject of America: The Outsider Inside."

13. For an excellent wide-ranging study, see David Wallace Adams, *Education for Extinction: American Indians and the Boarding School Experience, 1875–1928* (Lawrence: University Press of Kansas, 1995).

14. A rich and copious scholarship documents the central role played by missionaries, including support given tribes in struggles against the federal government—in particular, William G. McLoughlin, *Cherokees and Missionaries, 1789–1839* (New Haven CT: Yale University Press, 1984); Clyde A. Milner II, *With Good Intentions: Quaker Work among the Pawnees, Otos, and Omahas in the 1870s* (Lincoln: University of Nebraska Press, 1982); Francis Paul Prucha, *The Churches and the Indian Schools, 1888–1912* (Lincoln: Nebraska Press, 1979).

15. For details of published stories, see H. David Brumble III, *An Annotated Bibliography of American Indian and Eskimo Autobiographies* (Lincoln: University of Nebraska Press, 1981), and for an analysis of some of these accounts, see Michael Coleman, *American Indian Children at School, 1850–1930* (Jackson: University Press of Mississippi, 1993).

16. Some of the stories were too painful or difficult to tell. Some students never returned to their people; one group from Carlisle remained in Pennsylvania as farm and domestic workers.

17. Brenda J. Child, *Boarding School Seasons*; Scott Riney, *The Rapid City Indian School*.

18. Richard Jenkins, *Social Identity* (London: Routledge, 1996), 21.

19. James C. Scott, *Domination and the Arts of Resistance: Hidden Transcripts* (New Haven CT: Yale University Press, 1990), 87.

20. Scott, *Domination and the Arts of Resistance*, xii.

21. Here I am following the lead of Grandison in his pioneering work on the campuses of historical black colleges and universities, "Negotiated Space: The Black College Campus as a Cultural Record of Postbellum America," *American Quarterly* 51.3 (September 1999): 529–79.

22. Grandison, "Negotiated Space," xii, and James C. Scott, *Weapons of the Weak: Everyday Forms of Peasant Resistance* (New Haven CT: Yale University Press, 1985).

23. Michel-Rolph Trouillot, *Silencing the Past: Power and the Production of History* (Boston: Beacon Press, 1995).

24. Benedict Anderson, *Imagined Communities: Reflections on the Origin and Spread of Nationalism* (London: Verso, 1983), 15–16.

25. David Charter, "Canadian Natives Win £1bn for 70 Years' Abuse," *Times* (London), November 25, 2005 5, http://www.timesonline.co.uk/tol/news/world/us_and_americas/article596402.ece (accessed March 12, 2007); Graham Fra-

ser, "Ex-Residential School Students Get $1.9 billion," *Toronto Star*, April 26, 2006, sec. A, 4; "The Settlement Agreement on Residential Schools," The United Church of Canada, May 2006, http://www.united-church.ca/residentialschools/2006/0517.shtm (accessed January 22, 2007).

26. Genevieve Bell, "Telling Stories out of School: Remembering the Carlisle Indian Industrial School, 1879–1918" (PhD diss., Stanford University, 1998); Carmelita Ryan, "The Carlisle Indian Industrial School" (PhD diss., Georgetown University, 1962); Everett Gilcreast, "Richard Henry Pratt and American Indian Policy, 1877–1906: A Study of the Assimilation Movement" (PhD diss., Yale University, 1967). See also Linda F. Witmer, *The Indian Industrial School, Carlisle Pennsylvania, 1879–1918* (Carlisle PA: Cumberland County Historical Society, 1993), for a descriptive account with excellent archival photographs.

Prologue

1. Pratt to Sheridan, March 17, 1876, in Richard Henry Pratt, *Battlefield and Classroom: Four Decades with the American Indian, 1867–1904*, ed. Robert M. Utley (New Haven CT: Yale University Press, 1964), 171; Henry B. Whipple, *Lights and Shadows of a Long Episcopate* (New York: Macmillan, 1899), 30–36.

2. Pratt, *Battlefield and Classroom*, 112, 120.

3. Harriet Beecher Stowe, "The Indians at St. Augustine," *The Christian Union* (New York), April 25, 1877; reprinted in full in Pratt, *Battlefield and Classroom*, 158–62.

4. Jacqueline Fear-Segal, interview with Jim Anquoe Sr., February 12, 2003.

5. "Report of Kiowa Agent P. B. Hunt," in *Annual Report of the Commissioner of Indian Affairs* (Washington DC: GPO, 1880), 775. For an account of Kiowa schools at this time, see Clyde Ellis, *To Change Them Forever: Indian Education at the Rainy Mountain Boarding School, 1893–1920* (Norman: University of Oklahoma Press, 1996), chap. 2.

6. The treaties with the Kiowa, Comanche, Apache, Cheyenne, and Arapaho were signed in October 1867; the treaty with the Sioux was signed the following year in April 1868 and was also based on the recommendations of the commission (15 Stats. 581, 589, and 593: see Charles J. Kappler, *Indian Affairs: Laws and Treaties*, vol. 2, *Treaties* (Washington DC: GPO, 1904), 754, 764, and 770–75.

7. William Hagan, *United States–Comanche Relations* (Norman: University of Oklahoma Press, 1990), 29–32, 42–44; Robert H. Keller Jr., *American Protestantism and United States Indian Policy, 1869–82* (Lincoln: University of Nebraska Press, 1983). Hagan and Keller both criticize the Treaty of Medicine Lodge. For a detailed account of negotiations see Douglas Jones, *The Treaty of Medicine Lodge* (Norman: University of Oklahoma Press, 1966).

8. Kappler, *Indian Affairs: Laws and Treaties*, vol. 2, *Treaties*, 676–78, 686–93.

9. *Report to the President by the Indian Peace Commission*, Ho. Ex. Doc. No. 97, 40th Cong., 2nd sess., 1868, 2.

10. Francis Walker, *The Indian Question* (Boston: James R. Osgood, 1874), 17.

11. *Indian Question*, 77, 97.

12. *Congressional Globe*, 39th Cong., 1st sess., 1865–66, 2890–96; R. Alton Lee, "Indian Citizenship and the Fourteenth Amendment," *South Dakota History* 4 (Spring 1974): 198–222.

13. 16 Stat. 566.

14. Full details given by Pratt of the prisoners' alleged crimes are given by Pratt in *Battlefield and Classroom*, 138–144.

15. Robert Wooster, *The Military and United States Indian Policy, 1865–1903* (New Haven CT: Yale University Press, 1988), 174.

16. Agent James Haworth to CIA, February 27, 1879, Bureau of Indian Affairs, RG 75, letters received, Kiowa Agency, M234, National Archives.

17. James Mooney, *Calendar History of the Kiowa Indians* (Washington DC: GPO, 1898; repr., Washington DC: Smithsonian Institution Press, 1979), 344–45.

18. Robert M. Utley, *The Lance and the Shield: The Life and Times of Sitting Bull* (London: Pimlico, 1998), 279–80.

19. Quoted in Henrietta Mann, *Cheyenne–Arapaho Education, 1871–1982* (Niwot: University Press of Colorado, 1997), 23–24.

20. Report of Thomas Battey to Kiowa Agent, July 31, 1873, Bureau of Indian Affairs, RG 75, letters received, Kiowa Agency, M234, National Archives.

21. Shortly after the prisoners were taken from Fort Sill, Kicking Bear died suddenly. To this day, many Kiowa suspect he was poisoned for protecting his own supporters from imprisonment. See Utley, *The Lance and the Shield*, 40n4, and Jacqueline Fear-Segal, interview with Jim Anquoe Sr., February 12, 2003.

22. For Pratt's account see Pratt, *Battlefield and Classroom*, 104–15; for a white account giving a Cheyenne perspective on these events, see Peter John Powell, *People of the Sacred Mountain* (San Francisco: Harper and Row, 1981), 901.

23. Geronimo's band was treated in the same way. In 1886, nearly five hundred of his followers, including women and children, were transported to Florida and incarcerated in Fort Marion.

24. Ankopaaingyadete, meaning "In-the-middle-of-many-tracks", was abbreviated to Anko. See James Mooney, *Calendar of the History of the Kiowa Indians*, 145.

25. Anko's was one of three known Kiowa calendars and employed what James Mooney identified as a Kiowa system of calendar pictography (*Calendar of the History of the Kiowa Indians*, 339 and 144–45.

26. Karen Daniels Petersen, *Plains Indian Art from Fort Marion* (Norman: University of Oklahoma Press, 1971), 16.

27. Moira F. Harris, *Between Two Cultures: Kiowa Art from Fort Marion* (St. Paul MN: Pogo Press, 1989), 11; Janet Catherine Berlo, *Plains Indian Drawings, 1865–1935: Pages from a Visual History* (New York: American Federation of Arts and the Drawing Center, 1996), 12, 19.

28. Besides Bear's Heart, Wohaw, Edadhleuh, and Howling Wolf also drew their classroom.

29. "Indian Talk," *Southern Workman* 9.7, July 1880, 77.

30. Herman J. Viola, *Warrior Artists: Historic Cheyenne and Kiowa Indian Ledger Art Drawn by Making Medicine and Zotom* (Washington DC: National Geographic Society, 1998), 13; Petersen, *Plains Indian Art from Fort Marion*; Janet Catherine Berlo, *Native North American Art* (Oxford UK: Oxford University Press, 1998); Joyce M. Szabo, *Howling Wolf and the History of Ledger Art* (Albuquerque: University of New Mexico Press), 1994.

31. Ashis Nandy, *The Intimate Enemy: Loss and Recovery of Self under Colonialism* (Delhi: Oxford University Press, 1983), x–xi.

32. J. A. Mangan, "Images for Confident Control: Stereotypes in Imperial Discourse," in *The Imperial Curriculum: Racial Images and Education in the British Colonial Experience*, ed. J. A. Mangan (London: Routledge, 1993), 6–22.

33. David Wallace Adams, *Education for Extinction: American Indians and the Boarding School Experience, 1875–1928* (Lawrence: University Press of Kansas, 1995), 38–46.

34. Gillmore to Post, April 3, 1875, Office of the Chief of Engineers, RG 77, letters received, Chief Engineer, National Archives, in "Historic Structure Report for Castillo de San Marco," 273, typed manuscript, St. Augustine Historical Society.

35. Sidney Lanier, *Florida: Its Scenery, Climate and History* (Philadelphia: J. B. Lippincott, 1875; facs. repr., Gainesville: University of Florida Press, 1973), Brent Ashabranner, *A Strange and Distant Shore* (New York: Cobble Hill Books, 1996), 19.

36. Pratt, *Battlefield and Classroom*, 138–44, gives details of all the prisoners.

37. Lawrence J. Vale, *Architecture, Power, and National Identity* (New Haven CT: Yale University Press, 1992); Anthony D. King, *Colonial Urban Development: Culture, Social Power, and Environment* (London: Routledge, 1976).

38. Pratt, *Battlefield and Classroom*, 149.

39. Pratt to General Sheridan, March 1875, in Pratt, *The Indian Industrial School, Carlisle* (Carlisle PA: Indian School, 1901), 1

40. Pratt to General Sheridan, April 26, 1875, Pratt, *Battlefield and Classroom*, 106.

41. Stephen Lukes, *Power: A Radical View* (London: Macmillan, 1983).

42. See Michel Foucault's *Discipline and Punish* (New York: Vintage Books, 1977) for an exploration of the inner workings of surveillance.

43. William Cullen Bryant's 1873 letters to the New York *Evening Post*, quoted in J. E. Dovell, *Florida: Historic, Dramatic, Contemporary* (New York: Lewis Historical Publishing, 1952), 566.

44. Josephine Burgess Jacobs, "A Bull Fight in St. Augustine Florida, 1875," typed ms., St. Augustine Historical Society.

45. "Indian Sports and War Dance," publicity poster, n.d., St. Augustine Historical Society.

46. Joy S. Kasson, *Buffalo Bill's Wild West: Celebrity, Memory, and Popular History* (New York: Hill and Wang, 2000); George P. Horsecapture, *Powwow* (Cody WY: Buffalo Bill Historical Center, 1989).

47. Pratt, *Battlefield and Classroom*, 153; interview with Jim Anouh Sr., February 6, 2003; Clyde Ellis, *A Dancing People: Powwow Culture on the Southern Plains* (Lawrence: University Press of Kansas, 2003), 38–41.

48. Stephen Jay Gould, in *The Mismeasure of Man* (London: Penguin, 1981), 73–112, argues that concern with differing intelligence has always focused attention on the head.

49. William Stanton, *The Leopard's Spots: Scientific Attitudes toward Race in America, 1815–59* (Chicago: University of Chicago Press, 1960), 32–34. See Gould, *The Mismeasure of Man*, 54–69, for an excellent reexamination of Morton's methodology.

50. See Pratt, *Battlefield and Classroom*, 136–37. Many of these busts have survived and, although no longer displayed, are still at the Smithsonian.

51. Armstrong had insisted that no civilization was complete without educated women and was supported in this view by Secretary of the Interior Carl Schurz. So from the start, the future pattern of educating both sexes was established as accepted practice in Indian education. Helen W. Ludlow et al., *Twenty-Two Years' Work of the Hampton Normal and Agricultural Institute at Hampton, Virginia* (Hampton VA: Normal School Press, 1893), 314.

52. *Annual Report*, Hampton University Archives, 1878, 16.

53. Pratt, *Battlefield and Classroom*, 213.

54. Three Kiowa (Koba, Etahdleuh, and Ohettoint) and one Cheyenne (Cohoe) had also been among the most prolific and skilled artists at the fort.

55. *Eadle Keahtah Toh* 1.1, January 1880.

56. Pratt, *The Indian Industrial School, Carlisle*, 9.

1. White Theories

1. This is the paradigm for Robert F. Berkhofer Jr.'s classic book, *The White Man's Indian: Images of the American Indian from Columbus to the Present* (New York: Knopf, 1978).

2. Mike Hawkins, *Social Darwinism in European and American Thought, 1860–1945: Nature as Model and Nature as Threat* (Cambridge UK: Cambridge University Press, 1997); J. D. Y. Peel, ed., *Herbert Spencer on Social Evolu-*

tion: Selected Writings (Chicago: University of Chicago Press, 1972); George W. Stocking Jr., *Race, Culture, and Evolution: Essays in the History of Anthropology* (New York: Free Press, 1968).

3. John S. Haller Jr., *Outcasts from Evolution: Scientific Attitudes to Racial Inferiority, 1859–1900*, new ed. (Carbondale: Southern Illinois University Press, 1995), 3–39; Stephen Jay Gould, *The Mismeasure of Man* (London: Penguin, 1981), 56–60; William Stanton, *The Leopard's Spots: Scientific Attitudes toward Race in America, 1815–1859* (Chicago: University of Chicago Press, 1960), 175.

4. Bruce Dain, *A Hideous Monster of the Mind: American Race Theory in the Early Republic* (Cambridge MA: Harvard University Press, 2002), vii.

5. Ralph E. Luker, *The Social Gospel in Black and White: American Racial Reform, 1885–1912* (Chapel Hill: University of North Carolina Press, 1991), 268.

6. Richard Henry Pratt, *Battlefield and Classroom: Four Decades with the American Indian, 1867–1904* ed. Robert M. Utley (New Haven CT: Yale University Press, 1964), 190, 192.

7. Samuel Chapman Armstrong, *Proceedings of the Department of Superintendence*, Circulars of Information 3 (Washington DC: Bureau of Education, 1883), 139.

8. Pratt, *Battlefield and Classroom*, 265.

9. *Proceedings of the Lake Mohonk Conference of Friends of the Indian* (New York: Lake Mohonk Conference, 1885), 1.

10. Prucha, *The Great Father: The United States Government and the American Indians*, vol. 2 (Lincoln: University of Nebraska Press, 1984), 625.

11. *Proceedings of the Lake Mohonk Conference* (1886), 46.

12. *Proceedings of the Lake Mohonk Conference* (1886), 13.

13. *Proceedings of the Lake Mohonk Conference* (1886), 11.

14. Audrey Smedley, *Race in North America: Origin and Evolution of a Worldview* (Boulder CO: Westview Press, 1993), 252.

15. Gary B. Nash, *Red, White and Black: The Peoples of Early America*, rev. ed. (Englewood Cliffs NJ: Prentice-Hall, 1982), 292.

16. Audrey Smedley, *Race in North America*, 261; Stephen Gould, *The Mismeasure of Man*; see also Gould, 113–45.

17. *Proceedings of the Lake Mohonk Conference* (1885), 50.

18. Quoted in Ralph E. Luker, *The Social Gospel in Black and White*, 11, 12, 140, and 319.

19. Jonathan Baxter Harrison, *The Latest Studies on Indian Reservations* (Philadelphia: Indian Rights Association, 1887), 15.

20. Ralph E. Luker, *The Social Gospel in Black and White*, 26–27.

21. *Proceedings of the Lake Mohonk Conference* (1894), 56.

22. *Proceedings of the Lake Mohonk Conference* (1891), 8.

23. Lyman Abbott, "The Basis of Anglo-Saxon Understanding," *North American Review* 166 (May 1898): 513–21; Luker, *The Social Gospel in Black and White*, 139.

24. Quoted in Thomas W. Cowger, "Dr. Thomas A Bland, Critic of Forced Assimilation, *American Indian Culture and Research Journal* 16.4 (1992): 85.

25. *Proceedings of the Lake Mohonk Conference* (1892), 121.

26. *Proceedings of the Lake Mohonk Conference* (1892), 121; *Council Fire* 5.3, March 1882, 1. The magazine at this time was called the *Council Fire and Arbitrator*, but the following year it dropped the longer name and appears always to have been known to contemporaries as the *Council Fire*.

27. *Council Fire* 1.1, June 1878, 1; *Council Fire* 5.3, March 1882, 83.

28. *Council Fire* 7.1, January 1884, 7.

29. *Council Fire* 7.1, January 1884, 7.

30. *Report of the Indian Rights Association* (Philadelphia: Indian Rights Association, 1884), 5–6.

31. *Preamble, Platform, and Constitution of the National Indian Defense Association* (Washington DC: n.p., 1885), 4–5.

32. *Preamble, Platform, and Constitution of the National Indian Defense Association* 4–5.

33. *Preamble, Platform, and Constitution of the National Indian Defense Association*, 6.

34. *Council Fire* 6.6, June 1883, 91–92.

35. *Council Fire* 6.6, June 1883, 62.

36. D. S. Otis, *The Dawes Act and the Allotment of Indian Lands* (Norman: University of Oklahoma Press, 1973), explores how western demand for Indian lands and reformers' determination to break up reservations dovetailed and allowed the Allotment Act to pass easily through Congress. For a good biographical study of Bland see, Thomas W. Cowger, "Dr. Thomas A Bland, Critic of Forced Assimilation."

37. *Annual Report of the Commissioner of Indian Affairs* (Washington DC: GPO, 1894), 11–12.

38. Lee D. Baker, *From Savage to Negro: Anthropology and the Construction of Race, 1896–1954* (Berkeley: University of California Press, 1998), 56.

39. Robert W. Rydell, *All the World's a Fair: Visions of Empire at American International Expositions, 1876–1916* (Chicago: University of Chicago Press, 1984), 3.

40. *New York Times*, October 8, 1893, quoted in Lee D. Baker, *From Savage to Negro*, 60.

41. *Report of the Board of Indian Commissioners* (Washington DC: GPO, 1884), 8–10.

42. *Report of the Board of Indian Commissioners* (Washington DC: GPO, 1885), 116.

2. Native Views

1. Agent James Hawort to Supt. E. Hoag, May 4, 1875, Bureau of Indian Affairs, RG 75, letters received, Kiowa Agency, M234, National Archives.

2. Kicking Bird to CIA, n.d. (ca. 1872), Bureau of Indian Affairs, RG 75, letters received, Kiowa Agency, M234, National Archives.

3. *New York Times*, November 20, 1867, www.museumgreatplains.org/lawtoncentennial/medicinelodgetreaty.html (accessed March 8, 2007). For a full account of the treaty council, see Douglas C. Jones, *The Treaty of Medicine Lodge: The History of the Great Treaty Council as Told by Eye Witnesses* (Norman: University of Oklahoma Press, 1966).

4. Edward Red Hand, Cheyenne Keeper of the Sacred Arrows, quoted in Henrietta Mann, *Cheyenne-Arapaho Education, 1871–1982* (Niwot: University Press of Colorado Press, 1997), 23.

5. Mann, *Cheyenne-Arapaho Education*, 49.

6. Charles A. Eastman, *Indian Boyhood* (New York: Doubleday, 1914), 52.

7. Eastman, *Indian Boyhood*, 54.

8. Ruth McDonald Boyer and Narcissus Duffy Gayton, *Apache Mothers and Daughters: Four Generations of a Family* (Norman: University of Oklahoma Press, 1992), 19.

9. Eastman, *Indian Boyhood*, 59.

10. Ella Deloria, *Speaking of Indians* (New York: Friendship Press, 1944), 4.

11. John Stands in Timber, *Cheyenne Memoirs* (Lincoln: University of Nebraska Press, 1972), 12.

12. Eastman, *Indian Boyhood*, 51.

13. George A. Pettitt, *Primitive Education in North America* (Berkeley: University of California Press, 1946), 59.

14. Robert M. Utley, *The Lance and the Shield: the Life and Times of Sitting Bull* (London: Pimlico, 1998), 6, 14–15.

15. Boyer and Gayton, *Apache Mothers and Daughters*, 259–60.

16. Ella Deloria, *Speaking of Indians*, 63.

17. Both James Mooney and Clark Wissler regard this as the main defining feature of a plains tribe. Only the Comanche did not practice it.

18. John Stands in Timber, *Cheyenne Memoirs*, 92.

19. Ella Deloria, *Speaking of Indians*, 63–64.

20. Boyer and Gayton, *Apache Mothers and Daughters*, 45–49, 185–86, 201–3, 340–44.

21. Deloria, *Speaking of Indians*, 25.

22. Deloria, *Speaking of Indians*, 29.

23. Francis La Flesche, *The Middle Five: Indian Boys at School* (Boston: Small, Maynard, 1900; repr., *The Middle Five: Indian Schoolboys of the Omaha Tribe*

[Madison: University of Wisconsin Press, 1963]), x, vi. Citations are to the University of Wisconsin Press edition.

24. Miss Mable Gould to Mrs. H. R. Gould, February 3, 1898, Box 6 No. 32, Nebraska State Historical Society.

25. Lomawaima provides evidence for this in her study of Chilocco, *They Called It Prairie Light: The Story of Chilocco School* (Lincoln: University of Nebraska Press, 1994), 157–59.

26. *Cherokee Advocate*, October 22, 1870, quoted in William G. McLoughlin, *The Cherokees and Christianity, 1794–1870* (Athens: University of Georgia Press, 1994), 307–9.

27. Grant Foreman, *A History of Oklahoma* (Norman: University of Oklahoma Press, 1942), 197–98, 230–35.

28. McLoughlin, *Cherokees and Missionaries*, oo.

29. Devon A. Mihesuah, *Cultivating the Rosebud: The Education of Women at the Cherokee Female Seminary, 1851–1909* (Urbana: University of Illinois Press, 1993), 18–50.

30. Nancy Shoemaker, *A Strange Likeness: Becoming Red and White in Eighteenth-Century North America* (New York: Oxford University Press, 2004), 141.

31. Daniel Richter, *Facing East from Indian Country: A Native History of Early America* (Cambridge MA: Harvard University Press, 2001), 190.

32. The Navaho surfaced into this world from a series of lower worlds (Aileen O'Bryan, "The Dine: Origin Myths of the Navaho Indians," Bureau of American Ethnology Bulletin 163 [Washington DC: GPO, 1956], 1–13). According to N. Scott Momaday, *The Way to Rainy Mountain* (Tucson: University of Arizona Press, 1969), 3, 16, the Kiowa emerged from a hollow cottonwood log at the bidding of a supernatural progenitor.

33. Clark Wissler, *Red Man Reservations* (New York: Collier Books, 1971), 138–41.

34. Richard White, *The Middle Ground: Indian Empires, Republics in the Great Lakes Regions, 1650–1815* (Cambridge UK: Cambridge University Press, 1991); Nancy Shoemaker, *A Strange Likeness: Becoming Red and White in Eighteenth-Century North America* (Oxford UK: Oxford University Press, 2004), 141.

35. See John M. Coward, *The Newspaper Indian: Native American Identity in the Press* (Urbana: University of Illinois Press, 1999), 159–95.

36. Utley, *The Lance and the Shield*, 255.

37. Utley, *The Lance and the Shield*, 269.

38. Utley, *The Lance and the Shield*, 255, 275.

39. James C. Scott, *Domination and the Arts of Resistance: Hidden Transcripts* (New Haven CT: Yale University Press, 1990), 87.

40. Utley, *The Lance and the Shield*, 275. This time the signatures were collected and the Sioux lands sold and thrown open to white settlement.

41. Katherine Turner, *Red Man Calling on the Great White Father* (Norman: University of Oklahoma Press, 1951), xvi.

42. Martha Royce Blaine, *Some Things Are Not Forgotten: A Pawnee Family Remembers* (Lincoln: University of Nebraska Press, 1997), 41–42.

43. Charles A. Eastman, *From the Deep Woods to Civilization* (Boston: Little, Brown, 1916; repr., Lincoln: University of Nebraska Press, 1977), 25. Citations are to the University of Nebraska Press edition.

44. Eastman, *From the Deep Woods*, 32.

45. Clark Wissler, *Indian Cavalcade* (New York: Sheridan House, 1938), 173–76.

46. Pratt, *Battlefield and Classroom*, 222.

47. This story is told by both Luther Standing Bear and Pratt.

48. Ashis Nandy, *The Intimate Enemy: Loss and Recovery of Self under Colonialism* (Delhi: Oxford University Press, 1983), x–xi.

49. La Flesche, *The Middle Five*, 5.

50. La Flesche, *The Middle Five*, 24.

51. Agent G. W. Wilkinson, Report of Omaha Agency, in *Annual Report of the Commissioner of Indian Affairs* (Washington DC: GPO, 1883), 106.

52. Omaha petition, asking that Louis Sampson be the tribe's interpreter, to CIA, March 24, 1884, Bureau of Indian Affairs, RG 75, letters received, Omaha Agency, National Archives.

53. Agent G. W. Wilkinson, "Report of Omaha Agency," in *Annual Report of the Commissioner of Indian Affairs* (Washington DC: GPO, 1884), 119.

54. Two Crow to CIA, February 15, 1885, Bureau of Indian Affairs, RG 75, letters received, Omaha Agency, National Archives.

55. Agent C. H. Potter to CIA, December 12, 1885, Bureau of Indian Affairs, RG 75, letters received, Omaha Agency, National Archives.

56. Petition of White Ghost to CIA, March 18, 1881, Bureau of Indian Affairs, RG 75, letters received, Crow Creek Agency, National Archives.

57. Ruth Fire, interviewed by author, Crow Creek, September 10, 1974.

58. "Report of Crow Creek School," in *Annual Report of the Commissioner of Indian Affairs* (Washington DC: GPO 1896), 290.

59. John J. Mathews, *Wah Kon-Tah: The Osage and the White Man's Road* (Norman: University of Oklahoma Press, 1932), 71–72.

60. Maggie Tarbell Lazore, interviewed by Jacqueline Fear-Segal and Barbara Landis, St. Regis NY, August 4, 2000.

61. George A. Pettitt, *Primitive Education in North America* (Berkeley: University of California Press, 1946), 3–5.

62. Luther Standing Bear, *Land of the Spotted Eagle* (Boston: Houghton Mifflin, 1933; repr., Lincoln: University of Nebraska Press, 1978), 150. Citations are to the University of Nebraska Press edition.

63. Francis La Flesche, *The Middle Five*, 11.

64. Luther Standing Bear, *Land of the Spotted Eagle*, 119.

65. It was usual for this tribe to place a dead body in the open air, on a wooden structure.

66. John Joseph Mathews, *Wah'Kon-Tah: The Osage and the White Man's Road* (Norman: University of Oklahoma Press, 1932), 262–63.

67. Elaine A. Jahner, "Transitional Narratives and Cultural Continuity," in *American Indian Persistence and Resurgence*, ed. Karl Kroeber (Durham NC: Duke University Press, 1994), 156.

68. William T. Hagan, *Indian Police and Judges* (New Haven CT: Yale University Press), 165–67.

69. Frederik Barth, ed., *Ethnic Groups and Boundaries: The Social Organization of Cultural Difference* (Boston: Little, Brown, 1969), 32.

70. Thomas Wildcat Alford, *Civilization as Told to Florence Drake* (Norman: University of Oklahoma Press, 1936; repr., *Civilization and the Story of the Absentee Shawnee* [Norman: University of Oklahoma Press, 1979]), 90. Citations are to the 1979 edition.

3. Mission Schools in the West

1. James Axtell, *The Invasion Within: The Contest of Cultures in Colonial North America* (New York: Oxford University Press, 1985); Jorge Noreiga, "American Indian Education in the United States: Indoctrination for Subordination to Colonialism," in *The State of Native America: Genocide, Colonization, and Resistance*, ed. M. Annette Jaimes (Boston: South End Press, 1992), 371.

2. William McLoughlin, *Cherokees and Missionaries, 1789–1839* (New Haven CT: Yale University Press, 1984).

3. See Robert F. Berkhofer, *Salvation and the Savage: An Analysis of Protestant Missions and American Indian Response, 1787–1862* (Lexington: University of Kentucky Press, 1965), for an excellent study of this overlap.

4. For an excellent synthesis of scholarship on the Enlightenment see, Roy Porter, *The Enlightenment* (London: Macmillan, 1990).

5. Robert Sparks Walker, *Torchlights to the Cherokees: The Brainerd Mission* (New York: Macmillan, 1931); "Memorial of the American Board of Commissioners for Foreign Missions," March 3, 1824, *American State Papers*, 2, *Indian Affairs*, 446.

6. According to Cherokee/Osage scholar George Tinker, Christian missionaries should be judged as "partners in cultural genocide" because even their most benign work was fatally flawed by its complicity with the dictates of European culture. George E. Tinker, *Missionary Conquest: The Gospel and Native American Cultural Genocide* (Minneapolis MN: Fortress Press, 1993), 4.

7. Quoted in Stephen Jay Gould, *The Mismeasure of Man* (London: Penguin, 1981), 57.

8. *Inaugural Addresses of the Presidents of the United States* (Washington DC: GPO, 1968), 121.

9. James C. Scott, *Domination and the Arts of Resistance: Hidden Transcripts* (New Haven: Yale University Press, 1990), 18.

10. Lawrie Tatum, *Our Red Brothers and the Peace Policy of Ulysses S. Grant* (Philadelphia: J. C. Winston, 1899; repr. Lincoln: University of Nebraska Press, 1970), x. Citations are to the 1970 edition.

11. William T. Hagan, "The Reservation Policy: Too Little and Too Late," in *Indian-White Relations: A Persistent Paradox*, ed. Jane F. Smith and Robert M. Kvasnicka (Washington DC: Howard University Press, 1976), 160.

12. Tatum, 166.

13. *Annual Report of the Commissioner of Indian Affairs* (Washington DC: GPO, 1870), 474. To eliminate the corruption that was endemic in the Indian Service, widely judged to be a product of political appointments, Grant had first turned not just to Quakers but also to the military. He appointed serving army officers to administer the Indian agencies not assigned to the Quakers. Congress, angered over how these military appointments robbed them of political patronage, thwarted his plans and, in July 1870, banned army officers from taking up any civil post. Grant's countermove was to hand the running of the agencies over to church groups.

14. *Annual Report of the Commissioner of Indian Affairs* (1870), 474

15. *Annual Report of the Commissioner of Indian Affairs* (1871), 57.

16. *Annual Report of the Commissioner of Indian Affairs* (1900), 44.

17. Figures from Paul Stuart, *The Indian Office: Growth and Development of an American Institution, 1865–1900* (Ann Arbor MI: UMI Research Press, 1979), 125.

18. After this date, government funding of mission schools became the subject of increasing criticism and the sums became progressively smaller.

19. *Annual Report of the Commissioner of Indian Affairs*, 1888, xii–xv.

20. For full details of schools and their expenditures see John H. Oberley, "Report of the Indian School Superintendent," in *Annual Report of the Commissioner of Indian Affairs* (1885), 75–128.

21. *Proceedings of the Lake Mohonk Conference of Friends of the Indian* (New York: Lake Mohonk Conference, 1886), 66.

22. Section 8 of the Indian Appropriation Act of June 1888 authorized these new powers of the superintendent of Indian schools.

23. A useful thumbnail account of each commissioner's policy can be found in, Robert M. Kvasnicka and Herman J. Viola, eds., *The Commissioners of Indian Affairs, 1824–1977* (Lincoln: University of Nebraska Press, 1979).

24. *Proceedings of the Lake Mohonk Conference* (1889), 16–33.

25. For an analysis of how Morgan's anti-Catholicism drove the extension of federal power over all church schools, see Francis Paul Prucha, *The Churches and the Indian Schools, 1888–1912* (Lincoln: University of Nebraska Press, 1979), chap. 2.

26. *Proceedings of the Lake Mohonk Conference* (1889), 16–33.

27. Francis Paul Prucha, "Thomas Jefferson Morgan, 1889–1893," in Kvasnicka and Viola, eds., *The Commissioners of Indian Affairs, 1824–1977,* 193.

28. *Proceedings of the Lake Mohonk Conference* (1889), 16–19.

29. T. J. Morgan, "A Plea for the Papoose: An Address Given at Albany, New York," in Francis Paul Prucha, Americanizing the American Indians (Cambridge MA: Harvard University Press), 244.

30. *Proceedings of the Lake Mohonk Conference* (1889), 16–17.

31. Stephen R. Riggs, *Tah-koo Wah-kan; or, The Gospel among the Dakotas* (Boston: Congregational Sabbath-School and Publishing Society, 1869), chap. 10.

32. Samuel W. Pond Jr., *Two Volunteer Missionaries among the Dakotas; or, The Story of Samuel W. and Gideon H. Pond* (Boston: Congregational Sunday-School Publishing, 1893), 51–88; Samuel W. Pond, "The Dakotas or Sioux in Minnesota as They Were in 1834," *Collections of the Minnesota Historical Society* 12 (St. Paul: Minnesota Historical Society, 1908), 319–501; Rev. S. C. Bartlett, *Historical Sketch of the Missions of the American Board among the North American Indians* (Boston: American Board of Commissioners for Foreign Missions, 1880), 30–31.

33. In its written form, the language was comprehensible to all three groups of the tribe: the eastern Dakota, the central Nakota and the western Lakota.

34. Riggs, *Tah-koo Wah-kan,* 405.

35. "Report of the Santee Mission," in *Annual Report of the Commissioner of Indian Affairs* (1870), 703.

36. Martin Carnoy, *Education as Cultural Imperialism* (New York: David Mackay, 1974).

37. The individuating thrust of the schooling campaign is adroitly analyzed by Joel Pfister in *Individuality Incorporated: Indians and the Multicultural Modern* (Durham NC: Duke University Press, 2004).

38. Riggs, *Tah-koo Wah-kan,* 385.

39. *Report of the American Board of Commissioners to Foreign Missions* (1881), 86.

40. The names of the thirty-eight hanged (in no particular order) and the one reprived: Ptan Du-ta (Scarlet Otter); O-ya'-te Ta-wa (His People); Hin-han'-sun-ko-yag-ma-ni (One Who Walks Clothed in Owl Feathers); Ma-za Bo-mdu (Iron Blower); Wa-hi'na (possibly meaning I Came); Sna Ma-hi (Tinkling Water); Hda In-yan-ka (Rattling Water); He-pan (Secondborn Child); Tun-kan' I-ca'hda Ma-ni (One Who Walks by His Grandfather); Ka-mde'-ca (Broken to Pieces); He In'-kpa (The Tip of the Horn); Na-pe'-sni (Fearless); Ma-za Ku-te Ma-ni (One Who Shoots as He Walks); A-i'-ca-ge (To Grow Upon); Ho-i'-tan-in Ku (Returning Clear Voice); Ce-tan' Hun-ka' (Elder Hawk); Can-ka-hda (Near the Woods); Hda'-hin-hde (Sudden Rattle); O-ya'-te A-ku' (He Brings the People); Ma-hu'-we-hi (He Comes for Me); Ti-hdo'-ni-ca (One Who Jealously

Guards His Home); Wa-kan Tan-ka (Great Mystery or Great Spirit); Cas-ke'-da (Firstborn Child); Do-wan'-s'a (Sings a lot or Singer); Ta-te' Ka-ga (Wind Maker); Sun-ka Ska (White Dog); Wa-kin'-yan-na (Little Thunder); Baptiste Campbell (a mixed blood); Wa-hpe Du-ta (Scarlet Leaf); Wa-si'-cun (White Man); I-te' Du-ta (Scarlet Face); Ma-ka'-ta I-na' (One Who Stands on Earth); Hypolite Auge (a mixed blood); Ma-hpi'-ya A-i'-na-zin (One Who Stands on a Cloud, also known as Cut Nose); Tun-kan' Ko-yag I-na'-zin (One Who Stands Cloaked in Stone); Ta-te' Hdi-da (Wind Comes Home); reprived: Ta-te Hmi-hma (Round Wing) (http://www.isd77.k12.mn.us/schools/dakota/conflict/hang-names.htm [accessed January 27, 2006]).

41. Virginia Driving Hawk Sneve, *Completing the Circle* (Lincoln: University of Nebraska Press, 1995), 59–61.

42. Riggs, *Tah-koo Wah-kan*, 341–45.

43. Riggs, *Tah-koo Wah-kan*, 78–79.

44. Riggs, *Tah-koo Wah-kan*, 92.

45. Stephen R. Riggs, *Mary and I: Forty Years Among the Sioux* (Boston: Congregational Sunday-School and Publishing Society, 1880), 108.

46. Riggs, *Mary and I*, 102–3.

47. Riggs, *Mary and I*, 127–28.

48. Alfred L. Riggs, *What Does the Indian Worship?* (Santee NE: Santee Normal Training School Press, n.d.).

49. "Address of A. L. Riggs at National Council, Des Moines, Indiana," in Alfred L. Riggs, *Our Indian Missions: Seventy Years Review, 1834–1904* (Santee NE: Santee Normal Training School Press, 1904), 4.

50. "Report of the Santee Mission," in *Annual Report of the Commissioner of Indian Affairs* (1870), 703; "Report of the Santee Mission," in *Annual Report of the Commissioner of Indian Affairs* (1884), 167–68; Alfred L. Riggs to Commission of Indian Affairs, February 24, 1883, Bureau of Indian Affairs, RG 75, letters received, Santee Agency, National Archives.

51. Alfred L. Riggs, *Santee Normal Training School* (Santee NE: Santee Normal Training School Press, n.d., n.p.).

52. Charles A. Eastman, *From the Deep Woods to Civilization* (Boston: Little, Brown, 1916; repr., Lincoln: University of Nebraska Press, 1977), 30. Citations are to the University of Nebraska Press edition.

53. Riggs, *Tah-koo Wah-kan*, 172; *Report of the American Board of Commissioners to Foreign Missions* (1882), 78.

54. *Report of American Board of Commissioners to Foreign Missions* (1881), 87.

55. An unimposing, single-story printing office was joined to the dining hall.

56. Stephen R. Riggs, "Dakota Portraits," *Minnesota Historical Review* 2.8 (November 1918): 546.

57. Riggs, *Tah-koo Wah-kan*, 60, 341–45; Alice Fletcher, *Indian Education and Civilization* (Washington DC: GPO, 1888), 470–76.

58. Riggs, *Tah-koo Wah-kan*, 7–12; Pond, *Two Volunteer Missionaries*, 50–51.

59. Riggs, *Tah-koo Wah-kan*, 412.

60. Riggs, *Tah-koo Wah-kan*, 409–11.

61. Stephen R. Riggs and Gideon H. Pond, *The Dakota First Reading Book/ Dakota Oyawa Wowapi* (Cincinnati: Kendall and Henry, 1839); Stephen R. Riggs and Alfred L. Riggs, *Guyot's Elementary Geography in the Dakota Language/Maka-oyakapi* (New York: Scribner, Armstrong, 1876).

62. *Iapi Oaye/Word Carrier* 4.3, March 1875.

63. *Iapi Oaye/Word Carrier* 2.3, March 1873.

64. Gwyneth Tyson Roberts, *The Language of the Blue Books: The Perfect Instrument of Empire* (Cardiff: University of Wales Press), 1998, 52–58.

65. Alfred L. Riggs, *School Discipline* (Santee NE: Santee Normal Training School, n.d).

66. *Eadle Keatah Toh*, 1.9. March 1880, 3.

67. Daniel Defoe, *The Life and Surprising Adventures of Robinson Crusoe*, ed. J. D. Crowley (Oxford UK: Oxford University Press, 1972), 210, quoted and analyzed in Tony Crowley, *Language in History: Theories and Texts* (London: Routledge, 1996), 72.

68. Walter J. Ong, *Orality and Literacy: The Technologizing of the Word* (London: Methuen, 1982).

69. Benedict Anderson, *Imagined Communities: Reflections on the Origins and Spread of Nationalism* (London: Verso, 1983), 47.

70. For an excellent study of George Sword, see Douglas R. Parks and Raymond J. Demallie, "Plains Indian Native Literatures," in *American Indian Persistence and Resurgence*, ed. Karl Kroeber (Durham NC: Duke University Press, 1994), 106–48.

71. John O'Means (secretary of the American Board of Commissioners to Foreign Missions) to CIA, August 25, 1881, Bureau of Indian Affairs, RG 75, letters received, Santee Agency, National Archives.

72. *Annual Report of the Commissioner of Indian Affairs* (1887), xxii.

73. *Iapi Oaye/Word Carrier* 16.8, August-September 1887.

74. *Annual Report of the Commissioner of Indian Affairs* (1887), 20.

75. Bureau of Indian Affairs, *Correspondence on the Subject of Teaching the Vernacular in Indian Schools, 1887–88* (Washington DC: GPO, 1888).

76. Special Agent W. H. Sallmadge to CIA, June 20, 1888, Bureau of Indian Affairs, RG 75, letters received, Santee Agency, National Archives.

77. *Annual Report of the Commissioner of Indian Affairs* (1883), 245; *Annual Report of the Commissioner of Indian Affairs* (1884), 123; *Annual Report of the Commissioner of Indian Affairs* (1885), 138; *Annual Report of the*

Commissioner of Indian Affairs (1886), 193; *Annual Report of the Commissioner of Indian Affairs* (1893), 626.

78. *Annual Report of the Commissioner of Indian Affairs* (1883), 245; *Annual Report of the Commissioner of Indian Affairs* (1884), 123; *Annual Report of the Commissioner of Indian Affairs* (1885), 138; *Annual Report of the Commissioner of Indian Affairs* (1886), 193.

79. *Annual Report of the Commissioner of Indian Affairs* (1883), 298–303.

80. *Report of the President of the Indian Peace Commissioners*, Ho. Exec. Doc. No. 97, 40th Cong., 2nd sess., 1868, 16–18.

81. *Iapi Oaye/Word Carrier* 4.3, March 1875.

82. Thomas Crowley, *Language in History* (London: Routledge, 1996), 56.

83. *Annual Report of the Commissioner of Indian Affairs* (1894), 194, 198.

84. Ruth Spack, *America's Second Tongue: American Indian Education and the Ownership of English, 1860–1900* (Lincoln: University of Nebraska Press, 2002), 6–8.

85. *Annual Report of the Commissioner of Indian Affairs* (1886), 99–100.

86. *Correspondence on the Subject of Teaching the Vernacular*, 15.

87. Robert Phillipson, *Linguistic Imperialism* (Oxford UK: Oxford University Press, 1992), 224.

88. Edward Jacker, "Mental Capacity of the American India as Indicated by his Speech," *American Catholic Quarterly Review* 3 (1878): 274.

89. Captain E. Butler, *Our Indian Question* (New York: A. D. Watling, 1882), 43.

90. J. W. Powell, "From Barbarism to Civilization," *American Anthropologist* 1.2 (April 1888): 100.

91. John Wesley Powell, *First Annual Report of the Bureau of American Ethnology to the Secretary of the Smithsonian Institution, 1879–1880* (Washington DC: GPO, 1881), 79.

92. *Report of the Bureau of American Ethnology*, 16.

93. J. W. Powell, "From Barbarism to Civilization," 102.

94. Riggs, *Mary and I*, 35.

95. *Iapi Oaye/Word Carrier* 9.9, September 1880.

96. Riggs, *Mary and I*, 130.

97. *Iapi Oaye/Word Carrier* 3.1, January 1874.

98. Frederick Riggs, "A Necessary Use for the Vernacular," *Iapi Oaye/The Word Carrier* 24.11, November–December 1895.

99. The Catholics made an organized effort to gain Indian signatures for petitions requesting that tribal funds be used to support their reservations schools. See Francis Paul Prucha, *The Churches and the Indian Schools, 1888–1912* (Lincoln: University of Nebraska Press, 1979), 84–95, 117–34, 207–13.

100. *Annual Report of the Commissioner of Indian Affairs* (1909), 89.

101. Alfred L. Riggs, "Our Indian Missions: Seventy Years Review, 1834–1904," Address at National Council of the American Board, Des Moines IA, 5, Nebraska State Historical Society.

102. Riggs, "Our Indian Missions," 6.

4. Samuel Chapman Armstrong: Educator of Backward Races

1. The American Missionary Association, which sponsored Hampton's founding, established seven other teacher-training schools in Macon, Savannah, and Atlanta, Georgia; Charleston, South Carolina; Louisville, Kentucky; Nashville, Tennessee; and Talladega, Alabama. All seven began as advanced grammar schools and all aspired to collegiate status. See Joe M. Richardson, *Christian Reconstruction: The American Missionary Association and Southern Blacks, 1861–1890* (Athens: University of Georgia Press, 1986), 109–20; Robert Francis Engs, *Educating the Disfranchised and Disinherited: Samuel Chapman Armstrong and Hampton Institute, 1839–1893* (Knoxville: University of Tennessee Press, 1999); Samuel Chapman Armstrong, "From the Beginning," in *Twenty-Two Years' Work of the Hampton Normal and Agricultural Institute*, ed. Helen W. Ludlow et al. (Hampton VA: Hampton Normal School Press, 1891), 6.

2. Samuel Chapman Armstrong, "From the Beginning," 9.

3. Samuel Chapman Armstrong, *Proceedings of the Department of Superintendence*, Circulars of Information 3, (Washington DC: Bureau of Education, 1883), 139.

4. Engs, *Educating the Disfranchised*, 117.

5. Richard Henry Pratt, *Battlefield and Classroom: Four Decades with the American Indian, 1867–1904*, ed. Robert M. Utley (New Haven CT: Yale University Press, 1964), 190.

6. J. F. B. Marshall, "Reminiscences," in *Twenty-Two Years' Work*, 16.

7. Engs, *Educating the Disfranchised*, 115.

8. *Talks and Thoughts* 3.10, October 1888.

9. Armstrong, "From the Beginning," 9–10.

10. Marshall, "Reminiscences," 16.

11. See Eng, *Educating the Disinherited*, 83–84, for an account of how Armstrong wrested control and ownership of Hampton from the American Missionary Association.

12. Rayford W. Logan, *Howard University: The First Hundred Years, 1867–1967* (New York: New York University Press, 1969), 56.

13. Donal Lindsey, *Indians at Hampton Institute, 1877–1923* (Urbana: University of Illinois Press, 1995), 20

14. Morris, *Reading, 'riting, and Reconstruction: The Education of Freedmen in the South, 1861–1870* (Chicago: University of Chicago Press, 1981), 156–57.

15. Quoted in Engs, *Educating the Disfranchised*, 114.

16. Pratt, *Battlefield and Classroom*, 190.

17. Samuel Chapman Armstrong, *Ten Years' Work for Indians at Hampton Institute*, ed. Helen W. Ludlow (Hampton VA: Hampton Normal School Press, 1888).

18. Armstrong, "From the Beginning," 7.

19. Engs, *Educating the Disfranchised*, 144–45.

20. Samuel Chapman Armstrong, "Lessons from the Hawaiian Islands," originally published in the *Journal of Christian Philosophy* in (January 1884), quoted in Engs, *Educating the Disfranchised*, 74.

21. R. N. Lebow, *White Britain and Black Ireland: The Influence of Stereotypes on Colonial Policy* (Philadelphia: Institute for the Study of Human Issues, 1976), 104.

22. *Southern Workman* 5.7, July 1876.

23. Samuel Chapman Armstrong, *Indian Education at Hampton Normal and Agricultural Institute, Hampton, Virginia* (New York: George Nesbitt, 1881), 4.

24. *Annual Report*, 1879, Hampton University Archives.

25. Samuel Chapman Armstrong, in *Twenty-Two Years' Work*, 1.

26. Armstrong, *Twenty-Two Years' Work*, 2, 6.

27. *Southern Workman* 10.10, October 1881.

28. See Stephen Jay Gould, *The Mismeasure of Man* (London: Penguin, 1981), 31.

29. For an account of how Hampton's program worked to instill mutual humility in blacks and Indians, see Lindsey, *Indians at Hampton Institute*, and also David Wallace Adams, "Education in Hues: Red and Black at Hampton Institute, 1878–1893," *South Atlantic Quarterly* 76.2 (Spring 1977): 159–76.

30. Booker T. Washington, *Up from Slavery* (New York: Airmont Publishing, 1967), 69–70.

31. *Annual Report*, 1887, Hampton University Archives.

32. *Annual Report*, 1880, Hampton University Archives.

33. *Annual Report*, 1891, Hampton University Archives.

34. *Annual Report*, 1888, Hampton University Archives.

35. The two bands were very different. The Lower Yanktonai were central Sioux, or "Wiciyela," and although they had adopted some of the characteristics of the Plains tribes, they were more sedentary and peaceable than their Teton neighbors. As High Plains people, the Lower Brulé were far more individualistic and warlike, displaying an urge to raid as well as follow the buffalo herds. See Frederick W. Hodge, *Handbook of American Indians North of Mexico*, vol. 1 (Washington DC: GPO, 1907), 376–80.

36. Samuel Chapman Armstrong to CIA, January 20, 1884, Bureau of Indian Affairs, RG 75, letters received, Crow Creek Agency, National Archives.

37. Samuel Chapman Armstrong to CIA, January 20, 1884 and Agent William Dougherty to CIA, April, 1887, Bureau of Indian Affairs, RG 75, letters received, Crow Creek Agency, National Archives.

38. Samuel Chapman Armstrong, *Indian Education*, 4.

39. Harry Hand, "The Spider, the Panther and the Snake," part 2, *Talks and Thoughts* 7.11, November 1892, in student files, Harry Hand, Hampton University Archives.

40. Cora Folsom, "Historical Notes," typed ms., Folsom Box, Hampton University Archives.

41. Karen Daniels Petersen, *Plains Indian Art from Fort Marion* (Norman: University of Oklahoma Press, 1971).

42. *Annual Report*, 1879, Hampton University Archives.

43. Samuel Chapman Armstrong, "First Report to the Trustees," quoted in Francis G. Peabody, *Education for Life: The Story of Hampton Institute* (New York: Doubleday Page, 1918), 114–15.

44. Samuel Chapman Armstrong, "From the Beginning," 6.

45. Quoted in Engs, *Educating the Disfranchised*, 117.

46. *Annual Report*, 1888, Hampton University Archives; *Annual Report*, 1879, Hampton University Archives.

47. Edith Armstrong Talbot, *Samuel Chapman Armstrong* (New York: Doubleday, 1904), 214.

48. For an excellent study of a very different American Missionary Association school, which provided predominantly professional training, see Edmund L. Drago, *Initiative, Paternalism, and Race Relations: Charleston's Avery Normal Institute* (Athens: University of Georgia Press, 1990).

49. Louis Harlan, *Booker T. Washington*, vol. 1, rev. ed. (New York: Oxford University Press, 1983), 100.

50. For an instructive analysis of this relationship, see Harlan, *Booker T. Washington*, vol. 1, 52–77, and for details of Armstrong's intimate connection to all details of the early running of Tuskegee, see Booker T. Washington, *Booker T. Washington Papers*, vol. 2: 1860–1889, ed. Louis Harlan (Urbana: University of Illinois Press, 1972), 156, 248–49, 288–67, 522, and *Booker T. Washington Papers*, vol. 3: 1889–1895, ed. Louis Harlan (Urbana: University of Illinois Press, 1974).

51. Booker T. Washington, *Up from Slavery*, 44.

52. Washington, *Up from Slavery*, 43.

53. Washington, *Up from Slavery*, 79.

54. W. E. B. Du Bois, *The Souls of Black Folk*, ed. David W. Blight and Robert Gooding-Williams (Boston: Bedford Books, 1997), 62–72, 100.

55. Quoted in Henry J. Perkinson, *The Imperfect Panacea: American Faith in Education, 1865–1976*, 2nd ed. (New York: Random House, 1977), 51.

56. Drago, *Initiative, Paternalism, and Race Relations*, 108.

57. There have been mixed assessments of Armstrong's legacy. Donald Spivey, in *Schooling for the New Slavery: Black Industrial Education, 1868–1915* (Westport CT: Greenwood Press, 1978), was harsh in his criticism. August Meier, *Negro Thought in America: Racial Ideologies in the Age of Booker T. Washington* (Ann Arbor: University of Michigan Press, 1963), attributes the path taken by black education to Armstrong. James Anderson, *The Education of Blacks in the South, 1860–1935* (Chapel Hill: University of North Carolina Press, 1988), condemns him for curbing black aspirations and fostering passivity in the face of oppression. And Robert Engs, *Educating the Disfranchised*, urges a more balanced approach that would take into account the intricate and conflicting patterns of postbellum life, as well Armstrong's own background and history.

58. Quoted in Engs, *Educating the Disfranchised*, 157; Peabody, *Education for Life: The Story of Hampton Institute* (New York: Doubleday Page, 1918), 118.

59. Ivor F. Goodson, ed., *Social Histories of the Secondary Curriculum: Subjects for Study* (London: Falmer Press, 1985), 363.

60. Booker T. Washington, *The Story of the Negro: The Rise of the Race from Slavery* (New York: Doubleday Page, 1909), 127–28.

61. There were, of course, political reasons for Booker T. Washington to tell this story in the early twentieth century, but this should not detract from its probable truth.

62. Helen W. Ludlow, "Hampton's Indian Students at Home," in *The Hampton Institute, 1868–1865: Its Work for Two Races*, ed. Mary F. Armstrong (Hampton VA: Normal School Press, 1885).

63. For an account of one such meeting in Philadelphia given in the *Inquirer*, see Booker T. Washington, *Booker T. Washington Papers*, vol. 1: The Autobiographical Writings, ed. Louis Harlan (Urbana: University of Illinois Press, 1972), 180–82.

64. See Lindsey, *Indians at Hampton Institute*, 77–79, for an account of how Armstrong played a key role in persuading reformers to support the Dawes Act,

65. Armstrong, *Southern Workman* 10.10, November 1881, 109.

66. Commissioner Thomas J. Morgan, "A System of Education for Indians: General Principles," *Proceedings of the Lake Mohonk Conference of Friends of the Indian* (New York: Lake Mohonk Conference, 1889), 16–33.

67. Morgan, "A System of Education for Indians: General Principles," 16–33.

68. Pratt, *Battlefield and Classroom*, 235.

69. Richard Henry Pratt to Senator Dawes, April 7, 1880, in Pratt, *Battlefield and Classroom*, 62.

70. Estelle Reel, *Course of Study for Indian Schools of the United States* (Washington DC: GPO, 1901).

71. Reel, *Course of Study*, 210.

72. Reel to Frissell, November 20, 1901, Hampton University Archives.

73. Reel, *Course of Study*, 143, 144, 6.

74. *Annual Report*, 1888, Hampton University Archives.

75. Robert Francis Engs, *Freedom's First Generation: Black Hampton, Virginia, 1861–1890* (Philadelphia: University of Pennsylvania Press, 1979), 154.

76. Wilbert H. Ahern, "The Returned Students: Hampton Institute and Its Indian Alumni, 1879–1893," *Journal of Ethnic Studies* 10 (Winter 1983): 103; Peabody, *Education for Life*, 376.

77. William Parkhurst, "General A Reviewed," *Council Fire* 8.6, June 1885, 99–100, and "General A Reviewed," part 2, *Council Fire* 8.7, July 1885, 111–13.

78. Agent William W. Anderson to CIA, April 20, 1887, and December 9, 1887, and December 14, 1888, Bureau of Indian Affairs, RG 75, letters received, Crow Creek Agency, National Archives (quotation from April 20 letter).

79. *Report of the Board of Indian Commissioners* (Washington DC: GPO, 1887), 19.

80. *Congressional Record*, 49th Cong., 1st sess., 1886, 17, pt. 3, 2264–75.

81. Helen W. Ludlow, in Herbert Welsh, *Are the Eastern Industrial Schools for Indian Children a Failure?* (Philadelphia: Indian Rights Association, 1886), 10–20.

82. Many files in the Hampton University Archives are empty, but attention to maintaining a record and the continued survival of the institution mean that it is more complete than that of most other schools. Summaries of the records are published in Armstrong, *Ten Years' Work for Indians* and Helen W. Ludlow et al., *Twenty-Two Years' Work for Indians*.

83. Student files, Charlie Stone, Hampton University Archives.

84. *Southern Workman* 20.2, February 1891, in student files, Walter Little Eagle, Hampton University Archives.

85. *Southern Workman* 21.8, August 1892, in student files, Walter Little Eagle.

86. *Southern Workman* 14.12, December 1885, in student files, Walter Little Eagle.

87. "Speech of Wizi," *Southern Workman* 20.3, March 1891, in student files, Walter Little Eagle.

88. "Speech of Wizi," *Southern Workman* 20.3, March 1891, in student files, Walter Little Eagle.

89. "An Association Meeting," *Talks and Thoughts* 12.4, April 1897, in student files, Walter Little Eagle.

90. "An Association Meeting," *Talks and Thoughts* 12.4, April 1897, in student files, Walter Little Eagle.

91. *Southern Workman* 27.1, January 1898, in student files, Walter Little Eagle.

92. *Talks and Thoughts* 12.10, October 1897, in student files, Walter Little Eagle.

93. "An Association Meeting," *Talks and Thoughts* 12.4, April 1897, in student files, Walter Little Eagle.

94. *Talks and Thoughts* 17.2, February 1902, in student files, Walter Little Eagle.

95. *Talks and Thoughts* 6.6, June 1891; *Talks and Thoughts* 6.7, July 1891; *Talks and Thoughts* 7.3, March 1892; and *Talks and Thoughts* 7.9, September 1892, all in student files, Walter Little Eagle.

96. *Talks and Thoughts* 8.3, March 1893, in student files, Walter Little Eagle.

97. *Talks and Thoughts* 8.3, March 1893, in student files, Walter Little Eagle.

98. *Talks and Thoughts* 8.3, March 1893, in student files, Walter Little Eagle.

99. *Talks and Thoughts* 10.3, February 1895, in student files, Walter Little Eagle.

100. *Southern Workman* 27.1, January 1898; *Talks and Thoughts* 13.5, May 1898, all in student files, Walter Little Eagle.

101. Harry Hand to Miss C. M. Folsom, August 15, 1898, student files, Harry Hand, Hampton University Archives.

102. Harry Hand to Miss C. M. Folsom, August 15, 1898, student files, Harry Hand, Hampton University Archives.

103. Harry Hand to Miss C. M. Folsom, December 28, 1898, student files, Harry Hand, Hampton University Archives.

104. James C. Scott, *Domination and the Arts of Resistance: Hidden Transcripts* (New Haven CT: Yale University Press, 1990), xii.

105. Modest in its ambition and execution, Hand's project nevertheless provides a small retort to the missionaries of the Dakota Mission who had commandeered the Dakota language for their educational venture.

106. Peabody, *Education for Life.*

5. Thomas Wildcat Alford

1. For an analysis of Hampton's returned students records see, Wilbert H. Ahern, "The Returned Indians: Hampton Institute and its Indian Alumni, 1879–1893," *Journal of Ethnic Studies* 10 (Winter 1983): 101–24.

2. Thomas Wildcat Alford, *Civilization, as Told to Florence Drake* (Norman: University of Oklahoma Press, 1936; repr., *Civilization and the Story of the Absentee Shawnees* [Norman: University of Oklahoma Press, 1979]), 161. Citations are to the 1979 edition.

3. For an excellent examination of a similar phenomenon in the letters of eighteenth-century Indians see, David Murray, *Forked Tongues: Speech, Writ-*

ing and Representation in North American Indian Texts (London: Pinter Publishers, 1991), 49.

4. Alford, preface, in *Civilization.*

5. H. David Brumble III, "Albert Hensley's Two Autobiographies and the History of American Indian Autobiography," *American Quarterly* 37 (1985): 702–18.

6. Thomas Wildcat Alford to his teacher, Miss A. E. Cleaveland, July 14, 1882, Hampton University Archives.

7. Alford, *Civilization,* 81.

8. These issues are explored by A. Loomba in "Dead Women Tell No Tales: Issues of Female Subjectivity, Subaltern Agency and Tradition in Colonial and Post-Colonial on Widow Immolation in India," *History Workshop Journal* 36.1 (1993): 209–27.

9. Charles A. Eastman, *Indian Boyhood* (New York: Doubleday, 1914); Charles A. Eastman, *Indian Child Life* (Boston: Little, Brown, 1913); Charles A. Eastman, *Indian Scout Talks: A Guide for Boy Scouts and Camp Fire Girls* (Boston: Little, Brown, 1914).

10. Charles Eastman, *From the Deep Woods to Civilization* (Boston: Little, Brown, 1916; repr., Lincoln: University of Nebraska Press, 1977), xviii. Citations are to the University of Nebraska Press edition.

11. Eastman, *From the Deep Woods,* 187.

12. Eastman, *From the Deep Woods,* 195.

13. Raymond Wilson, *Ohiyesa: Charles Eastman, Santee Sioux* (Chicago: University of Illinois Press, 1999), 193.

14. Charles A. Eastman, *The Indian To-day: The Past and Future of the First American* (Garden City NY: Doubleday, Page, 1915), 80.

15. Gertrude Simmons Bonnin, "An Indian Teacher," *American Indian Stories* (Washington DC: Hayworth, 1921; repr., Lincoln: University of Nebraska Press, 1985), 95–99. Citations are to the University of Nebraska Press edition.

16. Gertrude Simmons Bonnin, "An Indian Teacher," 97–99.

17. Gertrude Simmons Bonnin, "Why I am a Pagan," *Atlantic Monthly* 90, December 1902, 801–3; Gertrude Simmons Bonnin, "Soft-Hearted Sioux," *Harper's Monthly* 101 (September 1901), 505–8; Gertrude Simmons Bonnin, "Trial Path: An Indian Romance," *Harper's Monthly* 101, October 1901, 741–44; Gertrude Simmons Bonnin, "Impressions of an Indian Childhood," *Atlantic Monthly* 85, January 1900, 37–47; Gertrude Simmons Bonnin, "An Indian Teacher Among Indians," *Atlantic Monthly* 85, March 1900, 381–86.

18. She was engaged twice before she married, each time to Indian men. While at Carlisle she was engaged to the Pine Ridge Sioux, Thomas Marshall, who died of measles in 1899. Then she was set to marry Carlos Montezuma, the Apache doctor, but broke the engagement when he would not return with her to the Yankton reservation. Finally, in 1902, she married Raymond T. Bonnin, a Yankton Sioux.

19. There is a growing scholarship on Zitkala-sa: Hazel Hertzberg, *The Search for an American Indian Identity* (Syracuse NY: Syracuse University Press, 1971); Paula Gunn Allen, *The Sacred Hoop: Recovering the Feminine in American Indian Traditions* (Boston: Beacon Press, 1986); Gretchen M. Bataille and Kathleen Mullen Sands, *American Indian Women: Telling Their Lives* (Lincoln: University of Nebraska Press, 1984); Dexter Fisher, "Zitkala-Ša: The Evolution of a Writer," *American Indian Quarterly* 5 (1979): 229–38; P. Jane Hafen, "Zitkala-Ša: Sentimentality and Sovereignty," *Wicazo Ša* 12.2 (Fall 1997): 31–41; Roseanne Hoefel, "Writing, Performance, Activism: Zitkala-Ša and Pauline Johnson," in *Native American Women in Literature and Culture*, ed. and intro. Susan Castillo and Victor M. P. Da Rosa (Porto, Portugal: Fernando Pessoa University Press, 1997), 107–18.

20. Bonnin, "The School Days of an Indian Girl", *American Indian Stories*, 47–80.

21. Alford, *Civilization*, 90.

22. Alford, *Civilization*, 73, 88–91.

23. Alford, *Civilization*, 90.

24. Alford, *Civilization*, 76

25. "Incidents in Indian Life at Hampton," quoted in Booker T. Washington, *Booker T. Washington Papers*, vol. 1: The Autobiographical Writings, ed. Louis Harlan (Urbana: University of Illinois Press, 1972), 118–19.

26. A very high proportion of Native Americans attending boarding schools, including Hampton, left without graduating.

27. Alford, *Civilization*, 106.

28. Alford, *Civilization*, 109, 111.

29. "The Native Wards," from the Philadelphia *Inquirer*, March 24, 1882, in Booker T. Washington, *Booker T. Washington Papers*, ed. Louis Harlan, vol. 2: 1860–1889, 182.

30. *Southern Workman* 11.7, July 1882, student files, Thomas Alford, Hampton University Archives.

31. Alford, *Civilization*, 165.

32. Alford, *Civilization*, 108.

33. Alford, *Civilization*, 106.

34. Alford, *Civilization*, 90.

35. Alford, *Civilization*, 102.

36. Alford, *Civilization*, 118.

37. Alford, *Civilization*, 111.

38. Alford, *Civilization*, 112.

39. *Southern Workman* 11.2, February 1882, student files, Thomas Alford.

40. In Robert Francis Engs, *Educating the Disfranchised and Disinherited: Samuel Chapman Armstrong and Hampton Institute, 1839–1893* (Knoxville: Uni-

versity of Tennessee Press, 1999), 132: "Whereas 90 percent of the school's black graduates taught school, only a small number of Indian graduates did so."

41. Alford, *Civilization*, 118.

42. Alford to Miss A. E. Cleaveland, March 11, 1889 and January 10, 1887, Hampton University Archives.

43. Alford, *Civilization*, 161.

44. Alford, *Civilization*, 162.

45. For an excellent account of this issue see, Colin G. Calloway, *First Peoples: A Documentary History of American Indian History* (Boston: Bedford, 2004), 1–11.

46. Henrietta Whiteman, "White Buffalo Woman," in *The American Indian and the Problem of History*, ed. Calvin Martin (New York: Oxford University Press, 1987), 170.

47. Alford, *Civilization*, 193.

48. Alford, *Civilization*, 193.

49. Alford, *Civilization*, 106.

50. Alford, *Civilization*, 147.

51. Alford, *Civilization*, 123.

52. Foreword by Angie Debo in Alford, *Civilization*, n.p.

53. *Southern Workman* 53.5, May 1924, student files, Thomas Alford.

54. Alford, *Civilization*, 199.

55. For a full list of American Indian autobiographies of varying length, see H. David Brumble III, *American Indian Autobiography* (Berkeley: University of California Press, 1988). For an analysis of these stories see, Michael Coleman, *American Indian Children at School, 1830–1950* (Jackson: University Press of Mississippi, 1993).

56. F. Scott Fitzgerald, *The Stories of F. Scott Fitzgerald*, vol.2: *"The Crack-Up" and Other Pieces and Stories* (Harmondsworth UK: Penguin Books, 1965), 39.

57. Malcolm McFee, "The 150% Man, A Product of Blackfeet Acculturation," *American Anthropologist* 70.6 (1968): 1096–1107.

58. See Margaret Connell Szasz, ed., *Between Indian and White Worlds: The Cultural Broker* (Norman: University of Oklahoma Press, 1994); James A. Clifton, ed., *Being and Becoming Indian: Biographical Studies of North American Frontiers* (Chicago: Dorsey Press, 1989); Daniel Richter, "Cultural Brokers and Intercultural Politics: New York Iroquois Relations, 1664–1701," *Journal of American History* 75.1 (June 1988), 40–67.

59. Many lives were permanently blighted by white schooling. For a comprehensive analysis of the crippling legacy of the Canadian schools, see J. R. Miller, *Shingwauk's Vision: A History of Native Residential Schools* (Toronto: University of Toronto Press, 1996).

60. Brumble, *American Indian Autobiography*, 72–97.

61. See, for example, Sam Blowsnake, *Crashing Thunder: The Autobiography of an American Indian*, ed. Paul Radin (New York: Appleton, 1926; first published in a slightly different form in 1920); Don C. Talayesva, Sun Chief, *Autobiography of a Hopi*, ed. Leo Simmons (New Haven CT: Yale University Press, 1942); Walter Dyk, Son of Old Man Hat, *A Navaho Autobiography*, Viking Fund Publications in Anthropology 8 (New York: Viking Fund, 1947); *Two Paiute Autobiographies*, as told to J. Stewart, Publications in American Archaelogy and Ethnology 33.5 (Berkeley: University of California Press, 1934). For a list of such narratives see Clyde Kluckhohn, "The Personal Document in Anthropological Science," in *The Use of Personal Documents in History, Anthropology*, ed. Louis R. Gottschalk (New York: Social Science Research Council, 1945), 164–75. For a more recent list, fully annotated, and indispensable to any study of American Indian autobiography see, H. David Brumble III, *An Annotated Bibliography of American Indian and Eskimo Autobiographies* (Lincoln: University of Nebraska Press, 1981).

62. Eastman, *From the Deep Woods*; Luther Standing Bear, *My People, the Sioux* (Boston: Houghton Mifflin, 1928; repr., Lincoln: University of Nebraska Press, 1975).

63. *Southern Workman* 11.7, July 1882, student files, Thomas Alford.

64. Alford to Miss A. E. Cleaveland, January 10, 1887, Hampton University Archives.

65. Alford, *Civilization*, 158.

66. Alford, *Civilization*, 42.

67. H. David Brumble III sees this tension as a defining feature of all Native American autobiography (*American Indian Autobiography* [Berkeley: University of California Press, 1988], 42). Some recent autobiographies have succeeded in exploiting this tension by emphasizing the inevitability of change and loss. N. Scott Momaday in *The Way to Rainy Mountain* (Albuquerque: University of New Mexico Press, 1969) combines historical, personal, and mythical narratives and suggests they are united by memory and imagination.

68. Alford, *Civilization*, 82.

69. Luther Standing Bear, *My People, the Sioux*; Luther Standing Bear, *My Indian Boyhood* (Boston: Houghton Mifflin, 1931; repr., Lincoln: University of Nebraska Press, 1988); Luther Standing Bear, *Land of the Spotted Eagle* (Boston: Houghton Mifflin, 1933; repr., Lincoln: University of Nebraska Press, 1978). Citations are to the University of Nebraska Press edition. The quote is from *Land of the Spotted Eagle*, 258–59.

70. Alford, *Civilization*, 199.

71. Alford, *Civilization*, 167.

72. Alford, *Civilization*, 167.

73. Alford, *Civilization*, 166–67; *Southern Workman* 53.5, May 1924, student files, Thomas Alford.

74. Alford, *Civilization*, 166; *The Four Gospels of Our Lord Jesus Christ, in Shawnee Indian Language*, trans. Thomas Wildcat Alford (Xenia OH: William A. Galloway, 1929).

75. *Southern Workman* 19.8, August 1890, student files, Thomas Alford.

76. Alford, *Civilization*, 167.

6. Richard Henry Pratt

1. Richard Henry Pratt, *The Indian Industrial School, Carlisle Pennsylvania: Its Origins, Purposes, Progress and the Difficulties Surmounted* (Carlisle PA: Indian School, 1908; repr., Carlisle PA: Cumberland County Historical Society Publications, 1979), 52.

2. Richard Henry Pratt, "Address before the National Educational Association, Ocean Grove, August 11, 1883, in *The Indian Industrial School, Carlisle* (Carlisle PA: Indian School, 1901), 1.

3. Pratt, *The Indian Industrial School*, 25.

4. Pratt, *Battlefield and Classroom*, 215.

5. Pratt, *Battlefield and Classroom*, 214.

6. Pratt, *Battlefield and Classroom*, 24.

7. Pratt, *Battlefield and Classroom*, 24.

8. *Morning Star*, 4.1, August 1883, 2.

9. Richard Henry Pratt, "The Indian No Problem," *Red Man and Helper*, 18.47, June 24, 1904, 8, and Pratt, "The Indian No Problem," 18.48, July 1, 1904, 8.

10. Richard Henry Pratt, *The Indian Industrial School*, 42.

11. Richard Henry Pratt, "Negroes and Indians: Address of Brigadier General Richard H. Pratt, U.S.A. Retired, Made before the Pennsylvania Commandery, Military Order of Foreign Wars of the United States," Bellevue Stratford Hotel, Philadelphia, January 14, 1913.

12. Pratt, *Battlefield and Classroom*, 215.

13. Pratt, "Negroes and Indians," 3

14. Records of the Carlisle Indian School, student record cards, Box 35, Bureau of Indian Affairs, RG 75, National Archives.

15. *Eadle Keatah Toh*, 1.11, June 1881, 3 (italics in source).

16. *The Indian Helper* 1.23, January 15, 1886, 2.

17. Pratt, *Battlefield and Classroom*, 121

18. "A Visit from the Braves," reprinted in the Carlisle *Valley Sentinel*, January 23, 1880, 5, Cumberland County Historical Society.

19. Pratt, *Battlefield and Classroom*, 121

20. *Indian Helper* 5.12 (November 8, 1889), 4.

21. Robert F. Berkhofer, *The White Man's Indian: Images of the American Indian from Columbus to the Present* (New York: Knopf, 1978), cogently ar-

gues that the savagery/civilization binary is paralleled by the equally potent noble/ignoble polarities.

22. For the original group picture, see Photographic Archives, Cumberland County Historical Society.

23. "United States Indian School, Carlisle, Penna., 1895," Dickinson College Library Rare Books Pamphlet Collection.

24. Chauncey Yellow Robe to Richard Henry Pratt, June 19, 1917, Carlos Montezuma Correspondence, Cumberland County Historical Society.

25. Chauncey Yellow Robe to Carlos Montezuma, June 10, 1913, Carlos Montezuma Correspondence, Cumberland County Historical Society.

26. Chauncey Yellow Robe to Richard Henry Pratt, June 15, 1916, Carlos Montezuma Correspondence, Cumberland County Historical Society.

27. Chauncey Yellow Robe to Richard Henry Pratt, June 15, 1916, Carlos Montezuma Correspondence, Cumberland County Historical Society.

28. Chauncey Yellow Robe to Carlos Montezuma, August 6, 1911, Carlos Montezuma Correspondence, Cumberland County Historical Society.

29. *First Proceedings of the Society of the American Indian*, 3–5, quoted in Hazel Hertzberg, *The Search for an American Indian Identity: Modern Pan-Indian Movements* (Syracuse NY: Syracuse University Press, 1971), 78.

30. Horace M. Kallen, "Democracy versus the Melting Pot," *The Nation*, February 18 and 25, 1915, reprinted in Kallen, *Culture and Democracy in the United States* (New York: Arno, 1970), 67–125.

31. Chauncey Yellow Robe to Carlos Montezuma, November 11, 1911, Carlos Montezuma Correspondence, Cumberland County Historical Society.

32. Hertzberg, *The Search for an American Indian Identity*, 31–78.

33. Richard Henry Pratt, "American Indians Chained and Unchained, Being an Address before the Pennsylvania Commandery," October 23, 1912" (n.p.: n.p., 1912), 4.

34. Pratt, *The Indian Industrial School, Carlisle* (Carlisle PA: Indian School, 1901), 4.

35. Pratt, "Negroes and Indians," 5.

36. Richard Henry Pratt to Governor Thad. C. Pound, January 21 1881, quoted in Pratt, *Battlefield and Classroom*, 261.

37. Richard Henry Pratt to his daughter, Nana Pratt Hawkins, January 5, 1917, U.S. Army Military Institute, Carlisle Barracks Collection, Richard Henry Pratt Box.

38. Pratt, *Battlefield and Classroom*, 190, 192.

39. Richard Henry Pratt, *The Indian Industrial School, Carlisle* (Carlisle PA: Indian School, 1901), 30. See Karen Daniels Petersen, *Plains Indian Art from Fort Marion* (Norman: University of Oklahoma Press, 1971), 102 and 132, for details.

40. Richard Henry Pratt to Anne Beecher Scoville, October 1, 1895, Hampton University Archives.

41. Annual Report of the Commissioner of Indian Affairs (1891): 592–93.

42. Built by Indian students as part of their vocational training program, today this house is one of the few surviving teaching buildings from the Indian school and is currently used as family housing by the U.S. War College.

43. Genevieve Bell, "Telling Stories out of School: Remembering the Carlisle Indian Industrial School, 1879–1918" (PhD diss., Stanford University, 1998), 198.

44. Samuel Chapman Armstrong, *Indian Education at Hampton Normal and Agricultural Institute, Hampton, Virginia* (New York: George Nesbitt, 1881), 4; *Annual Report of the U.S. Indian School at Carlisle, Carlisle, Penn.* (Washington DC: GPO, 1910), 9.

45. "United States Indian School, Carlisle, Penna., 1895," includes photographs of all the classes from 1889–1895, Dickinson College Library Rare Books Pamphlet Collection.

46. Richard Henry Pratt, "Negroes and Indians," 5.

47. Richard Henry Pratt, "Negroes and Indians," 6.

48. Richard Henry Pratt, "Negroes and Indians," 6.

49. For a revealing examination of this issue through personal letters, see Theresa Strouth Gaul, ed., *To Marry an Indian: the Marriage of Harriett Gold and Elias Boudinot in Lettters, 1823–1839* (Chapel Hill: University of North Carolina Press, 2005).

50. Bell, "Telling Stories out of School," 182.

51. Richard Henry Pratt to Senator Henry Dawes, April 4, 1881, in Pratt, *Battlefield and Classroom*, 265.

52. For an examination of Pratt's disputes with reformers see Everett Arthur Gilcreast, "Richard Henry Pratt and American Indian Policy, 1877–1906: A Study of the Assimilation Movement" (PhD diss., Yale University, 1967).

53. Richard Henry Pratt, "Address to the Lake Mohonk Conference," *Red Man* 13.6, January 1896, 2.

54. Pratt, *Battlefield and Classroom*, 291.

55. Pratt, *Battlefield and Classroom*, 118–19.

56. Pratt, *Battlefield and Classroom*, 120.

57. *Recorder*, October 11, 1892, quoted in Pratt, *Battlefield and Classroom*, 295.

58. Pratt, *Battlefield and Classroom*, 295–96; Lee D. Baker, *From Savage to Negro: Anthropology and the Construction of Race, 1896–1954* (Berkeley: University of California Press, 1998), 56.

59. Pratt, *Battlefield and Classroom*, 297.

60. "Our School," *Eadle Keatah Toh*, 1.9, March 1881, 3.

61. Interview with Maggie Tarbell, St. Regis NY, August 4, 2000.

62. Pratt, *Battlefield and Classroom*, 219.

63. "Our School," *Eadle Keatah Toh*, 1.9, March 1881, 3.

64. "Our School," *Eadle Keatah Toh*, 1.9, March 1881, 3.

65. "List of Indian Students attending Dickinson College," Indian School file, Dickinson College Special Collections.

66. *Valley Sentinel*, March 26, 1880, 6.

67. "Our School," *Eadle Keatah Toh*, 1.9, March 1881, 3.

68. Pratt, *Battlefield and Classroom*, 318.

69. The best study of Indian sport is John Bloom, *To Show What an Indian Can Do: Sports at Native American Boarding Schools* (Minneapolis: University of Minnesota Press, 2000).

70. *Red Man and Helper* 16.5, July 20, 1900, 3.

7. Carlisle Campus

1. See map of Carlisle Barracks, 1918, adapted by author from "Map of General Hospital No. 31," U.S. Army Military History Institute, Carlisle PA. Cemetary is superimposed to scale.

2. Photograph of School Building, 1880, Photographic Archives, Box 10 A-C-2, Cumberland County History Society; Photograph of Girls' Quarters, 1882, Photographic Archives, Box 12–6–2, Cumberland County History Society; Photograph of Boys' Quarters, 1887, Photographic Archives, Box 12–6–1, Cumberland County History Society.

3. Drawing in Thomas G. Tousey, *Military History of Carlisle and the Carlisle Barracks* (Richmond VA: Dietz, 1939), 195.

4. For an excellent study of how gates can proclaim themselves, see John A. Dolan, "'I've Always Fancied Owning Me Own Lion': Ideological Motivations in External House Decoration," in *At Home: An Anthropology of Domestic Space*, ed. Irene Cieraad (Syracuse, NY: Syracuse University Press, 1999), 60–72.

5. Luther Standing Bear, *My People, the Sioux* (Boston: Houghton Mifflin, 1928; repr., Lincoln: University of Nebraska Press, 1975), 133. Citations are to the University of Nebraska Press edition.

6. Arnold Van Gennep, *Les Rites de Passage* (Paris: E. Nourry, 1909; repr., Paris: A. and J. Picard, 1981), ch. 1; Mary Douglas, *Purity and Danger: An Analysis of Concepts of Pollution and Taboo* (London: Routledge and Kegan Paul, 1966).

7. Gaston Bachelard, *The Poetics of Space*, trans. Maria Jolas (Boston: Beacon Press, 1969), 38–73.

8. Most of the J. N. Choate photographs of the school are in the Photographic Archives of the Cumberland County Historical Society.

9. At many other Indian schools, proper entrances were built and photographed.

10. Photograph of bandstand and buildings, showing vista that greeted visitors, Photographic Archives, Box 1–86, Cumberland County History Society.

11. Kim Dovey, *Framing Places: Mediating Power in Built Form* (London: Routledge, 1999), 240.

12. Charles F. Himes, *A Sketch of Dickinson College* (Harrisburg PA: Lane S. Hart, 1879), 7–12.

13. Himes, *A Sketch of Dickinson College*, 46.

14. Himes, *A Sketch of Dickinson College*, 136.

15. Himes, *A Sketch of Dickinson College*, 46.

16. Himes, *A Sketch of Dickinson College*, 46–47.

17. The only college building not visible from Main Street was South College.

18. Himes, *A Sketch of Dickinson College*, 133.

19. Only one Dickinson building did not front Main Street during this time. This was North College, behind West College, which was purchased before the building of the railroad.

20. "School News," *Morning Star*, 4.4, 1884, 3.

21. Photograph of dining hall, Photographic Archives, Box 12-8-1, Cumberland County History Society.

22. Plan of Carlisle Barracks, U.S. Army Depot, 1870.

23. Open-air trolley at Pratt Avenue, Photographic Archives, Box 10 A-C-8, Cumberland County History Society.

24. *Redman and Helper*, 19.36, April 8, 1904, 3.

25. Photograph of Leupp Indian Art Studio, Photographic Archives, Box 14B-04-01, Cumberland County History Society. This building is still standing.

26. Photograph of new gates showing the two paths, Postcard Collection, Cumberland County History Society.

27. *Carlisle Arrow* 8.32, April 19, 1912, 143–44.

28. Photograph of new gates showing the two paths, Postcard Collection, Cumberland County History Society.

29. Photograph of laundry building, Box 55, folder 13, Cumberland County History Society.

30. For a fully annotated list of autobiographies see, H. David Brumble III, *An Annotated Bibliography of American Indian and Eskimo Autobiographies* (Lincoln: University of Nebraska Press, 1981); for an analysis of school autobiographies see, Michael C. Coleman, *American Indian Children at School, 1850–1930* (Jackson: University Press of Mississippi, 1993); for an autobiography by an ex-Carlisle student, see Luther Standing Bear, *My People, the Sioux* and *Land of the Spotted Eagle* (Boston: Houghton Mifflin, 1933; repr., Lincoln: University of Nebraska Press, 1978).

31. K. Tsisnina Lomawaima, *They Called It Prairie Light: The Story of Chilocco Indian School* (Lincoln: University of Nebraska Press, 1994); Henrietta Mann, *Cheyenne-Arapaho Education, 1871–1982* (Niwot: University Press of Colorado, 1997); Sally McBeth, *Ethnic Identity and the Boarding School Ex-*

perience of West-Central Oklahoma American Indians (Washington DC: University Press of America, 1983).

32. *Carlisle Arrow* 10.23, February 6, 1914, 145.

8. Man-on-the-Bandstand

1. This as nearly as possible reproduces the style of the text as it appeared in the *Indian Helper*.

2. *Indian Helper* 2.21, Jan 21, 1887, 3.

3. *Indian Helper* 4.25, February 8, 1889, 4.

4. *Indian Helper* 14.13, January 20, 1899, 3.

5. *Indian Helper* 2.38, April 29, 1887, 4.

6. *Indian Helper* 2.41, May 20, 1887, 3.

7. "Captain Richard Henry Pratt Mounted on Horseback," by J. N. Choate, ca. 1885, Photographic Archives, Box 14–32–4, Cumberland County Historical Society.

8. *Indian Helper* 2.41, May 20, 1887, 3.

9. *Indian Helper* Vol. 1.27, February 12, 1886, 3. The picture is half-an-inch high.

10. For an analysis of these photographs, see Lonna Malmsheimer, "'Imitation White Man': Images of Transformation at the Carlisle Indian School," *Studies in Visual Communication* 2.4 (Fall 1985): 54–74.

11. *Indian Boys' and Girls' Friend* 1.1, July 31, 1885, 1.

12. While fully endorsing Joel Pfister's opinion that Carlisle was a multifaceted institution, I want to suggest that the Man-on-the-bandstand was both more important and more complex an editor than Mr. SeeAll. See Joel Pfister, *Individuality Incorporated: Indians and the Multicultural Modern* (Durham NC: Duke University Press, 2004), 32–33.

13. *Indian Helper* 3.30, March 9, 1888, 2.

14. "Map of the Carlisle Barracks," 1870, Bureau of Indian Affairs, RG 75, subgroup c, Map 320, National Archives.

15. "The Bandstand," by J. N. Choate, 1879, Photographic Archives, PO 01, Cumberland County Historical Society, and "Indian Girls in First Uniforms," by J. N. Choate, October 1880, Photographic Archives, Cumberland County Historical Society, show the renovated bandstand.

16. "Superindendents's Quarters," by J. N. Choate, ca. 1880, Photographic Archives, Cumberland County Historical Society.

17. "Ground Plan of Carlisle Barracks, U.S. Cavalry Depot," showing location and use of buildings, made by U.S. Quartermaster's Department, 1877, Cumberland County Historical Society; "Dining Hall," by J. N. Choate, Photographic Archives, Box 12–8–1, Cumberland County Historical Society.

18. "Guardhouse," by J. N. Choate, 1880, Photographic Archives, Cumberland County Historical Society. A 1980 reconstruction of the bandstand stands in its original location. Today, visitors to the remnants of the Carlisle Indian

School, which now form part of the U.S. Army War College in Carlisle PA, can stand on its platform and survey the surrounding buildings.

19. *Indian Helper* 3.22, January 13, 1888, 2.

20. *Indian Helper* 1.27, February 12, 1886, 3.

21. *Indian Helper* 11.8, November 22, 1895, 3.

22. For Michel Foucault's reflections on panopticism, see *Discipline and Punish* (New York: Vintage Books, 1975), 195–228.

23. The panopticon thus allows seeing without being seen. For Foucault it is this asymmetry that is the very essence of power because ultimately the power to dominate rests on the differential possession of knowledge. See Foucault, "The Subject and Power," afterword to *Michel Foucault: Beyond Structuralism and Hermeneutics*, 2nd ed., ed. Hubert Dreyfus and Paul Rabinow (Chicago: University of Chicago Press, 1983), 208–26.

24. Jeremy Bentham, *Panopticon* (London: T. Payne 1791), 1.

25. Bentham, *Panopticon*, 1.

26. For a sound exploration of the photography and operation of the prison, see Norman Johnston, *Eastern State Penitentiary: Crucible of Good Intentions, Philadelphia* (Philadelphia: Philadelphia Museum of Art, 1994); Negley Teeters, *The Prison at Philadelphia, Cherry Hill* (New York: Columbia University Press, 1957).

27. David Rothman's *The Discovery of the Asylum: Social Order and Disorder in the New Republic* (Boston: Little Brown, 1971) is the seminal book that analyzes the development and spread of this idea.

28. In one of history's unsettling symmetries, the children of these same tribes would later be sent east to attend school at the Carlisle Barracks.

29. Foucault points this out in a footnote in "The Subject and Power," 317.

30. For the creation and workings of such imagined communities, see Benedict Anderson, *Imagined Communities: Reflections on the Origins and Spread of Nationalism* (London: Verso, 1983).

31. See Kaja Silverman, *Male Subjectivity at the Margins* (New York: Routledge, 1992), 1–8, for an interesting psychological analysis of the relationship between voyeurism and power.

32. *Indian Helper* 2.34, April 1, 1887, 2.

33. *Indian Helper* 3.23, January 20, 1888, 2.

34. *Indian Helper* 3.9, October 7, 1887, 3.

35. *Indian Helper* 13.1, October 15, 1897, 3.

36. *Indian Helper* 2.1, August 13, 1886. 3.

37. *Indian Helper* 1.45, June 18, 1886, 4.

38. *Indian Helper* 3.34, April 6, 1888, 3.

39. For a lucid psychoanalytical discussion of how a parent can subvert the parental role and demand that the child take care of the parent, see Alice Miller, *The Drama of the Gifted Child: The Search for the True Self*, trans. Ruth Ward (New York: Basic Books, 1981).

40. *Indian Helper* 4.40, May 24, 1889, 1.

41. If any photographs of the cemetery were ever taken they have not survived, but its location is marked on old maps. See U.S. General Hospital, No. 31, Carlisle PA, "General Map," October 18, 1918, U.S. Army Military History Institute.

42. *Indian Helper* 3.25, February 3, 1888, 3; *Indian Helper* 3.24, January 27. 1888, 3.

43. "A New Way to Get Well," *Indian Helper* 3.34, April 6, 1888, 2.

44. *Indian Helper* 3.25, February 3, 1888, 3.

45. *Indian Helper* 3.22, January 13, 1888, 2.

46. *Indian Helper* 14.16, February 10, 1899, 3.

47. *Red Man and Helper* 19.24, January 15, 1904, 3.

48. *Indian Helper* 14.39, July 21, 1899, 3.

49. Genevieve Bell, "Telling Tales out of School: Remembering the Carlisle Indian Industrial School, 1879–1918" (PhD diss., Stanford University, 1998), 209–48.

50. *Indian Helper*, 8.25, March 10, 1893, 1–4.

51. "Girls' Reading Room," by Frances Johnson, ca. 1900, Photographic Archives, Box JO-1-8, Cumberland County Historical Society.

52. For details of arson attacks see David Wallace Adams, *Education for Extinction: American Indians and the Boarding-School Experience, 1875–1928* (Lawrence: University Press of Kansas, 1995), 229–31, and Genevieve Bell, "Telling Tales out of School," 250–53.

53. *Indian Helper* 13.6, November 19, 1897, 2; *Indian Helper* 14.5, November 18, 1898, 3.

54. *Indian Helper* 13.14, January 21, 1897, 3.

55. *Indian Helper*, 3.2, August 19, 1887, 1.

56. Frank Lock, "Books as Ponies," *Indian Helper* 3.3, March 16, 1888, 3.

57. Marianna Burgess [Embe], *Stiya: A Carlisle Indian Girl at Home* (Cambridge MA: Riverside Press, 1891). Inside the title page it reads: "The story of Stiya and her trials is woven out of the experiences of girls at various times members of the Indian Industrial School at Carlisle, Pa. The fundamental facts, therefore, are true. Different Indian villages have contributed incidents and served for the pueblo of the story."

58. Embe, *Stiya*, 2–3.

59. *The Indian Helper* 5.5, September 20, 1889, contained the first episode of the story. The remainder appeared weekly, until no. 18, December 20, 1889.

60. *Indian Helper* 6.17, December 26, 1890, 2.

61. Lucy Tsinah was married to Burdette Tsinah, and both were students at Carlisle. Thank you to Barbara Landis at the Cumberland County Historical Society for biographical information on them both.

62. Leslie Marmon Silko, *Yellow Woman and a Beauty of the Spirit: Essays on Native American Life Today* (New York: Simon and Schuster, 1996), 161–65.

63. *Red Man and Helper* 16.4, July 13, 1900, 3.

64. *Red Man and Helper* 19.52, July 29, 1904, 2.

65. *Arrow* 1.12, November 10, 1904, 1–4.

9. Indian School Cemetery

1. Only one tombstone is given an entry in Loewen's *Lies Across America: What Our Historic Sites Get Wrong* (New York: New Press, 1999), 230–34, 458.

2. On three occasions I have been given or sent photographs that purported to be of the Carlisle Indian School cemetery, but on close examination none matched what we know about the layout and position of the cemetery.

3. Survey map of "United States Indian Industrial School for Proposed Borough Sewer," 1884, and "Map of the United States Barracks," 1909, RG 77, subgroup b, Records of the Office of Chief Engineers, National Archives.

4. Pratt, "Second Annual Report," *Eadle Keatah Toh*, 2.3, October 1881, 1. 3–5; "Fifth Annual Report," *Morning Star* 5.2, September 1884, 1, 4.

5. Renée L. Bergland, *The National Uncanny: Indian Ghosts and American Subjects* (Hanover NH: University Press of New England, 2000).

6. Philippe Ariès, *The Hour of Our Death* (New York: Alfred Knopf, 1981), 476.

7. Chris Brooks, *Mortal Remains: The History and Present State of the Victorian and Edwardian Cemetery* (Exeter UK: Wheaton, in Association with the Victorian Society, 1989), 7.

8. The African American graveyard has been razed and today has been turned into a children's playground; a plaque marks the site.

9. Carlisle Indian School student files, Amos La Fromboise, File 116, RG 75, National Archives.

10. St. John's Episcopal Church, Carlisle PA, Record of Burials, Number 231, 196; the Carlisle *Sentinel*, November 28, 1879; *American Volunteer*, December 4, 1879; the Carlisle *Herald*, December 4, 1879.

11. F. W. Beers, *Atlas of Cumberland County, Pennsylvania, from Actual Surveys* (New York: F. W. Beers, 1872), 41, 42, 46.

12. Quartermaster R. C. Bower to the quartermaster general of the army, November 28, 1921, Records of the Quartermaster General, RG 92, Entry 225, Consolidated Correspondence File, Box 275, Folder "Carlisle Barracks Cemetery," National Archives.

13. Assistant H. J. Conner to quartermaster, Medical Field Service School, Carlisle Barracks, July 25, 1923, Records of the Quartermaster General, RG 92, Entry 225, Consolidated Correspondence File, Box 275, Folder "Carlisle Barracks Cemetery," National Archives.

14. Adjutant General E. D. Townsend to quartermaster general, December 1, 1879, Records of the Quartermaster General, RG 92, Entry 225, Consolidated Correspondence File, Box 275, Folder "Carlisle Barracks Cemetery," National Archives.

15. Judge Advocate General H. M Dunn to Secretary of War Alexander Ramsey, January 20, 1880, Records of the Quartermaster General, RG 92, Entry 225, Consolidated Correspondence File, Box 275, Folder "Carlisle Barracks Cemetery," National Archives. Emphasis in original document.

16. Adjutant General E. D. Townsend to Richard Henry Pratt, January 28, 1880, Records of the Quartermaster General, RG 92, Entry 225, Consolidated Correspondence File, Box 275, Folder "Carlisle Barracks Cemetery," National Archives.

17. *Indian Helper* 15.27, May 5, 1900, 2.

18. Interview with William Ewing, Carlisle PA, March 16, 2000.

19. For official death figures, see Pratt's published "Annual Reports," in the *Annual Report of the Commissioner of Indians Affairs*; for ongoing research on the number and order of deaths, see Bell/Landis Cemetery Database, Cumberland County Historical Society.

20. Eight "recovered tombstones" are stored in the basement of the U.S. Army Military History Institute (Photograph by author, April 2000).

21. *Indian Helper* 5.33, June 15, 1900, 3.

22. *Indian Helper* 6.37, June 19, 1896, 3; *Indian Helper* 12.39, July 9, 1897, 3; *Indian Helper* 13.52, October 14, 1898, 3.

23. O. H. Bales to W. N. Hailman, superintendent of Indian schools, March 15, 1895, Thomas Marshall file, Dickinson College Special Collections.

24. Carlisle Indian School student files, Thomas Marshall, File 161, Bureau of Indian Affairs, RG 75, National Archives.

25. In his studio portrait, he is shown sporting a moustache (Photographic Archives, Box C-82, Cumberland County Historical Society) and in a photograph of the Dickinson graduating class of 1900, published early that year, Marshall blends in unremarkably with his white classmates, *Microcosm* 9.100 (Wilmington DE, 1899).

26. Simmons had attended White's institute at the same time as Marshall, and from July 1897 until January 1899 she taught at the Carlisle Indian School.

27. *Indian Helper* 14.26, April 21, 1899, 2.

28. *Dickinsonian*, April 28, 1899, 1, 4.

29. Position of cemetery and features in the landscape established from water and sewage map of U.S. General Hospital Number 31, Carlisle PA, October 18, 1918, Construction Division, War Department, Washington DC, Carlisle Barracks Cemetery file, U.S. Army Military History Institute.

30. R. C. Bower, Medical Field Service School quartermaster, Carlisle Bar-

racks, to quartermaster general of the army, Washington DC, November 28, 1921, Carlisle Barracks Cemetery file, U.S. Army Military History Institute.

31. P. M. Ashburn, colonel, Medical Corps., commandant, to quartermaster general, Washington DC, December 13, 1921, U.S. Army Military History Institute.

32. "Some twenty-six graves are marked with wooden markers which have rotted off and should be replaced with standard markers." K. J. Hampton to quartermaster, Medical Field Service School, Carlisle Barracks, June 20, 1927, U.S. Army Military History Institute.

33. Mitchill at office of the quartermaster general, Memorandum for Cemeterial Division, September 17, 1926, U.S. Army Military History Institute.

34. B. F. Cheatam, major general, the quartermaster general, memorandum to the surgeon general, September 18, 1926, U.S. Army Military History Institute.

35. Surgeon general, memorandum to the quartermaster, January 19, 1927, Carlisle Barracks Cemetery file, U.S. Army Military History Institute.

36. Isaac Longshore was buried in the Carlisle Indian School cemetery on June 27, 1918, Carlisle *Evening Sentinel*, June 6, 1918; interview with Andrew Cuellar (oldest surviving graduate of Carlisle), August 3, 2000, confirms Longshore's death and burial; plot size given in War Department, Quartermaster Corps. Form No. 117, Carlisle Barracks, Building No. 79 (Cemetery), 1931, U.S. Army Military History Institute.

37. Harrisburg *Patriot*, July 14, 1927, 4.

38. Carlisle *Sentinel*, July 14, 1927, 5.

39.*Sentinel*, July 14, 1927, 5, and Major George Sandrock, Medical Corps., Carlisle Barracks to Commanding General, Baltimore MD, November 6, 1934, Carlisle Barracks Cemetery file, U.S. Army Military History Institute; War Department Memorandum for Cemeterial Division, September 17, 1926, Carlisle Barracks Cemetery file, U.S. Army Military History Institute.

40. K. J. Hampton to quartermaster, Medical Field Service School, Carlisle Barracks, June 20, 1927, U.S. Army Military History Institute.

41. Map of Military Army Post (in negative), Carlisle PA, showing boundaries of proposed purchase of Henderson Tract, 1918, Cumberland County Historical Society.

42. These Civil War stones are still visible at Ashland.

43. Jack Mather, Old Cemetery plot A33, New Cemetery C1.

44. The eight surviving stones from the original cemetery expose just a few of these mistakes. These stones belong to the following children (in order of death): Leah Road Traveler, Arapaho; Warren Painter, Sioux; Lena Carr, Pueblo; John Bull, Gros Ventre; Thomas Suckley, Mandan; Mattie Ocumma, Cherokee; Fred Senoche, Sac and Fox; Tomiccouk, Alaskan.

45. Margaret Edgan, Old Cemetery plot B14, New Cemetery B23.

46. Barbara Landis, researcher at Cumberland County Historical Society, has succeeded in identifying all but two of the "unknowns."

47. John Dibble, major, Medical Corps., to Miss Elizabeth Parkinson of 21 East Pomfret Street, July 30, 1936, Carlisle Barracks Cemetery file, U.S. Army Military History Institute.

48. Pratt, *Battlefield and Classroom*, 239.

49. Luther Standing Bear, *My People, the Sioux* (Boston: Houghton Mifflin, 1928; repr., Lincoln: University of Nebraska Press, 1975), 159.

50. Major George Sandrock, Medical Corps., Carlisle Barracks to commanding general, Baltimore MD, November 6, 1934, Carlisle Barracks Cemetery file, U.S. Army Military History Institute.

51. War Department Quartermaster Corps. Form No. 117, Carlisle Barracks, Building No. 79 (Cemetery), June 1941, Bureau of Indian Affairs, RG 77, Military History Institute Cemetery file, National Archives.

52. Herbert Rasmussen, F40, Plot Map of New Cemetery, November 7, 1947, Carlisle Barracks Cemetery file, U.S. Army Military History Institute.

53. Having seen the photographs I took of the cemetery in 2000, Grayson, who visited it in the 1980s, reported at American Indian Workshop, Swansea, 2006, that at this time it was unkempt and dilapidated..

54. Carlisle *Sentinel*, August 29, 1984, sec 1., 5.

55. Harrisburg *Patriot*, August 29, 1984, sec. 2, 1.

56. The August 29, 1984, Harrisburg *Patriot* reported that "Mrs. Barr may be buried next to her husband if she so wishes" (sec. 2, 1). New Indian Cemetery, plot 28, row F.

57. Harrisburg *Patriot*, August 29, 1984, sec. 2, 1.

58. Carlisle *Sentinel*, August 29, 1984, 5; Harrisburg *Patriot*, August 29, 1984, 1.

59. L. J. Reho, "The Burial Grounds," MS., Cumberland County Historical Society.

60. This story is the subject of Barbara Landis's essay, "Putting Lucy Pretty Eagle to Rest," in *Boarding School Blues: Revisiting American Indian Educational Experiences*, ed. Clifford E. Trafzer, Jean A. Keller, and Lorene Sisquoc (Lincoln: University of Nebraska Press, 2006), 123–30.

61. Renée Bergland, *The National Uncanny*, 4.

10. Kesetta

1. Carlisle Indian School student files, Kesetta Roosevelt, File 1779, Bureau of Indian Affairs, RG 75, National Archives.

2. Names, dates, and locations of her "outing homes" are listed on her student cards.

3. Information provided by Daniel Castro Romero Jr., general council chairman of the Lipan Apache Band of Texas, in an e-mail to Jacqueline Fear-Segal, September 25, 2002.

4. Helena Pohlandt-McCormick, "'I Saw a Nightmare . . .': Violence and the Construction of Memory (Soweto, June 16, 1976)," *History and Theory* 39.4 (December 2000): 23–44. She further suggests that silence can also disrupt an individual's ability to think historically.

5. Daniel Castro Romero Jr. in an e-mail to Jacqueline Fear-Segal, September, 25, 2002.

6. Pohlandt-McCormick also strove to recover stories of the dead and disappeared so as to be able to present evidence of individuals "talking back" in relation to larger "collective narratives."

7. Glenn Welker and Daniel Castro Romero Jr., "The Castro Family History of the Lipan Apache Band of Texas," http://www.indians.org/welker/lipanap. htm (accessed September 9, 2006). Ramon Castro was listed as a leader in the Tehuacama Creek Treaty Tribal Leadership List, dated January 16, 1845, at Tehuacama Creek, Texas. Ramon was the only witness at the Treaty Council of Texas Tribes at Tehuacama Creek, Texas. This was an agreement with the Republic of Texas government and U.S. government from August 27, 1845, to September 27, 1845, signed at Tehuacama Creek, Texas.

8. www.tsha.utexas.edu/handbook/online/articles/AA/bma33.html (accessed March 12, 2007).

9. Dorman H. Winfrey and James M. Day, eds., *Texas Indian Papers*, vol. 4 (Austin: Texas State Library, 1961); Daniel Castro Romero Jr. and Glenn Welker, "The Castro Family History of the Lipan Apache Band of Texas," http://www. indians.org/welker/lipanap.htm.

10. Robert Wooster, *The Military and United States Indian Policy, 1865–1903* (New Haven CT: Yale University Press, 1988), 92.

11. John G. Keliher, "The History of the 4th U.S. Cavalry Regiment," http://www.25thida.com/4thcav.html (accessed February 1, 2007).

12. Randy Barnes, Genocide, http://www.americanindianmovement.org/txaim/genocide.html (accessed January 30, 2007).

13. Wooster, *The Military and United States Indian Policy*, 95, 180; Robert M. Utley, *Frontier Regulars: The United States Army and the Indian, 1866–1891* (New York: Macmillan, 1973), 11–12.

14. In the *Morning Star* 4.15, December 1884, an article entitled "A Happy Carlisle Indian Boy" reports that "In the bushes near the camp, the soldiers found Jack and Kesetta" (2).

15. Daniel Castro Romero Jr. in an e-mail to Jacqueline Fear-Segal, September 25, 2002.

16. Commissioner of Pensions Report for Charles Smith, November 17, 1919, National Archives, student record files, Richard Rosevelt.

17. Photograph in private collection of Celeste Sorgio, copy held at the Cumberland County Historical Society.

18. Carlisle's *Morning Star* 4.14, December 1884, 2, names the army family who took an interest in them as that of Captain T. J. Wint, not Smith.

19. *Morning Star* 4.14, December 1884, 2.

20. *Eadle Keatah Toh*, 1.2, April 1880, 2.

21. *Eadle Keatah Toh*, 1.2, April 1880, 2

22. Ruth McDonald Boyer and Narcissus Duffy Gayton, *Apache Mothers and Daughters: Four Generations of a Family* (Norman: University of Oklahoma Press, 1992), 45–49, 185–86, 201–3, 340–44.

23. *Morning Star* 4.3, October 1883, 3, and *Morning Star*, 4.8, March 1884, 3.

24. Jack Mather to Captain Pratt, November 29, 1884, in the *Morning Star* 5.4, December 1884.

25. Sarah Mather file, St. Augustine Historical Society.

26. Pratt, *Battlefield and Classroom: Four Decades with the American Indian, 1867–1904*, ed. Robert M. Utley (New Haven CT: Yale University Press, 1964), 121, 218, 228.

27. *Indian Helper* 2.24, January 21, 1887, 2.

28. Figures are taken from "Castillo de San Marcos National Monument: Apache Indians (Imprisoned)," a pamphlet printed by the National Park Service.

29. Boyer and Gayton, *Apache Mothers and Daughters*, 103; photograph, "Fort Marion, 1886," St. Augustine Historical Society.

30. Figures are taken from "Castillo de San Marcos National Monument."

31. "Saved by an Apache" as told by Ernest Johnstone, Syracuse, NY, typed ms., St. Augustine Historical Society.

32. Figures from "Castillo de San Marcos National Monument."

33. Figures from "Castillo de San Marcos National Monument."

34. In the *Indian Helper*, 3.25, February 3, 1888, we learn that Miss Longstreth, a long-standing friend of the school, has presented a gift of story and picture books to "the folks invalided in the hospital" (3).

35. Jack Mather was buried in the old cemetery in plot A33. In the new cemetery, he is in plot C1. There are two possibilities for explaining the discrepancy in his name: either his name was correct on the original marker and mistranscribed when the new plot map was made, and from there copied onto the new stone, or he was from the start buried under an inaccurate marker.

36. A week later, Sibyl Marko, one of the Chiricahua girls transported to the school the previous April, was laid to rest beside Jack Mather. She was the seventeenth of the twenty-one Chiricahua children who would be buried in the school cemetery.

37. By this time, in Texas, the Lipan Apache Band residing at Fort Griffin

had dwindled to fewer than twenty members (http://www.indians.org/welker/lipanap.htm).

38. All information comes from Kesetta Roosevelt's three Carlisle registration cards, Carlisle Indian School student files, File 1779, Bureau of Indian Affairs, RG 75, National Archives.

39. *Indian Helper* 5.5, September 20, 1889, 3.

40. *Indian Helper* Vol. 1.15, November 1885, 3.

41. On all three of Kesetta Roosevelt's enrollment cards it is noted in the "Agency" box that she is a "prisoner."

42. Joseph P. Paxson to superintendent of Carlisle Indian Industrial School, March 7, 1916, Carlisle Indian School student files, Richard Roosevelt, File 5196, Bureau of Indian Affairs, RG 75, National Archives.

43. Detailed descriptions of the weather are given in the papers, *Indian Helper* 11.11, December 13, 1896; *Indian Helper* 11.12, December 20, 1896, 3.

44. *Indian Helper* 11.12, December 20, 1896, 3.

45. "Our Girls in Country Homes," *Redman and Helper* 16.7, August 3, 1900, 3.

46. "Application of Melosina H. Diament for the Enrollment of Richard Roosevelt in the Indian School of Carlisle," August 15, 1907, Carlisle Indian School student files, Richard Kessetta, File 5196, Bureau of Indian Affairs, RG 75, National Archives.

47. *Redman and Helper* 18.17, November 7, 1902, 3.

48. "Statement of Account of J. Titus Slotter," October 15, 1907, Carlisle Indian School student files, Richard Kesetta, File 5196, Bureau of Indian Affairs, RG 75, National Archives.

49. *Arrow*, December 28, 1906. 5.

50. "Statement of Account of J. Titus Slotter"

51. "Statement of Account of J. Titus Slotter"

52. "Application of Melosina H. Diament for the Enrollment of Richard Roosevelt in the Indian School of Carlisle."

53. Student Record Card, Carlisle Indian School student files, Richard Kesetta, Bureau of Indian Affairs, RG 75, File 5196, National Archives, RG75.

54. *Arrow* 3.49, August 23, 1907, 3; *Arrow* 3.50, August 30, 1907, 3.

55. Reports for the years 1911, 1912, 1916,1 918 in Carlisle Indian School student files, File 5196, Bureau of Indian Affairs, RG 75, National Archives.

56. She had been called "Kesetta" since being captured. There is no record of what her Lipan name was but, according to Daniel Castro Romero Jr., her name is very similar to a Lipan clan name.

57. Postcard of "Dress Parade, Indian School, Carlisle, PA," Postcard Collection, PC-440.02–C2, Cumberland County Historical Society, There's also an enlarged version entitled "Indian School Band and Girls' Quarter, Carlisle PA."

58. Obituary of Mrs. Martha A. Sharp, Carlisle *Sentinel*, March 30, 1927, sec. 2, 3.

59. *Indian Helper* 12.48, September 10, 1897, 3.

60. *Indian Helper*, 14.7, December 2, 1892. 2.

61. *Indian Helper*, 14.7, December 2, 1892. 2.

62. *Arrow*, 9.8, January 3, 1913, 3.

63. George P. Donehoo, *A History of the Cumberland Valley in Pennsylvania* (Harrisburg PA: Susquehanna Historical Association, 1930), 84–85.

64. Snapshots in the family album assembled by Gerry Eichenberger for Dick Kaseeta's wife, Helen Kaseeta née Rice.

65. *Arrow*, 7.4, September 30, 1910, 1.

66. *Arrow*, 7.4, September 30, 1910, 1.

67. Carlisle *Sentinel*, October 30, 1968, sec. 1, 5.

68. Arthur E. Buchholz to John Francis, September 27, 1917, Carlisle Indian School student files, File 5196, Bureau of Indian Affairs, RG 75, National Archives.

69. Commissioner of Indian Affairs Cato Sells to Claud V. Peel, traveling auditor in charge, Carlisle School, July 27, 1918, Carlisle Indian School student files, File 5196, Bureau of Indian Affairs, RG 75, National Archives.

70. Flickinger interview, Cumberland County Historical Society.

71. George Yuda, interviewed by Jacqueline Fear-Segal, November 26, 2002, Carlisle, PA.

72. In a telephone conversation between Helen Kaseeta and Barbara Landis in June 1983, Mrs. Kaseeta said her husband chose to change the spelling of his name.

73. Memorial Gardens Cemetery lies on Route 11, two miles south of Carlisle.

74. Enrique Meastas and Daniel Castro Romero Jr., "Culcajen-Nde: Ancestry of the Lipan Apaches, Lipan Apache Band of Texas." This unpublished ms. traces the history of the Lipan Apache from fifteenth century to the eighteenth century. A more recent history is published on the Internet, http://www.indians.org/welker/lipanap.htm.

75. http://www.indians.org/welker/lipanap.htm.

76. David Charter, "Canadian Natives Win £1bn for 70 years' Abuse," *Times* (London), November 25, 2005, 5, http://www.timesonline.co.uk/tol/news/world/us_and_americas/article596402.ece(accessed March 12, 2007); Graham Fraser, "Ex-residential School Students Get $1.9 billion," *Toronto Star*, April 26, 2006, sec. A, 4; "The Settlement Agreement on Residential Schools," United Church of Canada, May 2006, http://www.united-church.ca/residentialschools/2006/0517.shtm.

This agreement means that all former students of Indian residential schools who were alive as of May 30, 2005, are eligible to receive a lump sum payment, called the Common Experience Payment (CEP), from the federal government in recognition of the general harms experienced in the schools. The payment will provide CDN $10,000 for the first year (or part thereof) and $3,000 for each additional year of attendance at a residential school. Former students sixty-five years of age and older are able to apply for an advance payment of $8,000.

77. One notable example was Paul Baldeagle, who taught school for many years in Bordentown NJ, and in retirement worked at the Firestone Library of the university (Princeton Collection of Western Americana WC034, Papers of J. Paul Baldeagle).

11. Susan Rayos Marmon

1. "Woman's World," *Alumni Quarterly* 78.1, Bloomsbury State College, September 1977, 5.

2. According to Foucault, every society has its "regime of truth", its "general politics of truth," a type (or types) of discourse "which it accepts and makes function as true" (Colin Gordon, ed., *Michel Foucault, Power/Knowledge: Selected Interviews and Other Writings, 1972–1977*. Harlow UK: Longman, 1980), 131.

3. Carlisle student record card, Susan Rayos, File 1954, Bureau of Indian Affairs, RG 75, National Archives. During all these years she is recorded as being enrolled at Carlisle, only being "discharged" in September 1906, when she was "employed in Indian Service."

4. Information about these children's parentage was taken from their Carlisle student cards, where, for all of them, their father is listed as Robert Marmon and their mother as deceased. Silko, however, refers to "two small children" from this marriage (Leslie Marmon Silko, *Storyteller* [New York: Arcade Publishing, 1981], 16).

5. *Indian Helper* 8.18, January 20, 1893, 2.

6. Robert Marmon's brother Walter also lived at Laguna and married a local woman. So there were a large number of Marmons in the next generation.

7. Anaya is spelt "Annallo" in Maria's Carlisle record, but Silko's spelling, "Anaya," will be used here.

8. *Red Man* 10.5, June 1890, 4; *Indian Helper* 2.17, December 3, 1886, 2.

9. Maurine Grammer, "Susie Rayos Marmon, 110, Laguna Matriarch," typed ms, Cumberland County Historical Society, 6.

10. "Woman's World," 5.

11. Leslie Marmon Silko, *Yellow Woman and a Beauty of the Spirit: Essay on Native American Life Today* (New York: Simon and Schuster, 1996), 31.

12. Gordon, ed., *Michel Foucault*, 131.

13. "Woman's World," 5.

14. Harriett Marmon, in an e-mail to Barbara Landis, cc Jacqueline Fear-Segal, October 10, 2005; Ellen L. Arnold, ed., *Conversations with Leslie Marmon Silko* (Jackson: University Press of Mississippi, 2000), 31.

15. Leslie Marmon Silko, *Storyteller*, 4.

16. Silko, *Storyteller*, 5–6.

17. Silko, *Storyteller*, 6.

18. Michel-Rolph Trouillot, *Silencing the Past: Power and the Production of History* (Boston: Beacon Press, 1995), xix.

19. Trouillot, *Silencing the Past*, 29.

20. Trouillot, *Silencing the Past*, xix.

21. Silko, *Yellow Woman*, 18.

22. Silko, *Yellow Woman*, 21.

23. Gordon, ed. *Foucault*, 131.

24. Silko, *Yellow Woman*, 101.

25. Silko, *Yellow Woman*, 160.

26. Silko, *Yellow Woman*, 161–65.

27. Leslie Marmon Silko, "Leslie Marmon Silko," interview by Donna Perry, in *Back Talk: Women Writers Speak Out* (New Brunswick NJ: Rutgers University Press, 1993), 317.

28. Silko, "Leslie Marmon Silko," 158.

29. Silko, "Leslie Marmon Silko," 61, 160.

30. Harriett Marmon, in an e-mail to Barbara Landis, cc Jacqueline Fear-Segal, October 10, 2005.

31. Silko, *Yellow Woman*, 59, and Arnold, ed., *Conversations*, 31, 139.

32. Silko, *Yellow Woman*, 57.

33. Silko, *Yellow Woman*, 54.

34. Grammer, "Susie Rayos Marmon," 6.

35. Silko, *Yellow Woman*, 101.

36. Silko, *Yellow Woman*, 41.

37. Silko, *Yellow Woman*, 105.

38. Parson's work is both explored and critiqued in Renae Bredin, "Falling into the Wrong Hands: Laguna Women and Ethnographic Strip Tease," *Readerly/Writerly Texts: Essays on Literature, Literacy Textual Criticism, and Pedagogical Theory* 2.1 (Fall/Winter 1994), http://www.readerly-writerlytexts.com/3falling.htm (accessed January 30, 2007).

39. James Clifford, *The Predicament of Culture: Twentieth Century Ethnography, Literature, and Art* (Cambridge MA: Harvard University Press, 1988), 45, explores indigenous influence on the authorial voice of ethnography.

40. Marietta Padilla, "The Social Perspective of the Impact of the English Language in Native American World," Summer Institute, 2001, 3, http;//si.unm.edu/Web%20Journals/articles2001/MPADIL~1.HTM (site now discontinued).

41. Padilla, "The Social Perspective of the Impact of the English Language in Native American World."

42. Silko, *Storyteller*, 7.

43. Arnold, ed., *Conversations*, 78; Silko, *Yellow Woman*, 53–57.

44. Silko, *Yellow Woman*, 57.

45. "'Yashtoah' is the hardened crust on cornmeal mash / that curls up. The very name 'yashtoah' means / it's sort of curled up, you know, dried, / just as mush dries on top" (Silko, *Storyteller*, 8).

46. This is the version of the story in *Yellow Woman*.

47. "Woman's World," 5.

48. Marietta Padilla explains that she too had to be sent away to boarding school, because the strain of merging these two worlds condemned her father (Susie's son Harry Marmon) and her mother to alcoholism ("The Social Perspective of the Impact of the English Language in Native American World").

49. Silko, *Storyteller*, 6.

Epilogue

1. *Sunday Patriot-News*, May 28, 2000, A6.

2. The superintendent's house dates back to 1821 but has a grand portico, added during Mercer's superintendency.

3. The girls' dormitory building burned down in 1924 and was not rebuilt.

4. Anne Wheelock Gonzales to Barbara Landis, June 18, 2000.

5. *Sunday Patriot-News*, May 28, 2000, A6.

6. Carlisle *Sentinel*, Saturday, May 27, 2000, A5.

7. Students and visiting parents are known to have conducted private ceremonies.

8. Fewer tribes were represented at Hampton, which is mirrored in the affiliations of children buried in the Hampton cemetery.

9. Jim West to Cousin Karin, May 29, 2000 (copy sent to author).

10. Jim West to Cousin Karin, May 29, 2000.

11. Joe Elias, "Thing of fear to Indians," *Sunday Patriot-News*, May 28, 2000, A6.

12. *News from Indian Country: The Independent Native Journal*, mid-May 2000, 13B.

13. Maggie Tarbell Lazore died in April 2001. There are now no known living Carlisle survivors.

14. Dorreen Yellow Bird, "Remembering 'Boarding Schools' and Their Impact," *GrandForksHerald.com*, May 16, 2000.

15. Jim West to Cousin Karin, May 29, 2000.

Bibliography

Primary Sources

American Board of Commissioners to Foreign Missions. Papers. Houghton Library, Harvard University.

Cumberland County Historical Society.

  Carlisle Indian School Oral History Project (1980–81).

    Henry Flickinger.

    Milton Flower.

    James Garvie.

    Arthur Mann.

    Ella Ruggles.

    Virginia Shelley.

    James Wardecker.

  Photographic Archives.

    Boudoir-Size Photograph Collection.

    Cabinet-Sized Photograph Collection.

    Diffendurfer Collection.

    Flat Box Collection.

    Framed Photograph Collection.

    Francis Benjamin Johnson Indian School Albums.

    Indian School Albums.

  Manuscript Archives.

    Yates, Humer, Smith, and Carroll. "Cemetery: A List of Those Buried There." MS., n.d.

    Cates. "The Carlisle Indian School Cemetery." Based on the earlier list by Yates et al., MS., 1994.

  Postcard Collection.

  Potamkin Collection.

  Stereoview Card Collection.

Dickinson College Archives and Special Collections.

  Indian School File.

  Carlisle Barracks Folder.

Hampton University Archives, Hampton VA.

  Annual Reports, 1878–1900.

  Student Files.

Indian Rights Association. Annual Reports, 1882–90. Historical Society of Pennsylvania PA.

Interviews

Jim Anquoe Sr., British Library, London, February 12, 2003.

Ruth Fire, Fort Thompson SD, September 10, 1974.

Rev. Clive Estes, Fort Thompson SD, September 13, 1974.

William Ewing, Carlisle PA, March 16, 2000.

James Hamilton, Macy NE, September 20, 1974.

Donna, Diane, and William Herne, St. Regis NY, August 4, 2000.

Maggie Tarbell, St. Regis NY, August 4, 2000.

George Yuda, Carlisle PA, November 26, 2002.

National Archives, Washington DC Records of the Bureau of Indian Affairs.

Cartographic Records. Records of the Carlisle Indian Industrial School. RG 75.26.

General Records of the Bureau of Indian Affairs.

Letters Received by the Office of Indian Affairs (both manuscript and microfilm). RG 75.4.

Letters Sent by the Office of Indian Affairs (both manuscript and microfilm). RG 75.4.

Report Books of the Office of Indian Affairs (both manuscript and microfilm). RG 75.4.

Records of the Education Division. Statistics Relating to Indian Schools. RG 75.10.

Records of the Office of Chief Engineers. Carlisle Barracks File. RG 77, subgroup B.

Records of the Quartermaster. RG 92.

Nebraska State Historical Society.

Correspondence of Mabel M. Gould.

Santee Normal Training School Correspondence and Printed Matter.

Richard Henry Pratt Papers. Beinecke Rare Book and Manuscript Library. Yale University.

St. Augustine Historical Society.

Fort Marion File.

Photographic Archives.

Smithsonian Institution, Washington DC

Alice C. Fletcher.

Correspondence and Personal Papers.

Field Book on the Omaha.

U.S. Army Military History Institute.

Carlisle Barracks Cemetery File.

Carlisle Barracks File.

Williamson Family Papers. Minnesota State Historical Society, St. Paul.

Periodicals

Carlisle Indian School Publications

The *Arrow* (1904–1908). Published weekly. Name changed to the *Carlisle Arrow* (1908–1918). Published weekly.

Eadle Keatah Toh (January 1880–March 1882). Name changed to the *Morning Star* in April 1882. Name changed to *Red Man* in January 1888. Name changed to *Red Man and Helper* in 1900. Published weekly until 1904.

Indian Craftsman (February 1909–January 1910). Name changed to *Red Man* in 1910. Published monthly. Merged with *Carlisle Arrow* in 1917; name changed to *Carlisle Arrow and Red Man*. Published weekly through June 7, 1918.

Indian Helper (1885–1900). Published weekly.

School News (June 1880–May 1883). Published monthly.

Hampton Normal and Agricultural Institute Publications

Southern Workman (1872–1938). Published monthly.

Talks and Thoughts (1886–1907). Published monthly.

Santee Normal Training School Publications

Iapi Oaye/Word Carrier (May 1871–March 1939). Published monthly (irregular).

Published Sources

Abbott, Austin. "Indians and the Law." *Harvard Law Review* 2 (November 1888): 167–79.

Abbott, Lyman. "The Basis of Anglo-Saxon Understanding." *North American Review* 166 (May 1898): 513–21.

Adams, David Wallace. *Education for Extinction: American Indians and the Boarding School Experience, 1875–1928.* Lawrence: University Press of Kansas, 1995.

———. "Education in Hues: Red and Black at Hampton Institute, 1878–1893," *South Atlantic Quarterly* 76.2 (Spring 1977): 159–76.

Ahern, Wilbert H. "The Returned Indians: Hampton Institute and its Indian Alumni, 1879–1893." *Journal of Ethnic Studies* 10 (Winter 1983): 101–24.

Alford, Thomas Wildcat. *Civilization, as told to Florence Drake.* Norman: University of Oklahoma Press, 1936. Reprint, *Civilization and the Story of the Absentee Shawnees.* Norman: University of Oklahoma Press, 1979.

Allen, Gunn, Paula. *The Sacred Hoop: Recovering the Feminine in American Indian Traditions.* Boston: Beacon Press, 1986.

Anderson, Benedict. *Imagined Communities: Reflections on the Origin and Spread of Nationalism.* London: Verso, 1983.

Anderson, James. *The Education of Blacks in the South, 1860–1935.* Chapel Hill: University of North Carolina Press, 1988.

Annual Report of the Associated Executive Committee of Friends on Indian Affairs. New Vienna OH: Peace Association of Friends in America, 1870–1900.

Annual Report of the Board of Indian Commissioners. Washington DC: GPO, 1870–1900.

Annual Report of the Commissioner of Education. Washington DC: GPO, 1885–1900.

Annual Report of the Commissioner of Indian Affairs. Washington DC: GPO, 1865–1916.

Annual Report of the Executive Committee of the Indian Rights Association. Philadelphia PA: Indian Rights Association, 1883–1889.

Annual Report of the Superintendent of Indian Schools. Washington DC: GPO, 1883–1900.

Annual Report of the Women's National Indian Association. Philadelphia, 1883–1890.

Archuleta, Maragaret, L., Brenda J. Child, and K Tsianina Lomawaima, eds. *Away from Home: American Indian Boarding School Experiences, 1879–2000.* Phoenix AZ: Heard Museum, 2000.

Ariès, Philippe. *The Hour of Our Death.* New York: Alfred Knopf, 1981.

Armstrong League of Hampton Workers. *Memories of Old Hampton.* Hampton VA: The Institute Press, 1909.

Armstrong, Mary F., ed. *The Hampton Institute, 1868–1865: Its Work for Two Races.* Hampton VA: Normal School Press, 1885.

Armstrong, Samuel Chapman. *Education for Life.* Hampton VA: Press of Hampton Normal and Agricultural Institute, 1913.

———. "From the Beginning." In *Twenty-Two Years' Work of the Hampton Normal and Agricultural Institute at Hampton, Virginia,* edited by Helen W. Ludlow et al., 1–11.

———. *Hampton Normal and Agricultural Institute.* Hampton VA: Hampton Normal School Printing Office, November 1887.

———. *The Hampton Normal and Agricultural Institute: Its Reply to a New Attack on Eastern Schools.* Hampton VA: Hampton Normal School Printing Office, January 1890.

———. *Hampton Report.* Hampton VA: Normal School Printing Office, 1889.

———. *Indian Education at Hampton Normal and Agricultural Institute.* New York: George Nesbitt, 1881.

———. "Lessons from the Hawaiian Islands." *Journal of Christian Philosophy* 3 (January 1884): 200–229.

———. *Proceedings of the Department of Superintendence.* Circulars of Information 3. Washington DC: Bureau of Education, 1883.

Armstrong, William H. *Warrior in Two Camps: Ely S. Parker, Union General and Seneca Chief.* Syracuse NY: Syracuse University Press, 1978.

Arnold, Ellen L., ed. *Conversations with Leslie Marmon Silko.* Jackson: University Press of Mississippi, 2000.

Ashabranner, Brent. *A Strange and Distant Shore.* New York: Cobble Hill Books, 1996.

Axtell, James. *The Invasion Within: The Contest of Cultures in Colonial North America.* New York: Oxford University Press, 1985.

Bachelard, Gaston. *La Poetique de l'Espace.* Paris: Presses Universitaire de France, 1957.

———. *The Poetics of Space.* Trans. Maria Jolas. Boston: Beacon Press, 1969.

Baker, Lee D. *From Savage to Negro: Anthropology and the Construction of Race, 1896–1954.* Berkeley: University of California Press, 1998.

Barnes, Randy. Genocide. http://www.americanindianmovement.org/txaim/genocide.html.

Barrows, William. *The Indian's Side of the Indian Question.* Boston: Lothrop, 1887.

Barth, Frederik, ed. *Ethnic Groups and Boundaries: The Social Organization of Cultural Difference.* London: Allen and Unwin, 1969.

Bartlett, Rev. S. C. *Historical Sketch of the Missions of the American Board among the North American Indians.* Boston: American Board of Commissioners for Foreign Missions, 1880.

Barton, Winifred W. *John P. Williamson, a Brother to the Sioux.* Chicago: Fleming H. Revell, 1919.

Bataille, Gretchen M., and Kathleen Mullen Sands. *American Indian Women: Telling Their Lives.* Lincoln: University of Nebraska Press, 1984.

Battey, Thomas C. *The Life and Adventures of a Quaker Among Indians.* Boston: Lee and Shepard, 1875.

Beaver, Robert Pierce. *Church, State and the American Indians: Two-and-a-Half Centuries of Partnership in Missions between Protestant Churches and Government.* St. Louis MO: Cordia, 1966).

Beers, F. W. *Atlas of Cumberland County, Pennsylvania, from Actual Surveys.* New York: F. W. Beers, 1872.

Bell, Genevieve. "Telling Stories out of School: Remembering the Carlisle Indian Industrial School, 1879–1918." PhD diss., Stanford University, 1998.

Bentham, Jeremy. *Panopticon.* London: T. Payne, 1791.

Bergland, Renée L. *The National Uncanny: Indian Ghosts and American Subjects.* Hanover NH: University Press of New England, 2000.

Berkhofer, Robert F., Jr. *Salvation and the Savage: An Analysis of Protestant Missions and American Indian Response, 1787–1862.* Lexington: University of Kentucky Press, 1965.

———. *The White Man's Indian: Images of the American Indian from Columbus to the Present.* New York: Knopf, 1978.

Berlo, Janet Catherine. *Plains Indian Drawings, 1865–1935: Pages from a Visual History.* New York: American Federation of Arts and the Drawing Center, 1996.

Berlo, Janet Catherine, and Ruth B. Phillips. *Native North American Art.* Oxford UK: Oxford University Press, 1998.

Berry, Brewton. *The Education of American Indians.* 91st Cong., lst sess., Health, Education, and Welfare Project 7–0813.

Blackmar, Frank W., "The Socialization of the American." *Journal of Sociology* 34 (January 1929): 653–69.

Blaine, Martha Royce. *Some Things Are Not Forgotten: A Pawnee Family Remembers.* Lincoln: University of Nebraska Press, 1997.

Bland, Thomas A. *Brief History of the Late Military Invasion of the Home of the Sioux.* Washington DC: National Indian Defense Association, 1891.

———. *Life of Alfred B. Meacham.* Washington DC: T. A. and M. C. Bland, 1883.

Bloom, John. *To Show What an Indian Can Do: Sports at Native American Boarding Schools.* Minneapolis: University of Minnesota Press, 2000.

Blowsnake, Sam. *Crashing Thunder: The Autobiography of an American Indian,* edited by Paul Radin. New York: Appleton, 1926.

Bonnin, Gertrude Simmons. "Impressions of an Indian Childhood." *Atlantic Monthly* 85, January 1900, 37–47.

———. "An Indian Teacher Among Indians." *Atlantic Monthly* 85, March 1900, 381–86.

———. "Soft-Hearted Sioux." *Harper's Monthly* 101, September 1901, 505–8.

———. "Trial Path: An Indian Romance." *Harper's Monthly* 101, October 1901, 741–44.

———. "Why I am a Pagan." *Atlantic Monthly* 90, December 1902, 801–3.

Bourke, John G. *On the Border with Crook.* London: Sampson Low, 1891.

Bowden, Henry W. *American Indian and Christian Missions: Studies in Cultural Conflict.* Chicago: University of Chicago Press, 1981.

Boyer, Ruth Mcdonald, and Narcissus Duffy Gayton. *Apache Mothers and Daughters: Four Generations of a Family.* Norman: University of Oklahoma Press, 1992.

Bradford, Amory, "Among Colored Educational Institutions." *Outlook,* June 19, 1897, 454–57.

Bredin, Renae. "Falling into the Wrong Hands: Laguna Women and Ethnographic Strip Tease." *Readerly/Writerly Texts: Essays on Literature, Literacy/Textual Criticism, and Pedagogical Theory* 2.1 (Fall/Winter 1994). http://www.readerly-writerlytexts.com/3falling.htm.

Brooks, Chris. *Mortal Remains: The History and Present State of the Victorian and Edwardian Cemetery*. Exeter UK: Wheaton, in Association with the Victorian Society, 1989.

Brumble, H. David, III. "Albert Hensley's Two Autobiographies and the History of American Indian Autobiography." *American Quarterly* 37.5 (Winter 1985): 702–18.

———. *An Annotated Bibliography of American Indian and Eskimo Autobiographies*. Lincoln: University of Nebraska Press, 1981.

Buntin, Martha, "The Quaker Indian Agents of the Kiowa, Comanche, and Wichita Reservations." *Chronicles of Oklahoma* 10 (June 1932): 204–18.

Bureau of Indian Affairs. *Correspondence on the Subject of Teaching the Vernacular in Indian Schools, 1887–88*. Washington DC: GPO, 1888.

———. *Easy Reading Lessons for Indian Schools*. Washington DC: GPO, 1975.

———. *Regulations of the Indian Department*. Washington DC: GPO, 1884. Revised ed. 1894.

———. *Rules for Indian Schools with Course of Study*. Washington DC: GPO, 1890.

———. *Teaching Indian Students to Speak English*. Washington DC: GPO, 1904.

Burgess, Marianna [Embe]. *Stiya: A Carlisle Indian Girl at Home*. Cambridge MA: Riverside Press, 1891.

Butler, Captain E. *Our Indian Question*. New York: A. D. Watling, 1882.

Carnoy, Martin. *Education as Cultural Imperialism*. New York: David Mackay, 1974.

Charter, David. "Canadian Natives Win £1bn for 70 Years' Abuse." *Times* (London), November 25, 2005, 5.

Child, Brenda J. *Boarding School Seasons: American Indian Families, 1900–1940*. Lincoln: University of Nebraska Press, 1998.

Clifford, James. *The Predicament of Culture: Twentieth Century Ethnography, Literature and Art*. Cambridge MA: Harvard University Press, 1988.

Clifton, James A., ed. *Being and Becoming Indian: Biographical Studies of North American Frontiers*. Chicago: The Dorsey Press, 1989.

Cohen, Felix. *Handbook of Federal Indian Law*. Washington, DC: GPO, 1945.

Coleman, Michael. *American Indian Children at School, 1850–1930*. Jackson: University Press of Mississippi, 1993.

Colyer, Vincent, *Peace with the Apaches of New Mexico and Arizona*. Report of Vincent Colyer. Washington, DC: GPO, 1872.

Condition of the Indian Tribes. Report of the Joint Special Committee Appointed under Joint Resolution of March 3, 1865. Washington DC: GPO, 1867.

Corwin, Hugh D. *Comanche and Kiowa Captives in Oklahoma and Texas*. Guthrie OK: Cooperative, 1959.

Coward, John. *The Newspaper Indian: Native American Identity in the Press, 1820–1890*. Urbana: University of Illinois Press, 1999.

Cox, Jacob Dolson, "The Indian Question." *International Review* (June 1879): 617–34.

Crowley, Tony. *Language in History: Theories and Texts*. London: Routledge, 1996.

Dain, Bruce. *A Hideous Monster of the Mind: American Race Theory in the Early Republic*. Cambridge MA: Harvard University Press, 2002.

Dawes, Henry L., "Have We Failed the Indian?" *Atlantic Monthly* 84.502, August 1899, 280–85.

Defoe, Daniel. *The Life and Surprising Adventures of Robinson Crusoe*. Edited by J. D Crowley. Oxford UK: Oxford University Press, 1972.

Deloria, Ella. *Speaking of Indians*. New York: Friendship Press, 1944.

Deloria, Vine, Jr., and Daniel R. Wildcat. *Power and Place: Indian Education in America*. Golden CO: Fulcrum Resources, 2001.

d'Errico, Peter. "Native Americans in America: A Theoretical and Historical Overview." In *American Nations: Encounters in Indian Country, 1850 to the Present*, edited by Frederick E. Hoxie, Peter C. Mancall, and James H. Merrell, 480–99. New York: Routledge, 2001.

Dickson, Charles. *Course of Study for the Indian Schools of the United States*. Washington DC: GPO, 1901.

Difficulties with the Indian Tribes. Ho. Ex. Doc. No. 240, 41st Cong., 2nd sess., 1869, concerning Relations with the Cheyenne, Comanche, Arapaho, Apache, and Kiowa Tribes in 1867.

Dippie, Brian W. *The Vanishing American: White Attitudes and U.S. Indian Policy*. Midddleton CT: Wesleyan University Press, 1982.

Dobbins, M. A. *Memorial and Affidavits Showing Outrages Perpetrated by the Apache Indians in the Territory of Arizona during the Years 1869–1870*. San Francisco: Francis and Valentine, 1871. Reprint, Tucson AZ: Territorial Press, 1964.

Dodge, Richard Irving. *Our Wild Indians: Thirty-three Years' Experience among the Red Men of the Great West*. Hartford CT: A. D. Worthington, 1882.

Dolan, John A. "'I've Always Fancied Owning Me Own Lion': Ideological Motivations in External House Decoration." In *At Home: An Anthropology of Domestic Space*, edited by Irene Cieraad, 60–72. Syracuse NY: Syracuse University Press, 1999.

Donehoo, George P. *A History of the Cumberland Valley in Pennsylvania*. Harrisburg PA: Susquehanna Historical Association, 1930.

Dorsey, J. O. *A Study of Siouan Cults*. llth Annual Report of the Bureau of American Ethnology. Washington DC: GPO, 1894.

Douglas, Mary. *Purity and Danger: An Analysis of Concepts of Pollution and Taboo*. London: Routledge and Kegan Paul, 1966.

Dovey, Kim. *Framing Places: Mediating Power in Built Form*. London: Routledge, 1999.

Drago, Edmund L. *Initiative, Paternalism, and Race Relations: Charleston's Avery Normal Institute*. Athens: University of Georgia Press, 1990.

Dyk, Walter. *A Navaho Autobiography*. Viking Fund Publications in Anthropology 8. New York: Viking Fund, 1947.

Du Bois, W. E. B. *The Souls of Black Folk*. Edited by David W. Blight and Robert Gooding-Williams. Boston: Bedford, 1997.

Eastman, Charles A. *From the Deep Woods to Civilization*. Lincoln: University of Nebraska Press, 1977.

———. *Indian Boyhood*. New York: Doubleday, 1914.

———. *Indian Child Life*. Boston: Little, Brown, 1913.

———. *Indian Scout Talks: A Guide for Boy Scouts and Camp Fire Girls*. Boston: Little, Brown, 1914.

———. *The Indian To-day: The Past and Future of the First American*. Garden City NY: Doubleday, Page, 1915.

Eastman, Elaine Goodale. *Pratt: The Red Man's Moses*. Norman: University of Oklahoma Press, 1935.

Ellis, Clyde. *To Change Them Forever: Indian Education at the Rainy Mountain Boarding School, 1893–1920*. Norman: University of Oklahoma Press, 1996.

———. *A Dancing People: Powwow Culture on the Southern Plains*. Lawrence: University Press of Kansas, 2003.

Engs, Robert Francis. *Educating the Disfranchised and Disinherited: Samuel Chapman Armstrong and Hampton Institute, 1839–1893*. Knoxville: University of Tennessee Press, 1999.

———. *Freedom's First Generation: Black Hampton, Virginia, 1861–1890*. Philadelphia: University of Pennsylvania Press, 1979.

Erikson, Erik. "Observations on Sioux Education." *Journal of Psychology* 7 (January 1939): 101-56.

Ewers, John. *Teton Dakota Ethnology and History*. Berkeley CA: U.S. Department of the Interior, National Park Service, 1937.

Febvre, Lucien. "Civilization: evolution of a word and a group of ideas," in Peter Burke, (ed.), A New Kind of History, London, Routledge and Kegan Paul (1973): 219–57.

Fields, Barbara J. "Ideology and Race in American History." In *Region, Race and Reconstruction: Essays in Honor of C. Vann Woodward*, edited by J. Morgan Kousser and James M. McPherson, 143–178. New York: Oxford University Press, 1982.

Fisher, Dexter. "Zitkala-Ša: The Evolution of a Writer," American Indian Quarterly 5 (1979): 229–38.

Fitzgerald, F. Scott. The Stories of F. Scott Fitzgerald, Vol.2, The Crack-Up and Other Pieces and Stories, Harmondsworth, Penguin Books (1965).

Fletcher, Alice C., Indian Education and Civilization, 48th Cong., 2nd sess., Senate Exec. Doc. No. 95, Washington DC: GPO, 1888.

———. *Indian Home Building*. New York: Women's National Indian Association, 1883.

———. *Lands in Severalty to Indians*. Salem MA: Salem Press, 1885.

———. *On the Lawlessness of the Indian Reservation System*. Boston: Indian Association, 1884.

———. "Personal Studies of Indian Life: Politics and 'Pipe-Dancing.'" *Century Magazine*, 45.3, January 1893, 441-55.

Fletcher, Alice C., and Francis La Flesche. *The Omaha Tribe*. 27th Annual Report of the Bureau of American Ethnology. Washington DC: GPO, 1911.

Foreman, Grant. *A History of Oklahoma*. Norman: University of Oklahoma Press, 1942.

Foucault, Michel. *Discipline and Punish*. New York: Vintage Books, 1977.

———. "The Subject and Power." Afterword. In *Michel Foucault: Beyond Structuralism and Hermeneutics*, edited by Hubert Dreyfus and Paul Rabinow, 208–26. 2nd ed. Chicago: University of Chicago Press, 1983.

The Four Gospels of our Lord Jesus Christ, in Shawnee Indian Language. Translated by Thomas W. Alford. Xenia OH: William A. Galloway, 1929.

Fraser, Graham. "Ex-residential School Students get $1.9 Billion." *Toronto Star*, April 26, 2006, sec. A, 4.

Gallaher, Ruth. "The Indian Agent in the United States since 1850." *Iowa Journal of History and Politics* 14.2 (1916): 73–239.

Galpin, S. A. *Report Upon the Condition and Management of Certain Indian Agencies in the Indian Territory now Under the Supervision of the Orthodox Friends*. Washington DC: GPO, 1877.

Gaul, Theresa Strouth, ed. *To Marry an Indian: The Marriage of Harriett Gold and Elias Boudinot in Letters, 1823–1839*. Chapel Hill: University of North Carolina Press, 2005.

Gilcreast, Everett. "Richard Henry Pratt and American Indian Policy, 1877–1906: A Study of the Assimilation Movement." PhD diss., Yale University, 1967.

Gladfelter, Valerie. "Caring and Control: The Social Psychology of an Authoritative Group, the Burlington Friends Meeting." PhD diss., University of Pennsylvania, 1983.

Goodale, Elaine. "How to Americanize the Indian." *New Englander and Yale Review* 52.242, May 1890, 452–55.

———. *The Senator and the School House*. Philadelphia, Indian Rights Association (reprinted from the New York, *Independent*, March 4, 1886).

Goodson, Ivor F., ed. *Social Histories of the Secondary Curriculum: Subjects for Study*. London: Falmer Press, 1985.

Gordon, Colin, ed., *Michel Foucault, Power/Knowledge: Selected Interviews and Other Writings, 1972–1977*. Harlow UK: Longman, 1980.

Gould, Stephen Jay. *The Mismeasure of Man*. London: Penguin, 1981.

Gossett, Thomas F. *Race: The History of an Idea in America*. Dallas TX: Southern Methodist University Press, 1963.

Grandison, Kenrick Ian. "Negotiated Space: The Black College Campus as a Cultural Record of Postbellum America." *American Quarterly* 51.3 (September 1999): 529–79.

Green, Charles L. "The Indian Reservation System of the Dakotas to 1889," *South Dakota Historical Collections* 14 (Pierre: South Dakota State Historical Society, 1928), 307–416.

Hafen, P. Jane. "Zitkala-Ša: Sentimentality and Sovereignty." *Wicazo Ša* 12.2 (Fall 1997): 31–41.

Hagan, William T. *Indian Police and Judges*. New Haven: Yale University Press, 1966.

———. "The Reservation Policy: Too Little and Too Late." In *Indian-White Relations: A Persistent Paradox*, edited by Jane F. Smith and Robert M. Kvasnicka, 157–69. Washington DC: Howard University Press, 1976.

———. *United States–Comanche Relations*. Norman: University of Oklahoma Press, 1990.

Hale, Grace Elizabeth. *Making Whiteness: The Culture of Segregation in the South, 1890–1940*. New York: Vintage Books, 1998.

Haller, John S., Jr. *Outcasts from Evolution: Scientific Attitudes to Racial Inferiority, 1859–1900*. New ed. Carbondale: Southern Illinois University Press, 1995.

Hampson, Norman. *The Enlightenment: An Evaluation of Its Assumptions, Attitudes and Values*. London: Penguin, 1990.

Harlan, Louis. *Booker T. Washington*. Rev. ed. New York: Oxford University Press, 1983.

Harris, Marvin. *The Rise of Anthropological Theory*. New York: Norton, 1968.

Harris, Moira F. *Between Two Cultures: Kiowa Art from Fort Marion*. St. Paul MN: Pogo Press, 1989.

Harrison, Jonathan Baxter. *The Latest Studies on Indian Reservations*. Philadelphia: Indian Rights Association, 1887.

Hawkins, Mike. *Social Darwinism in European and American Thought, 1860–1945: Nature as Model and Nature as Threat*. Cambridge UK: Cambridge University Press, 1997.

Head, F. H. "Our Ishmaelites." *Overland Monthly* 4, 1870, 105–ll.

Herskovits, Melville J. "Education and Cultural Dynamics." *American Journal of Sociology* 48.6 (May 1943): 737–49.

Hertzberg, Hazel. *The Search for an American Indian Identity*. Syracuse NY: Syracuse University Press, 1971.

Himes, Charles F. *A Sketch of Dickinson College*. Harrisburg PA: Lane S. Hart, 1879.

Hodge, Frederick W. *Handbook of American Indians North of Mexico*. Vol. 1. Washington DC: GPO, 1907.

Hoefel, Roseanne. "Writing, Performance, Activism: Zitkala-Ša and Pauline Johnson." In *Native American Women in Literature and Culture*, edited and introduced by Susan Castillo and Victor M. P. Da Rosa, 107–18. Porto, Portugal: Fernando Pessoa University Press, 1997.

Holt, Thomas C. "Marking: Race, Race-making, and the Writing of History." *American Historical Review* 100.1 (February 1995): 1–20.

Horsecapture, George P. *Powwow*. Cody WY: Buffalo Bill Historical Center, 1989.

Horsman, Reginald. *Race and Manifest Destiny: The Origins of American Racial Anglo-Saxonism*. Cambridge MA: Harvard University Press, 1981.

Hoxie, Frederick. *The Final Promise: The Campaign to Assimilate the Indian, 1880–1920*. Lincoln: University of Nebraska Press, 1983.

Hulme, Peter. *Colonial Encounters: Europe and the Native Caribbean: 1492–1797*. London: Methuen, 1986.

Hultgren, Mary Lou. *To Lead and To Serve: American Indian Education at Hampton Institute, 1878–1923*. Charlottesville VA: Virginia Foundation for the Humanities and Public Policy in cooperation with Hampton University, 1989.

Hyer, Sally. *One House, One Voice, One Heart: Native American Education at the Santa Fe Indian School, 1890–1990*. Santa Fe: Museum of New Mexico Press, 1990.

Indian Education: A National Tragedy or National Challenge. 91st Cong., 1st sess., Senate Report No. 92–501.

Information in Relation Massacre of United States Troops by Indians near Fort Phil Kearny. Washington DC: GPO, 1867.

Jacobson, Matthew Frye. *Whiteness of a Different Color: European Immigrants and the Alchemy of Race*. Cambridge MA: Harvard University Press, 1999.

Jacker, Edward. "Mental Capacity of the American Indian as Indicated by his Speech." *American Catholic Quarterly Review* 3 (1878): 268–89.

Jahner, Elaine A. "Transitional Narratives and Cultural Continuity." In *American Indian Persistence and Resurgence*, edited by Karl Kroeber, 149–80. Durham NC: Duke University Press, 1994.

James, Sydney. *A People Among Peoples: Quaker Benevolence in Eighteenth-Century America*. Cambridge MA: Harvard University Press

Jenkins, Richard. *Social Identity*. London: Routledge, 1996.

Johnston, Norman. *Eastern State Penitentiary: Crucible of Good Intentions.* Philadelphia: Philadelphia Museum of Art, 1994.

Jones, Douglas. *The Treaty of Medicine Lodge.* Norman: University of Oklahoma Pres, 1966.

Jordan, Winthrop. *White over Black: American Attitudes toward the Negro, 1550–1812.* Chapel Hill: University of North Carolina Press, 1968.

Kallen, Horace M. "Democracy versus the Melting Pot." *The Nation,* February 18 and 25, 1915, 190–94, 217–20. Reprinted in Kallen, *Culture and Democracy in the United States* (New York: Arno, 1970), 67–125

Kappler, Charles J. *Indian Affairs: Laws and Treaties.* 2 vols. Washington DC: GPO, 1904.

Kasson, Joy S. *Buffalo Bill's Wild West: Celebrity, Memory, and Popular History.* New York: Hill and Wang, 2000.

Keliher, John G. *The History of the 4th U.S. Cavalry Regiment.* http://www.25thida.com/4thcav.html.

Keller, Robert H. Jr. *American Protestantism and United States Indian Policy, 1869–82.* Lincoln: University of Nebraska Press, 1983.

Kelsey, Rayner W. *Friends and the Indians, 1655–1917.* Philadelphia: Associated Executive Committee of Friends, 1917.

Kluckhohn, Clyde. "The Personal Document in Anthropological Science." In *The Use of Personal Documents,* edited by Louis R. Gottschalk, 164–75. New York: Social Science Research Council, 1945.

Kvasnicka, Robert M., and Herman J. Viola, eds. *The Commissioners of Indian Affairs, 1824–1977.* Lincoln: University of Nebraska Press, 1979.

La Farge, Oliver, "White Man's Burden." *World's Work* 60, August 1931, 45–65.

La Flesche, Francis. *The Middle Five: Indian Boys at School.* Boston: Small, Maynard, 1900. Reprint, *The Middle Five: Indian Schoolboys of the Omaha Tribe.* Madison: University of Wisconsin Press, 1953.

Landis, Barbara. "Putting Lucy Pretty Eagle to Rest." In *Boarding School Blues: Revisiting American Indian Educational Experiences.* Edited by Clifford E. Trafzer, Jean A. Keller, and Lorene Sisquoc, 123–30. Lincoln: University of Nebraska Press, 2006.

Lanier, Sidney. *Florida: Its Scenery, Climate and History.* 1875. A facsimile reprint of the first edition with an introduction and index by Jerrell H. Shofner. Gainesville: University of Florida Press, 1973.

Latourette, K. S. "The Light of History on Current Missionary Methods." *International Review of Missions* 42 (1953): 137–43.

Lebow, R. N. *White Britain and Black Ireland: The Influence of Stereotypes on Colonial Policy.* Philadelphia: Institute for the Study of Human Issues, 1976.

Lee, Alton R. "Indian Citizenship and the Fourteenth Amendment." *South Dakota History* 4 (Spring 1974): 198–222.

Leupp, Francis E., *The Indian and His Problem*. New York: Charles Scribner's Sons, 1910.

Lindsey, Donal. *Indians at Hampton Institute, 1877–1923*. Urbana: University of Illinois Press, 1995.

Loewen, James W. *Lies Across America: What Our Historic Sites Get Wrong*. New York: New Press, 1999.

Logan, Rayford W. *Howard University: The First Hundred Years, 1867–1967*. New York: New York University Press, 1969.

Lomawaima, K. Tsianina. *They Called It Prairie Light: The Story of Chilocco School*. Lincoln: University of Nebraska Press, 1994.

Loomba, A. "Dead Women Tell No Tales: Issues of Female Subjectivity, Subaltern Agency and Tradition in Colonial and Post-Colonial on Widow Immolation in India," *History Workshop Journal* 36.1 (1993): 209–27.

Lord, Jeannette Mather. "John Brown: They Had a Concern." *West Virginia History* 20.3 (April 1959): 163–83.

———. "Hampton's Indian Students at Home." In *The Hampton Institute*, edited by Mary F. Armstrong.

———, ed. *Ten Years' Work for Indians at Hampton Institute*. Hampton VA: Normal School Press, 1888.

——— et al, eds. *Twenty-two Years' Work of the Hampton Normal and Agricultural Institute at Hampton, Virginia*. Hampton VA: Normal School Press, 1893.

Luker, Ralph E. *The Social Gospel in Black and White: American Racial Reform, 1885–1912*. Chapel Hill: University of North Carolina Press, 1991.

Lukes, Stephen. *Power: A Radical View*. London, Macmillan.

Malmsheimer, Lonna. "'Imitation White Man': Images of Transformation at the Carlisle Indian School." *Studies in Visual Communication* 2.4 (Fall 1985): 54–74.

Mangan, J. A. "Images for Confident Control: Stereotypes in Imperial Discourse." In *The Imperial Curriculum: Racial Images and Education in the British Colonial Experience*, edited by J. A. Mangan, 6–22. London, Routledge, 1993.

Mann, Henrietta. *Cheyenne–Arapaho Education, 1871–1982*. Niwot: University Press of Colorado, 1997.

Marietta, Jack. The Reformation of American Quakerism, 1748–1783, Philadelphia: University of Pennsylvania Press (1984): xiii–xv.

Mark, Joan. *Four Anthropologists: An American Science in its Early Years*. New York: Science History Publications, 1980.

Mathews, John Joseph. *Wah'Kon-Tah: the Osage and the White Man's Road*. Norman: University of Oklahoma Press, 1932.

McBeth, Sally. *Ethnic Identity and the Boarding School Experience of West-*

Central Oklahoma American Indians. Washington DC: University Press of America, 1983.

McFee, Malcolm. "The 150% Man, A Product of Blackfeet Acculturation." *American Anthropologist* 70.6 (1968): 1096–1107.

McLoughlin, William G. *Cherokees and Missionaries, 1789–1839.* New Haven CT: Yale University Press, 1984.

Meier, August. *Negro Thought in America, 1880–1915: Racial Ideologies in the Age of Booker T. Washington.* Ann Arbor: University of Michigan Press, 1963.

Memorial of the Yearly Meeting of Friends, Relative to the Treatment of the Indians. Ho. Misc. Doc. No. 29, 40th Cong., 3rd sess., 1868.

Mihesuah, Devon A. *Cultivating the Rosebud: The Education of Women at the Cherokee Female Seminary, 1851–1909.* Urbana: University of Illinois Press, 1993.

Miller, Alice. *The Drama of the Gifted Child: The Search for the True Self.* Trans. Ruth Ward. New York: Basic Books, 1981.

Miller, J. R. *Shingwauk's Vision: A History of Native Residential Schools.* Toronto: University of Toronto Press, 1996.

Milner, Clyde A., II. *With Good Intentions: Quaker Work Among the Pawnees, Otos, and Omahas in the 1870s.* Lincoln: University of Nebraska Press, 1982.

Minutes of the Associated Executive Committee of Friends on Indian Affairs. 1870–1900.

Momaday, N. Scott. *The Way to Rainy Mountain.* Albuquerque: University of New Mexico Press, 1977.

Mooney, James. *Calendar History of the Kiowa Indians.* 17th Annual Report of Bureau of American Ethnology. Washington DC: GPO, 1898. Reprint, Washington DC: Smithsonian Institution Press, 1979.

Mooney, James. *The Ghost Dance Religion and the Sioux Outbreak of 1890.* 14th Annual Report of the Bureau of American Ethnology. Washington DC: GPO, 1896.

Morris, Robert Charles. *Reading, 'riting and Reconstruction: The Education of Freedmen in the South, 1861–1870.* Chicago: University of Chicago Press, 1981.

Murchison, S. *Digest of Decisions Relating to Indian Affairs.* 2 vols. Washington DC: GPO, 1901.

Murray, David. *Forked Tongues: Speech, Writing and Representation in North American Indian Texts.* London: Pinter Publishers, 1991.

Myers, William J. *Carlisle Barracks and Army Medicine.* Carlisle PA: privately printed, 1997.

Nandy, Ashis. *The Intimate Enemy: Loss and Recovery of Self under Colonialism.* Delhi: Oxford University Press, 1983.

Nash, Gary B. "The First Decade in Pennsylvania: The letters of William Markham and Thomas Holme to William Penn." *Pennsylvania Magazine of History and Biography* 90 (1966): 314–516.

Nash, Gary B. *Red, White, and Black: The Peoples of Early America.* Rev. ed. Englewood Cliffs NJ: Prentice-Hall, 1982.

National Park Service. "Castillo de San Marcos National Monument: Apache Indians (Imprisoned)." N.d.

Noreiga, Jorge Noreiga. "American Indian Education in the United States: Indoctrination for Subordination to Colonialism." In *The State of Native America: Genocide, Colonization, and Resistance,* edited by M. Annette Jaimes, 371–402. Boston: South End Press, 1992.

Nye, W. S. *Carbine and Lance: The Story of Old Fort Sill.* Norman: University of Oklahoma Press, 1937.

O'Bryan, Aileen. "The Dine: Origin Myths of the Navaho Indians." Bureau of American Ethnology, Bulletin 163. Washington DC: GPO, 1956.

Omi, Michael, and Howard Winant. *Racial Formation in the United States.* New York: Routledge, 1994.

Ong, Walter J. *Orality and Literacy: The Technologizng of the Word.* London: Methuen, 1982.

Otis, D. S. *The Dawes Act and the Allotment of Indian Lands.* Norman: University of Oklahoma Press, 1973.

Padilla, Marietta. "The Social Perspective of the Impact of the English Language in Native American World." University of Minnesota, Center for Advanced Language Research Acquisition, Summer Institute, June 2001, 3. http://si.unm.edu/Web%20Journals/articles2001/MPADIL~1.HTM (site now discontinued).

Parkhurst, William. "General A Reviewed." *Council Fire* 8.6 (1885): 99–100,
———. "General A Reviewed." Part 2. *Council Fire* 8.7 (July 1885): 111–13.

Pascoe, Peggy. "Ideologies of Race in Twentieth-Century America." *Journal of American History* 83.1 (June 1996): 44–69.

Peabody, Francis G. *Education for Life: The Story of Hampton Institute.* New York: Doubleday Page, 1918.

Peel, J. D. Y., ed. *Herbert Spencer on Social Evolution: Selected Writings.* Chicago: University of Chicago Press, 1972.

Perkinson, Henry J. *The Imperfect Panacea: American Faith in Education, 1865–1976.* 2nd ed. New York: Random House, 1977.

Petersen, Karen Daniels. *Plains Indian Art from Fort Marion.* Norman: University of Oklahoma Press, 1971.

Pettitt, George A. *Primitive Education in North America.* Berkeley: University of California Press, 1946.

Pfister, Joel. *Individuality Incorporated: Indians and the Multicultural Modern.* Durham NC: Duke University Press, 2004.

Philbrick, John D. *City School Systems in the United States.* U.S. Bureau of Education, Circular No. 1. Washington DC: GPO, 1885.

Phillipson, Robert. *Linguistic Imperialism.* Oxford UK: Oxford University Press, 1992.

Pohlandt-McCormick, Helena. "'I saw a nightmare . . .': Violence and the Construction of Memory (Soweto, June 16, 1976)." *History and Theory* 39.4 (December 2000): 23–44.

Pond, Samuel W. "The Dakotas or Sioux in Minnesota as They Were in 1834." *Collections of the Minnesota Historical Society* 12, 319–501. St. Paul: Minnesota Historical Society, 1908.

———. *Two Volunteer Missionaries Among the Dakotas.* Boston Congregational Sunday-School Publishing House, 1893.

Porter, Roy. *The Enlightenment.* London: Macmillan, 1990.

Powell. J. W. *First Annual Report of the Bureau of American Ethnology to the Secretary of the Smithsonian Institution, 1879–1880.* Washington DC: GPO, 1881.

Powell, J. W. "From Barbarism to Civilization." *American Anthropologist* 1.2 (April 1888): 97–123.

Pratt, Richard Henry. "Address before the National Educational Association, Ocean Grove, August 11, 1883." In Pratt, *The Indian Industrial School, Carlisle.* Carlisle PA: Indian School, 1901.

———. "Address to the Lake Mohonk Conference." *Red Man* 13.6, January 1896, 2.

———. "Second Address to the Lake Mohonk Conference." *Red Man* 12.4, December 1893, 3.

———. "American Indians Chained and Unchained, Being an Address before the Pennsylvania Commandery," October 23, 1912.

———. Annual Reports of the U.S. Indian School at Carlisle, Carlisle PA. In Annual Report of the Commissioner of Indian Affairs, 1879–1916.

———. *Battlefield and Classroom: Four Decades with the American Indian, 1867–1904,* edited by Robert M. Utley. New Haven CT: Yale University Press, 1964.

———. *The Indian Industrial School, Carlisle.* Carlisle PA: Indian School, 1901.

———. *The Indian Industrial School, Carlisle, Pennsylvania: Its Origins, Purposes, Progress and the Difficulties Surmounted.* Carlisle PA: Indian School, 1908. Reprint, Carlisle, PA: Cumberland County Historical Society Publications, 1979.

———. "The Indian No Problem." *Red Man and Helper,* 18.47, June 24 and July 1, 1904, 8.

———. "Negroes and Indians: Address of Brigadier General Richard H. Pratt, U.S.A. Retired, Made before the Pennsylvania Commandery, Military Order of Foreign Wars of the United States." Bellevue Stratford Hotel, Philadelphia, January 14, 1913.

Preamble, Platform, and Constitution of the National Indian Defense Association. Philadelphia: Rufus H. Darby, 1885.

Proceedings of the Lake Mohonk Conference of Friends of the Indian. New York: Lake Mohonk Conference, 1883–1900.

Proceedings of the National Education Association. 1870–1900.

Proceedings of the Superintendent of the National Education Association. Circulars of Information 4. Washington DC: Bureau of Education, 1884.

Prucha, Francis Paul. *Americanizing the American Indians: Writings by the "Friends of the Indian," 1880–1900.* Cambridge MA: Harvard University Press, 1973. Reprint, Lincoln: University of Nebraska, 1978.

———. *The Churches and the Indian Schools, 1888–1912.* Lincoln: University of Nebraska Press, 1979.

———. *The Great Father: The United States Government and the American Indians.* Vols. 1 and 2. Lincoln: University of Nebraska Press, 1984.

Qoyawayma, Polingaysi [Elizabeth Q. White]. *No Turning Back: A Hopi Woman's Struggle to Live in Two Worlds.* Albuquerque: University of New Mexico Press, 1964.

Reel, Estell. *Course of Study for Indian Schools of the United States.* Washington DC: GPO 1901.

———. *Statistics of Indian Tribes, Agencies, and Schools.* Washington DC: GPO, 1899.

Report to the President by the Indian Peace Commissioners. Ho. Exec. Doc. No. 97, 40th Cong., 2nd sess, 1868.

Richardson, James D., *A Compilation of the Messages and Papers of the Presidents.* 20 vols. New York: Bureau of National Literature, 1897–1917.

Richardson, Joe M. *Christian Reconstruction: The American Missionary Association and Southern Blacks, 1861–1890.* Athens: University of Georgia Press, 1986.

Richter, Daniel. "Cultural Brokers and Intercultural Politics: New York Iroquois Relations, 1664–1701." *Journal of American History* 75.1 (June 1988): 40–67.

———. *Facing East from Indian Country: A Native History of Early America.* Cambridge MA: Harvard University Press, 2001.

Riggs, Alfred L. "Address of A. L. Riggs at National Council, Des Moines, Indiana." In *Our Indian Missions: Seventy Years Review, 1834–1904,* 7. Santee NE: Santee Normal Training School Press, 1904.

———. *Santee Normal Training School.* Santee NE: Santee Normal Training School Press, n.d., n.p.

———. *Santee Normal Training School Prospectus.* Santee NE: Santee Normal Training School Press, 1885.

————. *School Discipline*. Santee NE: Santee Normal Training School Press, n.d.

————. *What Does the Indian Worship?* Santee NE: Santee Normal Training School Press, n.d.

————. "What Shall We Do With The Indian?" *The Nation*, October 1867, 356–90.

Riggs, Frederick. "A Necessary Use for the Vernacular." *Iapi Oaye/The Word Carrier* 24.11 (November–December 1895).

Riggs, Mary R. *Early Days at Santee*. Santee NE: Santee Normal Training School Press, 1928.

Riggs, Stephen R. "Dakota Portraits." *Minnesota Historical Review* 2.8. (November 1918): 481–568.

————. *Mary and I: Forty Years Among the Sioux*. Boston: Congregational Sunday-School and Publishing Society, 1880.

————. "Protestant Missions in the Northwest." *Collections of the Minnesota Historical Society* 6, 117–88. St. Paul: Minnesota Historical Society, 1894.

————. *Tah-koo Wah-kan; or, The Gospel among the Dakotas*. Boston: Congregational Sunday-School and Publishing Society, 1869.

Riggs, Stephen R., and Alfred L. Riggs. *Guyot's Elementary Geography in the Dakota Language/ Maka-oyakapi*. New York: Scribner, Armstrong, 1876.

Riggs, Stephen R., and Gideon H. Pond. *The Dakota First Reading Book/Dakota Oyawa Wowapi*. Cincinnati: Kendall and Henry, 1839.

Riney, Scott. *The Rapid City Indian School, 1898–1933*. Norman: University of Oklahoma Press, 1999.

Roberts, Gwyneth Tyson. *The Language of the Blue Books: The Perfect Instrument of Empire,* Cardiff: University of Wales Press, 1998.

Rothman, David. *The Discovery of the Asylum: Social Order and Disorder in the New Republic*. Boston: Little Brown, 1971.

Royce, Charles C. *Indian Land Cessions in the United States*. 18th Annual Report of the Bureau of American Ethnology. Washington DC: GPO, 1899.

Ryan, Carmelita Ryan. "The Carlisle Indian Industrial School." PhD diss., Georgetown University, 1962.

Rydell, Robert W. *All the World's a Fair: Visions of Empire at American International Expositions, 1876–1916*. Chicago: University of Chicago Press, 1984.

Saxton, Alexander. *The Rise and Fall of the White Republic: Class Politics and Mass Culture in Nineteenth-Century America*. London: Verso, 1990.

Scott, James C. *Domination and the Arts of Resistance: Hidden Transcripts*. New Haven CT: Yale University Press, 1990.

————. *Weapons of the Weak: Everyday Forms of Peasant Resistance*. New Haven CT: Yale University Press, 1985.

Seton, Earnest Thompson, and Julia M. Seton. *The Gospel of the Red Man: An Indian Bible.* Los Angeles: Willing, 1948.

Shoemaker, Nancy. *A Strange Likeness: Becoming Red and White in Eighteenth-Century North America.* New York: Oxford University Press, 2004.

Silko, Leslie Marmon. "Leslie Marmon Silko." Interview by Donna Perry. *Backtalk: Women Writers Speak Out,* 313–48. New Brunswick NJ: Rutgers University Press, 1993.

———. *Storyteller.* New York: Arcade Publishing, 1981.

———. *Yellow Woman and a Beauty of the Spirit: Essays on Native American Life Today.* New York: Simon and Schuster, 1996.

Silverman, Kaja. *Male Subjectivity at the Margins.* New York: Routledge, 1992.

Smedley, Audrey. *Race in North America: Origins and Evolution of a Worldview.* Boulder CO: Westview, 1993.

Sneve, Virginia Driving Hawk. *Completing the Circle.* Lincoln: University of Nebraska, 1995.

Spack, Ruth. *America's Second Tongue: American Indian Education and the Ownership of English, 1860–1900.* Lincoln: University of Nebraska Press, 2002.

Spivey, Donald. *Schooling for the New Slavery: Black Industrial Education, 1868–1915.* Westport CT: Greenwood Press, 1978.

Spring, Joel. *The Cultural Transformation of a Native American Family, 1763–1995.* Mahwah NJ: Lawrence Erlbaum Associates, 1996.

Standing Bear, Luther. *My Indian Boyhood.* Boston: Houghton Mifflin, 1931. Reprint, Lincoln: University of Nebraska Press, 1988

———. *Land of the Spotted Eagle.* Boston: Houghton Mifflin, 1933. Reprint, Lincoln: University of Nebraska Press, 1978.

———. *My People, the Sioux.* Boston: Houghton Mifflin, 1928. Reprint, Lincoln: University of Nebraska Press, 1975.

Stands-in-Timber, John. *Cheyenne Memoirs.* Lincoln: Nebraska University Press, 1972.

Stanton, William. *The Leopard's Spots: Scientific Attitudes toward Race in America, 1815–59.* Chicago: University of Chicago Press, 1960.

Statutes at Large.

Stewart, J. *Two Paiute Autobiographies.* As told to J. Stewart. University of California Publications in American Archaelogy and Ethnology 33.5. Berkeley: University of California Press, 1934.

Stocking, George W., Jr. *Race, Culture, and Evolution: Essays in the History of Anthropology.* New York, The Free Press, 1968.

Stuart, Paul. *The Indian Office: Growth and Development of an American Institution, 1865–1900.* Ann Arbor MI: UMI Research Press, 1979.

Swanton, John. "The Indian Tribes of North America." Bureau of American Ethnology, Bulletin 145. Washington DC: GPO, 1952.

Szabo, Joyce M. *Howling Wolf and the History of Ledger Art*. Albuquerque: University of New Mexico Press, 1994.

Szasz, Margaret Connell. *Education and the American Indian: The Road to Self-Determination since 1928*. 3rd rev. and exp. ed. Albuquerque: University of New Mexico Press, 1999.

———. *Indian Education in the American Colonies, 1607–1783*. Albuquerque: University of New Mexico Press, 1988.

———, ed. *Between Indian and White Worlds: The Cultural Broker*. Norman: University of Oklahoma Press, 2001.

Talbot, Edith Armstrong. *Samuel Chapman Armstrong*. New York: Doubleday, 1904.

Talyesva, Don C., Sun Chief. *Autobiography of a Hopi*. Edited by Leo Simmons. New Haven CT: Yale University Press, 1942.

Tatum, Lawrie. *Our Red Brothers and the Peace Policy of Ulysses S. Grant*. Philadelphia: J. C. Winston, 1899. Reprint, Lincoln: University of Nebraska Press, 1970.

Teeters, Negley. *The Prison at Philadelphia, Cherry Hill: The Separate System of Penal Discipline, 1829–1913*. New York: Published for Temple University Publications by Columbia University Press, 1957.

Tinker, George E. *Missionary Conquest: the Gospel and Native American Cultural Genocide*. Minneapolis MN: Fortress Press, 1993.

Trafzer, Clifford E., Jean A. Keller, and Lorene Sisquoc, eds. *Boarding School Blues: Revisiting American Indian Educational Experiences*. Lincoln: University of Nebraska Press, 2006.

Trennert, Robert A., Jr. *The Phoenix Indian School: Forced Acculturation in Arizona, 1891–1935*. Norman: University of Oklahoma Press, 1988.

Trouillot, Michel-Rolph. *Silencing the Past: Power and the Production of History*. BostonL Beacon Press, 1995.

Trout Gallery. *Visualizing a Mission: Artifacts and Imagery of the Carlisle Indian School*. Carlisle PA: Dickinson College, 2004.

Turner, Katherine. *Red Man Calling on the Great White Father*. Norman: University of Oklahoma Press, 1951.

Utley, Robert M. "The Celebrated Peace Policy of General Grant." *North Dakota History* 20 (July 1953): 121–42.

———. *Frontier Regulars: The United States Army and the Indian, 1866–1891*. New York: Macmillan, 1973.

———. *The Lance and the Shield: The Life and Times of Sitting Bull*. London: Pimlico, 1998.

Vale, Lawrence J. *Architecture, Power, and National Identity*. New Haven CT: Yale University Press, 1992.

Van Gennep, Arnold. *Les Rites de Passage*. Paris: E. Nourry, 1909. Reprint, Paris: A. and J. Picard, 1981.

Vaughan, Alden T. "From White Man to Red Skin: Changing Anglo-American Perceptions of the American Indian." *American Historical Review* 87.4 (October 1982): 917–53.

Viola, Herman J. *Warrior Artists: Historic Cheyenne and Kiowa Indian Ledger Art Drawn by Making Medicine and Zotom*. Washington DC: National Geographic Society, 1998.

Vogt, Evon Z. "The Acculturation of American Indians." *Annals of the American Academy of Political and Social Science* 311 (May 1957): 137–46.

Vollbrecht, John L. *St. Augustine's Historical Heritage*. Rev. ed. Jacksonville: North Florida Web Press, 1995.

Walker, Cheryl. *Indian Nation: Native American Literature and Nineteenth-Century Nationalisms*. Durham NC: Duke University Press, 1997.

Walker, Francis. *The Indian Question*. Boston: James R. Osgood, 1874.

Walker, Robert Sparks. *Torchlights to the Cherokees: The Brainerd Mission*. New York: Macmillan, 1931.

Walker-McNeil, Pearl Lee. "The Carlisle Indian School: A Study in Acculturation." PhD diss., American University, 1979.

Wallace, Ernest, and E. Adamson Hoebel. *The Comanches: Lords of the Southern Plains*. Norman: University of Oklahoma Press, 1952.

Warrior, Robert. *The People and the Word: Reading Native Nonfiction*. Minneapolis: University of Minnesota Press, 2005

Washington, Booker T. *Up from Slavery*. New York: Airmont, 1967.

Welker, Glenn. "The Castro Family History of the Lipan Apache Band of Texas." http://www.indians.org/welker/lipanap.htm.

Welsh, Herbert. *The Apache Prisoners in Fort Marion, St. Augustine, Florida*. Philadelphia: Indian Rights Association, 1887.

———. *Are the Eastern Industrial Training Schools for Indian Children a Failure?* Philadelphia: Indian Rights Association, 1886.

———. *Civilization Among the Sioux Indians: Report of a Visit to Some of the Sioux Reservations of South Dakota and Nebraska*. Philadelphia: Indian Rights Association, 1893.

———. *A Dangerous Assault upon the Integrity of the Civil Service Law in the Indian Service*. Philadelphia: Indian Rights Association, 1893.

———. *Four Weeks among some of the Sioux Tribes of Dakota and Nebraska*. Philadelphia: H. F. McCann, 1882.

———. *How to Bring the Indian to Citizenship and Citizenship to the Indian*. Philadelphia: Indian Rights Association, 1892.

———. *The Indian Problem*. Philadelphia: Indian Rights Association, 1886.

Whipple, Henry B. *Lights and Shadows of a Long Episcopate*. New York: Macmillan, 1899.

White, Richard. *The Middle Ground: Indian Empires, Republics in the Great Lakes Regions, 1650–1815*. Cambridge UK: Cambridge University Press, 1991.

Whiteman, Henrietta. "White Buffalo Woman." In *The American Indian and the Problem of History*, edited by Calvin Martin, 162–70. New York: Oxford University Press, 1987.

Wilson, Raymond. *Ohiyesa: Charles Eastman, Santee Sioux*. Urbana: University of Illinois Press, 1983.

Winfrey, Dorman H., and James M. Day, eds. *Texas Indian Papers*. Vol. 4. Austin: Texas State Library, 1961.

Wissler, Clark. Indian Cavalcade. New York: Sheridan House, 1938.

———. *The Indians of the United States*. New York: Doubleday, Doran, 1940. Reprint, *Red Man Reservations*. New York: Collier Books, 1971.

Witmer, Linda F. *The Indian Industrial School, Carlisle Pennsylvania, 1879–1918*. Carlisle PA: Cumberland County Historical Society, 1993.

Wooster, Robert. *The Military and United States Indian Policy, 1865–1903*. New Haven CT: Yale University Press, 1988.

Index

In the Indigenous Education series

American Indians, the Irish,
and Government Schooling
A Comparative Study
Michael C. Coleman

White Man's Club
Schools, Race, and the Struggle
of Indian Acculturation
Jacqueline Fear-Segal

Indian Education in the
American Colonies, 1607–1783
Margaret Connell Szasz